Thirst for Growth

Robert Gottlieb
Margaret FitzSimmons

Thirst for Growth

Water Agencies
as Hidden Government
in California

The University of Arizona Press   Tucson & London

The University of Arizona Press
Copyright © 1991
The Arizona Board of Regents
All Rights Reserved
⊗ This book is printed on acid-free, archival-quality paper.
Manufactured in the United States of America.

96   95   94   93   6   5   4   3   2

Library of Congress Cataloging-in-Publication Data

Gottlieb, Robert.
   Thirst for growth : water agencies as hidden government in
California / Robert Gottlieb, Margaret FitzSimmons.
      p.   cm.
   Includes bibliographical references (p.) and index.
   ISBN 0-8165-1134-9
   ISBN 0-8165-1418-6 (pbk.)
      1. Water districts—California, Southern.   2. Water-supply—
Government policy—California, Southern.   3. Water-supply,
Agricultural—Government policy—California, Southern.   4. Municipal
water supply—Government policy—California, Southern.
   I. FitzSimmons, Margaret.   II. Title.
   HD1694.C2G68   1991   90-20184
   333.91′212′097949—dc20   CIP

British Cataloguing-in-Publication Data
A catalogue record for this book is available from the British Library.

To Our Families and
Our Community of Friends and to
Casey and Andy and
Anne, Libby, Maggie, Molly, and Michael
Who We Know Will Walk More Gently

Contents

vii

Illustrations

ix

A Note on Method and Acknowledgments

This project originated from two related sets of events: the appointment of one of the authors, Robert Gottlieb, to what was to become a seven-year tenure, from December 1980 to December 1987, as a member of the Metropolitan Water District board of directors, representing the City of Santa Monica; and the research of both authors, through their work in the Environmental Analysis and Policy Area of the UCLA Graduate School of Architecture and Urban Planning, on the resource economy of California and the West. In 1985, we were fortunate to receive a grant from the John Randolph Haynes and Dora Haynes Foundation to examine the issues of accountability and innovation in public water agencies, thus formally launching more than four years of research that included collection of qualitative data through interviews, personal observation, and review of documentary evidence, and a comprehensive review of agency activity.

In the course of that research, thousands of agency documents—from annual reports and SEC filings to board letters and memoranda—were reviewed, and more than one hundred and fifty interviews were conducted. All the formal interviews were undertaken by the authors, though additional information—also cited as "interviews"—was gathered by several research assistants who worked on the project, especially Louis Blumberg, Rubell Helgeson, and April Smith. Information was also derived from the notes taken at various meetings by the senior author, especially during his tenure on the MWD Board.

During this period, when that author saw his role as "participant-observer" within MWD and the larger water industry, he had the opportunity to view events and decisions as they were occurring. The analysis derived from this in part reflects debates the author experienced and in which he participated. This opportunity to draw both on direct observation and on participation provides a framework for analysis of events as a form of contemporary history where research, though objective in its comprehensiveness, is capable of making choices in its conclusions, as we have done in this project.

This research was initially prepared in report form for the Haynes Foundation, which has been a major actor over the years in analysis and evaluation of the system of governance that has developed in Southern California, including that of the water agencies. We intend our effort to fit into that tradition of review, analysis, and proposals for action and so to offer guidelines for future activities.

A project of this magnitude required considerable assistance from others. We would first like to thank the directors of the Haynes Foundation, and its executive director, Diane Cornwell, for their generous support and their willingness to extend deadlines as the research itself became more extensive. We would also like to thank our invaluable researchers—Elizabeth Atwell, Louis Blumberg, Rubell Helgeson, Michael Kitahara, Leslea Meyerhoff, Ioannis Pissimissis, Sue Ruddick, April Smith, and Cathy Wharton—who were quickly able to learn their way in the obscure world of public water agencies in order to locate the wide range of information and source materials we requested of them. Finally, we are greatly indebted to Richard Berman for the preparation of the maps.

We would also like to thank those within the water agencies who took time and effort to provide information and to give us their point of view on a host of subjects. We especially want to thank Carl Boronkay, Myron Holburt, Richard Balcerzak, Dawn Chin, Karen Dorff, Jay Malinowski, JoAnn Lundgren, Bob Gomperz, Ray Corley, Wiley Horne, Michael McGuire, Dan Ashkenaizer, Robert Gough, Greg Leddy, Fred Vendig, Warren Abbott and Tim Quinn (of MWD); Larry Michaels, Lester Snow, Pete Rios, Linden Burzell, Art Bullock, Janet Raviart, Cindy Heinz, and Paul Engstrand (San Diego CWA); Jane Bray, Robert Berlien, Ralph Helm, and Tom Stetson (Upper District—San Gabriel); Charles Shreves, Ron Hull, and Patricia Warren (IID); Stuart Pyle, Tom Clark, George Ribble, and Pam Schilling (Kern); and Alan Capon, Tom McCauley, Goodwin Glance and Dale Kyle (Burbank).

Numerous board members and other water-industry participants were of special help to us, particularly Tim Brick, Mike Nolan, Robert Ghirelli, Rich Atwater, Neil Ziemba, Paula Bisson, Timothy Vendlinski, Harry Griffen, Mike Madigan, Conrad Riebold, Burton Jones, Howard Hawkins, Gene

Lundquist, Ron Lampson, Ron Khachigian, Willard Sniffen, John Benson, Bill Condit, Lester Bornt, David Osias, and Duane Georgeson. We also thank the various community members and press people who gave us time and information and opened up their files, thus providing us an invaluable look at those "outsiders" who have become key to the process of agency decision making: Joyce Johnson, John Means, Tom Schroeter, Ron Campbell, John Fleck, Dorothy Green, Charles Cooper, Phil Pryde, Don Wood, Cheryl Clark, the late Emily Durbin, Will Baca, Maxine Leichter, Henry Nowicki, Bill Boyarsky, Myron Levin, and Willy Morris.

Finally, we would like to thank the faculty, students, and staff of the UCLA Graduate School of Architecture and Urban Planning, with whom we were able to share our insights and discuss our findings. GSAUP, as it's known, was, as we knew it would be, an ideal place to join the issues of public innovation and democratic accountability in a research design that aimed to be both thorough and passionate.

Introduction

To the water agencies of southern California, the region they serve is a desert, and only their efforts have made possible its flowering as a modern metropolis—today a world city, a massive industrial and commercial complex and a vast agro-industrial empire. There is a certain irony in this perception, since early European settlement of Los Angeles was based on what the Spanish explorers, more accustomed to life in a seasonally arid environment, saw as the remarkable water wealth of the region. The Pueblo of Los Angeles was sited beside a freely flowing river, a river that provided year-round water for irrigation and household use in a climate where rain fell only in the winter months. The Zanja Madre, the primary irrigation ditch of the Pueblo, was managed by the region's first water bureaucrat. Later, farmers who drove wells into the soils of the fertile Los Angeles basin found that artesian water gushed from those wells and that the accumulated pressure of the vast store of local groundwater made irrigation of their crops almost effortless.

The early water problems of Los Angeles were problems of surplus, not dearth. In 1815, the river flooded the settlement, forcing relocation of the central plaza and the church. Settlement of the coastal basin and its tributary valleys was restricted by the marshes that covered huge areas, wetlands in which the indigenous people found an important source of food and materials for their livelihood. Snowfall trapped on the slopes of the then heavily forested San Gabriel mountains melted slowly through the late spring and flowed through the soil, the creeks, and the broad and coalescing alluvial fans to feed the San Gabriel and Los Angeles rivers year round. And the brimming gravels of the San Fernando Valley, charged by the spreading streams that descended from the western San Gabriels and the Transverse ranges, ran through reed-filled swampland, sank into the beds of their courses, and then welled up over the rock threshold of the Valley to flow by the Pueblo. Even now, engineers building skyscrapers in downtown Los Angeles must design their foundations to rest securely in the still-saturated gravels of old riverbeds.

Throughout Southern California the question has been not whether there was water, but where there was water; and where there were lands that could be bought cheap, but sold dearly if water was brought to them. The question was not whether there was water to support local agriculture but whether there was water to grow crops for export, not whether the resource could support the local economy but how that economy could be made to grow, to increase the wealth of its leaders, and to draw in more and more people to settle more and more land and take more and more jobs.

In fact the region has never yet suffered a drought (if this word is used only for those times when developed water supply is inadequate to immediate human needs), although rainfall averages less than three inches a year in the deserts of the Imperial Valley and only thirteen inches a year in downtown Los Angeles, considerably lower than in other parts of California and the West. In 1976–77 and 1986–90, when other urban areas in California found water so scarce that they imposed sometimes severe mandatory rationing on their water users, Southern Californians faced no such imposed restrictions. Only after the dry period, which began in 1986, seemed likely to extend to a fifth year did the MWD board approve a small mandatory cutback in deliveries to member agencies.

Water politics in Southern California have always been politics of growth, of heating up the local economy by finding strategies to subsidize an increased and reallocated supply of a necessary natural resource so that, no matter how rainfall might fluctuate from year to year, economic growth would anticipate no checks and no limits. Out of this agenda has grown a remarkable complex of powerful and hidden institutions, institutions that continue to be driven by this old program of uncontrolled and unmanaged growth and which, even now, find their primary constituency among those who continue to present growth as the panacea through which to resolve all the region's urban problems.

These institutions are the water agencies of the region, a complex of nominally public bodies whose policies and agendas affect the everyday life of Southern California citizens in complex and hidden ways. Together, they have assembled the most remarkable series of public-works projects in human history, projects whose scale dwarfs in their own time the Pyramids of Egypt. These include the controversial and pace-setting Los Angeles Aqueduct, which devastated Owens Valley while setting the pattern of explosive urbanization in the South Coast Basin; Hoover Dam, the All-American Canal, and the Colorado River Aqueduct, which extended and sustained a vast agricultural empire while establishing the lines of development throughout six Southern California counties; and the California State Water Project, which was designed to make permanent the regional cycle of expansion. These agencies and structures bring water to Southern California from a total drainage area of more than 250,000 square miles. The relocation of this water not only supports growth in Southern California but also subordinates the populations and economies of the regions from which the water is drawn.

Together, the various water agencies in Southern California represent an enormous investment of capital in the development of a regional infrastructure. In combination, the two largest urban water agencies—the Metropolitan Water District and the San Diego County Water Authority—and the two largest agricultural agencies—Kern County Water Agency and the Imperial Irrigation District—alone control more than two billion dollars in capital assets in plant and equipment and manage more than one billion dollars in bonded indebtedness. Their combined annual revenues exceed 450 million dollars. The water agencies of Southern California serve nearly 15 million people, including the third- and fourth-largest agricultural counties in the United States and several of the fastest-growing Standard Metropolitan Statistical Areas (SMSAS) in the nation.

For more than ninety years Southern California water agencies have acted largely free from general public oversight. Though the scale of their operations has become immense, their policies have rarely stimulated extended controversy or intense local debate. In the last few years, however, this remarkable complex of government bodies has faced greater public attention and concern as the growth consensus on which they depended has weakened and as changing popular perception of what water issues are significant has forced them to address a new agenda.

This book examines a select group of Southern California water agencies, reviewing the interests from which they originate, their historical development, their increasing interconnection, and their responses to the challenge to be innovative and accountable to the public. The agencies selected represent the spectrum of agency power, scale, and responsibility, ranging from the giant imported-water wholesaler, the Metropolitan Water District of Southern California, to the troubled groundwater agencies representing the City of Burbank and the San Gabriel Valley, and from the rapidly urbanizing region served by the San Diego County Water Authority to the irrigated agricultural territories of the Kern County Water Agency and the Imperial Irrigation District. We look at their relative roles in an increasingly integrated and centrally controlled water economy, at the forces which have encouraged their integration and interdependence, and at their varying responses to common but novel themes such as water management efficiency, water quality, water reallocations, and the present role of water supply in the matrix of urban growth and development. We ask whether it is time that these public bodies rethink their agendas in order to respond appropriately to popular concerns and to find a new role in the further design of the Southern California region.

In the scholarly and professional literature, there have been a number of studies of historical and current aspects of western water policy in recent years. This project differs from the existing literature in several ways: we argue that local agencies rise out of local initiatives, rather than from a general logic of water development in arid environments, and that the nature of those local initiatives is not entirely predictable; we suggest that in Southern California, at least, it is local initiatives, not more widespread constituencies, that stimulate and support federal investment; we treat this as a current, not simply a historical problem; and we find that urban interests and forces increasingly dominate rural interests in water development. We mean to offer a contribution to the ongoing debate on water policy and on the dimensions of further growth in Southern California, but we believe that this research also contributes to a more general analysis of the origins of government forms and policies in relation to economic activities, and of the relationship between local, regional, and national political-economic changes. Finally, we suggest that our analysis addresses some important questions about how we, as a society, incorporate and develop the natural environment within which our activities are embedded and on which our actions depend. If water policy has at last come into question, it is only partially because we have become more sensitive to the issue of growth management, the quality of basic resources, and the public subsidy of private interests; it is also because we are increasingly aware as a society that we may need to walk more softly on the earth—to design with nature rather than against it—and to fit our common choices to the real and patterned world in which we live.

Part I

The Agencies and the Regional Water Economy

The water agency has been a pivotal institution in both urban and agricultural development in the United States, having evolved into an instrument for the interests of the development community. Water policy has reflected the goals and objectives of local elites. It has been the primary forum for local economic development in most western regions from the time of formation of irrigation districts at the end of the nineteenth century. A hundred years earlier similar forces led to city water departments along the Atlantic seaboard to make possible and influence the growth of the eastern urban corridor.

As an institutional form, the water agency offers a particular window into the workings of local government and the linkages between local initiatives and the revenue and enforcement powers of government at higher levels.

I

*Also, like other public works agencies, water agencies are
a hidden component of local government. Their present
agendas, framed by growth politics, reflect the tensions
and purposes from which the agencies were formed and
within which they developed over time.*

*Water issues are local issues that have become em-
bedded in, and given rise to, an increasingly elaborate
articulation of local, state, and federal powers and organizations. Early local initiatives (for example, the formation
of water districts to support the continued growth of the
cities of the Eastern Seaboard) looked to their own state
legislatures as the source of extended power and as the
forum to reconcile competing claims. Later, in the settlement of the Middle West and the West, local concerns
about water control and resource development stimulated
the formation and growth of two federal agencies, the
Army Corps of Engineers and the Bureau of Reclamation
of the Department of the Interior. Although local interests
continued to shape and control water issues, water policy
became associated with larger regional, statewide, and
national forces, leading to a complex (and often hidden)
political geography of water and political and economic
power.*

*In the East, cities like Boston, New York, and Phila-
delphia found early that continued growth of their industry and commerce, further development of urban land, and
continued immigration required new water supplies from
beyond existing city limits. They applied to their states for
rights to distant sources of water and for financial support*

and taxing powers. Later in the South and Midwest, urban, mercantile, industrial, and agricultural interests together turned to the federal government—in particular, to the U.S. Army Corps of Engineers—to control local rivers for navigation and flood control in order to support local economies. As a result, the Corps of Engineers became the largest water-related agency in the country and continues today as a key federal participant in local development programs and strategies.

In the West, perceived as a desert where scarce water might limit growth both in agriculture and in urban areas, an even more powerful set of local agencies appeared. Though some settlers (for example, the Mormon communities of the Great Basin Kingdom along the Colorado River) became adept at husbanding and marshalling local *water resources, most agricultural, mining, and commercial investors laid plans to capture and* import *additional water for their activities. By the 1890s, led by the railroads, which had proved their success at gaining federal subsidies, these groups sought federal intervention and support in this effort. Their claims led to establishment of the U.S. Reclamation Service (later the Bureau of Reclamation), the agency that was to control and stimulate much subsequent private development of the once-public lands of the West. Federal intervention neither centralized policy decisions nor established the priority of a national agenda; the choices that framed the activities and set the purpose of water development remained locally rooted. The Corps of Engineers, through its regional offices, sought to meet*

3

local needs. Though the Bureau maintained an apparently more centralized structure, Bureau plans were initiated locally and contracts between the Bureau and local users of federal water set up a special relationship with local interests. In Washington the western water industry set up lobbyists and established congressional blocs in order to maintain this local-federal nexus. At the heart of that nexus stood the local water agency.

This relationship between local and federal agency was later duplicated between local and state agency, particularly in California where the water industry succeeded in engaging state resources in construction of the California Aqueduct.

The development of the Southern California water industry (and its varied agencies) during the past seventy-five years portrays this relationship of local, statewide, and federal interests. At the height of this special relationship, these local water agencies designed billion-dollar public-works projects, structured policies that would affect millions of people and bring millions of acres under irrigation, and enlisted federal, state, and local politicians and bureaucrats to support these efforts. But today water agencies, though still a central source of policymaking and economic and political power, face the most substantial challenges since their formation. These challenges rise from a substantial realignment of their constituencies and from growing public concern about their purposes and agendas.

I

"The Mighty MET":
A Center of Power

The Metropolitan Water District of Southern California (MWD) sits at the center of the web of water compacts and political relationships that integrate water supply, growth, and economic development issues throughout Southern California. MWD's central position in Southern California water policy results from two factors: it was the first umbrella agency to be established to tie together water policy and water delivery infrastructure across a complex set of urban and rural jurisdictions; and it has successfully won and defended a formal role as intermediary between its client urban water agencies and its neighbor agricultural agencies, and between this whole group of actors and the state and federal powers involved with water development.

MWD is a giant among public water agencies, serving an area of 5,135 square miles and a population of 15 million. Though MWD itself is a water wholesaler with only twenty-seven clients, these MWD member agencies in turn serve 127 cities in six counties (Ventura, Los Angeles, Riverside, San Bernardino, Orange, and San Diego)[1] (see fig. 1). In the 1989–90 fiscal year MWD delivered 2.55 million acre-feet of water—greater than the combined water supply of Denver, Phoenix, Los Angeles, and Dallas. No other water agency in the country comes close to this.[2] Through its direct effect on member agencies and its role as mediator of the water relations between urban Southern California and surrounding agricultural regions, MWD influences water politics and sets water policy standards for the region as a whole.

5

MWD's twenty-seven member agencies range in size from the cities of San Marino (13,300 people) and San Fernando (17,700 people) to the city of Los Angeles with its three million residents and the huge San Diego County Water Authority, which serves nearly 1,500 square miles. The area served by MWD includes all or part of four of the largest Standard Metropolitan Statistical Areas (SMSAS) in the United States. In combination these SMSAS constitute the second largest industrial center in the United States and a major commercial and financial headquarters, a level of economic activity that would make Southern California the tenth-ranked national economy in the world.[3]

MWD's role in the growth and development of Southern California has been crucial. Although in its original charter MWD activities were limited to the provision of municipal and industrial water within a specific area known as the South Coastal Plain, the district has since the 1940s stretched that definition to annex unincorporated, undeveloped, and agricultural areas in other cities and counties. In the process, MWD has helped to construct the patterns and parameters of Southern California development. At the same time, it has become a major locus of economic and political power: an ally, and at times an extension of such informal centers of power as the State and Local Government Committee of the Chamber of Commerce, the Committee of 25, the Central City Association, and the California Business Roundtable.

The enabling legislation establishing the district was enacted by the Legislature of the State of California in 1927.[4] This Act set up the Metropolitan Water District of Southern California as the agency representing a coalition of municipalities advocating the construction of an aqueduct from the Colorado River to serve the growing Southern California region. MWD gained exclusive rights to allocate this new water and, by extension, to direct the pattern of urbanization and development for the region.[5] Similar arrangements were established in the late 1950s regarding MWD's second major supply source, the State Water Project. Through these relationships, the Metropolitan Water District became the forum for coordinated planning of the Southern California region.

Annexation and Development

The MWD coalition emerged out of bitter conflicts over Southern California's first major imported water supply, the Los Angeles Aqueduct system, which tapped the Owens River watershed east of the Sierra Nevada Mountains for the City of Los Angeles. Completion of the aqueduct in 1913 touched off an extraordinary round of annexations to Los Angeles, induced by access to this new supply of water, which dramatically increased the physical extent of the city. Imported water seemed the sine qua non of

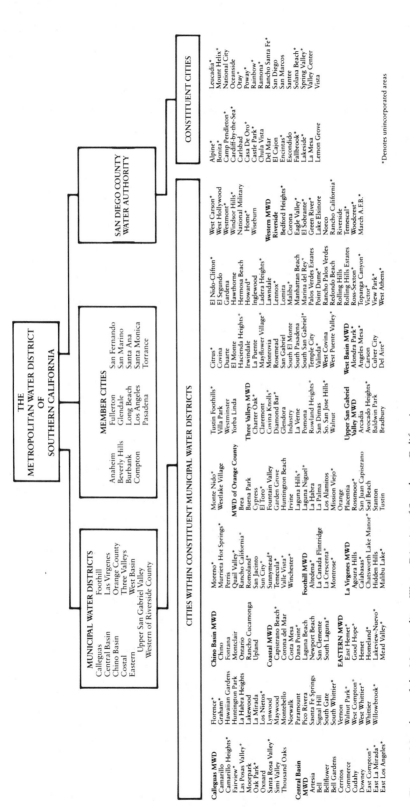

Figure 1. Members of the Metropolitan Water District of Southern California

further urbanization: without it, an area could be bypassed by development; with it, local landowners could reap the benefits of the land boom. Still, several existing cities (including Pasadena, Santa Monica, Compton, and Burbank) resisted annexation to Los Angeles, relying instead on their own groundwater and on the hope that other imported sources might become available.[6]

The conflicts over annexation and disposition of the Owens River supply lasted from 1913 to 1928. At first, this regional controversy undermined a united Southern California front during negotiations to divide rights to the Colorado River. But by the mid-1920s, in the midst of a new wave of immigration that doubled the population of the region and of a series of dry years that forced the City of Los Angeles to increase its withdrawals from the Owens watershed, pressure for unity and for an end to distributional conflict prevailed. In November 1928, the voters of thirteen cities (participants in the initial legislation) voted whether to join the new water district. Of these, two (Glendora and Orange) voted against the measure (and consequently never joined the district); two others (San Bernardino and Colton) withdrew within a few years.[7]

The Los Angeles Chamber of Commerce had been at the center of the planning and formation of both the district and the Colorado River legislation. A special fifteen-member committee of the chamber, chaired by Joseph Jensen (an influential oil industry executive), was created to establish a united regional front. The committee's report, Jensen later said, "formed the basis of the organization of the Metropolitan Water District".[8] Even the prominent role assumed by the city of Pasadena in the formation of the district was designed to disguise the fact that the District was dominated by Los Angeles.

According to the charter, representation to the Board of Directors of the new district was to be determined on the basis of each member agency's share of the total assessed valuation of land served by the district, with each agency appointing at least one member. This allocation of power was justified by the argument that the new district, which had been granted powers to tax and to issue bonds as part of its charter, would meet its capital expenses (in construction of the proposed aqueduct) by a uniform *ad valorem* tax on land within its service area. Formal votes were to be registered on the basis of each agency's share of total assessed value.

For years, the representatives of the city of Los Angeles dominated the MWD Board (see fig. 2), due both to their number (seven of the nineteen directors from the original thirteen member agencies) and to their personal power. The MWD's first manager (or chief engineer), F. E. Weymouth, came from the City of Los Angeles Water Department. W. P. Whitsett, an important local developer and a Los Angeles representative, became the board's first Chair.[9]

*Figure 2. The original Board of the Metropolitan Water District: (left to right)
Harry L. Heffner, San Marino; Franklin Thomas, Pasadena; Harvey E. Bruce,
Burbank; A. W. Franzen, Anaheim; W. P. Whitsett, Los Angeles; Will O. Harris,
San Bernardino; S. H. Finley, Santa Ana; W. Turney Fox, Glendale; George H.
Hutton, Santa Monica; Paul Schwab, Beverly Hills; C. A. Hutchinson, Colton;
James H. Howard, Pasadena; Hiram W. Wadsworth, Colorado River Aqueduct
Association, which sponsored establishment of the Metropolitan Water District;
and Clayton R. Taylor, Pasadena.*

Despite the clout of the Los Angeles appointees to the board, the benefits
of the new district for the citizens of Los Angeles seemed uncertain. The $220
million bond issue to construct the Colorado River Aqueduct approved in
1931 was financed through tax revenues, of which the city of Los Angeles
would provide more than 82 percent, based on its percentage of total assessed valuation. Unlike some of the other original member agencies, the
city had more than enough water (from its groundwater sources and the Los
Angeles Aqueduct) to meet existing and projected needs. For Los Angeles
itself, Colorado River water was not a necessary but a *surplus* water supply,
designed to accommodate and extend the regional boom. When, during the

Depression, immigration slowed while the aqueduct was under construction, the citizens of Los Angeles were obliged to pay for water that could not be immediately used; nor could city representatives predict just when such need within Los Angeles might arise.[10]

This confluence of declining growth and disproportionate payments precipitated the first major battles over district policy. Controversy over the sizing and financing of the Colorado River Aqueduct erupted in the midst of economic depression and fiscal crisis within the City of Los Angeles. But many of the city's business and political leaders (including the Chamber Committee of Fifteen) continued to support the new water district and its imported water project as a stimulant to future growth, denying that it was an economic burden.[11] Future development of the region's industrial base and future population growth depended absolutely, according to one MWD report, on the "availability of an abundant supply" of water.[12] These leaders hoped this growth would extend beyond the city limits, throughout Los Angeles County, and into adjacent counties otherwise seen as limited by local water supplies. The city's business leaders, including the real estate, retail and commercial, and financial men who took the lead on infrastructure issues, saw their interests—and the district's interests—in broader regional terms, not as limited to the interests of the city itself. Water to fuel new growth in outlying areas was of general economic benefit, these leaders argued—though of course it also benefited their own investments—even if city residents had to subsidize it.[13]

The Depression of the 1930s hit Los Angeles and the Southern California region particularly hard. The enormous debt burden the region had assumed to construct the Colorado Aqueduct caused alarm within the financial community, which feared that this might limit further investment in Southern California, given the uncertain nature of the aqueduct venture.[14] But by the early 1940s, the economic climate had improved due to the war boom in aircraft, steel, and rubber and other industries, though the population growth rate had not yet returned to the high levels of the 1920s.[15] The first sales of Colorado River water were extremely small, increasing the financial burden of debt service on the city of Los Angeles since taxes were used to make up revenue shortfalls and meet operating costs as well as debt service charges. Water sales continued depressed through the 1940s; sales were so low in fact that they were insufficient "to keep a single pump operating."[16] District leaders realized that "any attempt to place all or most of the financial load on water sales would result in a prohibitive price and no sales."[17] As a consequence, district directors decided to set the price of Colorado River water at a low rate to encourage sales, continuing to derive the bulk of the district's revenue base from taxes, with tax rates reaching a historical high (50 cents per $100,000 assessed valuation) during the mid and late 1940s.[18] To offset this ongoing revenue problem, as well as to encourage

growth, MWD embarked on an ambitious annexation policy designed to attract new members and thus stimulate future sales. An aggressive campaign
sought to lure new areas to the district based on no-interest (later, low-inter-
est) annexation charges, low water rates, which did not reflect the district's
capital and operational expenses, and even occasional gimmicks, such as
"free" water for a limited time.[19] The district still faced hurdles, however,
concerning the boundaries and land-use characteristics of prospective applicants. The original member agencies were wary that annexed areas would
constitute only a portion of a groundwater basin or sub-basin. Annexation
of smaller units could dilute the voting power of the original members and
create inefficient managerial units competing for the same supply. The district board decided to force smaller entities to consolidate into larger units,
representing either county boundaries or basin boundaries within counties,
as a condition of annexation.[20]

MWD board members were also concerned about the charter restrictions
limiting the provision of water to municipal and industrial use. Potential
areas for annexation included substantial agricultural and undeveloped
land, creating a tension between the district's need to stimulate any growth
in demand to increase sales and a narrower interpretation of the prerequi-
sites for district membership. The drive toward expansion undermined the
original management strategy of annexation of defined, coherent entities
(see fig. 3). The first new area to annex to MWD, the Coastal Municipal
Water District in Orange County, which joined MWD in 1942 during World
War II, never did expand into the regional "South Orange County" unit
anticipated at its annexation. The largest annexation, the San Diego County
Water Authority (in 1946), resulted from concern that lack of water might
constrain future growth in San Diego rather than from management or structural efficiencies. This San Diego annexation, furthermore, expanded the
MWD service area beyond the formal boundaries of the South Coastal Plain
and included both agricultural and undeveloped land.[21]

The Laguna Declaration

By the late 1940s, district policies were fully integrated into
the growth agendas for the region. The new, postwar population and industrial boom revised growth projections upward and again stimulated expansionary talk about "Greater Los Angeles," as the area's top business leaders
described their region. At the same time, an evolving Southern California–
wide water industry, led by MWD, began to talk of developing a second major
source of supplemental water. Though MWD water sales were still well below
the capacity of the Colorado River system, district leaders were worried that
Arizona's claims might result in eventual reduction of MWD entitlements to

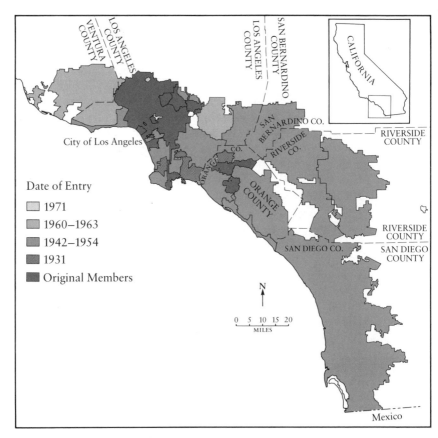

Figure 3. The Growth of the Metropolitan Water District

Colorado River water through congressional or court action. By 1949, district leaders, led by Joseph Jensen (see fig. 4) who became chairman that year, had become convinced that a new imported water project, either through the State of California or independently organized and financed by MWD, was essential to maintain the momentum of the boom.[22]

This growth-centered position was resisted by the representatives of some original member agencies, including those Los Angeles directors who differed with their board chairman. These directors, some of whom also had opposed the San Diego annexation, feared that certain new annexations, especially those involving undeveloped and agricultural areas with low assessed valuation, would create a continuing burden on the city.[23]

These conflicts came to a head in the early 1950s when the agricultural areas of Pomona and Ontario sought to annex to the district. The MWD board initially resisted these requests on the grounds that they violated the charter provisions that specified that MWD water was to be for domestic and municipal use. But Pomona and Ontario threatened to establish a separate contract with the State of California, which had begun to proceed with plans to develop a facility on the Feather River (a Sacramento River tributary in northern California) for diversion to central and Southern California. The MWD board, worried about maintaining monopoly control over any project bringing water south of the Tehachapis, ultimately worked out an agreement with the two applicants. As a result, the board, at a special meeting, issued a declaration setting its new policy. This crucial document came to be known as the Laguna Declaration (based on the location of the meeting).

As a result, between 1950 and 1954 seven new members, all serving what were then extensive agricultural areas, joined MWD (see fig. 3). These members together covered most of the arid agricultural areas to the east and south of Los Angeles, extending the area receiving MWD water from 770 square miles (in 1942) to more than 4,500 square miles by 1954.[24] The effect of this was to dilute the value of the average square mile served by MWD; in 1942, while MWD membership was still limited to urban users, the average

Figure 4. Joseph Jensen, chairman of the MWD Board, 1949–1974. MWD photograph by Al Monteverde.

assessed value per square mile served was approximately $9.87 million (in current dollars). In 1954, after the annexations to the southeast, average assessed value per square mile was only $5.33 million, substantially lower than the 1942 figure despite the post-war boom. Since land in the city of Los Angeles had the highest current market value, Los Angeles taxpayers still paid most of MWD's operating and capital costs. While the most developed of these annexed areas, the rapidly urbanizing Central Basin MWD, made up 17 percent of MWD's tax base at the time of its entry in 1954, the other six agencies which joined MWD in the 1950s (including Orange County) together made up only 13 percent of total assessed value but 44 percent of the area.[25]

Since 1952, the Laguna Declaration (see fig. 5) has become the single most important MWD policy statement. Prior policy had been summed up in a 1938 declaration by the district's Water Problems Committee, which linked "the ultimate capacity of the [Colorado River] aqueduct" with the extension of the district service area "within certain definite limits" based on MWD's ability to assure an "adequate supply" of water.[26] The Laguna document reversed that equation and now stipulated that adequate supplies would be developed "to meet expanding and increasing needs in the years ahead." To do that, *it assured all current* and future *clients that it would secure any new source of water required to meet any such future needs.* As a tradeoff, annexing areas would forego independent arrangements for new sources of water and all distribution facilities would be centralized through the MWD system. MWD would maintain its monopoly on imported water and in turn would provide such water (and water from any future sources) to any member which requested it, whatever the cost.[27]

Thus, the new policy combined expansion with centralization of the imported water system designed to meet that expansion, well in advance of authorization of MWD's second major source of water, the California State Water Project. Statement of this policy, however, did not eliminate opposition within the MWD service area. The Los Angeles Department of Water and Power (LADWP), representing the city of Los Angeles, argued that each member agency of MWD should contract separately with the State of California, which was planning to build and operate the new state water project. By doing so, the DWP hoped it could reduce the city's own financial exposure if it decided to contract for a lesser entitlement than what the member agencies of the MWD system as a whole would require. The city of Los Angeles had an independent water supply, which made it less dependent on MWD imported water, and had already begun to explore building a second aqueduct to the Mono Lake area (completed by 1970). But MWD directors led by Jensen opposed the Los Angeles position and insisted that MWD remain the single contracting agency, with the city of Los Angeles and the other member agencies obliged to contract through MWD.[28]

MWD also hoped to strengthen its monopoly by forcing areas outside its

LAGUNA DECLARATION

STATEMENT OF POLICY

The Metropolitan Water District of Southern California is prepared, with its existing governmental powers and its present and projected distribution facilities, to provide its service area with adequate supplies of water to meet expanding and increasing needs in the years ahead. The District now is providing its service area with a supplemental water supply from the Colorado River. When and as additional water resources are required to meet increasing needs for domestic, industrial and municipal water, The Metropolitan Water District of Southern California will be prepared to deliver such supplies.

Taxpayers and water users residing within The Metropolitan Water District of Southern California already have obligated themselves for the construction of an aqueduct supply and distribution system involving a cost in excess of $350,000,000. This system has been designed and constructed in a manner that permits orderly and economic extensions and enlargements to deliver the District's full share of Colorado River water as well as water from other sources as required in the years ahead. Establishment of overlapping and paralleling governmental authorities and water distribution facilities to service Southern California areas would place a wasteful and unnecessary financial burden upon all of the people of California, and particularly the residents of Southern California.

Approved by the Board of Directors of
The Metropolitan Water District of Southern California
December 16, 1952

Figure 5. The Laguna Declaration

system to annex to the district and to forego separate contracts with the state. Communities in the San Gabriel Valley and San Bernardino (to the east of Los Angeles) nonetheless opted for independence and separate contracts, but only after withstanding intense political pressure by MWD.[29] Though in the end MWD failed to achieve full monopoly over the delivery of SWP water within Southern California, it did lay the groundwork for a new series of annexations and for a continuing push for expansion of the supply and delivery infrastructure.

Growth and Consolidation

With authorization of the State Water Project by the State Legislature in 1959, the MWD entered a second period of growth and consolidation. As its near monopoly over access to the new state project evolved, the district once again sought to annex new areas to boost sales and fill in "windows" (areas not tied into the MWD system, but surrounded by annexed areas). The district's territory now stretched throughout six counties in Southern California. Urban expansion in Orange, San Diego, Riverside, and even Los Angeles County (still with considerable undeveloped or semi-developed area) followed the lines of annexation to the MWD system.

MWD water supplemented local supplies, usually of groundwater. But groundwater management policies in this period were designed conservatively (with the encouragement of MWD leaders) to guard against potential overdraft (overuse of groundwater basins) by relying increasingly on imported MWD supplies.[30] Imported water became the condition for new development, and real estate and financial investors, mapping their own plans for expansion, sought alliances within MWD and the larger water industry. Several new directors from newly annexed agencies were directly involved, in their own communities, in investments dependent on the expansion of district water supplies. One such person, E. Thornton Ibbetson (an ally of Joseph Jensen who would himself eventually become chairman of the MWD board), linked his involvement in water issues with his real estate activity quite directly. Ibbetson's firm, Union Development Corporation, was heavily involved in the newly urbanizing areas of Lakewood, Bellflower, and Paramount in south Los Angeles County near the Orange County border. These communities, once agricultural lands, were initially subdivided by Ibbetson and other developers without concern about the availability of water. Well water in the area had been anticipated to meet the requirements of increased residential use. But now problems of overdraft caused concern that future development might be limited. As a result, Ibbetson had helped establish a local water company, to supply his residential developments, which subsequently joined the Central Basin Water Users Association. When the Central Basin district, established to monitor and control the area's groundwater basin, annexed to MWD to supplement its more strictly controlled groundwater sources, the Central Basin board selected Ibbetson as its representative to MWD. Embodying the link between water availability and urban development, Ibbetson became one of the leading advocates of expansion policies for MWD through the 1960s and 1970s, a key member of the board's old guard, and board chairman in 1983.[31]

The 1950s to 1970s were halcyon years for MWD. Already a significant regional power, the district now entered strongly into state and national arenas. Southern California was becoming synonymous with unchecked urban and economic growth supported by unlimited water. MWD executives (led by board chairman Joseph Jensen and his inner circle and top management such as R. A. Skinner and Henry Mills) set out to accomplish two related goals: to expand the MWD service area while pressing for major new sources of imported water; and to build the vast infrastructure, including the large set of internal distribution facilities, required to support such expansion. MWD was now both a massive engineering and construction agency and a powerful political and lobbying operation, influencing the policies and positions of state legislators, congressmen and even senators and governors.[32] MWD's strategy was to pursue the objectives set out in the Laguna Declaration: to establish an ever expanding source of imported water.[33]

Seeking the Final Solution

Though expansion remained the unifying objective, the MWD leadership began to divide over how to achieve that objective, a division made worse by the vacuum that developed in Jensen's last years. During the 1960s (with Jensen, in his eighties, beginning to lose his capacity to govern effectively), signs of disagreement began to appear. Some tensions had already emerged over MWD differences with other state project contractors, especially the Kern County Water Agency that immediately established itself as the largest single *user* of state project water once it hooked into the state system in 1968.[34] Once again, the allocation of costs became an issue, this time between MWD and the Kern agency that paid a lesser overall rate (in part because of smaller entitlements to state water) than did MWD. During the early 1960s, MWD management, led by then Assistant General Manager R. A. Skinner, had arranged a compromise between the two big contractors over how payments would be structured. By the late 1960s and early 1970s, as both systems came on line, it became apparent to several of the MWD staff (particularly its general counsel, John Lauten) that such arrangements represented implicit subsidies for the large agricultural agency which, by extension, penalized the district.[35]

This situation was compounded by Kern's unwillingness to proceed with a new transfer facility in the state project system, called the Peripheral Canal, which would allow a much greater flow through the Sacramento Bay Delta during the dry summer months, especially during critically dry years when the need for imported water would be greatest. Moreover, the construction of a bypass facility was directly linked to the more ambitious plans to build additional facilities in the North Coast area of Northern California.[36] The Kern agency's initial reluctance about the Peripheral Canal was not to its objective but to its timing, since the agricultural agency hoped to stretch the time before it would have to assume new capital payments. The old guard within MWD, however, agreed with State Director of Water Resources William Gianelli that any postponement of the Peripheral Canal could have lasting political consequences.[37]

Part of that concern was due to the increasing role of the environmental movement in state and national water issues. Environmentalists (from Northern California in particular, including representatives from several of the nationally based, professionally staffed environmental organizations with regional headquarters in the Bay area) had come to focus on the Sacramento Bay Delta and San Francisco Bay, arguing that increased water withdrawals from the California State Water Project and the federal government's Central Valley Project were causing serious environmental problems for the Delta and the Bay. Preventing construction of a Peripheral Canal, or any other transfer facility, became a prime objective of this new movement, and the tactics of these environmental groups, in circumstances of dissension among the water agencies, effectively blocked passage of legislation during the years of Reagan's governorship.[38]

As environmental issues came to the fore, the dissension within MWD also was exacerbated, particularly after John Lauten became general manager in 1974. Lauten (the district's first general manager who had not earlier been one of its own engineers) differed with colleagues and board members over how to respond to environmental issues. Lauten was especially concerned that MWD comply with the new procedures established by the California Environmental Quality Act (CEQA), already a major battleground for water development following a California Supreme Court ruling (*Friends of Mammoth*) which spelled out specific requirements for compliance, including environmental impact statements. Several MWD staff disputed Lauten's interpretation of CEQA, and they found allies among board members who themselves had become increasingly factionalized.[39] These board divisions intensified during Jensen's last years as a leadership vacuum developed. "During those last years," recalled Jensen protege Ibbetson, "he [Jensen], like so many of us, had trouble letting go. He had been an institution for so long. Out of respect for him, we didn't push to have a new chairman."[40]

After Jensen died, these leadership struggles were not resolved. The first post-Jensen chairman to serve a full term, Howard Hawkins (owner of a fertilizer company and a former politician from the San Gabriel Valley) immediately clashed with Lauten, and Hawkins' support was actively solicited by Lauten's rivals on the MWD staff, especially Robert Will (the district's general counsel), Alan Williams (public relations director and political troubleshooter), Sacramento lobbyist Robert Fairbanks, and David Kennedy (an engineer who became assistant general manager in 1975). Each of these figures had established separate channels with Hawkins and other board members, creating what one management figure characterized as "independent power bases" which eroded Lauten's position and undercut the unity of purpose that had characterized the growth and consolidation era of the 1960s.[41] This maneuvering came to a head during complex negotiations for the Peripheral Canal. MWD's inability to speak with a single voice made obvious the need for new district leadership, at both the board and management level, who could intensify the search for an acceptable transfer facility that would "complete the State Water Project."[42]

At first, the new MWD leadership selected in 1979 seemed unable to pursue this end. The new general manager, Evan Griffith, was a likable engineer who had risen through the ranks of the district and was thought of fondly by a significant faction of directors who yearned for the time when the problems of the day were construction problems. But Griffith, out of place in the internecine warfare of Sacramento, turned over his political functions to David Kennedy (who had been passed over in the Griffith selection but who still wielded considerable power from his own ties with board members). Kennedy developed a strong working relationship with the new board chairman, Earle Blais, an attorney and former mayor of Burbank.[43]

Though Blais had been on the MWD board for nearly twenty years, he at first did not appear the powerful chair that Jensen had been and Hawkins had hoped to be. But Blais quickly established himself as a forceful advocate of what he called the district's "final solution," construction of the Peripheral Canal.[44] Focusing his considerable energies on this single objective and enlisting Kennedy as his chief negotiator and tactician, Blais attempted to re-create a sense of mission for MWD.

Passage of the Peripheral Canal became the overwhelming priority for the Blais and Kennedy leadership. To secure that objective, Blais and Kennedy recognized that tradeoffs had to be arranged with the agricultural contractors, with Governor Jerry Brown, who maintained an ambivalent posture on further water development, and with those environmentalists who were prepared to accept the project in return for environmental guarantees. Blais locked the district into difficult positions, such as his suggestion to Robert McCarthy (the new President of the Kern County Water Agency) that Kern support the Peripheral Canal in return for MWD opposition to mandatory groundwater controls in the Central Valley, despite the additional water for Southern California implicit in such controls. Blais offered the same quid pro quo to the Friant Water Users Association, whose members controlled more than one million acres along the east side of the San Joaquin Valley.[45]

The Peripheral Canal became the centerpiece of the Blais era. District priorities came to be heavily focused on this cause célébrè for the Southern California water industry.[46] The long-standing objectives of growth and expansion of the region itself and of the water development necessary to support such growth became symbolized by the campaign to secure passage of the canal.

Between 1980, when compromise legislation was finally arranged, and 1982, when voters were to decide, in a referendum election, whether to keep the legislation intact, the Blais-Kennedy MWD activities resembled a crusade more than a political effort to secure an important objective. Blais's pronouncements on the subject, linking passage of the referendum to the district's—and the region's—"destiny," caused some directors and staff members to worry privately whether MWD was becoming overexposed by this high intensity rhetoric about the dire consequences that would follow defeat of the Peripheral Canal.[47] The contrast between the widely disseminated public message of potential disaster and doom (one Blais ally drew a portrait of future shortages where residents would be forced to drink toilet bowl water to meet mandatory cutbacks[48]) and the less visible, more complex portrait of a district capable of relying on "alternatives," with a less dramatic projection of future shortages (offered for example to bond analysts[49]) made the district more vulnerable when these conflicting assessments were made public. Blais became a strong and powerful leader within MWD by force of his personality and his compelling attempt to reunify the district, but he ultimately made the district "controversial" to the public by the nature of the campaign he directed.

By staking so much on the Peripheral Canal and the referendum election, Blais unwittingly helped set the new terms for a policy and political transition in regard to water development and the role of both the agencies and the larger water industry. The election campaign revealed that large majorities in Northern California (and a significant minority in Southern California) opposed the cycle of expansion implicit in the Laguna Declaration. The overwhelming defeat of the canal (more than 60 percent opposed statewide, with more than 95 percent opposed in several Northern California counties, and nearly 40 percent or more opposed in much of Southern California[50]) sent shock waves through the Southern California water industry. With the heart of the Blais-Kennedy strategy in disarray, the district found itself with an outdated and increasingly unpopular mission, facing a developing set of challenges which promised to erode traditional approaches. The "final solution" had turned out to be elusive.

Change and Resistance to Change

At the time of the Peripheral Canal referendum, with attacks on MWD credibility and activity growing, the district leadership sought to explore public attitudes toward water issues and water agencies (such as MWD) as part of its new attention to "image." The public relations firm of Novick-Rappaport Associates sampled residents in the six-county area to assess their opinions on major district themes. The survey posed questions about the adequacy of Southern California's water supplies, about perceptions of the "seriousness of Southern California's water problems," and about the nature and degree of concern over how to "(solve) our water problems." Other questions addressed concerns about water quality, awareness of the various agencies, and impressions of water agency activity. In effect, the survey was designed to provide "a benchmark measure of public opinion against which to measure the effectiveness of Metropolitan's communications programs and their impact on the public's thinking about water."[51]

The results of the survey, published in August 1983, suggested that the district orientation was not shared by the public. Only 24 percent of those surveyed agreed that water availability was a "very serious problem right now" and only a third (32 percent) were very concerned about future availability. On the other hand, more than 85 percent thought there was enough water to meet existing needs, while a majority assumed the situation "was either the same or getting better." Water quality was seen by the majority of those surveyed as of serious concern, and the overall impression of the district itself was mixed. The Novick-Rappaport survey produced little initial interest among MWD staff or MWD board members, who remained convinced the canal election was a temporary setback. Six months after the referendum, Earle Blais stepped down as chairman just before completing his second term. The new chairman, E. Thornton Ibbetson, continued the Blais program, appointing the former chairman to head a special committee designed to continue (through lobbying and related political activities) the quest to "complete" the State Water Project.[52] Blais once again teamed up with David Kennedy, who had left MWD to head the State Department of Water Resources, appointed by newly elected Governor George Deukmejian. With encouragement from the water industry, Deukmejian and his water director put together a new plan (dubbed "Duke's Ditch" by the press), which proposed to transfer water through the Delta by enlarging existing channels rather than by a peripheral canal.[53]

With Blais working behind the scenes in Sacramento and Ibbetson providing carte blanche to his special committee, MWD once again plunged into seeking additional Northern California water exports to the south. To MWD's surprise, this time several Southern California legislators broke ranks with the water industry to ally with their Northern California counterparts to block legislation. The old coalitions, so strenuously put together over the years, were eroding, and the defeat of Duke's Ditch raised the possibility that the core of the water industry strategy for expansion could be permanently damaged.[54]

Defeat in the legislature, following rejection by the public, brought MWD up short. The old guard still maintained power but it had become essentially reactive, dependent on management to set direction for the agency. The departure of Kennedy and the retirement of general manager E. L. Griffith, at about the time of Blais' resignation, meant a full change of top personnel. The three leading candidates for general manager were Robert Gough (an MWD assistant general manager who oversaw the financial end of the district's operations), Carl Boronkay (the district's general counsel, who had previously worked for the state attorney general on coastal and environmental issues), and William Gianelli (Ronald Reagan's former state water director, recently retired as assistant secretary of the army for civil works, overseeing the programs for water resources of the Army Corps of Engineers). The selection of Boronkay was less an indication by the board of their desire for a change of direction than of personal preference for the witty and personable lawyer.[55]

The Boronkay era soon came to display a dynamic tension between change and resistance to change. Boronkay put in place a young middle management in planning, water quality, resources, and economics, who hoped to reorient the district by responding to the new issues and challenges facing the water industry.[56] Several of the staff saw Boronkay as an enlightened leader and would characterize district initiatives as "B.C." (before Carl) or "A.C." (after Carl).[57] Though not reformers by training or instinct, the new management team saw themselves as "contemporary" strategists, capable of developing the latest approaches and innovations, especially in the areas of water management, reallocations, and water quality.

Many of these innovations, however, resulted less from independent thinking by the new management team than from changes forced on the district by outside pressure or circumstance. The most visible new initiative, the water transfer-conservation funding trade proposed between the Imperial Irrigation District and MWD, was entertained by the two districts only after enormous pressure including court actions, political criticism, and proceedings initiated by the State Water Resources Control Board. Similar external intervention and public pressure were responsible for the significant changes in the water quality arena. Even emergence of new efforts, some successful and some not, in conjunctive use and water pricing were largely adaptations of programs that had been explored in other agencies throughout the country, and elsewhere in Southern California, for a decade or more prior to the Boronkay era.

In regard to the IID exchange, for example, during the Blais era, Blais, Kennedy, and General Manager Griffith had dismissed the idea of MWD's financing conservation programs, such as lining unlined canals in the Imperial service area, in exchange for additional water to be earmarked for MWD. In opinions published in the *Los Angeles Times*, in speeches during the Peripheral Canal campaign, and in letters to the Environmental Defense Fund (one of the leading advocates of the exchange) and the State Department of Water Resources, MWD leaders excoriated the exchange proposal, denying its legitimacy and claiming it was not feasible.[58] Only two years later, however, after defeat of the canal and at about the time that Duke's Ditch was being debated, negotiations between the two districts commenced as an almost inevitable consequence of Imperial's own limited options. The issue of who initiated this new course of action became a sensitive matter for Boronkay and his team, who wished to claim credit for a potentially innovative program popular with the press and legislators but also wanted to indicate to the old guard MWD board leadership that their actions were still "mainstream" and not dictated by outside pressure.[59]

That same sensitivity emerged in regard to the water quality issue with its threat of radical, new—and expensive—departures in the treatment of MWD's supplies. New regulations by the Environmental Protection Agency regarding potentially carcinogenic by-products of the disinfection process, first promulgated in 1979 and reviewed again in the late 1980s, forced MWD to revise its own treatment methods. For the expansion-minded district leadership, the substantial cost of complying with new water quality regulations was a necessary but unfortunate side show to the district's main mission—making still more water available for current and future growth.[60]

The question of greater efficiency in management and pricing of water supplies also engendered controversies about new programs and approaches. During earlier periods, MWD leaders had tended to downplay the possibilities of greater efficiency, particularly of more flexible conjunctive use of MWD imported water with local groundwater sources. Though the district had sought—not always successfully—to play a role in establishing groundwater basin-wide management units, it later found itself on the defensive when many of these same units resisted district attempts to interfere with the management of their local supplies. This extended to opposition to "seasonal" pricing programs designed to stimulate greater and more efficient storage of imported water in groundwater basins, as well as the physical enlargement or expansion of existing groundwater storage facilities.[61]

During the Blais era, district management had quietly sought to develop groundwater-based conjunctive use programs *outside* the district service area but had dismissed arguments that an enlarged conjunctive use program, including efforts *inside* the district service area, constituted an "alternative" approach to build-and-expand programs such as the canal and Duke's Ditch.[62] Under Boronkay, district management began to propose a range of conjunctive use programs, primarily physical programs involving more efficient use of existing surface and groundwater storage facilities. MWD managers successfully argued that such programs could be beneficial—in increased supplies—to the local agencies as well. These conjunctive-use concepts, however, were less successful when applied to water pricing, since local agency resistance to seasonal pricing, and especially to any marginal pricing approach, remained widespread.[63]

Despite the external pressures and uneven results, the new MWD initiatives were substantial by comparison with those of earlier periods. For example, beginning in 1986 the general manager released an annual survey of district efforts to secure additional supplies. Each year, the "alternative" approaches, such as conjunctive-use programs and "market" transfers or reallocations long advocated by many district critics, appeared to increase, suggesting a new direction for MWD supply strategies.[64] At the same time, however, the Boronkay management continued to emphasize the expansionary focus of district activities and the continuing objective of enlarging the State Water Project.

This sense of "split personality," as one district critic characterized it,[65] intensified as the Boronkay management group consolidated its position. During the late 1980s, as the region entered yet another boom cycle, MWD management put together a major and expensive new program seeking to vastly enlarge the district's internal distribution system especially to accommodate growth in San Diego, Riverside, and Orange counties. This estimated $2.8 billion program was structured on the basis of old agendas regarding allocation of costs (already developed areas were to subsidize new, high-growth areas) and included some crucial structural inefficiencies (peaking capacities were to be *increased* rather than reduced). The primary emphasis of the program, ultimately, involved the expansion of the physical infrastructure rather than the management of demand.[66] Instead of responding to the increased need to manage growth, given the growing environmental and infrastructural crises throughout the region, MWD leadership once again appeared to welcome the notion of a permanent cycle of expansion. "We are not in the growth management business," MWD leaders continued to proclaim, preparing to extend the expensive distributional requirements that accommodated and underwrote such growth.[67] "If the water agencies are not in the growth business," Tim Brick, an MWD director and one of the agency's sharpest critics, declared, "then I don't know who is!"[68]

The Boronkay leadership, moreover, continued to seek expansion of the state project despite the continuing erosion of support for the issue *throughout the state*. In 1987, MWD leaders, both management and the board, strongly supported the introduction in the legislature of yet another water industry initiative for state project expansion. This measure was once again defeated, with significant opposition from Southern as well as Northern California and with a "neutral" stance by Governor Deukmejian, whose water director, David Kennedy, divorced himself from the water industry strategy in favor of his own, low-key, "incremental" strategy. Despite the defeat, which MWD's own Sacramento lobbyist characterized as a "crisis point" in the erosion of support for the water industry, the MWD leadership still refused to reorient its approach to the state project.[69]

Aware of its political problems, MWD management decided first to hire a Northern California–based public relations firm (a firm associated with one of the biggest industrial polluters, Chevron, affecting San Francisco Bay) to help improve the agency's image in the North. Boronkay himself sought to promote the "new" MWD in discussions with editorial boards, legislators, businessmen, and other "opinion leaders" from the northern part of the state.[70] That conciliatory effort, however, was significantly undermined when MWD (with other members of the water industry) launched an all-out campaign against a draft report put forth in the fall of 1988 by the staff of the State Water Resources Control Board.

The state board had been charged by the U.S. Court of Appeals to review the complex, intertwined matter of surface flows through the Sacramento–San Joaquin Delta and San Francisco Bay system and its impact on the various contending interests inside and outside the water industry, including the fragile and declining environmental condition of both the Delta and San Francisco Bay.[71] This review process, the Bay-Delta Hearings, was a crucial moment in the changing fortunes of the water industry. Unlike the State Department of Water Resources (which had charge of the State Water Project and was primarily responsive to its main constituency, state project contractors), the State Water Resources Control Board was directly involved with water quality and environmental protection. Water industry ties were still a factor, but the whole Bay-Delta Hearings process, whose first phase had culminated in the draft report of the state board's staff, suggested the changing terms of water policy in the state.[72]

The state contractors, led by MWD, felt seriously aggrieved when the Draft Report called for limits on the amount of water exported through the delta as well as for establishment of a new "water ethic." Through the first phase of the hearings, MWD, which spent more than $3 million to influence the hearings (including a heightened media and "public awareness" campaign in the South), raised old arguments about future shortages and economic crisis if MWD were not able to maintain its state project supply and indeed to increase its withdrawals through construction of a new facility. When the Draft Report was released, the MWD board *and* its management were livid.[73] North-South war talk reminiscent of the Peripheral Canal campaign returned to the district meeting rooms. New special committees within the district were established, there was talk of launching a new referendum or initiative campaign, and MWD leadership proposed hiring a political consulting firm to prepare for the battle. There was also a proposal about creating new lobbying coalitions, led by development interests, a prospect that caused Chris Reed (a MWD board member) to scoff at management's claim to be removed from the growth issue.[74]

By 1989, the state contractors, who extensively lobbied their one-time champion Governor George Deukmejian, were temporarily successful in derailing the draft report.[75] For a time, the war talk subsided, though MWD began raising the prospect of reintroducing the Peripheral Canal, this time promoting it, as a *water quality* measure, in terms of its potential in reducing the organic buildup contributing to the problem of disinfection by-products.[76] While the Bay-Delta Hearings had now been disrupted and the battle lines were once again being redrawn, MWD and other members of the Southern California water industry found themselves in the unenviable position of trying to protect what just a few years previously they had taken for granted.

The renewed war talk and threat of another battle over the Peripheral Canal had, in a way, brought the MWD back full circle. This time, however, the terms of debate had shifted. The water industry, especially its most visible participants such as MWD, appeared to be groping for direction. Change and resistance to change—two steps in one direction and then another step backwards—characterized much of the district's activities. With an inflexible and recalcitrant but essentially directionless governing body and a management unable to fully pursue and implement new strategies, MWD remained in turmoil, reflecting the drift of the water industry itself.

2

Growth and Identity

he San Diego County Water Authority (CWA) and its constituency have been the major beneficiary of the Metropolitan Water District's pursuit of regional development. CWA serves one of the fastest growing areas in the country and the third largest metropolitan area in the state, and the authority has been at the center of the debates in the San Diego area about growth, change, and the complex intangible known as community identity. Though organized as a "pass-through" water wholesaler, the water authority has served as a forum and instrument for those who have sought water development to encourage urban growth.

The CWA service area is vast, covering 1,417 square miles (907,288 acres), about a third of San Diego County but all of its coastal area, the most developed and urbanized zone. Ninety-seven percent of San Diego County's 2.2 million people are served by CWA, which delivers MWD water to its own twenty-four member agencies.[1] These range from the city of San Diego itself, the largest member (with a population of more than one million), to undeveloped agricultural areas such as the De Luz Heights Municipal Water District at the northern end of the county (with a total of 269 residents, a density of 0.02 people per acre). Frequent annexations to CWA continue to expand its area, at about 2,000 acres annually in recent years. These annexations are usually located in the northern and eastern ends of the county where most new urban growth is found (see fig. 6).[2]

San Diego's weather, particularly along the coast, is mild and temperate, with a mean temperature of 62.3 degrees within the city limits. The area is also quite dry; average annual rainfall along the urbanized coast is about 10 inches a year, below the average (14.5 inches) for the entire MWD service area. The mountains of San Diego County receive up to 40 inches, but the inland desert areas get only about 6. As in the rest of the MWD service area, nearly all rain falls during the winter season, which lasts from November through March. Summertime (peak) demand for water averages about 150 percent of the monthly norm.[3]

Water Dependency

San Diego County's coastal hills and plains are composed primarily of uplifted marine and alluvial sedimentary deposits. The landscape of CWA's service area is varied, including valleys, mesas, foothills, and portions of the mountains, to the east of which lie the high and low desert. The sparsely populated inland half of the county has little imported water, but the eastern low desert sits over a large groundwater basin.[4] There is little groundwater along the coast, and the high growth rate (encouraged by the mild climate and coastal location) and lack of local water have been key to the region's water policy.

San Diego has always defined itself in relationship to the patterns of growth and urban development in Los Angeles. CWA's water policy since the authority was first formed in 1943 has displayed contradictory instances of identity with or antagonism to the development agenda of Los Angeles, its larger metropolitan neighbor to the north. Initially, MWD was perceived as an extension of that agenda; and San Diego's earliest plans to find a source of imported water arose from a local desire to develop the open lands of the county without influence from Los Angeles.

San Diego merchants, real estate developers and landowners, and lawyers (most of whom were active in the Water Committee of the San Diego Chamber of Commerce) hoped that local growth, particularly in the inland areas, could be stimulated by securing an outside source of additional water.[5] Aware of Los Angeles' design on the Colorado River, the chamber leaders sought to lay their own claim to the river's water. At first, San Diego had led the League of the Southwest, a political coalition of southwestern interests lobbying for Colorado River development, as well as the Boulder Dam Association, an organization of California interests whose first president, John L. Bacon, was then San Diego's mayor.[6] But during the mid-1920s, Los Angeles had succeeded in displacing San Diego from this regional leadership in organizations claiming water from the Colorado. The formation of the Los Angeles–based MWD was perceived by San Diego leaders as a further direct

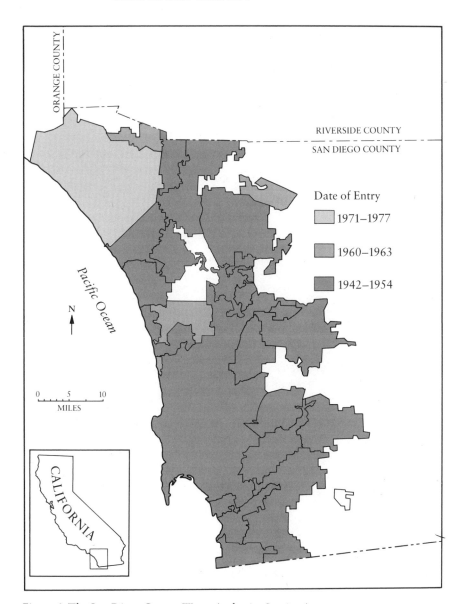

Figure 6. The San Diego County Water Authority Service Area

threat to their community's opportunity to share the Colorado supply. Chamber leaders turned to Phil Swing, a recently retired congressman and long-time water leader from the Imperial Valley who had co-authored the legislation establishing the Boulder Canyon Project (later renamed the Hoover Dam).

Swing, hired as the city's "special water counsel," was immediately successful in obtaining for San Diego a fifth priority on the Colorado River for 112,000 acre-feet of water. This entitlement, just below MWD's fourth priority of 550,000 acre-feet, was part of the Seven Party Water Agreement that allocated California's share of the Colorado among the various California users. Signed in 1931, it established a system of priorities designating rights to the river in an order of preference based on historical claims of prior use or filings.[7] The first three priorities, totaling 3.85 million acre-feet, belonged to the agricultural users in the Imperial and Coachella valleys to the east of San Diego.[8] San Diego's rights were based on its 1926 application for diversion of 112,000 acre-feet (the amount of its eventual fifth priority) for city water supply purposes. These numbers and priorities, though they did not reflect actual use of Colorado River water at the time the Colorado Aqueduct was under construction, were to have enormous significance to long-term claims on the river.[9]

In the 1930s, an incipient San Diego water industry emerged to review the prospects of future water development in the region. Led by Swing, the Chamber Water Committee (the heart of this new water industry) considered building a separate aqueduct system to the Colorado through the Imperial Valley and the inland areas. These discussions were complicated by divisions between the City of San Diego group (which included Swing) and others with interests in the development of San Diego's "North County" region, especially the Fallbrook area. While both groups favored tapping the Colorado, they were divided over other issues, particularly the disposition of local water sources in the North County area, to which the city sought access against the self-protective plans of North County.[10]

These divisions delayed any San Diego effort to build a separate pipeline. As MWD constructed its own system, San Diego water leaders debated whether hooking into the MWD system would eliminate or exacerbate their disagreements over the control of San Diego's own water. Meanwhile, the City of San Diego, though still hoping to import water from the Colorado, began to construct its own storage facilities to capture rainfall runoff.[11] These local arguments, however, were superseded by the intervention of the United States Navy.

In the early 1940s, the navy, which had a large base in the San Diego area, focused on the issue of its water supply. With war in the Pacific (and the anticipation that U.S. economic and political interests might well expand in the Pacific Basin after the War), the U.S. military presence on the West

Coast was expanding. The Department of Defense specifically wanted to expand its base in San Diego, which would increase the growth of the San Diego region. In 1940, the local navy payroll totalled $30 million; three years later it had jumped to $150 million. Military facilities in the region (with some federal housing projects) used more than 40 percent of the water delivered by the City of San Diego, which at the time controlled most of the developed water in the county.[12]

As it became a more dominant presence, the navy decided that imported water was essential to its current activities and future plans and pressured the local water industry to set aside its debates and establish a central water authority to secure imported water. Failing this, the Defense Department was prepared to make arrangements unilaterally to obtain the Colorado River water necessary to its expansion plans. The Defense Department had decided, given the location of its naval facilities and pressures of time, that the MWD's Colorado River Aqueduct would be its preferred route and that it would not support the alternative of a new Imperial Valley aqueduct to be financed and controlled solely by San Diego water interests. The navy, in effect, handed down an ultimatum to the water industry: act now or be preempted.[13]

Without resolving its internal divisions, the local water industry established its own organization, the San Diego County Water Authority. Legislation drafted by Phil Swing (who became the new organization's first general counsel) was introduced in the California legislature by San Diego State Senator Ed Fletcher (a participant in the early deliberations of the local water industry). The authorizing act, modeled after MWD's original charter, was passed in 1943 and the new agency was organized officially in June 1944. That same year, the CWA was obliged to accept the navy's agreement with MWD to build an extension of the MWD's Colorado Aqueduct system designed to bring an immediate supply of imported water to San Diego.[14] For the next two years, the newly organized water authority chafed at its secondary status and the decisions forced on it by the navy.[15] First, the navy/ MWD agreement foreclosed the option of the Imperial route and thus of an independent transfer. Moreover, the navy had insisted, in its concern to secure a supply to serve existing needs quickly, on constructing the new pipeline at a capacity that would carry only half the region's entitlement. This undercut the local water industry's hopes for a full-capacity pipeline that would stimulate future growth. And while navy money might stimulate the local economy in the short run, the navy's presence could also begin to have negative impacts once military activities wound down after the war. Caught between the fears of possible recession and the taste of rapid growth that the war had brought, CWA leaders were still divided over the role of this plan of water development on the prospects for future growth.[16]

The newly organized water authority represented an uneasy alliance between the city of San Diego and the North County agricultural landowners who looked forward to developing their land. The city representatives made significant concessions, including the agreement that the water authority would seek sources of water only outside San Diego County, thus structuring itself (like MWD) as an agency dealing exclusively with imported water. Also like MWD, CWA relied on real property taxes to pay its expenses, including repayment of the $2 million bond issue to construct the branch lines from the Colorado River Aqueduct to the CWA delivery area. As in the Los Angeles case, this meant that urban landowners within the City of San Diego would pay 82 percent of the CWA's capital costs, though they had less voting power than did the Los Angeles representatives to MWD: City representatives would be allowed no more than 50 percent of the weighted votes and as little as 25 percent where votes were based on one vote per director.[17]

This combination of dependency on imported water for future growth and the uneasy relationship between the City of San Diego and other member agencies led to a series of crucial policy disputes whose resolution shaped the direction of the new water authority. Forced to deal with MWD by the navy, CWA leaders decided then to annex to MWD and to rely entirely on the Los Angeles–based agency's system. In exchange for annexation, CWA was obliged to relinquish its 112,000 acre-feet fifth-priority entitlement to Colorado River water to MWD, when CWA annexed to the larger district in 1946.[18]

Once integrated into the MWD system, the CWA needed to resolve two related issues: (1) the question of its own internal annexations; and (2) whether to expand its Colorado River supply by building a second barrel of the aqueduct from MWD. In 1948, two irrigation districts north of the San Diego city limits sought to annex to the CWA system. By annexing these districts, CWA would then consist of four irrigation districts, four cities including San Diego, and the Fallbrook Public Utility District. Furthermore, the largest of the original irrigation districts had itself decided to annex an additional area.[19]

At the time these annexations were proposed, CWA directors were also obliged to confront the capacity issue. While the branch line from the MWD system could meet existing demand (and even increase existing storage in a series of dry years), various CWA leaders, including the first CWA chairman Fred Heilbron, argued that a second barrel was crucial to the area's continued growth. Heilbron and his allies insisted that San Diego was once again poised for take-off, despite relatively disappointing population growth in the late 1940s. The long-anticipated recession appeared to be interrupted locally by the renewed military activity of the Cold War. The Heilbron faction insisted that, by building the second barrel, renewed growth could be stimulated by eliminating any possible constraints of future water supply.[20] The annexation requests and the arguments over the second barrel led to open (and contentious) debate within both the CWA and MWD boards.[21] One City of San Diego CWA director, a downtown department-store owner named Arthur Marston, opposed the annexations on the grounds that the new areas had no local source of water and would therefore intensify imported water dependency. Other city officials, including its public works director and several members of the city council, also argued strenuously that construction of the second barrel would further exacerbate the unequal assessment of costs. The San Diego officials envisioned a situation like that of Los Angeles, where the city would pay the costs of expansion to develop additional water that the city would only need after further growth occurred.[22] Such expansion of capacity, furthermore, would only fuel the push for future annexations. These positions, however, were overridden by a majority of the CWA directors, including chairman Heilbron, himself a City of San Diego CWA representative, a former city council member, and an original participant in the Chamber Water Committee. Heilbron had succeeded in constructing a "growth bloc" both within CWA and among allies in the business community attracted to Heilbron's vision of a continuing cycle of expansion.[23]

These early conflicts over annexation and increased capacity also became a factor in the water authority's relationship with MWD, a relationship central to CWA's structure and purpose. The MWD board, led by Joseph Jensen, took an active interest in CWA internal matters. Jensen threatened at times to have MWD pursue a separate relationship with the North County area if the question of annexations, the CWA's "pass-through" status, and the construction and location of the second barrel were not resolved to his approval. Other MWD directors were concerned about annexations of additional irrigation districts to CWA, further jeopardizing MWD's definition as a supplier of water exclusively for municipal and industrial use. CWA chairman Heilbron, who was also San Diego's first representative to the MWD board, in turn threatened to have CWA develop its own relationship with the state regarding initial plans for a state water project. Three years prior to the Pomona and Ontario annexations, the San Diego matters set off the debates that would eventually culminate in MWD's 1952 Laguna Declaration.[24]

Ultimately, Heilbron obtained approval for the annexations and the second barrel, and, with this, recognition within MWD that San Diego was a new and important player on the block. As soon as it joined the MWD system, San Diego became by far the largest purchaser of imported water; it maintained this position through the 1940s and 1950s, relinquishing its top position only briefly (to Orange County MWD) during the early 1960s.[25] Jensen and Heilbron also resolved their differences, with Heilbron becoming secretary to the MWD board, a position he would hold for more than seventeen years until 1970, a few years before his death in 1973.[26] The water authority stood ready to assume the mantle of leadership on the growth issue.

"More MET Than MET"

The Heilbron-led County Water Authority soon found itself at the center of the growth-development forces within the Southern California water industry. "We were more MET [Metropolitan Water District] than MET" recalled long-time CWA General Manager Linden Burzell, referring to the CWA's support and enthusiasm for MWD-directed policies regarding growth and expansion.[27] Burzell, appointed to his post when Heilbron (though advanced in years) still controlled the water authority's affairs, saw Heilbron as the major figure in shaping CWA strategies and perspectives. Like Jensen at MWD, Heilbron ruled CWA in an arbitrary and authoritarian manner, even insisting that the CWA general manager not attend MWD board meetings, thus leaving MWD matters (the very essence of CWA activity and definition) entirely to Heilbron and San Diego's other MWD representatives.[28]

Burzell recalled his first encounter with Heilbron, shortly after Burzell's appointment as CWA general manager, as representative of Heilbron's style of leadership. Burzell had an appointment with the CWA chairman in order for Heilbron to sign several months of board meeting minutes, a minor administrative matter. But Heilbron kept the new general manager waiting some time in his outer office before calling Burzell to his desk. "He hardly looked up as I sat there," Burzell recounted, while Heilbron "reviewed invoices and other papers relating to (his own) plumbing business. After a while, he came across a tire invoice, and in a fit of temper, he called one of his sons in, who was over sixty years of age, and began to rant and rave about not asking him before buying these tires. After some minutes of this, the son was dismissed. Fred Heilbron then looked at me and calmly said, 'And what can I do for you?'" "Apparently," Burzell concluded, "he had a purpose in all this."[29]

By the mid- and late-1960s, with the San Diego area starting to boom again, the water authority continued to increase its dependence on MWD imported water and new MWD distribution facilities to meet increased demand within its service area. During the 1960s, San Diego's purchases of MWD water tripled (102,000 acre-feet purchased in 1958–59; 356,000 acre-feet purchased in 1971–72) while its *per capita* water use increased by more than 25 percent. San Diego remained MWD's single largest user of water and was taking more than twice the amount purchased by its closest competitor (in 1971–72, when CWA purchased 356,000 acre-feet, West Basin MWD—the second largest user of imported water—purchased 169,000 acre-feet from MWD).[30] The CWA clearly benefited from MWD policies, both in terms of expanding capacity with the construction of the State Water Project and in the allocation of costs within the MWD system. As CWA continued to expand, it incorporated several new agricultural areas that were significant to the county economy and which were major water users but which had relatively low land values. As a result, CWA's ratio of tax payments to water use became increasingly favorable, especially by contrast to the city of Los Angeles, which had a much higher assessed valuation (and therefore high tax payments) but an increasingly smaller share of MWD water. By 1965, when San Diego finally permanently established itself as MWD's largest user (responsible for more than 30 percent of the total MWD water delivered to member agencies), it paid 10 percent of the taxes paid to MWD. Los Angeles, which paid 30 percent of the taxes, received only 10 percent of the water that year.[31] Even MWD Chairman Jensen complained of the imbalance in payments between San Diego and Los Angeles, though he continued to pursue further MWD expansions that only perpetuated that imbalance.[32]

But while Los Angeles representatives argued against subsidies which favored San Diego, San Diego water industry leaders worried about the other component of the taxes–water-sales payment structure, the system of "preferential rights" (legal entitlements for member agencies based on that agency's prior tax assessments). A preferential right was a legal right to water allocations that would be exercised in periods when imported water supplies were insufficient for each MWD member agency to obtain the water it required at that moment. Thus, the system would only come into play when the available imported water came to be outstripped by demand, an unlikely scenario for the medium- and even long-term, since the system was designed for overcapacity. MWD policies, in fact, were based on a cycle of expansion to prevent such a scenario of shortages from ever occurring.[33] By the 1950s, however, CWA leaders began to focus on the MWD preferential rights system as creating major potential adverse effects for San Diego. The use of water as a stimulant to growth was based on the argument that shortages "could never happen here"; with the system of preferential rights in place, the San Diego leaders feared that if such shortages should occur, San Diego would be the first to suffer. Preferential rights also reinforced the perception that San Diego was at "the end of the pipeline" both literally and figuratively. Having increased the area's dependence on imported water and promoted the use of these supplies to induce growth, but then finding itself defined as "last in line," the CWA again felt that it now lacked autonomy and independence. While the preferential rights issues still remained rather vague during the 1950s and 1960s, the concern about the agency's "dependent" status already had become a significant issue in that period.[34]

To overcome this dilemma of dependency, CWA water leaders sought to increase their influence within MWD. Two Heilbron proteges, Harry Griffen and Hans Doe (who represented urban and agricultural districts outside the City of San Diego), became leaders both within MWD and in the statewide water industry. After Heilbron's death at ninety-five (only a year after Jensen, himself eighty-seven years old, died in office as well), Griffen and Doe (who had first been appointed in 1956 and 1954, respectively) cemented their relationship within CWA and in the behind-the-scenes activities that characterized MWD during the discordant 1970s. Griffen and Doe were particularly successful in developing relationships with MWD member agencies outside Los Angeles County, especially the expanding agencies in Orange and Riverside counties. This "growth bloc" within MWD ensured that MWD continued to focus on expansion of the state project and pushed for the construction and favorable location of expensive distribution and treatment facilities to serve their areas. At the same time, San Diego water leaders continued to maneuver to protect San Diego's favorable balance of payments while seeking to abolish or modify the preferential rights system.[35]

By the late 1970s, San Diego had established a secure position within the MWD system, though its concerns over future growth and water availability failed to diminish. But, just as MWD itself was about to be set back unexpectedly by its defeat in the Peripheral Canal referendum, the San Diego water industry (as import-dependent and growth-conscious as ever) would also find itself facing new difficulties.

The Search for Independence

The defeats of the Peripheral Canal and Duke's Ditch were particularly troublesome for the San Diego water industry. The CWA had become heavily engaged in the canal referendum election, establishing its own expensive advertising campaign parallel to MWD's $625,000 "Water Watch" advertising extravaganza. Both campaigns were designed to promote the same message: that economic health depended on imported water and it was thus crucial to complete the "missing link" to the State Water Project. Like MWD, the water authority itself became "news" with its high profile effort to warn residents that the area's "end of the pipeline" status made San Diego particularly vulnerable.[36]

At first, the San Diego water industry leaders could take credit that, in their region at least, voters and legislators were responsive to their message. Nearly 73 percent of San Diego County votes were cast in favor of the canal in the 1982 referendum; two years later, the San Diego delegation, unlike Los Angeles legislators, held fast in their support of the governor's water plan.[37] Still, the defeats of the two state expansion projects placed the San Diego water industry in the uncomfortable position of having to answer its own self-generated dilemma: without additional state project water, where would San Diego's future water supply come from?

These concerns were exacerbated by newly articulated fears about the growth–water-development relationship. During 1984, as Duke's Ditch headed for defeat, business leaders at the Chamber of Commerce, which included key participants in the water industry, began sending a new message to water authority leaders. "The Chamber guys were beginning to ask us to tone it down, to take a lower profile," recalled Larry Michaels, the new CWA general manager who had replaced Burzell. "They were now worrying that with all the clamor about preferential rights, 'end of the pipeline' status, and future water shortages, that such talk would act as a disincentive for future investment in the region."[38] The decision by a Japanese "high-tech" electronics firm (an industry much coveted by the area's business leaders) to select an Oregon location over San Diego was widely interpreted as linked to the fear of water shortages. A new source of crisis had emerged.[39]

The search for water independence suddenly rose once more to the top of the water industry's agenda. Studies connecting water to growth, released during the early 1980s, put further pressure on CWA to come up with new approaches.[40] These eventually centered on three possible programs: storage, reclamation, and water transfers.

The most developed of these efforts was the plan to construct the Pamo Dam, a storage facility proposed for the undeveloped Pauma Valley at the northern end of the City of San Diego. The Pamo project had originally been conceived by the San Diego City Water Department that held title to several thousand acres kept in reserve for a future storage site. During the late 1970s and early 1980s, the city's water leaders, fearful that an environmental review process undertaken at the city level might be politically explosive, turned to the water authority to develop the idea, given the water authority's lower visibility.[41] At first, CWA decided to explore the project jointly with MWD, and initial engineering studies and consulting work were financed by MWD.[42] But with pressure for "alternatives" and "water independence" beginning to drive CWA decisions, water authority leaders abruptly ended discussions with MWD and announced that the Pamo Dam, now defined as an essential part of the strategy to secure a water supply for the region, would be financed and undertaken solely by the CWA.[43]

At the time that the Pamo project began to preoccupy the water authority, CWA leaders also became absorbed by another, more fanciful proposed storage project: a dam on the Yampa River in the Upper Colorado River Basin, to be built to hold water to transfer to San Diego. This idea, called the Galloway plan after the speculator who put it together, was brought to the attention of the water authority at a time when water crisis talk in San Diego had become even more intense.[44] Yet another tax-payments–water-use conflict between Los Angeles and San Diego had been temporarily resolved, but without any concomitant resolution of the preferential rights issue. Subsequent attempts by San Diego legislators to introduce legislation eliminating preferential rights from the MWD system were easily stymied by the larger Los Angeles delegation, which included several key legislative leaders.[45] With the complex preferential rights discussion transformed into an issue by the canal referendum and editorials bemoaning San Diego's "last-in-line" status, the Galloway plan, though farfetched, suddenly took on greater urgency.

For the San Diego water leaders and their business allies, a combination of the Galloway plan and the Pamo Dam project became the cornerstone of a new water authority strategy. The third prong of that strategy, developing water reclamation and conservation (more advanced sewage treatment to reclaim water, new drought-resistant landscaping, and a new technology known as "aquaculture") was perceived to have more limited bearing on securing additional supplies, given its expense.[46] Galloway, in contrast, was appealing precisely because project sponsors offered contractual assurance that the water the project delivered to San Diego would cost only 90 percent of that from MWD.[47]

The new water authority strategy was fashioned in part by a new coalition that had emerged to take the leadership at CWA. Led by Harry Griffen, who continued to exercise influence at the water authority, the new leadership bloc included both City of San Diego representatives and non-city–agricultural representatives, such as Michael Madigan (a former executive assistant to one-time San Diego mayor Pete Wilson and, subsequently, an executive with one of San Diego's largest development firms), Francesca Krauel (an attorney with close ties to political leaders such as Assemblyman Larry Stirling), John Hennigar (a local agricultural water agency manager soon to be a candidate for the CWA general manager's position), and Dale Mason (an insurance executive in the North County area).[48]

The desire to place CWA "on the map"—to have it become a more effective player in the larger water industry—was especially appealing given the agency's recent and humbling defeat in its effort to overturn the preferential rights system. Galloway was particularly attractive since it appeared to minimize the risk to the water authority but seemed likely to gain much-needed recognition for CWA's search for alternatives. The CWA needed only to commit an initial $10,000 for an option on the plan, while the project sponsors promised to assume all legal risks—and costs—if and when opposition were to occur. As a kind of "market" or "transfer" plan, moreover, the project appealed to the "business" orientation of the water authority leaders, who were also favorably impressed by its innovative and forward-looking veneer.[49] Most importantly, Galloway promised CWA control over an annual water supply estimated at 300,000 to 500,000 acre-feet, nearly the entire amount provided by MWD.[50]

The response to Galloway, when the plan was announced and the option was exercised, was explosive. MWD leaders (particularly Boronkay and his staff) were livid. Galloway, they insisted, in several forcefully worded letters to MWD board members, was impractical, illegal, and undermined years of patient coalition building with several Colorado River Basin states long wary of California's design on the river.[51] Environmental groups attacked the project for its unnecessary and environmentally destructive attempt to create a storage facility on one of the West's few remaining undeveloped rivers. And water industry leaders, politicians, and the media from the basin states (particularly Colorado) sharply criticized the plan as yet another attempt by California to "steal" Upper Basin water.[52]

Despite these external attacks, San Diego water leaders were initially pleased with the local attention the plan generated and with its deflection of the local concerns that had built up during the early 1980s. For one, the high profile the water authority received on this presumed "market" issue brought a large number of interested inquiries, particularly from California agricultural interests who for the first time seriously began to explore the possibility of selling their water rights.[53] Most importantly, San Diego business, political, and media leaders strongly supported this new quest for additional water. The *San Diego Union* and *Tribune*, the area's two papers,[54] were lavish in their praise for Galloway and the CWA, relieved that the paralysis of the state project and the preferential rights struggle was being overcome. Elected officials, such as Assemblyman Stirling, also praised CWA, while chastising project opponents, especially MWD—now a target of regional anger and frustration. "The San Diego County Water Authority has suffered the slings and arrows of a multitude of people who apparently do not understand the situation regarding our future water supply," Stirling commented in a press release issued two weeks after the Galloway plan was made public.[55] "Instead of criticism and censure, the San Diego County Water Authority should be admired for their courage and farsightedness in trying to solve this problem before it reaches crisis proportions." The "Los Angeles–based" MWD, on the other hand, had "not kept the best interests of San Diego in the forefront of its efforts." "We are no longer," Stirling warned, "going to be the tolerated step-child of the Metropolitan Water District."

Despite the initial excitement, the Galloway project never amounted to more than an idea. The formidable obstacles involved in such a plan—agreements, for example, had to be secured from hostile Upper and Lower Basin states as well as MWD itself whose aqueduct and distribution facilities had to be used to transport the water—were compounded by the range of legal obstacles, not the least of which was the Seven Party agreement that established priorities on the use of any Colorado River water entering California. The original option agreement, for a three-month period, kept being extended (without further cost to San Diego) to a point that even the original CWA leadership group that had lauded the project began to dismiss its significance. "I don't even think about it anymore," commented CWA leader Madigan, just a few days before he and other CWA leaders unanimously—and perfunctorily—extended the option yet another six months.[56] Galloway eventually faded quietly from view, in sharp contrast with its explosive, heavily publicized beginnings.

The same fate awaited the water authority's other new project, the Pamo Dam. When the authority decided to pursue the project on its own, it immediately required a funding mechanism. A bond measure, Proposition B (to authorize $90 million in general revenue bonds), was prepared for the November 1984 election. During the low-key campaign for its passage, the arguments about the need for a viable supply were reintroduced along with the first representations that without Pamo, the northern part of the county could be vulnerable to an emergency, such as an earthquake, or to mechanical failures in the pumping system or pipeline failures due to age or corrosion. Ironically, despite their lengthy board discussions concerning MWD participation and their decision to go it alone, the CWA leaders decided to include in the crucial ballot argument the statement that MWD participation would help insure the repayment of the bonds. In October 1984, just a few weeks after Galloway had exploded on the scene, the ballot argument issue came before the MWD board, resulting in a formal rebuke by both the MWD board chairman and its assistant general manager.[57]

Despite widespread support from top local officials and media, including then–San Diego Mayor Roger Hedgecock and both the *Union* and *Tribune*, the water authority got only a 55 percent vote in support of its proposition, far less than its impressive tally two years earlier in the Peripheral Canal election. CWA leaders dismissed the lower vote totals as reflexive opposition to bond issues, but the substantial no vote on Proposition B heartened Pamo's primary opponents, a coalition of environmental groups led by the chairwoman of the San Diego Sierra Club, a self-taught water activist named Emily Durbin.[58]

Over the next several years the Pamo issue became more contentious, with environmentalists (concerned about the project's growth implications in North County and its negative impact on one of the few scenic, undeveloped areas in the region) mobilizing the public against the project. In turn, Pamo became the first priority of water authority leaders, despite its relative low annual yield (about 10,000 acre-feet) and its increasing economic and political costs. CWA's pursuit of Pamo led to its public identification as a major proponent of regional growth and expansion, despite its oft-stated claim that it never got involved with growth-related issues.[59] Durbin and her allies were successful in convincing the Environmental Protection Agency to intervene in the permit review process being undertaken by the Army Corps of Engineers, and, in a major policy reversal, EPA temporarily blocked the project, claiming the permit review had inadequately considered project alternatives and negative environmental impacts.[60] With water authority prestige and clout on the line, CWA leaders, including its General Manager Larry Michaels, who spent much of his time on this issue, decided to press on, despite the EPA intervention and the additional threat of a Sierra Club lawsuit.[61] More than any other CWA policy, Pamo, it appeared, would ultimately define the water authority's quest for independence.

Redefining the Terms

By 1987, it had become clear that the search for independence was not going well. The flurry of interest in San Diego as a potential buyer in a market arrangement began to dissipate as the water authority leadership, retreating from the sharp attack by MWD over the Galloway affair, referred all such inquiries to the larger agency. Even the attempts by the Imperial Irrigation District to sound out San Diego (replacing MWD) as a potential partner for its negotiations were referred by CWA back to MWD. Privately, San Diego leaders suggested that if MWD-IID negotiations were to fail, then San Diego would be willing to talk.[62] Larry Michaels, especially, argued that San Diego would eventually have a possible role, if not after the first deal, then in subsequent deals. This posture, however, remained passive at best, and it eliminated San Diego as a factor in the negotiations over water transfers.[63] The Pamo conflict exposed the water authority's uncertainties even more fully. General Manager Michaels was particularly vulnerable, since he had been identified with the project even prior to his selection as general manager. Michaels had initially been opposed as general manager by the new leadership bloc at the board, who had pushed instead for one of their own members, John Hennigar. One opposing board member stated that Michaels's selection was based in part on resentment of the new bloc's power and "arrogance." The bloc's position that a water authority general manager had to be politically oriented (in this new era of the search for independence) was also rejected in favor of support of a more technically oriented manager—a requirement that Michaels, with his engineering background, met.[64]

Once selected, however, Michaels deferred to the new leadership bloc, and together they pushed Pamo to the top of the CWA agenda. As the project came to be challenged and problems mounted, Michaels's position became even more tenuous. Once again the leadership bloc intervened, forcing Michaels's resignation by arguing again that the general manager's position required someone with political, not just technical, skills. Pamo's troubles, now defined as political constraints to water development, were Michaels's downfall.[65]

The search for Michaels's replacement created further stress on the water authority quest for independence. Divisions within the board reappeared once again, and Michaels's eventual successor, a young Tucson water manager named Lester Snow, was also selected over the opposition of the leadership bloc. Snow, one of a small but increasing number of water agency managers responsive to new concerns about management efficiency and the need to restructure water industry approaches away from traditional supply-enhancement development strategies, entered a politically charged atmosphere with an uncertain mandate.

Snow's first major policy initiative—an inevitable decision given the difficulty of overturning EPA—was to get the CWA board to agree to stop pursuing the Pamo Dam. Instead of formally declaring Pamo "dead," CWA announced it was putting the project aside for the time being, though without identifying what new circumstances might cause the project to revive. Like Galloway, it seemed clear that Pamo was destined simply to fade away.[66]

With Pamo on the back burner, CWA began to review its approach toward stretching, rather than expanding, its supply base—a crucial change of perspective for the pass-through agency. Under Snow's prodding, discussions with MWD over the possible development of a conjunctive-use approach using existing storage facilities—a strategy long advocated by CWA's critics—were expanded.[67] CWA turned, as did MWD at this time, to strategies for more efficient use of the existing system, though these had earlier been dismissed as insignificant to resolving the problem of supply.[68] Even San Diego's opposition to seasonal pricing, a key factor in preventing adoption of the program at MWD, was modified by Snow's new emphasis on an increased and more flexible storage system, which could take advantage of a seasonal price differential.[69]

The return to attention to the MWD relationship, which Snow helped refocus on the prospects of stretching existing supplies, was compounded by the board's continued attention to supporting the growth agenda. Water authority leaders, especially Madigan, were effective opponents of the slow growth movement in San Diego, which gathered strength through the 1980s, though it suffered setbacks in 1988 in its quest to use the initiative process to impose controls on growth.[70] The water authority leaders also resumed their strong support of MWD efforts for the State Water Project and the areawide distribution system, which had significant benefits for the region in terms of MWD's policy of melding all system costs equally among its member agencies. The San Diego water leaders, despite their new emphasis on local storage, also helped steer MWD policy toward *increasing* peaking capacity both through building the new distribution facilities and through increasing the pipeline size to *greater* than that of the existing system, which already had been designed at 130 percent of capacity.[71]

In the late 1980s, the San Diego County Water Authority seemed as uncertain of its mission and unclear about its strategy as it had been at its inception more than forty years earlier. Though CWA's support for growth remained constant, it was still plagued by the problem of identity. Soon after Lester Snow had joined the water authority, the CWA was confronted unexpectedly with an entirely new focus, albeit one still bound up with the question of San Diego's "identity." Southern California Edison (Los Angeles County–based) proposed to take over the San Diego Gas and Electric utility, which served much the same service area as did CWA. This threw the business and political leaders of San Diego into turmoil since, as with water, San

Diego saw itself as dependent on outside sources for supply of energy.[72] The Edison takeover, favored by the SDG&E executives, inflamed San Diego's existing tensions with Los Angeles.[73]

Soon after the Edison takeover plan was announced, San Diego city and county leaders, many of them business and growth-oriented conservatives, began to consider the idea of a public takeover of the utility. The most likely vehicle for such a takeover was the County Water Authority, given its over-lapping jurisdictions, interrelated activities and condemnation powers.[74] Other publicly owned water utilities, including Los Angeles's own Depart-ment of Water and Power, were also electrical utilities.

A public takeover of San Diego Gas and Electric, exercised through the County Water Authority, was an appealing prospect for the local leaders (including CWA leaders) who shared the concept of community "identity." The problem was how to accomplish such a "public" takeover, given the hostility of Edison and SDG&E and their considerable resources to oppose such a "municipalization" effort.[75]

Beyond the tactical maneuvers, however, lay a broader set of questions that CWA had not resolved. For Snow, the San Diego water industry's critical issues had become "perception of equity, environmental feasibility, and polit-ical acceptance."[76] The purpose and mission of the agency, however, had become less rather than more focused, combining growth agendas with un-certain forays into new areas, such as the SDG&E takeover study. These efforts have been framed by the issues of public accountability. By seeking to go beyond its former passive, pass-through role and pursuing such matters as a public "takeover," CWA has also brought to the fore the question of what "public" it will serve, and on what terms.

3

The Politics
of Groundwater

The Upper San Gabriel Valley Municipal Water District (Upper District) and related San Gabriel agencies and the City of Burbank's water and power utility, the Public Service Department (Burbank), are both heavily engaged in the politics of groundwater. Each has partial rights to a huge groundwater basin, each basin a major component of the natural water system of the Southern California area. Each has used this groundwater as its primary source of local water, and each shares its basin with other agencies. Both agencies have relied increasingly on the MWD system to supplement or substitute for their own local sources, and thus these agencies provide an opportunity to examine how local agencies have been enlisted in (or, in the USGVMWD case, created through) the region-wide agenda to expand imported water supplies.

This shift to imported water, even where water agencies had substantial groundwater rights, was intensified by the discovery of contaminated wells in the San Gabriel Valley and the San Fernando Basin in late 1979 and the early 1980s. This discovery had an immediate and major impact on the operations of these agencies. Locales within each agency's groundwater area have been designated as Superfund sites on the basis of the substantial contamination of the groundwater on which the agencies have depended. In the process, such agencies, organized to perform the routine tasks of distribution and delivery, have instead found themselves thrust into the highly visible and fluid problem of water quality. Without any clear guidance or precedent, subject to the activities and decisions of agencies of government located outside the traditional institutional setting of the water industry, these groundwater managers face some of the most difficult and volatile water issues today.

The Nature of Groundwater

Groundwater is that water stored below the ground in struc-tural basins that have been filled, over hundreds of thousands of years, with a complex bedding of material washed down from the surrounding moun-tains. As these materials are deposited, the spaces between the particles are filled with the water that transports them. If the basin is hydraulically bounded (either by the structure of the basement rock or, at the seacoast, by the counter-pressure of ocean water pushing through the sand) this water is retained. Subsequent rainfall, streamflow, and intentional percolation of water into the basin may replace (recharge) water which flows from (or is withdrawn from) the basin, but the base storage capacity of the basin is set by its geology, not by the rate of recharge. For this reason, *groundwater basins are managed most effectively when they are thought of as reservoirs of water, not as new sources.*

The Southern California area contains, within its current urban bound-aries, more than 140 million acre-feet of such potential storage. These reser-voirs were fully charged until wells were driven into them, beginning in the late nineteenth century. In areas like Anaheim, where this well water was first used for irrigation, the accumulated pressure of water trapped under impervious clay layers within the complex bedding of the basin led to arte-sian flow (well water flowed to the surface under pressure, without pumping) for a number of years after the wells were first driven.

As these various reservoirs were more fully developed for agricultural and then for urban water use, however, the rate of water withdrawal quickly passed the natural rate of recharge. This condition is termed basin overdraft. Short-term, minor overdraft may have little effect, if seasonal or intentional recharge quickly makes up this water deficit. But long-term patterns of over-draft can lead to two significant physical changes in the usefulness of the basin. The first—salt-water intrusion—occurs along the coastal margin as the withdrawal of water inland reduces the mass, and thus the pressure, of freshwater pushing against the salt water at the coast; when this happens salt water flows into the sediments along the coast, introducing the salts it carries into those sediments so that the water in this zone is no longer usable. The sec-ond—subsidence—occurs when, as groundwater is withdrawn, the sediment pore space in which it has been stored collapses under the pressure of the overlying materials. Salt-water intrusion and subsidence are both irreversible.

Groundwater accumulates within valleys that also provide flat land for urban development. So throughout Southern California most new land development for industrial, residential, or commercial use has been placed atop these reservoirs. The potential water-quality effect of this was treated as insignificant for many years, since it was thought that any contaminants on the soil surface would be adsorbed by (attached to) soil particles and would not percolate into the groundwater. The only contamination (other than salt-water intrusion) considered important until the mid-1970s was the other source of solution of minerals in groundwater, the total dissolved solids (TDS) which the water accumulated as it passed through the mineral materials of the basin. Where TDS are particularly high, they are likely to be from samples collected within salt-water intrusions in the coastal zone.

We now know that a whole complex of contaminants can travel from the surface into the groundwater, where these contaminants accumulate. The physical and chemical composition and the thickness of the material (along with the specific chemical characteristics of the particular contaminants) between the ground surface and the water table determine the rate at which contaminants travel toward the groundwater mass. Where the groundwater is effectively layered, contaminants may be trapped above the uppermost clay layers to enter lower zones only where natural breaks in these clays (or inadequately sealed wells) provide an opening for such flow. Because rates of surface contamination vary (depending on land use), the permeability of the soil varies, and the pattern of subsurface flow is complex, contaminants tend to be concentrated into plumes within the general groundwater mass.

The first finding of human contamination of groundwater was the discovery of high concentrations of nitrates in the groundwater of agricultural areas like the eastern San Gabriel Valley.[1] These nitrates appeared to result from agricultural fertilizers, especially from the rapid growth in use of synthetic fertilizers after 1920. But the health effects of nitrate contamination seemed relatively insignificant.[2] And the discovery of nitrate contamination did not signal the possibility of other contamination immediately, since nitrates were thought to be unusually mobile (able to flow) in the soil column. Water quality thus remained a secondary concern, at best, in decisions regarding the management of the groundwater resource.

The Institutions of Groundwater Management

The established institutional patterns of groundwater management made it difficult to address either the problem of overdraft or of contamination immediately. Any effective effort required institutional change.

From 1847 to the present, an intricate corpus of water-rights law has evolved in California. This law combines judicial decisions, legislative statutes, and constitutional amendments. The "California doctrine" recognizes rights based on a number of factors: ownership of parcels adjacent to the watercourse (*riparian* rights); prior capture of water (*appropriative* rights); and title to overlying land (*groundwater* rights). For historical reasons some of these rights are usufructory (that is, limited to use and not permitting sale), and others are fully developed property rights.

Water law in California is a marriage of forms derived from English common law, from the informal customs of early settlers, and from the arbitration of contemporary disputes. Though rights to water are often limited in ways that property rights in land are not, water rights are normally vested in land title (that is, they are transferred with the sale of land).[3]

The allocation of water becomes a complex process whenever demand exceeds supply. English common law (and its derived forms in the water law of more humid states within the United States) is not adequate to manage the disputes that arise in more arid regions. Although the current state of water rights entitlement in California is clearly transitional, a clear historical tendency can be discerned: over the last one hundred years the state (through the legislature and judiciary) has moved persistently to assert its jurisdiction over the common resource, in order to grant individuals increasingly secure and private title to water.

Like all other property rights, water rights are social relations that protect some members of society against the claims of others. Even when such rights take the form of rights-in-common (as in riparian rights), they serve to exclude some (those not members of the commons) from access to the resource.[4]

Appropriative rights, based on the dictum "first in time, first in right," grant priority to prior appropriators to the amount of water to which each is accustomed at the expense of latecomers, no matter their need. Appropriative rights have been codified from customary usage in the early American settlement in the West and represent the basic form of rights within the most arid western states; unlike riparian rights, they do not originate in English common law.

Like appropriative rights, rights to groundwater, as developed in California, represent a break with the common-law tradition. Where the common-law rule had entitled the landowner to everything beneath his land (and hence all water that could be extracted from the land), the California Supreme Court in 1903 ruled this not suitable to California.[5]

Groundwater in California has, over the years, become a major contributor of water for all uses. Approximately 15 million acre-feet of groundwater were withdrawn each year by the 1970s, with an overdraft of approximately 2.2 million acre-feet.[6] Rights to groundwater, as established by judicial decisions, have been based on two rules: the overlying use right and the correlative rights doctrine. In dependence on physical contiguity and in the requirement of correlative rights, groundwater rights resemble riparian rights but are not as clearly defined as rights in common. Like riparian rights, groundwater rights are normally not affected by priority of capture. Where overdraft occurs, however, the courts have held that prescriptive rights to groundwater can develop.

Overlying users can protect rights to groundwater in several ways: by obtaining a declaratory judgment before overdraft occurs that establishes a paramount overlying right against subsequent nonsurplus allocation; by injunctive relief when overdraft begins; or by retaining an established right, to the extent that this right is exercised during the prescriptive period. In several instances courts have apportioned groundwater rights in overdrafted basins on the basis of previous rates of withdrawal. This criterion may stimulate competitive withdrawal in unadjudicated basins where adjudication is anticipated. Except where adjudication has taken place, groundwater rights are not measured or recorded. Only appropriative rights to surface water are fully recorded, making the assessment of individual rights and of the degree to which private rights fully occupy a resource quite difficult. But the importance of groundwater to the Southern California water economy has led to the adjudication (in the last forty years) of all of the major urban groundwater basins.

Adjudication, the apportionment of rights among existing users, has not been the only or the clearly preferred strategy of groundwater management. While this process confirms individual rights, it also limits them, in that by law adjudicated basins must limit subsequent withdrawals to "sustainable or safe yield." With this limitation, producers in adjudicated basins may face a disadvantage in competition with producers in other areas, who do not face this constraint. Therefore California groundwater users have frequently set up water districts (like the Upper San Gabriel Valley Municipal Water District) in parallel with the Watermaster institution, which manages adjudicated groundwater, creating a second quasigovernmental agency to undertake groundwater replenishment programs and to levy taxes, including pump taxes (rate taxes based on withdrawal).[7] Setting up such a district has distinct advantages for major water users: together they can undertake projects beyond the means of any individual, expanding the supply by bringing in water from outside the region. Where control of the district is based on landownership (the usual case in agricultural areas), large landowners have effective control over the entire resource[8]; and the cost of this supplemental imported water is reduced (for those for whom it provides most benefit) by the special tax status of the district as a peri-statal (tax-exempt bonds) and by the opportunity to pass on some portion of the cost to a broader base of users through rate structures or property taxes (*ad valorem* taxes based on land value, not water use).

For a local agency like Burbank, adjudication reduces its autonomy and limits its authority to set its own rate of groundwater withdrawal. For the Upper San Gabriel Valley Municipal Water District (USGVMWD), however, adjudication created its role, as local users sought to avoid the use limits that the adjudication process mandated, by importing water to offset the water drawn from the San Gabriel aquifers. But the adjudication process is directed toward managing water supply, not water quality, and has not provided in either case an institutional form that has aided water agencies in responding to the problems of groundwater contamination, an issue which now preoccupies both agencies.

Burbank

The city of Burbank is located directly to the north and slightly to the west of downtown Los Angeles. With an estimated population of 93,800 and a land area of 17.14 square miles, Burbank is just one of eighty-eight separate municipalities within Los Angeles County.[9] With neighboring Pasadena to the east and Glendale to the west and south, the city (incorporated in 1911) represents one of the oldest, most developed urban core areas in the region. Burbank has a large industrial base, centered around Lockheed's major facility and the various film and television studios, both of which located within or near the city limits in the 1920s. Most of the land in the city is developed, with new construction primarily limited to higher-density residential infill or to redevelopment of former studio properties.

Burbank sits over the San Fernando Valley Groundwater Basin, located in the Upper Los Angeles River Area, which extends for 328,000 acres over the entire watershed of the Los Angeles River and its tributaries. Burbank's section of the basin is bounded on the north and northwest by the Verdugo Mountains, to the east by the San Rafael Hills and to the west by the Santa Monica Mountains (see fig. 7). Water use throughout the San Fernando Basin is primarily municipal and industrial, and pumping is restricted by court decision to 104,000 acre-feet per year, divided between the cities of Los Angeles, Glendale, La Crescenta, San Fernando, and Burbank.[10] For more than sixty years, Burbank relied primarily on the San Fernando Basin for its water supply, ultimately drilling eleven wells, and supplemented its local production with water purchased from MWD. However, as a consequence both of the adjudication of rights to water in the San Fernando Basin and of the subsequent discovery of trace amounts of volatile organics in several of the city's wells, Burbank's usable local water supply, which had

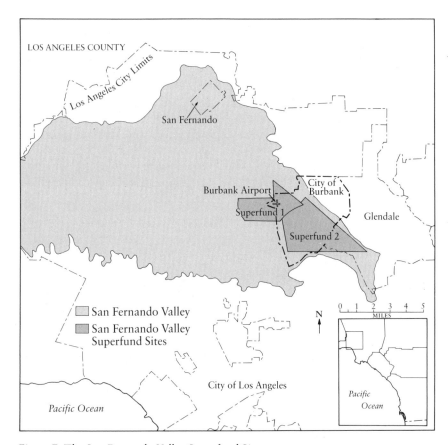

Figure 7. The San Fernando Valley Superfund Sites

provided as much as 83 percent of the city's water as late as 1968, declined significantly.[11] Of its ten wells, only three were found to have contaminants below water quality standards and were thus available for operation. The city has purchased 100 percent of its water from MWD since June of 1986.[12]

In addition to these wells, the city manages and operates its own electrical utility, established in 1934 when Burbank itself purchased a share of Hoover Dam power, on the basis of its participation as an original member agency of the Metropolitan Water District.[13] Water and power operations were combined and the Public Service Department set up as the city's utility. Most of the Public Service Department's approximately $100 million budget today is committed to its power side, which provides eight times the revenue base of water sales. And whereas electricity use is predominantly industrial (accounting for about 50 percent of total sales) and commercial (about another 25 percent), more than 65 percent of all water sales are for residential use, with industrial use as low as 10 percent of total sales.[14]

For some years city water use has stabilized at about 23,000 acre-feet annually (although the ratio of imported water to groundwater has changed dramatically in that time).[15] As a result, much of the Public Service Department's activity has been focused on the power side of the utility's operations. But the growing problem of contamination and the politics related to the origins of this pollution and to the issues of monitoring and clean-up have recently become a difficult (and unresolved) policy matter for the city and its utility, increasingly subject to intervention by outside parties. The politics of groundwater, seen as a settled, though lost, question after adjudication of the basin, has forced its way back onto Burbank's agenda.

A Company Town

Long known as a city famous for its landmarks, such as the giant Lockheed plant and the huge studios, Burbank was also one of the region's earliest bedroom subdivisions, in the wake of the first plans to bring imported water into the region. Located at the eastern edge of the vast tract of undeveloped land acquired by the powerful real-estate syndicate led by Harry Chandler of the *Los Angeles Times* and including W. P. Whitsett (MWD's first chairman), Burbank's land base had first been subdivided, during the boom of 1887, by a handful of speculators who purchased the tract from a New Hampshire–born dentist named David Burbank.[16] At the time of incorporation, when fewer than five hundred people lived within what were to become the Burbank city limits, most of the land was in alfalfa and a wide range of other crops including table grapes (and wineries), peaches, apricots, and melons, and the area also included fifteen dairies with one thousand cows. The city was connected to the Pacific Electric streetcar system in 1911, the year of its incorporation, and urban settlement and new industrial activity quickly began to alter Burbank.[17]

During this period, various settlements within the Los Angeles region went through rapid population growth and the emergence of a new industrial infrastructure based on oil, movies, and the budding aircraft industry. As Burbank changed, its population increased twenty-fold, and much of the area's agricultural land was acquired for other purposes, including the establishment of the city's two most prominent companies. The Lockheed aircraft plant was sited in 1927 three miles east of what were then the city limits to house the major facility of Allen and Malcolm Lockheed, two brothers who built one of the first aircraft plants in the country in 1916 and incorporated their company a decade later. When it set up its Burbank plant, Lockheed was producing about fifty planes a year. "A great step in the town's desire to attract new industries and payrolls," commented newspapers at the time.[18] Similarly, in 1926, a Burbank site was selected to house what was then the world's largest film studio (soon to be acquired by Warner Brothers), which led one local newspaper to proclaim that this had laid the groundwork for a "boom unprecedented in real estate history in Southern California."[19]

These events, in turn, focused attention on the city's infrastructure and its ability to meet anticipated growth. Water and energy use were a central concern. Having first organized itself as a separate city, Burbank had decided to forego annexation to the city of Los Angeles, a precondition for access to water from the Los Angeles Aqueduct.[20] By the mid 1920s, the rapid expansion and changing land use of the city caused Burbank (with neighboring Pasadena and Glendale, and several other cities in the region with groundwater resources), to seek to join the city of Los Angeles to obtain additional water—and power—from the Colorado River. Though anticipating the need for future supplemental water, Burbank was also particularly attracted to the new energy supply to be generated at Hoover Dam. As a consequence, the city bought out the Burbank facilities of Southern California Edison in 1934, in advance of signing contracts with the federal government for Hoover power three years later.[21]

By the 1940s, its water and power infrastructure in place, the city resumed both population growth and industrial expansion, primarily centered around the Lockheed plant and the Warner studio. Lockheed, which went bankrupt but reorganized during the Depression as part of the consolidation in the aircraft industry, became a huge enterprise during World War II. At one point, it employed more than 35,000 workers, nearly equivalent to the entire population of the city. Lockheed came to be identified with Burbank in terms of both image and its impact on the community. Lockheed was the community's largest energy user, a major water user, and a pivotal force in the town's political, business, and cultural life. The company cut back operations at the end of the war (though it shifted part of its production to commercial aircraft), but the advent of the Korean War and renewed military expenditures with the Cold War caused Lockheed to continue to grow, weathering various industry cycles.[22]

Burbank's other major industry also grew when the NBC television studios were located across from the Warner Brothers lot in 1952.[23] Residential population growth leveled off during the 1950s and 1960s, but the city's industrial character became even more pronounced as the remaining land zoned for light and heavy industry was occupied by firms tied to the aerospace and entertainment giants. This in turn further oriented the utility towards its energy role. Expanding energy use dominated the utility's agenda since water use, with declining residential growth rates, remained relatively constant. The city of Burbank, its present—and future—immersed in its relationship to its two giant industries, had become, in its planning for utility services, a company town.

Adjudication Woes

By the early 1970s, the agenda of the Burbank Public Service Department seemed settled. By the time its general manager, Alan Capon, retired in 1973, the utility had made the transition from a small water retailer relying on local wells and also selling power from its new Hoover Dam contracts, to a larger, more diverse organization. Increases in water use during the 1950s and 1960s had been met largely with purchases from MWD, while growing power demands led the utility to explore several new energy sources, eventually including (among other projects) a small but expensive share in the Intermountain Power Project (a huge Utah coal-fired generating plant), a sizable commitment for a small utility.[24] Following the Arab oil embargo and the subsequent crisis, the utility's attention shifted even further to the energy side and utility managers introduced a new pricing structure, which included a summer demand charge designed to reduce summertime peak demands for energy.[25]

The water side of the utility, on the other hand, had become quite routine. The city's secure relationship with MWD seemed strengthened by the growing prominence of Burbank's MWD director, Earle Blais, who became chair of MWD's Legal and Claims Committee in the late 1960s and chairman of the board a decade later. Burbank's water concerns were centered on the continuing legal attempts by the City of Los Angeles to restructure the use and disposition of the San Fernando Valley Groundwater Basin.

By the 1940s, urban development and industrial activity in the San Fernando Valley had led to long-term overdraft problems in the San Fernando Basin. The City of Los Angeles, which drew on this groundwater extensively, had begun to worry that increased pumping by other parties, including Burbank and Glendale, might also affect the status of the city's imported Owens Valley water, which was being stored in the San Fernando Basin. In 1955, Los Angeles decided to take legal action, filing suit in superior court to establish title to the groundwater.[26]

The Los Angeles suit, which was referred first to the then–State Water Rights Board and finally came to trial more than ten years after the initial filing, became one of the key adjudication suits in Southern California. The trial court's decision, issued in 1968, not only allocated rights to water among the different parties but also established regulations for pumping and management of the supply.[27] Implementation was delayed until the California Supreme Court upheld the ruling in 1975 and the parties then reached agreement over the specific volumes of water involved.

The court judgment allowed some flexibility to the local agencies—for example, each party could over- or underpump its rights by 10 percent during any given year, to be paid back (or taken) in subsequent years. In establishing such flexibility it became possible to develop further the storage capacity of the basin, an idea pursued by the State Department of Water Resources, which was seeking storage sites for State Project water.[28] But, uncertain about their future rights to San Fernando Basin water, the smaller involved parties (including Burbank) reworked their water strategy on narrower grounds, shifting away from an uncertain groundwater supply toward greater dependence on MWD's imported water.[29] After the adjudication settlement, which limited Burbank's extractions to 20 percent of its historical use, the city quickly increased its intake of MWD water and began to explore a new MWD program, designed to encourage additional storage of imported water.[30] Still reeling from its losses of local supply stemming from the adjudication, the utility also found itself confronting its most difficult issue to date: serious and extensive contamination of its wells (and others) located throughout the San Fernando Basin. A new and troubling era for this groundwater agency had arrived.

San Gabriel

The San Gabriel Valley is located at the eastern end of Los Angeles County, bounded on the north by the San Gabriel Mountains, the west by the San Rafael and Merced hills, the south by the Puente Hills and the east by a low divide between the San Gabriel and the Upper Santa Ana river systems (see fig. 8). It includes the cities of Alhambra, El Monte, Monrovia, Baldwin Park, West Covina, Duarte, Azusa, and Glendora, among others.

Much of the valley lies over the Main San Gabriel Basin, a vast surface and underground water system that includes two principal rivers, the San Gabriel and the Rio Hondo. These systems drain about 115 square miles of valley land and 335 square miles of mountains and foothills. The basin comprises about 110,000 acres, mostly alluvial deposits that make the basin a natural groundwater storage reservoir. The surplus groundwater flows, with the San Gabriel River, through the Whittier Narrows (the lowest point in the valley) and across the coastal plain of Los Angeles County, passing through the Central and West Basins, the two other interrelated groundwater storage basins linking this vast underground system that stretches from the San Gabriel Mountains to the ocean.[31]

By the late 1980s, 111 different water producers in the San Gabriel Valley (including municipalities, water companies, industrial users such as breweries and rock and gravel companies, and individual landowners) had rights

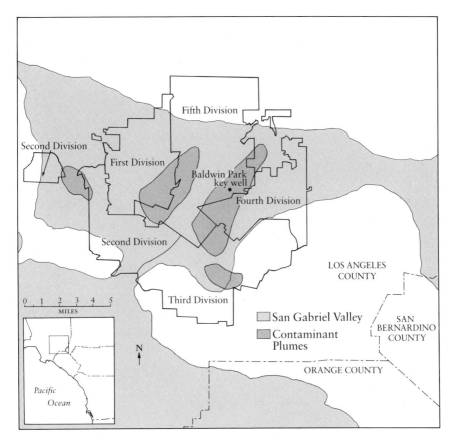

Figure 8. The Upper San Gabriel Valley Municipal Water District

to the groundwater underlying the Main San Gabriel Basin. In 1987, these producers used 256,000 acre-feet of water, of which 237,000 were pumped from the ground (with the remaining 19,000 acre-feet captured from surface water sources). At the same time, the three regional agencies (including the Upper San Gabriel Valley Municipal Water District) purchased another 78,000 acre-feet of water to replenish the basin.[32]

The San Gabriel Valley, now largely urbanized (with an estimated 1988 population of 900,000) has evolved into a complex of bedroom communities with a diverse mix of light and heavy industry and a declining level of agricultural (including dairy) production. Though some undeveloped land can still be found in the eastern end of the valley and in the foothills to the north, much of the valley experienced the shift to urban land use after World War II.

Prior to the war, the San Gabriel Valley had grown slowly, but this changed dramatically in the late 1940s and 1950s with early industrial development and new urban subdivisions. This growth substantially increased the amount of water used within the Upper Valley, ultimately leading to legal action by those water agencies whose service areas were located below Whittier Narrows but who depended on continued outflow from the Upper Basin. Fearing a successful lawsuit that might limit basin withdrawals and lead to a need for imported water, San Gabriel Valley interests (the existing water agencies and private water companies, along with various prominent developers, ranchers and industrialists) combined to form the San Gabriel Valley Water Association to protect their water position. In 1960, one year after suit was filed by downstream agencies, the local valley interests set up the Upper San Gabriel Valley Municipal Water District (USGVMWD) to secure whatever supplemental water might be needed after resolution of this litigation. Three years later the Upper District annexed to MWD. Most of the cities and water users in the valley at the time affiliated with the Upper District, though four cities—Azusa, Alhambra, Sierra Madre, and Monterey Park (the Four Cities, or San Gabriel Valley Municipal Water District)—had formed their own separate district and ultimately decided to contract separately with the State of California for State Project water. As a result, the Upper District service area came to include most (92,000 acres) but not all of the 110,000 acres in the Main San Gabriel Basin (and also 4,500 acres in the Raymond Basin to the north and 780 acres to the west in South Pasadena).[33] The split between the municipal agencies resulted in a series of lawsuits and adjudication efforts culminating in 1972 in a complex basin-wide agreement to regulate and manage the Main San Gabriel Basin.[34] By the late 1970s, the San Gabriel Valley water industry had become an intertwined array of water users and region-wide agencies. Four separate entities—the Upper District, the Four Cities (or San Gabriel Valley Municipal) Water District, the Main San Gabriel Basin Watermaster (overseeing the adjudication) and the industry-related Water Association—all played a crucial and sometimes overlapping role.

The discovery of contaminated wells in San Gabriel compounded this already complex structure of agency activity. The arrival of EPA, with the Superfund designation of San Gabriel's groundwater, brought an entirely new dimension to water-policy decision making. All the regional water agencies, including the Upper District, which in 1984 contracted with the EPA to provide public outreach as part of the San Gabriel Superfund process,[35] were drawn into the politics of groundwater quality and, by extension, into a range of other new issues. Superfund not only added new players but ultimately put into question the terms by which water policy in general had been dealt with within the complex and fragmented world of San Gabriel water.

Filling in the Valley

For nearly a hundred years, the surface and underground water supplies of the San Gabriel Valley have been coveted by Southern California urban development forces. During the late nineteenth century, the nascent Los Angeles water industry explored the possibility of diverting the San Gabriel River to support and stimulate the growth they hoped for, before deciding on the Owens Valley watershed as the best source for imported water. The anticipation that growth would push eastward into the San Gabriel Valley—already considered part of Greater Los Angeles by local boosters—was one key reason for the decision.[36]

The early real estate booms and busts so characteristic of Los Angeles, however, did not extend eastward at first, and the San Gabriel Valley remained sparsely populated through much of the first half of the century. Most valley land was in irrigated agriculture, primarily walnuts and oranges, based on modestly expanding well water use. The San Gabriel Basin stood at the center of what came to be known as the "inland citrus district," which stretched from Pasadena to San Bernardino.[37] The limited urban development that did exist was located mostly at the western edge of the valley, closer to downtown Los Angeles. With water use predominantly agricultural, the rate of increased groundwater withdrawals was nowhere near that of the more rapidly urbanizing Central and West Basin areas, which were already beginning to experience overdrafts by the 1930s.[38]

From World War II on, however, the San Gabriel Valley grew rapidly, shifting from agriculture to urban development, tied in part to the emergence of more extensive manufacturing. Defense contracts stimulated medium and light manufacturing, which became the main source of employment in the valley by the late 1950s. The rapid shift from orchards to cities and suburbs paralleled the massive post-war urbanization transforming most of rural Los Angeles County. In 1950, 307,000 people lived in the incorporated areas of the San Gabriel Valley; ten years later there were 563,000, with another 354,000 in unincorporated areas. Most growth was still concentrated in the western part of the valley in Pasadena, Alhambra, Arcadia, and Monterey Park, but the urban areas moved east during the 1960s and 1970s, though more slowly than during the 1950s. By the 1980s, nearly the entire valley had been urbanized and population growth leveled off to rates commensurate with other developed parts of the county.[39]

Housing development, industrial growth, and the shift from agriculture to urban land use in the San Gabriel Valley influenced the nature of both water production and consumption. Water-use patterns shifted from agricultural to municipal and industrial, at first lowering *per capita* demand for water while simultaneously raising the overall amount of water consumed and the volume of water lost to sewage.[40] This reduced the water returning to the surface and underground river systems. As a consequence, the main San Gabriel Basin itself began to experience the first signs of overdraft by the late 1940s and early 1950s, compounding problems in the Central and West Basins, which were already experiencing serious problems, including salt-water intrusion, from their own overdraft.

In 1954, major pumpers in the San Gabriel Basin began meeting to discuss the possibility that legal action would be brought against them by the downstream users. In January 1956 the major San Gabriel users, including several private water companies, a number of cities (including Alhambra), and a variety of agricultural and industrial interests (including the rock and gravel industry), formally organized themselves into the San Gabriel Valley Water Association to represent basin interests.[41] Three years later, the downstream users filed a suit, known as the Long Beach Action, regarding the San Gabriel River. This case, brought by Long Beach, Compton, and the Central Basin Municipal Water District, sought to insure that San Gabriel Valley water users would be required to supply a set volume of water from the San Gabriel River system.[42] Both the Central and West Basin areas had by then adjudicated their own basins to limit overall use of groundwater, to prevent further overdrafts, and to set allocations among users based on their historic use. Now these users wanted to force limits upstream, because increasing consumptive withdrawal in the San Gabriel Valley reduced the water that flowed through the Whittier Narrows to the users downstream.

The Long Beach action forced the hand of the San Gabriel water users, setting off a chain of events that would reshape the water system in the San Gabriel Valley. The adjudication process in all three basin areas had stimulated the various urban, industrial, and agricultural interests to pursue the idea of importing water into this water-rich region to sustain and continue the explosive growth of the post-war years. With water development directly associated with urban growth throughout Southern California, this fear of the future limits of presently bountiful local water led to increased support for the State Water Project, to sustain the growth-development equation indefinitely.

These negotiations between the various San Gabriel groundwater users were affected by MWD's policy of expansion following the Laguna Doctrine, which tied its support for new sources of imported water to its own monopoly status over those sources. In line with this commitment, MWD continued to promote an aggressive annexation policy, especially of groundwater users who turned to MWD as a supplemental supplier once adjudication terms were set. Under MWD chairman Joseph Jensen's continuing leadership, MWD sought to insure that agencies in those groundwater areas annexing to the MWD would join as centralized units representing an entire, adjudicated groundwater basin. Groundwater management entities could then limit groundwater use both to reduce their overdraft and to tie future growth to imported water.[43] To underwrite this process, MWD sponsored a ballot measure, "Proposition W," which allowed it to issue $50 million in short-term notes to be secured by annexation charges levied on territories annexing to the district. The Proposition W campaign, headed by a major regional land developer, Preston Hotchkis,[44] was designed to help ensure that annexations would generate adequate additional demand for water from the proposed State Water Project.[45]

By 1959, when the Long Beach action was initiated, the MWD annexation campaign had moved into full gear. MWD had already made overtures to water users and political and business figures in the San Gabriel Valley, suggesting that they pursue annexation to MWD as the best way to obtain the supplemental water necessary for continuing urban and industrial expansion while meeting the possible terms of a legal settlement with the downstream users. Moreover, the two downstream user groups had themselves already annexed to MWD as part of their own adjudication-centralization-expansion strategy.[46]

Most of the San Gabriel water users and business and political leaders were amenable to MWD annexation. They were concerned, however, about the cost of the expensive distribution facilities required to hook the valley into the MWD system. Several of the cities in the valley, particularly Alhambra (one of the more developed and important valley water users), also feared that annexation to MWD would mean a serious loss of autonomy. "Alhambra was the key," recalled water lawyer Ralph Helm, who would become the Upper San Gabriel Valley MWD's first legal counsel. "They thought MWD was autocratic."[47]

The tensions between MWD and Alhambra and its allies came to a head in the attempt to establish a Valley-wide organization to annex to MWD. When the Upper San Gabriel Valley Municipal Water District was formed in 1960, it was not entirely clear whether the new district would annex to MWD, though its leadership leaned in that direction.[48] Another available option involved obtaining a separate contract with the State of California for State Project water, a position advocated by the "four cities": Alhambra, Monterey Park, Sierra Madre, and Azusa. The four cities, in a defensive move, in 1959 had established their own water district, the San Gabriel Valley Municipal Water District.[49] With moves and counter-moves at their most intense, the controversy came to rest on whether the Upper District would indeed proceed with annexation to MWD, without including the Four Cities.

Soon after its formation, the Upper District commissioned studies to explore both how much supplemental water might be required and how best to obtain it. The valley's need for supplemental water, these studies estimated, would jump from 7,000 acre-feet to more than 52,000 acre-feet in less than a decade, and would thereafter increase to 88,000 acre-feet by 1980 and to 131,000 acre-feet by 1990.[50] The Upper District's preliminary investigation suggested that annexation to MWD might be more expensive, depending on which of its feeder systems were used to serve the area. The San Gabriel interests, as a condition of annexation, wanted MWD to ensure that the San Gabriel agencies would not pay more than what they might pay as state contractors.[51]

This issue came to a head at an informal session arranged during a national gathering of the American Water Works Association (AWWA). MWD representatives (led by Jensen), and Upper District representatives (including several of its board members, general counsel Helm, and the Upper District's first general manager, Carl Fossette) ultimately agreed to a tradeoff: MWD leaders would work out a less expensive arrangement and, in turn, Upper District leaders would seek annexation to MWD. Jensen pursued this agreement despite its incompatibility with MWD's stated policy of annexing only centralized groundwater units, since Jensen, Helm recalled, "wanted to increase the sales of State Project water badly and would do considerable things to attract people to MWD."[52] After the deal was cut at the AWWA meeting, Upper District leaders moved quickly to annex, launching a successful drive to get area residents to back joining MWD.[53] While MWD was willing to accommodate the Upper District to get the annexation, it was at the same time prepared to "play hardball," one participant recalled, with the Four Cities (San Gabriel Valley Municipal Water District).[54] The Four Cities District, despite MWD opposition, successfully negotiated its own contract for State Project water with the State Department of Water Resources, which had long been interested in breaking the MWD monopoly for purchase of State Project water south of the Tehachapis. MWD subsequently sought to persuade one of the Four Cities (Sierra Madre) to deannex from its district to join the Upper District and thus to become part of the MWD system. These moves were countered by the head of the State Department of Water Resources, William Gianelli, whose position was in turn characterized by the MWD general counsel as "arbitrary, unreasonable, and capricious."[55]

MWD tactics in the San Gabriel Valley compounded an already messy situation. After the Four Cities signed their own separate contract with the State of California, they sought at one point the joint use of a proposed San Gabriel Valley pipeline to deliver State project water to the valley. MWD refused, insisting that two separate facilities be built, despite additional, duplicated expenses. "MWD was telling them," Upper District director Howard Hawkins recalled of the discussions, "that they wouldn't build a joint facility to the State Project because [the San Gabriel District] had refused to join MWD. It was as simple as that."[56] Imported water would come to the valley to meet anticipated growth, but through parallel distribution systems, involving contending agencies without a coherent management approach.

Setting Up the System

With imported water at hand, the Upper District and its four cities rival now needed a mechanism to divide up local water. The Long Beach action had been settled in 1965 with a stipulation that the San Gabriel users would deliver more than 98,000 acre-feet of water from the San Gabriel River to downstream users.[57] This settlement, combined with the creation of the two districts and their separate contractual arrangements with the State Department of Water Resources, placed increasing pressure on all valley water users to set up a system governing groundwater use.

The problems in establishing such a system were enormous. To begin with, there were then more than 200 "producers" in the valley—water agencies, private water companies, and a wide variety of individual agricultural, municipal, and industrial entities—almost all of whom would claim rights to a portion of the San Gabriel groundwater basin. Moreover, the existence of more than one contractor for imported water necessitated an agreement, or adjudication, to settle not only who got what rights to the water but how much water could be pumped. With the Long Beach Agreement adding pressure to resolve the issue quickly, legal action aimed at adjudication was filed by the Upper District in 1968, setting off a scramble between twenty-eight interest groups.[58]

The adjudication process was striking in its complexity and breadth. Dozens of attorneys, engineers, water managers, landowners, dairy owners, and industry executives worked for months at a time over specific and elaborate details to sort out different claims and strategies to arrive at a workable solution. Often, the attorneys would meet in one room to define the legal parameters of an agreement, while the engineers got together separately to deal with how such an agreement could be physically achieved and implemented, with each producer lobbying each group for an ultimate resolution most favorable to it.[59]

From the outset, one central question was what limits to set on the water to be pumped in any given year. The Central and West Basin adjudication agreements had established fixed shares of water among producers and a lower "safe yield" limit beyond which pumping could not occur. A number of the San Gabriel parties, particularly the Upper District's consulting engineer, Thomas Stetson, wanted to modify that approach by establishing an "operating safe yield" that functioned more flexibly than did earlier Southern California adjudications.[60] This concept would establish a *range* of use, based on an upper and lower limit that might vary annually depending on storage levels and previous and projected rainfall patterns. Levels for the upper and lower limits would be set in relation to a representative well, the "Baldwin Park key well."

This approach was initially resisted by the rock and gravel firms, several of which were active in the basin. They feared that if too much flexibility was structured into the system, particularly if the upper limit was set too high, they would suffer economic losses when forced to mine underwater.[61] Though their alternative "long-term yield" approach was ultimately rejected in favor of the operating safe yield, the mining interests succeeded in setting the upper limit at a figure of 250 feet above the base level of the Baldwin Park key well, even though this would reduce the effective storage capacity of the basin.

This conflict over the upper limit was just one of several during the adjudication. There were differences between some of the older, long-standing water "producers" or pumpers, particularly agricultural interests, and new pumpers (representing industry and urban users) who did not have the same historical rights to the water. Those with riparian rights to surface flows of the San Gabriel River were reluctant to have their rights quantified, though this would be necessary to complete the adjudication. Other arguments revolved around the boundaries of the basin, and some pumpers remained antagonistic to the adjudication process to the very end. Finally, however, four years after the legal action was instituted, informal agreements based on the operating safe yield principle were worked out and formal judgment was entered in January 1973.[62]

The terms of the San Gabriel adjudication were as complex as the process to establish it. A Watermaster, created to oversee the agreement, would ·consist of nine members: six producer representatives to be selected by the San Gabriel Valley Water Association from among its own ranks; two more to be chosen from the five-member board of the Upper District; and the final member from the board of the San Gabriel Valley Municipal Water (Four Cities) District.[63] The Watermaster would be staffed by some of those who helped work out the agreement: consulting engineer Tom Stetson, who was also advising the Upper District; attorney Helm, who represented both the Upper District and the Four Cities; and Jane Bray, the top staff representative of both the Upper District and the Water Association.[64]

The adjudication agreement and the establishment of Watermaster set in place the complex though relatively unified structure of governance of the groundwater basin and the contending member units of the water industry. Four different operating entities had now been established: Watermaster to manage the groundwater basin; the Upper District to obtain MWD water and link the imported and local water systems; the Four Cities agency to contract directly for State Project water on behalf of the dissident cities; and the Water Association to represent the producer interests. Moreover, the number of producers active in the basin, particularly the large number of small, private water utilities and the variety of industrial users with their own water rights, compounded the already complex set of relationships. During the 1970s, the system appeared to function smoothly as growth rates began to level off and MWD imports remained modest. And though the adjudication afforded some important flexibility, most water producers tended to simply "peak off" the MWD system by increasing imports only when demands exceeded annual limits.[65] As long as pumping could continue and MWD water was readily available when needed, the producers seemed content with the system. Water supply management had arrived in the valley to stay.

Enter Superfund

For nearly all Southern California water agency managers, drinking water quality was given little thought through the 1970s. Organizations such as the Upper District and the San Gabriel Watermaster, like the Watermaster for the San Fernando Basin, had considered water quality issues only incidentally in their original charters.[66] Contamination of groundwater was thought unlikely and easily contained. Even existing contamination, such as nitrates in the San Gabriel Valley or high TDS in MWD's Colorado River supply, was seen as limited and manageable, secondary to the primary mission of supply and delivery. So when the Aerojet-General Corporation, a major San Gabriel industry, revealed in December 1979 that a well in the city of Azusa contained 1800 parts per billion (ppb) trichloroethylene (TCE)—a chlorinated solvent widely used in a number of industries including aerospace—the water agencies initially minimized the matter.[67]

But the new problem of organic chemicals, far from fading, began to mushroom. Indeed, within months after the Aerojet discovery, new test results suggested that contamination in both the San Gabriel and San Fernando basins was extraordinarily widespread. In the San Fernando Basin, 25 percent of the first set of wells tested showed trace levels of two common volatile organic contaminants, TCE and another widely used solvent, perchloroethylene (PCE).[68] In the San Gabriel Basin, the findings were even more dramatic: of the first 246 wells tested by the State Department of Health Services (DOHS), thirty-seven exceeded five parts per billion of TCE, the current "action level" set by DOHS.[69] Though "action levels" were still only "advisory,"[70] they placed pressure on water agencies to intervene in some manner, by blending the contaminated well water with other sources such as the imported MWD water, by developing a new method to treat the water, or simply by shutting down the wells—as most agencies, including Burbank and several of the municipalities and private water companies in San Gabriel, opted to do. The disadvantage of blending or of shutting down wells, the least expensive alternatives, was that this only postponed and possibly intensified the problem, since the contaminants moved with the groundwater, possibly as much as ten feet a year or more, often in an unpredictable way, and thereby endangered nearby wells. Moreover, in both the heavily developed San Gabriel and San Fernando basins, the degree and volume of pumping intensified the concentration and movement of the contamination. Wells testing clean one month might begin to show trace levels the following month, and then exceed standards or action levels several months later. Ultimately, without some form of intervention, the growing and wandering trace contaminants could threaten significant areas of the basins.[71]

Treatment was an expensive and unanticipated operational cost, resented by the water agencies that were still dubious about the seriousness of the problem. Even testing was expensive, and most agencies preferred to have other government agencies, whether the Department of Health Services or the Regional Water Quality Control Boards, undertake those functions. By the early 1980s, as additional tests continued to demonstrate the magnitude of contamination,[72] water agencies such as Burbank and the Upper District found themselves continually on the defensive, wary of any suggested operational changes and uncertain as to how to analyze the issue, let alone to suggest a strategy of intervention. Reluctant to take action, the agencies were relieved when outside parties led by the federal Environmental Protection Agency (EPA) intervened instead. In the San Gabriel and San Fernando groundwater basins that meant intervention via EPA's vast new program established pursuant to the 1980 Comprehensive Emergency Response, Compensation, and Liability Act (CERCLA), or Superfund.

In retrospect, EPA came to regret its intervention. The combination of public outcry, expanded media coverage, and especially of pressure from public officials such as California Assemblywoman Sally Tanner had caused the federal agency to place the San Gabriel and San Fernando basins on its national priorities list of hazardous sites requiring Superfund cleanup.[73] But contaminants in a groundwater basin had varied and multiple sources, compounding the difficulty of locating parties responsible and therefore potentially liable to pay for the cleanup. Moreover, both the San Gabriel and San Fernando basin situations presented their own institutional problems related to the particular history and focus of the various agencies involved.

San Gabriel: Clean-Up Paralysis

In San Gabriel, EPA was immediately confronted with the different, though overlapping, regional entities—the Upper District, the Four Cities District, Watermaster, and the association—as well as with dozens of parties with rights to the water. These included the purveyors, such as the municipalities and private water companies, and other pumpers such as the rock and gravel companies and the dairies. At first, EPA attempted to bypass this structure by assigning the lead role to the State Department of Health Services. Within a short time, however, DOHS had dropped out, deferring to the local actors.[74] EPA then turned to the Upper District, impressed by the political and public relations skills of that agency's general manager, Jane Bray. Contracting with the Upper District to develop a community relations plan in 1984, EPA hoped that out of this new relationship, a new regional leadership role could be established to cut through the problems of the multiple jurisdictions and the generally passive approach of the water agencies. To develop that role, however, turned out to be more difficult than anticipated.

The contamination problems were far more serious and ubiquitous than originally understood. First, new tests showed that the contamination was not only widespread (there were, in fact, four different sites that became linked together into a single Superfund site) but that it might be joining into a giant plume of pollution, flowing toward the Whittier Narrows and the Central and West Basin areas. Second, the wide range of industrial activity in the valley and the existence of a variety of possible sources (including a number of small-quantity generators of hazardous wastes), rather than a single point source for any particular contaminant, made it difficult for EPA to move quickly and directly against any of the responsible parties. In contrast, other Superfund sites often involved single source polluters who could be held liable for all or a portion of the clean-up costs. The San Gabriel situation, moreover, was compounded by the existence of several historical point sources, such as an unregulated industrial dump that operated during the 1940s and 1950s located in an area then without a sewage system.[75]

Finally, the costs were phenomenal and there was no clear means of identifying particular polluters, a necessary preliminary to forcing them to pay. In one embarrassing set of events, EPA, already criticized for its lack of action, found that it itself had to pay more than $1.5 million to set up an adequate treatment facility designed to clean the water in one particular well, the only water source for two hundred families.[76] Meanwhile, tests had shown that, at the very least, more than 65,000 acre-feet of water already contained contaminants in excess of existing standards.[77] The extent of the contamination, moreover, would increase; despite the pollutants being removed, one EPA study noted that if current pumping practices continued, the extent of contamination could increase by fifteen square miles in ten years, with forty to fifty more wells exceeding drinking water standards.[78] If someone did not act effectively, an entire groundwater basin could ultimately be lost as drinking water; yet at the same time the nature of the problem, the costs, and the sources of contamination made it problematic to speak of "clean up" as a generic or comprehensive strategy. By 1988, six years (and $8.5 million) after the San Gabriel Valley Superfund site was declared, still-growing information about the extent of the problem ran up against the paralysis that had seized both EPA and the water industry.

To try to break this impasse, EPA set up a January 1988 meeting of all the key parties involved, including representatives from the state and regional water quality control boards, private water companies and municipal agencies, the Upper District, Four Cities, the association and the Watermaster, and even MWD and the State Department of Water Resources. At the meeting, EPA laid out its overall assessment of what the problems were, what clean-up alternatives existed, and what institutional barriers and issues needed to be addressed.[79]

The problems seemed intractable. Even the large sums available through Superfund were nowhere near sufficient to cover the costs of clean-up beyond simply treating "at the wellhead," that is, on a well-by-well basis which would fail to prevent the spread of contamination, particularly below the Whittier Narrows. Even a partial restoration of the basin, that is by extraction and treatment from those areas with high contamination levels, could cost as much as $700 million over a twenty-year period, with annual costs as much as $20 to $30 million.[80] Moreover, most of those costs were not likely to be borne by the polluters, given the technical and political difficulties of assigning responsibility. By 1988, EPA had spent $8.5 million, mostly for contractors to study the problem (including how to identify the polluters, a process that EPA was now saying had ended in failure).[81] In its frustration, EPA tried to transfer authority back to the local interests, insisting there had to be a new management structure created. EPA argued that no single existing entity on the regional or state level was capable of dealing comprehensively with the issues of groundwater contamination in this or other basins.

To that point the water agencies, like others, had assumed that EPA would take care of business. Superfund, in their minds, represented an unlimited pot of clean-up gold. This perception acted as a disincentive for the water agencies to change their own ways, either by developing their own clean-up strategy or by facing the need to pursue some form of regulation and intervention to prevent further contamination or to control the movement of existing contamination.[82]

The pressure to intervene, combined with growing fears about a pollution problem that seemed out of control, had begun to force the water agencies, including the Upper District, to try to figure out how to respond themselves to the situation, not just to rely on EPA. When San Gabriel was first declared a Superfund site, neither the Upper District nor any of the other region-wide bodies, such as Watermaster, had expressed willingness to become involved in the volatile and politically sensitive matter of identifying responsible parties or forcing change in any particular industrial or disposal practices.[83] As the Superfund impasse deepened, the local agencies began to fear that their inaction could generate public anger and thus calls for administrative change.

Targets for such potential intervention varied, including light and heavy industry, underground storage tanks, numerous landfill sites (some of which had been closed), residential septic tank and cesspool sites, and pesticide use among agricultural users, parks, cemeteries, and golf courses.[84] But the key to controlling existing and future contamination was restricting the use of chlorinated solvents; without directly confronting such existing industrial practices, it would be "questionable whether any attempt to improve the groundwater quality and to prevent new areas of the Basin from being contaminated [would] be successful."[85]

Slowly and hesitantly at first, the water agencies began to review their options. Watermaster, at one point, assigned people to monitor all active landfills within the Main San Gabriel Basin in order to identify any illegal dumping of hazardous wastes.[86] But by 1988, both EPA and the Regional Water Quality Control Board, the primary state agency attempting to identify responsible parties, seemed no closer to resolution of this or several of the other related clean-up issues. Despite its promise of resolution, Superfund was creating, in this area as well as others, its own lengthy institutional morass.

Under pressure from EPA on the one hand, which wanted to shift some responsibilities back to the local water industry, and public disquiet over the issue on the other, a small committee of key water-industry figures in the valley began to meet to address the issues laid out by the federal agency. This committee, which included Robert Berlien, the new general manager of the Upper District (who, like Jane Bray before him, maintained an equivalent staff role with both Watermaster and the association, while drawing part of his salary from EPA),[87] sought to develop the beginnings of a new strategy. At a June 1988 hearing called by the State Water Resources Control Board, the group issued a statement presented by the Upper District's consulting attorney, Arthur Kidman, that indicated a new willingness to act. The group advocated the formation of an entirely new water-quality-oriented San Gabriel organization made up of representatives from the Watermaster, the Upper District, the Four Cities District, and the association as well as from the County Board of Supervisors, the Health Department, and the Regional Water Quality Control Board. This body would be given broad powers to deal with basin contamination, and would be able to intervene in pumping, treatment, and enforcement. Clean-up costs, the group suggested, could be partially recovered through a fee or tax on leaking landfills and leaking hazardous materials storage facilities as well as a tax or license fee on all businesses that used toxic chemicals.[88]

The Kidman statement, as it came to be called, came as a bombshell to other members of the San Gabriel water industry, many of whom first heard these proposals at the June 1988 hearing. Fearing dilution of their own powers (and the political implications of a more aggressive interventionist approach), several key San Gabriel water purveyors maneuvered, successfully, to have the proposal for a new agency withdrawn. By 1990, the idea of a new posture by the water agencies had given way to the call for additional powers to be granted to Watermaster, the nine-member agency that had functioned as a kind of inbred water industry grouping since it had been set up to oversee the adjudication of the main San Gabriel Basin.[89] The long, drawn-out process of Superfund had, moreover, yet to resolve the key issue for the valley: how to stop (or at least slow) continuing contamination, let alone prevent future degradation of the water. Congressional hearings on the San Gabriel situation, one year after the Kidman Report was presented and more than a year and a half after EPA suggested the mechanism for developing a plan, indicated both growing public concern and growing frustration over the lack of results.[90] At stake was the viability of the basin itself.

Burbank: Confronting Lockheed

If the problems in the San Gabriel Basin, with its multiple purveyors and jurisdictions and range and diversity of polluters, appeared complex and intractable, then the problems of the San Fernando Basin, particularly those caused by Burbank's largest industrial employer—and polluter—were, though more straightforward in origin, potentially as politically contentious. As the primary, though not exclusive, source of the contamination of the North Hollywood–Burbank well field (where much of the most severe contamination in the San Fernando Basin could be found), the Lockheed company was pivotally located in the Superfund process. In its opportunity to accept, or resist, acknowledging its role and to participate in clean-up and reduce its generation of toxic wastes, Lockheed was in a unique position to influence the program. And the Burbank utility, directly affected by those choices, found itself sharing some of the unwanted spotlight with its largest and most powerful customer.

Just a few months after Aerojet had discovered TCE contamination in the San Gabriel Valley, the State Department of Health Services sampled and analyzed water from wells in the San Fernando Basin, including several in the Burbank area where Lockheed's facilities were located. This survey found high levels of TCE and PCE, including at the Lockheed site.[91] These results set off a series of investigations and another round of tests designed to identify the sources of contamination. As part of that process, the Regional Water Quality Control Board, in response to legislation and community pressure, began to develop a systematic inventory of underground storage tanks (including Lockheed's) in the basin area, while requiring tank owners to participate in a leak detection program.[92] Lockheed was first ordered to pursue its own tests in November 1983, a process that took more than a year and a half. These investigations resulted in the discovery that at least eighteen different sites contained concentrations of chemicals in the soil significant enough to cause further review. Ordered by the regional board to undertake a groundwater monitoring program, Lockheed's tests continued to show the possibility of serious contamination, particularly at Lockheed's oldest plant, which had been a major World War II plating and painting facility.[93] Investigations regarding City of Burbank wells, meanwhile, identified five wells exceeding state standards for TCE and PCE and potential contamination of others. As a result of these findings, the city stopped pumping from its wells in June of 1986 and began ordering 100 percent of its water from MWD.[94]

Each of these tests, however, extended the time between initial discovery and remedial action. Finally, in August 1987, seven years after the discovery of contamination in wells under Lockheed facilities, the Regional Water Quality Control Board, armed with substantial documentation from the varied sources of sampling and analysis, ordered Lockheed to begin mitigation of the contamination.[95] Lockheed at first resisted the order, arguing that other sources of contamination upstream from the plant might have had some responsibility and that further tests needed to be conducted.[96] Both the regional board and the basin's primary user, the city of Los Angeles, insisted that Lockheed proceed. Los Angeles Mayor Tom Bradley at one point even threatened legal action against the huge aerospace company in order to speed things along.[97]

While Lockheed continued to lock horns with a number of agencies, the Burbank utility and its governing bodies adopted a passive stance. From 1984 through 1987, the Lockheed water quality issue was barely mentioned at the meetings of the Public Service Department's advisory board; it first received attention in a January 1986 report. The board first devoted its full attention to this problem at a July 1987 meeting more than a year after the wells were shut down, when the issue—and the growing confrontations over Lockheed's responsibilities—were already at their peak.[98] Similarly, the Burbank City Council virtually ignored the issue. Water quality was only mentioned twice during council proceedings until October 1987: once through a motion urging EPA not to cut back any of the Superfund monies earmarked for the Burbank area, and on a second occasion to discuss the council's unanimous decision to oppose Proposition 65, a statewide groundwater quality initiative put on the ballot by environmental groups (see chapter 8). In October 1987, in the wake of the threat of legal action against Lockheed by Los Angeles, the council took up the measure in detail for the first time. At the meeting, council members attempted to downplay any adversarial relationship and to insist that Lockheed was, in fact, doing everything they could to cooperate. "Are we really making an effort to work with them, rather than a push-type thing?" Council member Al Dawson admonished the utility's acting general manager.[99]

In 1987, monitoring wells drilled near the Burbank Well Field showed concentrations as high as 18,000 micrograms per liter (parts per billion— ppb) for PCE and 3,600 ppb for TCE. Lockheed likewise discovered in early

1989 concentrations in its water as high as 10,000 ppb for PCE and 2,000 ppb for TCE. By 1988 and 1989, it had become clear that contamination was not only widespread but in some areas even more severe than anticipated. Two more Burbank wells, now a total of seven of the eleven, were found to exceed TCE and/or PCE standards. Action seemed imperative.[100]

One answer was close at hand. In the nearby North Hollywood area, EPA had agreed to fund an advanced treatment system, involving air stripping to remove volatile organic solvents, in conjunction with the Los Angeles Department of Water and Power.[101] EPA then proposed a similar plan for the Burbank site.[102] Lockheed, meanwhile, under the gun on this issue and other health and environmental workplace-related concerns, decided to shift from a defensive to a more aggressive posture. In April 1988, it created a new set of environmental positions within the company to seek ways to reduce liability. Company officials "became a lot more fearful with the recognition that corporate liability could also lead to personal liability," commented Ed Fader, Lockheed's new environmental specialist.[103] As a result, Lockheed began to develop a new "advanced treatment" method on site, while at the same time more actively pursuing negotiations to limit liability. Ultimately, a more cooperative mood emerged between EPA, the municipal utilities including Burbank, and the huge aircraft company, partly in recognition that EPA was also pursuing other responsible parties and that Lockheed would not have to assume all of the clean-up costs.[104]

What still remained to be resolved was the actual magnitude of the costs of clean-up and who, ultimately, would pay.[105] Lockheed's dominant presence in the east San Fernando Basin, while creating tension for Burbank because it was a major local employer, ultimately did provide an easier target for regulatory negotiations than did the dispersed and less easily identifiable polluters in the adjacent San Gabriel Valley. What the agencies in both basins had discovered, however, was that the problem had become bigger than those agencies were prepared to handle, whether by themselves or in conjunction with others. Water contamination ultimately had changed the terms of agency discourse and activity.

4

A Desert Conundrum

The Imperial Irrigation District (IID) is one of the more contentious agricultural water districts in the country. Formed in the wake of an extraordinary manmade disaster, initially near bankruptcy (as its clients defaulted on their own properties), the IID and its agricultural clients have witnessed a remarkable regional evolution based on imported Colorado River water. IID takes about 2.5 million acre-feet of water from the Colorado River each year, almost all allocated to its member landowners, many of whom reside outside the Imperial Valley and lease their valley land. Imperial's farming operations produce a good share of the country's winter vegetables, especially lettuce. The irrigation district, the retail water and power supplier of the valley's landowners and residents, is the heart of the local water industry and a major political and economic power in the region in its own right. The scene of bitter labor disputes, devastating floods, tremendous poverty, and enormous wealth, the story of the Imperial Valley and its water industry is a desert conundrum; an arid land made profitable by tapping an unpredictable water supply whose disposition today might well determine the valley's future.

The Imperial Irrigation District (fig. 9) serves a vast area, encompassing over one million acres including all of Imperial County and that small portion of Riverside County into which the Salton Sea extends.[1] This land, in the southeastern corner of the state, due east of the MWD and San Diego CWA service areas, is primarily desert, a broad lowland where average precipitation is as little as three inches a year. Average temperatures in the summer months can range as high as 110 degrees Fahrenheit.[2] As a result, the valley has the highest per capita consumption of electricity in the country, largely due to air conditioning.

The valley, over the past forty years, has become one of the country's leading agricultural areas. Its entire harvested area is irrigated with huge volumes of imported water, since local rainfall provides less than 10 percent of the water any crop grown here would require. Winter vegetable crops make up about half the total value of all agricultural commodities sold from the valley, $454 million out of a total annual gross sales of $976 million in 1988.[3] Though lettuce ($200 million in 1988) is the most valuable crop grown in the valley, vegetables together require only about 120,000 of the valley's million acres (and that only for the winter season). Much of the valley is planted in alfalfa (189,000 acres in 1988) or, in the summer, in cotton (24,000 acres in 1988); both of these crops have very high water requirements in the hot summer desert sun (more than five acre-feet per acre planted). Valley agriculture also includes 500,000 head of cattle and some 105,000 feeder sheep; the county ranks first in the United States in pen-fed cattle.[4]

As in other rural areas in the state, the distance between wealth and poverty in the valley is extreme. Imperial County, with a population of 115,000, has the highest unemployment rate (22.4 percent in 1988)[5] in California, and the lowest per capita income ($11,107 in 1988). Large pockets of poverty exist throughout the valley in rural labor camps and small towns that remain economically depressed despite the substantial agricultural activity. Agriculture is the primary employer; about a third of the regular labor force have jobs in agriculture, and many off-farm jobs are tied to the agricultural sector. Most of the poor are immigrants from Mexico who have long formed a transient agricultural labor pool and who lately have taken many of the low-paying service jobs in the towns.[6] The Imperial Irrigation District is at the center of the valley's system of agricultural production. It provides Colorado River water to more than 500,000 acres in the valley, averaging nearly 3.7 acre-feet of water for each acre of land.[7] This high ratio is required by the extremely high alkalinity of the water, a factor that increases the need for effective drainage. Over the last twenty years, IID has delivered an average of 2.5 million acre-feet to its customers.[8] The Colorado River water for the valley is diverted at Imperial Dam, and then conveyed through the Bureau of Reclamation's 80-mile-long All-American Canal. The water then enters IID's 1625-mile distribution system where it is delivered to about five thousand farm delivery gates as well as to domestic and industrial users located in nine cities and towns in the valley, all entirely dependent on IID.[9]

The IID also has a power generation and distribution function that dates

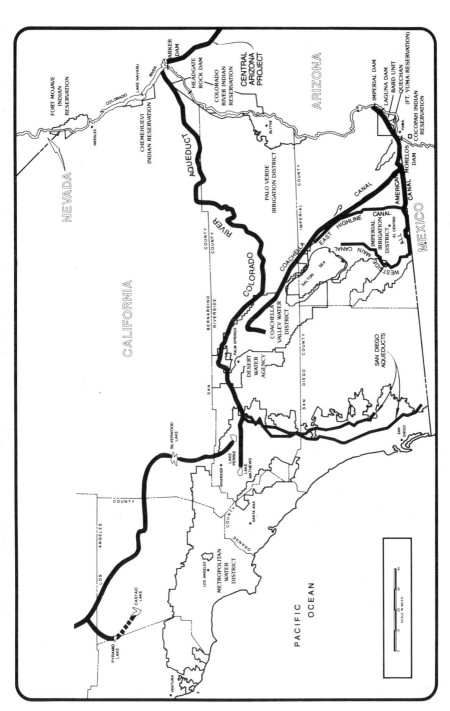

Figure 9. The Imperial Irrigation District and the Distribution of Colorado River Water in California

back to the construction of Imperial Dam and the All-American Canal. In 1943, IID purchased the properties of the investor-owned utility and became the sole distributor of electricity in Imperial County and the Coachella Valley. More than 300 kilowatts of electricity are consumed each year in the sparsely populated county, with residential—and industrial—energy bills an important policy issue for the community. Over the years, the power and water divisions of IID have been integrated in the district's financial accounting methods, which, in turn, has created political conflicts between the district's big water customers, the agricultural users, and its major power consumers, residents, local businesses, and small-scale industry.[10]

The IID also acts as the local agent for the federal Soil Conservation Service, which has helped install the drainage system in the area. The district provides office space and clerical staff for the Soil Conservation Service, which in turn has paid for most of the surveying and engineering work for this drainage program. Partly as a consequence of development of the drainage system, the IID has also become a major landowner within its own service area, today controlling as much as 100,000 acres; most of that land is located under water in the Salton Sea, itself a consequence of the IID's and the valley's own checkered irrigation history.[11] Perhaps most importantly, IID has evolved into a dominant regional political, social, and cultural institution, supporting local events, originating its own programs, and functioning as the single most important agency of government for the area's most important industry—agriculture. As such, IID's actions have taken on added significance for various constituencies in the region, and its history broadly encompasses the changes that have taken place in the valley itself.

Subsidies and Survival

IID was founded on July 14, 1911, when voters in the Imperial Valley elected to form a public agency to acquire the irrigation works of the California Development Corporation (CDC), then facing bankruptcy.[12] The CDC had been organized a decade earlier by two construction engineers employed by the Southern Pacific and two land agents of the Kern County Land Company. They had created the company as part of yet another attempt to try to divert water from the Colorado River. These diversion schemes were designed to stimulate development in this otherwise arid, valueless land. Taming the Colorado was the great challenge of the irrigators, many of whom were essentially land speculators attracted to the vision of an agricultural oasis in the desert capable of feeding the new urbanizing communities to the east of the valley.[13]

The problem with the Colorado River, which wound its way along the twisting California-Arizona border on its way to the Gulf of California, was its unpredictability, particularly its propensity to flood during especially wet years. Attempts to regulate the flow for irrigation, first made possible with the CDC's construction of Imperial Dam (then called Alamo Dam) in 1901, near the United States–Mexico border, were often misjudged, and the first efforts to farm the land were problematic at best. The CDC activity, moreover, sought to utilize sources of private capital (especially the Southern Pacific, which provided a $200,000 loan to the company in early 1905), partly in an attempt to prevent federal intervention through the Bureau of Reclamation.[14]

The initial mishaps, however, became catastrophes with the great flood of March 1905 and the collapse of the CDC infrastructure. For several months, the Colorado rampaged through the valley, flooding out farms, spreading over the lands, and settling within a dry inland basin known as the Salton Sink. The irrigators were helpless to control the river, even after the Southern Pacific took over a majority interest in CDC as collateral for its loan and desperately began to erect a new series of dams and channels to reroute Big Red (as the river was known) back to its outlet to the Sea of Cortez (the Gulf of California). For almost two years the Colorado remained out of control, with nearly half the entire flow of the river continuing to flood the valley. After six futile attempts to hold back the river by the Southern Pacific–run CDC, a fifteen-mile-long levee constructed in 1907 finally succeeded in re-diverting the flow.[15]

Once the river was again under control, the irrigators were finally able to take stock of their difficult situation. For one, the Salton Sink had become a massive, inland sea with no outlet back to the river. Moreover, the Southern Pacific, formerly the biggest champion of the valley's future, was now beginning to explore ways to extricate itself—and recoup its investment—from its overtaxed water-works system. As a consequence, other landowners in the valley, their own investments in jeopardy, decided to establish a local water and power district to salvage their lands and the valley's future.[16]

By 1911, the Southern Pacific, which had already instituted a series of lawsuits against CDC board members, was also pressing hard for the landowners to buy out the CDC system. The vote to establish IID, with its powers to sell bonds and buy property, allowed the transfer of the CDC system, which the railroad company was able to sell for nearly three times the cost it had incurred, including its original $200,000 loan.[17]

The new water district, representing a reconstituted landowner bloc, was immediately beset by problems inherited from CDC, including continual problems of flooding, silt build-up, salinity, and a controversial relationship with a large, 860,000-acre land company on the Mexican side of the border controlled by Harry Chandler, the owner of the *Los Angeles Times*. The Chandler arrangement, based on an earlier deal the CDC had made with the

Times publisher to construct diversion works and canals south of the border, required the IID to deliver up to 50 percent of its Colorado River water to the Mexico-based Chandler land company.[18]

Almost from the moment it was formed, IID, hemmed in by its obligations and its enormous operating expenses, went into substantial debt. The early hostility to federal intervention, marked by CDC's ill adventures, now became a call for federal help, including loans and grants to help the district maintain its existing system as well as funding for possible new projects, including improvements for Alamo Dam and the construction of a new facility, the All-American Canal. This project was to be designed to regulate the river flow at the border, to bypass the facilities and channels on the Mexican side while substantially increasing the amount of river water flowing back into the Imperial Valley. This new push for a federal relationship was led by Mark Rose, a large landowner in the East Mesa area of the valley, and IID's own general counsel, Phil Swing, who became the area's congressional representative (and later settled in San Diego). Rose and Swing became the leaders of the valley's water industry, centered around IID and the political maneuvering and lobbying for passage of the Boulder Canyon (or Swing-Johnson) Act which included authorization of the All-American Canal.[19]

While helping orchestrate the passage of this legislation, Swing also attempted to secure an exemption for the valley from the 160-acre limitation provision of reclamation law. Aside from the Southern Pacific, which still held substantial land in the valley, many other Imperial landowners held lands far in excess of the 160-acre limit established for Bureau of Reclamation—related federal water projects. Exemption from the 160-acre limit became a major policy goal of the IID and the local water industry. Although Swing was unsuccessful in setting the exemption in the act itself, he and other Imperial lobbyists obtained it, in the form of a letter written by Secretary of Interior Ray Lyman Wilbur, from the Hoover administration in its waning days in 1933. This exemption cemented the ties between IID and its landowner clients who now became champions of federal support for irrigation and valley development.[20]

Despite these victories, the Depression was a bleak period for the valley. Sharp and, at times, violent labor conflicts scarred the region, with the irrigation district allied with many of the larger landowners and their employer coalition, the Associated Farmers.[21] Meanwhile, a number of the smaller landowners had begun to default on payments and the district itself, as a consequence, hovered near bankruptcy. These problems were exacerbated by a series of land purchases and default proceedings in this period, including a 1936 buy out of the Chandlers' Mexican land company's United States facilities. The *Times* publisher, concerned about land seizures and demonstrations on his properties in the Mexicali Valley, soon sold his lands in Mexico to the Mexican government.[22] Moreover, IID's own irrigation system remained faulty and inadequate as its landowner clients continued to face the growing problem of salinity and poor drainage. During the late 1930s, the district management decided to establish a new drainage policy based on using the Salton Sea as an outlet for agricultural runoff. To implement the program, the district was obliged to purchase thousands of acres from the Southern Pacific as well as other lands bordering or actually below the Salton Sea.[23]

As the district eagerly awaited the completion of the All-American Canal which became operational in 1941, it began to turn to other federal agencies, including the Reconstruction Finance Corporation and the Rural Electrification Agency, to help finance its new drainage program, retire its substantial debts, and establish a new revenue base through power sales from the All-American Canal. The district thus became even more dependent on various federal loans, subsidy programs, and other forms of intervention in maintaining its water and power system as well as its new drainage program.[24] The war improved economic prospects in the valley, due, in part, to increased markets for produce and a new cheap labor pool provided by an agreement between the United States and Mexican governments in 1942. By the conclusion of the war, both the district, once again solvent, and its landowner clients, more prosperous than ever with the growth of production, were ready to respond to a new era of expansion.

Through the late 1940s and 1950s, the valley experienced a tremendous boom in land sales and crop plantings. Substantial new acreage was brought into production, particularly in cotton, which, with lettuce, were now the major crops in the area. Land holdings became more concentrated than before the war as the tendencies toward absentee ownership, already prevalent during the 1920s and 1930s, intensified. Many of these absentee landowners, such as the Irvine Corporation, the largest landowner in the valley, or the Bixby Ranch and the Union Development Corporation, controlled by MWD leaders Preston Hotchkis and E. Thornton Ibbetson, were Southern California–based.[25] IID itself became a major participant in land transactions, both selling properties acquired from bankruptcy proceedings during the 1930s and acquiring other properties, including those adjacent to the Salton Sea. Long-time farmer and IID board member Lester Bornt recalled that such sales at times involved friends and associates of IID board members.[26] With land deals, new irrigation, and water availability at the heart of the boom which had transformed the area into one of the largest agricultural producers in the country, the district came to be perceived as the dominant economic and political force throughout the valley.

Contradictions of the Sea

By the 1960s and 1970s, the district's policies explicitly encouraged the expansion of irrigated production and the economic fortunes of the valley, due to IID's active land sales policies, which made additional acreage available for production; its pricing policies; and its efforts to establish the Salton Sea as an income-generating recreational area. Pricing subsidies were especially crucial to the production boom. These included the low cost of Colorado River water, based on federal pricing subsidies; the co-mingling of IID's water and power revenues, which also subsidized prices for water users; and the system of charges for the IID system, based on actual sales rather than on assessed valuation or other fixed sources of revenue as in most other water systems. This last policy locked the district into depending on sales for income and thus was a disincentive to reduce overall Colorado River use.

More substantial water use was perceived by the district and its landowner clients to be a reflection of the economic condition of the region. These were boom years for the Imperial Valley, as both farm income and irrigated acreage increased significantly. The budding recreation industry grew as well: the varied uses of the Salton Sea and the instrumental role played by IID in shaping those developments was another key to the regional boom.

When the sea was first created by the floods of 1905, it made a huge inland waterway of more than 75,000 acres of cultivated lands. In the next several decades, the sea became an immense sump; as water evaporated, the levee system stabilized the area, and the drainage policies of IID were put into place. While the sea had a salt balance of about 77 million tons of salt (a concentration of about 3,350 parts per million) at the time of its formation, evaporation and the inflow of irrigation water increased salinity over time, to nearly ten times that amount by the 1950s.[27]

During the same period, this huge lake and its surrounding marshes also became a wildlife refuge. By the 1950s, the sea had become a winter home for waterfowl such as the Canada and Snow geese and a shelter for more than three hundred and fifty species of birds, including thousands of migratory ducks and fish-eating grebes. Moreover the sea, despite agricultural drainage and high alkalinity, also supported fish (due to efforts by the State Department of Fish and Game to turn the refuge area into a sport fishery). "The Fish and Game people were constantly trying to find the sturdiest, most salt-resistant fish they could," recalled one long-time valley landowner.[28] Fish and Game finally succeeded in locating several fish species for the sea, including the orange-mouth corvina, the gulf croaker, and the sargo perch, each of which survived in the inhospitable environment and fed on the pile worms, barnacles, and amphipods the state agency transplanted from the ocean. By the 1950s, the Salton Sea had become an anomaly: a man-made, extremely saline, drainage sump that was also a wildlife refuge.[29]

In the mid-1950s, the IID initiated its own Salton Sea policy. On the one hand, it instituted some modest conservation programs designed to stabilize the level of the Sea, which was rising due to district-sponsored drainage. At the same time, the district, now the major landowner of properties adjacent to the sea, launched its own leasing and land sales program to transform sea-front properties into recreational homes, marinas, and stores. District publications in this period lauded the opening of new facilities and helped promote the area as a major recreational center, calling the sea "a fishing paradise."[30] The district counted on obtaining flooding easements, both to allow new residential and commercial construction on properties bordering the sea and to protect the district (the owner of some of those properties) from liability. "The District managers such as Bob Carter [IID general manager from 1959 until 1983] were convinced that once they had those flooding easements the District would be protected," recalled former IID Director John Benson. "'We can't get sued,' Carter would say, and then he'd turn around and do things that just got us deeper and deeper in the hole until we were ready to take a fall."[31]

For a time, district strategy appeared to succeed. The level of the sea did not appear to rise, though this might have been due to the filling of Glen Canyon Dam during most of the 1960s and 1970s. The salt level of the sea, however, began to rise again sharply, climbing past 40,000 parts per million, even higher than ocean water. Still, fish survived; the sea had even become home to a fourth species, the Mozambique tilapia, originally imported by area farmers who dumped this small panfish into drainage canals for weed control. The tilapia, a freshwater algae eater, entered the sea where it flourished, providing food for the larger, sturdier, and now more abundant corvina. With sea-front properties booming, the fish surviving, and the legends growing, fishing agencies and local fishing organizations proclaimed that the Salton Sea had become the most productive sport fishery in California.[32]

The contradictions of the sea—and of district policy—finally came home to roost during the late 1970s, when a series of wet years on the Colorado River following the filling of Glen Canyon Dam upset the balance. Inexorably, the level of the Salton Sea rose and flooding struck the businesses and properties along the waterfront. Moreover, agricultural production in the valley was at its peak, and IID's limited conservation programs were overwhelmed by the increased volume of tail waters draining into the sea. Though the fish might have been happier (salt levels declined slightly during the wet years), the marina commercial and residential property owners washed out by the floods were not. Their unhappiness became focused on the sea's long-term booster, the water district.[33]

Salton Sea–related flooding extended to agricultural land near the margin of the sea, much of which was owned by two brothers, John and Stephen Elmore. Second-generation landowners, both brothers were politically well connected and active in valley affairs but had been continually frustrated in their attempts to convince district leaders to expand conservation programs and better regulate drainage activities to protect their land from encroachment. Though aware of the intended suit by residential and commercial sea-front owners, the brothers hired David Osias, a San Diego attorney, to begin proceedings on their own behalf.[34]

Osias and the Elmores initiated action against the district before the State Water Resources Control Board and the State Department of Water Resources, based on California Water Code Section 275. Under this provision, the state agencies were to determine whether IID was in violation of Code procedures by wasting water (in lieu of putting that water to beneficial use). This contention also formed the basis of the civil suit brought by the Elmores requesting damages be awarded against IID, whose position began to look increasingly untenable.[35] By 1982, these various suits, which became linked to the debates on the Peripheral Canal, thrust the IID and its policies to the center of the state's water politics, a position the district would occupy over much of the decade. As the level of the sea rose and the floods continued, the district was paralyzed by its own conflicting goals.

Maneuvers and Negotiations

The next move had as much to do with state-wide water politics as with the district's own legal bind. The Elmore suit before the State Water Resources Control Board set in motion a chain of political events that directly threatened existing water policies and assumptions. At first, however, all seemed to be business as usual. Nearly the entire California water industry mobilized in support of their beleaguered counterpart in Imperial.[36] Key officials and leaders of the urban Metropolitan Water District and the San Diego County Water Authority strongly backed IID as did members of the agricultural wing of the water industry.[37] The Imperial Board of Supervisors also offered support, portraying the Elmore suit as a conflict between "outsiders" (that is, the State Water Resources Control Board) and a united valley. The biggest fear of the IID and its allies was that the irrigation district would be forced to adopt a new, conservation-oriented approach and that the political fallout from such a program would ultimately undermine the strategies and objectives of the state-wide industry.[38]

These concerns were related to both the specific circumstances and the conceptual framework underlying the Elmore suits. The Elmores argued that IID had failed to implement a number of possible conservation-related programs that would have had far more substantial effects than had its limited efforts since the 1950s—programs that would be necessary if the level of the Sea were to recede to pre-flood levels. Moreover, even if the additional water to be saved from such programs were not put to "beneficial use" in the valley itself, such water would still be available for urban Southern California, which had the next set of priorities to water from the Colorado River.

To implement such a conservation program, the Elmores and their attorney suggested a trade-off between MWD, which needed the water, and the IID, whose landowner-clients feared higher water bills for expensive programs, such as concrete linings for the canals that carried water through the valley.[39] This idea, also picked up by the Environmental Defense Fund (an environmental organization active in the Peripheral Canal fight and interested in the concept of water markets as an alternative to new water development), had, according to Paul Engstrand (the general counsel of the San Diego County Water Authority) "long been obvious to many of us in the water industry."[40] It would be a variation of the "water market" concept: instead of a farmer selling water rights and/or land to an urban buyer, the urban water district would fund the construction and operation of a set of conservation facilities in exchange for the conserved water.

Just how much water could be conserved was another question. While IID argued futilely that its conservation program was already substantial, studies by state and federal agencies, including a pivotal 1981 report by the State Department of Water Resources in response to Elmore's complaint, pointed to far greater potential savings.[41] DWR estimated that upwards of 438,000 acre-feet of water could be conserved, in addition to IID's existing programs, a number that compared favorably with the additional amounts of water that would be available to Southern California from the proposed Peripheral Canal. Those findings were immediately injected into the referendum battle, further politicizing an already contentious set of proceedings.

With the defeat of the Peripheral Canal in 1982 and the launching of hearings on the Elmore complaint by the State Water Resources Control Board the following year, IID's position weakened considerably. The threat of loss of its civil suits placed the district in a financially precarious position. Even MWD, which had backed IID strongly during the canal campaign, now qualified that support to suggest that it would be willing to participate in a conservation agreement if the IID were also willing.[42] With the state board hearings about to reach their climax, IID friends such as Myron Holburt, then head of the Colorado River Board but soon to become assistant general manager of MWD, began to argue that the political situation had changed and that IID was vulnerable.[43] And, as IID staff and directors began to reconsider their position, they were encouraged by other outside voices suggesting that this conservation trade could transform the irrigation district into the "new water market brokers of the Southwest".[44]

By early 1984, the valley had become a hotbed once again for entrepreneurs, speculators, and large firms interested in transforming water (specifically, conserved water) into profit. The key player was the Ralph M. Parsons Company, a multinational engineering and resource development firm based in Pasadena in the Los Angeles metropolis. Parsons had initially been approached by a water marketing consultant named Tom Havens.[45] Havens, a

self-confident entrepreneur, had been based in Colorado but, like his ac-
quaintances from the Colorado-based Galloway group, had decided to focus
on Southern California and to carve out a role for himself in the volatile
world of California water supply issues. Havens saw an opportunity to link
the Reagan era emphasis on "privatization" to the IID situation by restructuring the conservation–funding-trade idea into a full-blown water market
with private parties handling the transactions. Paying for conservation
facilities could then be redefined as selling the water to the highest bidder.[46]

To carry out this plan, Havens turned to the Parsons company, which
had already entered the privatization field in the water and sewage treatment
area.[47] Together they approached IID directors who had begun to hold discussions with MWD on the conservation–funding trade. The IID directors
had entered negotiations without an overall plan and with the presumption
that their asking price—initially about $30 to $40 per acre-foot for the conserved water—would be directly pegged to the costs of the conservation-
related facilities. The Havens-Parsons consortium sought to convince them
otherwise.[48]

Led by John Benson, a long-time valley landowner and the first to urge
his fellow district directors to open negotiations with MWD, the IID board
decided to contract with Parsons to review their situation and to come up
with a new strategy regarding the conservation–funding exchange or the
"SWAP" (as it began to be called by the valley press). The contract stipulated
that Parsons would undertake an Environmental Impact Report on the conservation measures; develop a marketing strategy to pay for the facilities and
"sell" the water; and put together a negotiating posture for the district to
assume with MWD or other potential buyers. The payment to Parsons would
be based on a percentage of the funds or "profits" resulting from the transactions; that is, the bigger the sale (in amount of water sold and its sale price),
the bigger the fees for Parsons.[49]

Parsons quickly sought to revise the IID approach. Rather than minimizing the potential for conservation, the Parsons EIR argued that a huge potential volume of water (as much as 512,000 acre-feet) could be conserved,
even more than DWR's controversial assessment had suggested several years
earlier.[50] Moreover, Parsons argued that IID had additional bargaining
power (and could potentially increase its asking price) since it had other
buyers aside from MWD, including the Department of Water Resources, the
local geothermal industry, and most significantly the San Diego County
Water Authority.[51] A former Parsons employee, Larry Michaels, was San
Diego's general manager and the chief proponent of the idea that the San
Diego CWA, in the wake of Galloway, might make its own arrangements
outside the MWD system.[52]

As negotiations between IID and MWD intensified during 1984 and
1985, the Parsons role became more and more intertwined with the SWAP's

prospects. As the key behind-the-scenes player in the IID and MWD negotiations, Parsons sought a two-track approach. On the one hand, Parsons and IID hoped to conclude an initial agreement with MWD for the first 100,000 acre-feet of water conserved. The cost estimates for the conservation facilities, in turn, were defined as higher than earlier estimates, by including additional costs and a relatively indeterminate concept of impacts.[53] Moreover, IID would also receive an unstated subsidy equal to these funds already earmarked for conservation that IID would have been forced to spend irrespective of an agreement.

Arranging a successful MWD and IID agreement was only the first step in Parson's overall strategic plan. Step two involved the successful completion of any follow-up deals above and beyond the first 100,000 acre-feet of water conserved. These deals, the Parsons advisers argued, would become the basis of IID's water marketing approach, involving sale of water (rather than simply payment for conservation facilities) to the highest bidder, presumably the San Diego CWA. Such a sale, of course, would reflect the greater value of the water, thus commanding a much higher price than the $100 per acre-foot price established in the first agreement. This first agreement, moreover, would be undertaken on the basis that both MWD and IID, given their different approaches, would "agree to disagree" about the nature of their transaction, with MWD identifying it as a conservation trade, while IID reserved the right to consider it a "sale."[54]

By the summer of 1985, Parsons had convinced the IID board to pursue this two-track approach.[55] A tentative agreement or memorandum of understanding (MOU) was reached between MWD and IID negotiators for that first 100,000 acre-feet of water.[56] The price, as expected, was set at $100 an acre-foot or $10 million annually over thirty-five years. The "agree to disagree" provision was included, as was a cancellation procedure requiring a fifteen-year notice to be given no earlier than after the first twenty years of the agreement had elapsed. With both negotiating parties assuring the other that the agreement was well in hand, the political process that began with the Elmore suit appeared settled.

The Politics of Contention

This agreement, however, turned out to be as problematic as the political process itself. While the MWD board of directors quickly, unanimously, and with little discussion approved the MOU, the majority of the Imperial board soon displayed a bad case of political afterthought.[57] Public concerns over the SWAP in the valley had intensified in just a few months, as a vociferous opposition argued that the price was too low, the loss of the water too fundamental, and the role of the "outsiders" (especially

Southern California–based MWD and Parsons) too substantial.[58] The IID board members felt particularly vulnerable to the latter claim with its suggestion that the SWAP would turn Imperial into another "Owens Valley" (where the Los Angeles Department of Water and Power maintained an almost imperial presence more than seventy-five years after authorization and construction of that first "water market" deal, the Los Angeles Aqueduct). Opposition had formed among town and city residents already suspicious of the big landowner-oriented irrigation district, but had spread to elected officials and landowners in the farm bureau and other agricultural organizations.[59]

With elections less than a year away, the IID directors retreated, rejecting the MOU by a three-to-two vote and subsequently reducing (eventually eliminating) the consulting relationship with Parsons.[60] Negotiations with MWD were reconstituted, then suspended for the elections, continued again, and once more broken off after the IID board attempted to appeal directly to MWD directors, bypassing MWD's own negotiators.[61] Meanwhile, IID itself was being pressed by an unfavorable ruling from the State Water Resources Control Board, a big out-of-court settlement with the Elmores on their civil suit, and a major loss on the class action suit brought by Salton Sea property owners.[62] These rulings increased both political and economic pressure on IID, which continued to rely on the increasingly elusive hope that the much anticipated deal with San Diego would somehow extricate the district from its multiple problems.

The idea of dealing with San Diego was particularly attractive to the Imperial board for a variety of reasons. The notion of a "special" Imperial–San Diego relationship dated back to the period when the valley was the eastern extension of San Diego County and its representatives (such as Phil Swing) played a pivotal role in both areas. Many of Imperial's "absentee" landowners were San Diego–based, while some of the largest of the "local" Imperial farmers maintained second, summer homes in the San Diego area. "Any time I need to contact some of our key landowners during the summer months," commented an *Imperial Valley Press* reporter, "I know I'm more likely to find them in San Diego than in the Valley."[63] After the Galloway proposal became public, IID board members became convinced that San Diego was their trump card in the negotiations with MWD. They would joke about it during the SWAP negotiating sessions, make passing comments to their San Diego counterparts at water industry gatherings, and discuss it informally with San Diego political, business, and water agency figures when the opportunity arose. Most critically, the Imperial board attempted, although without success, to pursue the matter directly at moments when negotiations with MWD seemed at a stalemate.[64] Despite San Diego's rhetorical interest in an "independent" water supply, any arrangement with Imperial (as with Galloway) would require MWD approval in light of the complex institutional and physical requirements for transfer of Colorado River water.

Moreover, by 1985, after the Imperial board's rejection of the MOU, the San Diego board had itself retreated to a position that left the negotiating field to MWD.

Despite the initial, Parsons-induced enthusiasm about "markets" and anticipation of a high price for the conserved water—possibly as much as $250 an acre-foot, given the Galloway price tag of 90 percent of the MWD rate or $180 an acre-foot based on 1985–86 rates[65]—the Imperial board was still beset by external factors. Each year that passed without an agreement increased the threat of intervention from the State Water Resources Control Board. By not securing an immediate agreement the district postponed the opportunity to develop an income source at a time when it was increasingly strapped for funds. Already by 1985, the district had been forced to scramble for funds to pay a $4 million obligation resulting from one of the Salton Sea lawsuits; to pay this, the district board and management sought, in closed sessions and later open meetings, to devise ways to tap funds from the power side of operations (without creating any further public backlash), thereby reopening a long-standing controversy between power and water customers.[66] Costs incurred from the Salton Sea suits and declining sales in the mid-1980s increased pressure on the district to derive additional revenues from higher water rates. At one point, district management, responsive to their primary constituency (the larger landowners who were better able to absorb losses during periods of decline), sought to establish a minimum water charge; this fee strongly disadvantaged smaller landowners, especially those who had been forced to take their lands out of production. As a result of these and other actions, the Imperial board members, elected every four years, found themselves increasingly vulnerable.[67]

During the 1986 and 1988 elections, four of the five incumbent directors retired or were defeated.[68] Buffeted by internal opposition in the valley, by financial, legal, and political constraints, and by a nonresponsive San Diego County Water Authority, the Imperial water industry seemed at an impasse. Without board consensus and lacking a coherent negotiating strategy, the district once again turned to outsiders to salvage a deal and recapture the dream that water would provide the economic margin for the valley.

Off Again, On Again

By 1988, after several protracted rounds of negotiation that MWD General Manager Carl Boronkay characterized as an "off again, on again soap opera",[69] the SWAP appeared no closer to resolution than when discussions had commenced four years earlier. Desperate to break the impasse, the Imperial board once again turned to outsiders, hiring in June 1988, after a one-month search, water engineering consultant Robert Edmonston of the Bookman-Edmonston firm to represent the district in negotiations. As a condition of employment, Edmonston insisted he become IID's sole negotiator and that all contacts with MWD be through him.[70] Edmonston, a powerful and respected member of the water industry fraternity, was an effective choice and was well situated to obtain a number of IID's objectives. Also, political pressures about the SWAP within the valley had begun to subside. Elected officials such as Imperial Supervisor James Bucher (called "Lord Jim" by his detractors such as Imperial board member John Benson[71]) had modified or dropped their opposition as negotiations dragged on and the threat of intervention by the State Water Resources Control Board loomed larger.[72] Attendance at board meetings, which had been high during the 1985–86 period, had dwindled by the time Edmonston entered the picture. Several of the new board members, including one-time critics of the SWAP, had modified their opposition to an MWD agreement, particularly after the continual rebuff from San Diego.[73] Even the opposition that had been generated by the sport fishery-oriented defenders of the Salton Sea had dissipated, after one of the sea's leading boosters unexpectedly departed from the area, revealing his organization to be little more than a mailing list.[74] Sustaining water politics at the community level, even in the volatile Imperial environment of the mid 1980s, turned out to be more difficult than anticipated.

While the situation in Imperial was evolving, the situation at MWD was also subject to change. Despite MWD's passive board and an apparently unyielding negotiating posture, MWD's managers were also sensitive about the failure to conclude a deal that had initially been heralded as ushering in a new era for the water industry.[75] Through much of the 1980s, the Imperial-MWD SWAP had symbolized the possibility—and limits—of water transfers. MWD, which still maintained designs on increasing its supply from the State Water Project, needed to demonstrate its willingness—and ability—to secure additional water by nontraditional arrangements. Not being able to conclude an arrangement could ultimately backfire on MWD, given the visibility of the negotiations.[76]

The most difficult obstacle, however, appeared to be the potential veto power of the Imperial electorate. At the height of the debate over the original MOU and the attacks against the lack of accountability by Imperial board members, a motion was introduced proposing that any agreement with MWD be subject to voter approval in the IID service area.[77] Though the measure passed by a four to one vote, Imperial board members soon began to have second thoughts about their hasty, politically motivated action. Had they locked themselves into an untenable situation, board members wondered, a situation compounded by the apparently volatile mood shift of Imperial residents and public officials regarding the negotiations?[78] By the 1988 elections, as the Edmonston-MWD negotiations came to a conclusion, a majority of the Imperial board, led by newly elected board member Don Cox, moved to bypass the election requirement. Cox argued that a public vote undermined the "system of representative government (by) putting the decision in the hands of people who do not have the time or interest to study the issues completely. . . . Anytime you put this out to the public," the new director concluded, "you're not sure what's going to happen."[79]

With some political difficulties under control, Edmonston and his new negotiating counterpart, long-time water industry colleague and MWD Assistant General Manager Myron Holburt, were finally able to conclude an agreement. The new MWD-IID agreement (not substantially different from that discussed in the original negotiations) stipulated that the giant urban district pay for sixteen different conservation projects. In addition, in a major concession to Imperial, MWD also agreed to provide payments for a number of "indirect costs," such as the decline in revenues resulting from the loss of hydroelectric energy from reduced water use. Ultimately, the cost of the project was estimated at $128 an acre-foot, including about $23 an acre-foot for the indirect costs, many of which were in effect direct payments to Imperial.[80]

The boards of both water agencies moved quickly this time to uphold the agreement, with only one—MWD—dissenting vote.[81] With the election requirement eliminated, the Imperial water industry began to focus on the next stage. Talk of markets was once again couched in terms of alternative transfer arrangements, such as MWD paying landowners to keep lands fallow during dry years in order for the urban district to receive additional Colorado River water. Though the extended negotiations with MWD, with their emphasis on conservation facilities, had been litigation-driven, Imperial landowners, with their substantial rights to the Colorado River, began to visualize water as a high-priced commodity, as marketable as the winter vegetables that had established the valley as a profitable center for irrigated agriculture.

This landowner scenario, however, remained complicated by the institutional and economic realities affecting the valley. Less than a month after agreements were signed, the water swap was once again jeopardized, this time by threatened litigation from the Coachella Valley Water District, which served the adjacent agricultural valley. Coachella, which maintained its own priority rights to the Colorado River, considered itself the primary loser from the MWD-IID agreement and wanted compensation or benefit.[82]

Coachella's intervention not only delayed implementation of the agreement but also led to a new effort, spurred by a new organization of Imperial landowners, the "Imperial Valley Water Users for Fairness," which included Stephen Elmore, to convince the IID board to renegotiate its agreement with MWD, particularly in regard to liability for environmental damage resulting from the conservation program and to the question of loss of local control. With time running out on the agreement, another compromise was reached both with Coachella and the Imperial dissidents. Finally, in December 1989, a year after first signing off on the Edmonston-Holburt document and more than five years after negotiations had begun, the IID-MWD swap was made final, becoming a part of water history.[83]

The lengthy, difficult negotiation drew attention to the continuing institutional hurdles located in existing allocations and distributional agreements worked out over the years by often-contending local water interests in the Colorado River system. All of the parties involved in, or affected by, the agreement, including bystanders such as the San Diego County Water Authority, recognized that the 100,000 acre-feet to be saved and reallocated made up only part of the long-term potential of the SWAP. Both IID and MWD staff spoke of a minimum of 250,000 acre-feet that might eventually be available, and that figure might well be increased. But the politics of water reallocation, compounded by institutional inertia and distributional rivalries, still presented potential problems.

Attention to the circumstances of this negotiation, prolonged by the further delay in reaching final agreement, also continued to expose to a broader public the great disparity in incomes and overall quality of life between the large landowners and other valley residents. Agriculture was on the rebound once again in Imperial and landowner prospects for realizing profits on their investments seemed improved, especially with the new view of water as an item for trade or sale. But the benefits of this new arrangement were as concentrated as those of the previous patterns of water distribution in the Imperial Valley had been; the valley itself remained a land where some had great expectations and others found little to hope for.

5

The Search
for Cheap Water

The Kern County Water Agency (KCWA) has become a
major player on the statewide water scene, although it
was first formed only to pass through water from the
State Water Project to local irrigation districts and city agencies. Some of the
largest agricultural land operations in the country are serviced by The
Agency; many of these huge farms came into cultivation only with State
Project water after 1968. The agency provides water to these landowner
clients and also to the City of Bakersfield and surrounding communities, the
county's largest urban area. In water debates within California, KCWA has
been a powerful representative of agriculture's interests, but its internal politics have become increasingly contentious as a result of new economic and
institutional uncertainties.

KCWA received its first water from the California Aqueduct in 1968. The
agency immediately became the single largest user of State Project water
(although its entitlements are only half those of the Metropolitan Water
District, the system's largest contractor).[1] The questions of water availability
and price have guided agency activities and policies and the needs of its
member agencies. And, in the midst of changes in both the cost and the
amount of State Project water available to project contractors, the agency
and its constituents continue the search—for secure but less expensive
water—that has dominated its mission since it was founded more than
twenty-five years ago.

Kern County is a major agricultural area, averaging in recent years from 800,000 to nearly a million acres under irrigation. Major crops are cotton (which alone takes a third of the water available in the county), alfalfa, grapes, and almonds. These four crops represent more than two-thirds of the acreage and water use in the KCWA service area. The estimated value of these crops, in 1986, was nearly $1.4 billion. More than 2.65 acre-feet of water is required for each acre of land.[2] Located at the southern end of the San Joaquin Valley, approximately 100 miles north of Los Angeles and 280 miles south of San Francisco, the KCWA service area is largely arid, with between five and eight inches a year of rainfall, mainly from October through March. Although the county maintains strong ties to (and shares economic and geographic characteristics with) Central California, it has also developed political and institutional ties with the Southern California area south of the Tehachapis, the mountain chain dividing Los Angeles and Kern counties.

KCWA's service area is about forty miles wide and extends about seventy miles from north to south (see fig. 10). Approximately 1,250,000 acres in the county overlie a continuous groundwater basin filled with sands, gravels, and associated clays deposited by erosion of the Sierra Nevada range. Groundwater in the western and northwestern ends of this basin is of very poor quality and is too saline to use. The overall area is naturally a "closed" drainage basin, since the rivers that flow from the Sierra Nevada terminate in Tulare Lake with no outlet to the ocean; this causes a significant drainage problem for Kern agriculture.[3]

During 1988, the agency contracted for 1,074,600 acre-feet of State Project water. This contract figure peaked at 1,153,400 acre-feet in 1990, when full entitlements became available to all state contractors.[4] KCWA delivers its State Project water to sixteen different member agencies, including several water districts that receive municipal and industrial (m&i) water. KCWA's largest customer is the Wheeler Ridge–Maricopa Water Storage District, whose two biggest landowners over the years—the Tejon Ranch and Tenneco (as successor to the Kern Land Company)—had been the oldest and most influential in the region. The Bakersfield urban area, which receives water via an Improvement District (I.D. No. 4), has no direct representation to KCWA, though its taxpayers contribute significantly to agency revenues. There are seven agricultural districts overlying the usable part of the groundwater basin; one of these districts recharges groundwater, while the other six offer imported water directly to their customers as a supplemental supply to be used in conjunction with, or in place of, groundwater. Three additional agricultural districts either overlie that part of the groundwater basin that is not usable or have no local groundwater source; these districts rely heavily on State Project water as a primary source for irrigation, and land in production in these districts has increased significantly since imported water became available.[5]

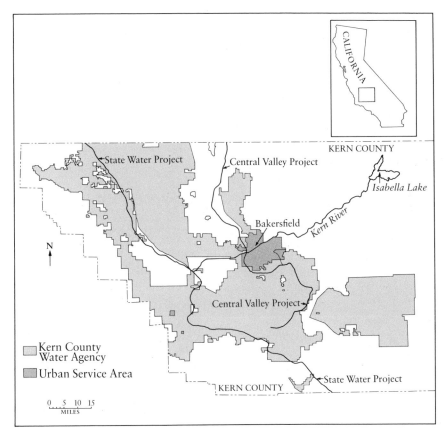

Figure 10. The Kern County Water Agency and the San Joaquin Valley

The four main sources of water in the Kern area include State Project water; groundwater wells, which provide as much as 40 percent of the water for the Kern area; the Kern River, which originates in the Sierra Nevadas; and the Central Valley Project water, delivered via the Friant-Kern Canal. The Kern River's yield ranges from 200,000 to more than two million acre-feet, depending on the snow pack in the Sierras, and fluctuates seasonally, with the major flow from April through July. Its average yield is 670,000 acre-feet annually. A storage facility, Isabella Dam, completed in 1950, provides 570,000 acre-feet of storage and allows regulating water flow to meet the demands of heavy summer irrigation. The CVP's Friant-Kern Canal, completed in 1951, provides an average of 400,000 acre-feet of water annually to four county districts, each of which also uses groundwater. Though the four sources provide some operational flexibility, the Kern water system has been organized to supplement and expand rather than coordinate and extend existing water.

Concentration, Expansion, and Overextension

The history of Kern County agriculture has been characterized by concentration of landownership and expansion of production. Cattle barons dominated the early Anglo history of the area, as they did most of the Central Valley. When in 1874 the Southern Pacific Railroad connected the little town of Bakersfield to San Francisco, it provided a means for settlers to enter the area and for agricultural produce to reach the northern market. But instead of settlement and small farms, the area witnessed the takeover of "large tracts of the best land and vital water rights . . . by a few non-resident land holders."[6]

The two biggest landowners were the Miller-Lux partnership and their chief competitors, the Haggin-Tevis-Carr consortium, which founded the most powerful company in Kern, the Kern County Land Company. Henry Miller, a German immigrant, began his career as a butcher in San Francisco. As his operations expanded, he decided to integrate them vertically, investing in livestock and then combining forces with Charles Lux, a competitor. The Miller-Lux partnership secured options to lease lands and graze their herds throughout the San Joaquin Valley and other parts of the state. By the 1870s, they had obtained more than a hundred thousand acres in Kern County, taking advantage of the provisions of the Swamp Act of 1850.[7] They were soon challenged by James Ben-Ali Haggin and his brother-in-law Lloyd Tevis, who entered Kern County soon after the Miller-Lux interests had consolidated their holdings.

Haggin and Tevis, with their lawyer and chief troubleshooter James Carr, were at the top of the California elite. Also based in San Francisco, they were leading investors in the Wells Fargo Bank, with major holdings in land, utilities, railroad and transportation, and mining operations scattered over the West. The Haggin group, through their manipulation of the Desert Land Act of 1877 and their association with the Southern Pacific railroad, developed a vast "grasslands empire," amounting to 1.4 million acres in Kern, Arizona, and New Mexico.[8]

Both the Haggin group and the Miller-Lux group were adept at using water rights theories to eliminate competitors and consolidate their own holdings. The Miller-Lux group cited riparian doctrine since they owned the land adjoining the river and wanted to prevent landowners upstream from diverting water, while the Haggin group used prior appropriation doctrine in attempting to destroy rival landowners who refused to sell their lands to the Kern County Land Company. Ultimately, the two land monopolists clashed, and their resulting court battle, California's classic water rights case, *Lux v. Haggin*, tilted California water law towards riparian doctrine.[9] Meanwhile, both sides bribed officeholders, manipulated the press and sought to control elections to shape the outcome. "Money flowed like water in the fight," wrote Henry Miller's biographer.[10] After the court decision, the two groups cut their own deal, reinforcing their shared monopoly by building a reservoir on the Kern River to which only they had access.[11]

The connection between water rights and land monopoly that comes to view in *Lux v. Haggin* continued to stimulate land concentration after 1900. The Kern County Land Company expanded to control much of the land south and west of the Kern River, including huge landholdings around the growing settlement at Bakersfield. The Miller-Lux holdings became more dispersed, though Henry Miller's descendents continued to emphasize control of water, creating captive water districts and planning Isabella Dam.[12]

During this period, land development was limited by overuse of groundwater. Overdraft had occurred as early as the 1930s, when the advance of pumping technology with electrically powered pumps opened up additional acreage to irrigation.[13] Overdraft led Kern landowners to join their counterparts throughout the valley to push for the Central Valley Project (CVP), arguing that imported water would improve the condition of the groundwater basin. Once CVP water became available in 1951, however, it became clear that cheap CVP water instead provided an incentive to increase the amount of irrigated acreage, ultimately exacerbating the overdraft. The same problem developed with the construction (by the Army Corps of Engineers) of Isabella Dam, which allowed more marginal land to be brought into production. By the late 1950s, the Kern overdraft was estimated at 700,000 acre-feet per year despite the regulated flow of the Kern River through Isabella Dam and the imported water supply arriving through the Friant-Kern Canal.[14] The land concentration and expansion so characteristic of the region had also become a continuing problem of overextension.

An Agency is Born

By the mid-1950s, Kern landowners confronted a set of problems—and opportunities—that were both structural and political. A consensus emerged that the way to deal with the overdraft region required additional sources of water tied to the emerging plans to construct a new statewide water system. This new supply would not only control the overdraft but also allow further opportunity for expansion. In 1956, the landowners, led by the Kern County Land Company, created their own Kern County Water Association. This association became the negotiator in attempts to secure this new imported water supply, including importation for

93

use by lands with no access to groundwater (or groundwater of high enough quality to allow irrigation). These lands had previously not been able to receive imported water, because they were outside the area served by the Friant-Kern Canal. In order to proceed, the association was able to get the state legislature to pass legislation establishing the new Kern County Water Agency.[15]

The water association had three key goals: subsidies, to keep the price of the water low enough to encourage new irrigation; elimination of acreage restrictions, that is, the 160-acre limit imposed—at least in name—on certain federal projects such as the CVP; and creation of a contracting agency on a countywide basis to secure the entire tax base of the county. To succeed, the water association had to counter opposition from organized labor, including a budding farm-worker movement that objected to the acreage exemption; from potential urban contractors such as the MWD, concerned that price breaks to Kern County would increase their financial burden; and from urban interests and anti-tax groups from Bakersfield (wary of the concept of a county water agency with the power to secure taxes from all landowners).[16]

While the legislature debated whether to proceed on a new state water project, the water association moved quickly to gain support. With the County Farm Bureau and the region's major newspaper, the *Bakersfield Californian* (a strong backer of local agricultural interests), the water association began a political campaign on the need for water in the county. A sponsored study argued that local landowners' "capacity to pay" was limited without a price break.[17] Through political alliances with other Central Valley investors, the association lobbied the legislature (whose upper house was still dominated by rural senators since, at that time, each county had two senators irrespective of its population) on the need for a state project to free California agriculture from the federal acreage exemptions. And KCWA and MWD, the two largest proposed contractors for the state water, entered protracted negotiations over the parameters of the contracting system.

The Kern landowners achieved most of their objectives. The 1959 Burns-Porter Act (authorizing the State Water Project) eliminated any reference to acreage limitations.[18] In turn, direct preferential pricing for agricultural water was also eliminated, traded off against the absence of acreage restrictions.[19] The MWD-Kern negotiations, however, reestablished two crucial types of pricing subsidies that worked to the benefit of agriculture.

First, two categories of water allocation were established: "full-cost" entitlements, based on the capital and operational costs for delivering the water, and a lower-priced "surplus" water charge based solely on transportation costs. Surplus water would be available if contractors used less than their full entitlements. Kern was, in effect, assured of substantial surplus water in the early years of the project, since it would come on line earlier than MWD. At the same time, Kern's rate of annual increment in entitlement (and thus its proportional share of capital costs) was set lower, for the first decade of project operation, than that of MWD, although it was clear that Kern landowners, and not the more flush MWD system) would use most of the water.[20]

A second key subsidy was related to the allocation of costs of pipeline size. In the agreement that was worked out, system charges incorporated "capacity" factors, that is, building the pipeline to the capacity needed to meet the "peak" needs of any given contractor, as well as "volume" factors, the volume of water flowing through the system to meet all contract entitlements. Charges based on "capacity" disadvantaged Kern, since the system's summertime "peak" use would be primarily for irrigation, while "volume" charges were less favorable to MWD, which had a 50 percent entitlement to the system where Kern's entitlement was smaller at 27 percent. Ordinarily, pricing mechanisms would be based on capacity charges, given the additional expense of building a larger system to handle any increase in the peak. Kern, however, strongly resisted such an approach, and, ultimately, MWD and Kern worked out a compromise, known as the "Skinner compromise" after the MWD official who proposed it.[21] This approach split the charge between capacity and volume, providing a significant price break for the Kern landowners. MWD agreed to these positions because it feared that without the price breaks, the Kern landowners might pull out of the system as they threatened. Moreover, MWD officials, as David Kennedy later commented, feared agriculture's power in the state legislature and their long-time dominance of water industry activities.[22] Despite Joseph Jensen's power, the Kern landowners were still able to call most of the shots.

Though they had gained reduced payments and subsidized prices, the Kern County Water Association now sought to lower the price of water to agriculture even further. Led by Allen Bottorff of the Kern County Land Company, the association proposed that the agency, which had been established to contract for State Project water, have the power to initiate a countywide "zone of benefit" tax to secure additional revenues and thereby further lower the unit cost of water to the individual landowner. To institute such taxes, the contracting agency had to be established on a countywide basis with some powers residing with the county board of supervisors. Moreover, it had to be approved by the Kern electorate in a special election.[23]

Once again, the water association was able to mobilize its forces, led by the rural landowners in alliance with other political and business leaders in the region. A coalition of landowners, oil companies, the board of supervisors (long sympathetic to agricultural interests), the *Bakersfield Californian*, and civic groups such as the League of Women Voters supported the formation of the Kern County Water Agency on the grounds that the new State Water Project would represent an economic bonanza for the county, more than offsetting any tax burden.[24] Opposition appeared primarily among taxpayer groups who complained about subsidies to farmers and were able to tap urban antagonisms to the agricultural landowners. In November 1963, after a low-key, though tense, election campaign, agency advocates prevailed by a very small margin.[25]

A Speculative Spiral

Agreement on the State Water Project and establishment of the Kern County Water Agency immediately set off a land spree within the Kern area. In 1967, just one year before the arrival of the State Project's California Aqueduct in Kern, the venerable and massive Kern County Land Company (with 300,000 acres in Kern County) was sold to Tenneco, an oil- and gas-based conglomerate based in Houston.[26] Long-time landowners in the county, such as the Tejon Ranch (owned by the Chandlers, publishers of the *Los Angeles Times*)[27] and the Blackwell Land Company (controlled by the Lazard Freres banking family)[28] moved to contract for water for lands that had been used either for grazing or dry farming or that had remained idle for lack of water. Similarly, various oil companies began to explore the possibility of using their undeveloped lands for irrigated agriculture, given the availability—and price—of this new supply of water. Many of these lands had been considered marginal for agricultural activity, but the arrival of the California Aqueduct with its subsidy-laden, multi-tiered pricing struc-ture provided an incentive for these and other landowners to contract for substantial amounts of water in anticipation of an irrigation boom.[29]

The boom was not long in coming. The transformation of Kern agricul-ture took only a few years, once water began to arrive in the California Aqueduct. Several hundred thousand acres were newly irrigated, and a whole new cropping pattern was established. Recent investors, such as Pru-dential Life Insurance and Standard Oil of California, either converted unde-veloped land or took over existing properties and expanded operations.[30] Long-time landowners, like the Tejon Ranch, speculated that by connecting to the state system with its promise of plentiful and cheap water they could restructure underutilized lands either for more profitable agriculture or, ulti-mately, for urban subdivision.[31]

With new purchases and related expansion of irrigated acreage becom-ing a speculative spiral, the Kern landowners raced to establish new water districts to contract for State Project water through KCWA, as well as to raise the capital to put in place their own distribution systems. The tendency toward concentration and overextension, already prevalent in the county from the days of *Lux v. Haggin*, was enormously magnified with the arrival of the aqueduct. A handful of landowners dominated most of the key water districts affiliated with KCWA, and these districts, in turn, dominated the agency.[32] Much of their focus was on the economics of converting their land. Some of that conversion was aided by tax shelters available during the early 1970s,[33] but most of the landowners' attention continued to be on the price of water.

During the first ten years of the State Project's operation in the Kern area, most new imported water was priced at the surplus rate—an average of 60 percent of all water delivered during that period and more than 80 percent in some years, despite the annual increase in entitlements structured into the agreement.[34] Thus, the mean unit cost of delivered water remained well below the cost of entitlement water, that price which reflected the capital expenses of the State Project. Even in 1979, when KCWA entitlements had increased to 516,300 acre-feet, the agency purchased 524,247 acre-feet of "surplus water" beyond the entitlement. That entitlement water cost KCWA member agencies more than $15 million (or about $29 an acre-foot) while the bill for the same amount of surplus water came to only $2.3 million (or approximately $4 an acre-foot), reducing the overall unit cost to $17 per acre-foot.[35] The various subsidies—the surplus rate, the capacity-volume split, and the timing of the increases in the entitlements—not only offset the start-up costs of new irrigation but also contributed to the speculative environment in land purchases, cropping decisions and, perhaps most importantly, long-term estimates of the price of water and of the profitability of expanded production.[36] Kern landowners, hooked on cheap water, anticipated these benefits would remain intact into the 1980s and beyond.

During the 1970s, the agency's deliberations were dominated by competition over surplus water among its member agencies. KCWA board members and agency staff were constantly subject to pressures over the allocation of surplus water. Most board members, though elected from geographical districts rather than appointed through the member agencies, had close ties with the landowner-dominated member agencies and shared their perspective about keeping costs low and water supplies abundant. The conflicts that emerged, some of which were quite sharp, were more distributional than strategic and tended to focus on the role of the agency staff, especially of its general manager who was often buffeted between competing member agency interests.[37]

Despite these internal conflicts, the agency and its members were largely satisfied with the arrangements and operations of the state project through the mid-1970s. Though they continued to support a long-term plan to expand the State Water Project, the Kern landowners, unlike their MWD counterparts, were less anxious while Reagan was governor in California to develop a new facility, due to existing costs of financing their internal distribution systems.[38] But for Kern, like most in the water industry, the 1976–77 drought forced a reevaluation of the agency's emphasis on state water politics. The drought, according to KCWA director Gene Lundquist, "came as a shock to the agency. . . . For the first time," Lundquist recalled, "we began to realize that without expansion of the state system some time soon, we could be vulnerable in future years."[39] A few member agencies felt particularly vulnerable, and (especially during 1977) quickly sought to cover their exposure and potential loss of crops by arranging to obtain new sources of water. They asked MWD to forego use of its State Project entitlements. MWD could make this support available, since the drought was not as severe in the Colorado River system, and it could increase its supply of Colorado River water to offset the foregone SWP water.[40] In one instance, MWD made available more than 20,000 acre-feet of additional water to Kern's Wheeler Ridge–Maricopa member agency.[41] These arrangements established new ties between the two huge state project contractors and strengthened a shared perspective toward expansion of the state system. By the early 1980s, the attention of the agency had shifted back to another cycle of expansion of the state water project, the Peripheral Canal.

Putting Out Fires

While the agency began to mobilize on the Peripheral Canal, it also encountered a series of county issues that had the potential to jeopardize its unity and sense of mission. These problems—water quality, taxation issues, and conjunctive management of ground and surface water supplies—all came to a head in the late 1970s and early 1980s, threatening to unravel the internal compromises that held the agency together.

Water quality had emerged, during the 1970s, as an intractable, though secondary, problem. The primary concern was drainage, since the Kern area was part of the Upper San Joaquin Valley drainage basin, a closed system with no outlet to the sea. With expanded irrigation, mineral salts accumulated in the area. The agency joined other San Joaquin Valley interests in arguments for a federally financed Master Drain for the entire valley to transport drainage water through the Sacramento–San Joaquin Delta and out into San Francisco Bay.[42] At the same time, the agency became involved in plans made by the Los Angeles Department of Water and Power to construct a nuclear power plant near the Wasco area, which would use agricultural drainage water as a coolant, and which would generate energy for the State Project as well as for KCWA member agencies.[43] Both the Master Drain and nuclear power projects, however, became politically untenable, postponing any drainage solution and putting the agency on the defensive on water quality.

These problems were compounded by the developing controversy over groundwater quality that emerged in the late 1970s and early 1980s. The Kern County Health Services Department evaluated groundwater quality in the county and issued a draft report in 1980. The tone of this report was mild, but the agency and its landowner clients forced a revision, so that the final report paid much less attention to the role of agriculture in water quality problems. Similarly, the agency and its clients strongly opposed any state-initiated, conjunctive-use program to integrate management of groundwater and surface water supplies, making it impossible for the state (during the Brown administration) to proceed with its plans to store surplus State Project water in the Kern area.[44]

The same sense of short-term crisis emerged in the debates of the early 1980s on KCWA's established "zone-of-benefit" taxation system. This system was organized around a series of "zones": different charges based on the presence or absence of groundwater, the condition of that groundwater, and whether the area was served or not served by the State Project. The system was justified by the argument that SWP water contributed economic benefits to the community as a whole—as well as specific areas or zones—with increased irrigation and hence agricultural activity having both direct and indirect "multiplier" effects on the regional economy. Furthermore, zone-of-benefit revenues, which helped reduce the cost of the SWP water, also presumably helped the groundwater overdraft by making the price of imported water more competitive with the costs of pumping groundwater, and therefore protected a common groundwater pool.[45] The amount of the tax subsidy of imported water varied over the years, though it ranged as high as 15 to 20 percent of the total revenues needed to pay for the SWP water.[46]

By the late 1970s and early 1980s, opposition to the zone-of-benefit arrangements began to mount as increased purchases of SWP water sent the zone-of-benefit charges skyrocketing. In just three years, from 1980 to 1982, the zone-of-benefit bill jumped from $1.6 million to an estimated $8 million.[47] These increases would be borne primarily by the oil companies, who were paying more than 50 percent of the charges, and by urban residents, who accounted for another 25 percent of these tax revenues collected, given the higher assessed value of urban land.[48] One estimate prepared for the City of Bakersfield indicated that by the year 2035, when SWP contracts expired, more than $1 billion in subsidies from urban taxpayers to agriculture would have been generated by the zone-of-benefit charges.[49]

The pressure on KCWA to revise the zone of benefit charges intensified during the early 1980s. A lawsuit was filed in 1981 by the Independent Oil Producer's Association, which led the oil companies in this dispute. Unlike Chevron and Shell, the county's largest taxpayers, the independents were not directly engaged in agricultural production and therefore did not receive any direct benefits in lower water bills to partially offset the zone-of-benefit charges.[50] Urban residents, moreover, were doubly penalized since the water they received from the State Project was already priced at a higher (m&i) rate reserved for urban water use, and they had no direct recourse to KCWA policy, since the Improvement District established to receive urban water was run by the staff and board members of KCWA.[51] The growing concerns of Bakersfield residents culminated in an advisory election on the issue in 1982, in which urban voters by more than two-to-one expressed opposition to the system. The anti–zone-of-benefit vote (68 percent) was considerably higher than the vote on that same election day (54 percent) in favor of the Peripheral Canal.[52]

Since the zone-of-benefit vote was only advisory, it encouraged the agency to consider a response that would somehow, as one agency director commented, "put out the fire".[53] A public relations firm was hired to structure public hearings designed to provide the appearance of participation in the discussion on how to change the system.[54] The Supervisors were also brought in again, though they left the behind-the-scenes negotiations to KCWA, the landowners, and the oil companies.[55] The resulting "compromise" measure, while modestly lowering the bill for the oil companies, turned out to be a kind of "sleight-of-hand" (as one water industry participant put it) for the urban areas, giving the appearance of lower rates but the reality of slight increases due to juggling definition of the zones.[56] Moreover, one of the leading urban critics of the system of charges and of the structure of the Improvement District No. 4, the Bakersfield city manager, was summarily dismissed from his position in part due to water industry lobbying.[57] Ultimately, the zone-of-benefit issue faded from view as the concern over equity in pricing was supplanted by the problem of agricultural decline and the new issues this engendered.

The Cheap Water Crisis

For the Kern water industry and its landowner client-participants, the prospect of an agricultural decline, or even recession, seemed unthinkable. With the appearance of the State Project, agriculture seemed impregnable: an inexpensive and abundant water supply, a strong and ever-increasing export market, a healthy and vibrant future for the crops that dominated the region. The dramatic rise of Kern agriculture had cemented California's place as the number one producer in the country, with a system that some had begun to say was "recession-proof." The primary agenda item for the Kern water industry during the early 1980s was State Project expansion, not reducing its own activity.

When prices of other commodities and agricultural activity in other states collapsed in 1981 and 1982, the impact on California agriculture seemed at first remote. Both production and water use were still high, suggesting uninterrupted expansion and even a possible increase in national market share for those crops, such as cotton, grown elsewhere in the United States. But by 1983 and 1984, both production- and water-use figures began to decline (precipitously, in cotton) and it was suddenly clear that Kern County agriculture was also in trouble.[58]

Agriculture's decline—nearly 100,000 acres were taken out of production in Kern between 1982 and 1984[59]—was exacerbated by growing concern over the price of water. During the late 1970s and early 1980s, the price of water, including but not limited to the price of entitlement water, had begun to increase at a rate significantly higher than anticipated when contracts were first signed in the late 1960s. The problem was magnified in 1983, when the price of energy for the State Project jumped after electricity contracts were renegotiated. The amount of energy needed by the system had also increased, forcing the State Department of Water Resources to develop new "off aqueduct" energy sources that proved to be far more expensive than anticipated.[60] Suddenly, the price of water put negative pressure on the production system rather than providing a subsidy.

The price factor was especially a problem in areas with limited groundwater resources and in those areas where distribution facilities required additional energy to pump water uphill into more inaccessible and marginal areas. This was the case of two of KCWA's largest member agencies, Wheeler Ridge–Maricopa and the Berrenda Mesa Water District, both of which had taken the lead in encouraging the State Project and in requesting additional amounts of surplus and entitlement water once the project got underway. Both agencies, each of which served only a few landowners, had been at the center of the speculative spiral and now were among the first to feel the impact of the irrigation boom's collapse.

In Wheeler Ridge–Maricopa, four landowners dominated: the Tejon Ranch (the largest landowner), closely followed by Tenneco, and then Standard Oil of California and the Southern Pacific Company. These four companies owned more than 70 percent of the land and accounted for three-fourths of imported water sales, and each had benefited greatly from the economic changes brought by imported water.[61] State Project water had stimulated an economic boom, with cotton acreage more than doubling from 26,000 acres in 1968 to nearly 59,000 acres in 1980 and grape acreage skyrocketing from 823 acres in 1968 to 10,693 in 1980.[62] As early as 1971, Wheeler Ridge–Maricopa managers estimated that the land value in the district had appreciated from $38 million to $120 million just from the presence of the SWP.

The Berrenda Mesa Water District also combined land concentration and close political control with an extraordinary escalation in land values. Berrenda Mesa was dominated by two entities: the Blackwell Land Company (controlled by members of the Lazard family, from the international investment-banking firm of Lazard Freres and Company) and the Berrenda Mesa Farming Company (a farm management operation, growing almonds and pistachios, but whose main crop was tax benefits for its limited partners).

By the early 1980s, these two companies accounted for 73 percent of the total cultivated acreage and 90 percent of the total crop value within the district, whose economic worth had dramatically increased with the availability of State Project water. Berrenda Mesa's managers estimated that the per acre value of the lands serviced by the SWP had risen astronomically from a 1966 estimate of $186 average value per acre to $5005 in 1983. "Long-range appreciation in land value," the Berrenda Mesa managers had concluded, "is one of the major incentives for corporate agricultural development in the district."[63]

These two districts were among the first in Kern County to feel the impacts of agricultural decline. The Tejon Ranch's cotton production, much of it organized through tax-sheltered partnerships set up during the 1970s, was one of the first casualties. Lands planted just a few years earlier were left fallow in 1982 and then again in 1984 and 1985, with only crop subsidy programs responsible for limited subsequent planting.[64] In the Berrenda Mesa area, the withdrawal of more than 3,000 acres in cotton in 1983 led to several bankruptcies in 1984 and 1985 when some of the district's smaller landowners, unable to pay their large water bills (based on entitlements as well as use), began to default.[65] The soil of both districts required substantial amounts of water to be applied for each acre irrigated, and the increased water bills—sometimes hundreds of thousands of dollars—came to be perceived as the crucial factor which pushed landowners into insolvency.[66]

By 1985, led by their landowner-clients, both districts decided it was time to bail out. The solution each sought was to sell the rights to their water, either to cover all costs, including long-term debt on the internal distribution facilities as in the Wheeler Ridge–Maricopa case, or to recoup the original investment and make a profit as in the Berrenda Mesa case. Without cheap water, the districts decided, water markets would offer the next best option.[67]

With the decline in the rate of growth of markets for local commodities leading to bankruptcies and to decisions to let land lie fallow or retire it from production, Kern landowners began to focus on reducing their financial exposure. Both Wheeler Ridge–Maricopa and Berrenda Mesa, under pressure from major landowner-clients, surveyed their areas to see how much imported water, at current prices, was no longer wanted in their districts and how best to dispose of or market it. Thirty-five thousand acre-feet of water, much of it from Tejon Ranch and Tenneco, were available to be offered for sale by Wheeler Ridge–Maricopa, and another 50,000 from Berrenda Mesa.[68] Other water districts in the Kern area, including the Belridge, Lost Hills, Cawelo, and Devil's Den water agencies, also indicated interest in reducing, or even eliminating, their water entitlements through some kind of market arrangement.[69]

Wheeler Ridge–Maricopa and Berrenda Mesa pursued somewhat different objectives. Wheeler Ridge–Maricopa, under strong urging from the Tejon Ranch, which had already decided to retire nearly 9,000 acres with contracts for upwards of 23,000 acre-feet of water, wanted to bail out as rapidly as possible by finding a seller to pick up all costs, including the costs of constructing internal distribution facilities. Berrenda Mesa, on the other hand, decided to sell the water—and the land in default—at a rate as high as $800 to $1000 an acre-foot, which would not only cover costs but realize a profit on the contracted water.[70]

Once these positions were made public, all hell broke loose within the agency and throughout the water industry in the state. Several water districts, including the urban Castaic Lake Water District (serving a rapidly growing area in northern Los Angeles County) and the Orange County Water District, expressed interest in buying the water but ran into strong opposition from KCWA and MWD. KCWA was most concerned with keeping entitlements from the State Project within the Kern area, while MWD (as with Galloway) wanted to maintain control over State Project water within its service area. Tensions between the Kern agency and some of its landowner-clients heightened in this period, with one agency board member even attacking the Tejon Ranch for its desire to be bailed out from its "speculative investments" that had now turned sour; "they gambled and lost," the director, Gene Lundquist, argued.[71] The agency, meanwhile, desperately sought to find buyers among its member agencies but found this difficult because of the high price of the water.[72] Finally, after the agency threatened to increase zone-of-benefit charges to pay for the Wheeler Ridge–Maricopa water, Improvement District No. 4, the urban contractor within Kern, agreed to take over the costs for some of the water. The situation with Berrenda Mesa, meanwhile, remained unresolved.[73]

In the midst of agricultural disinvestment and the search to transfer unused water, public agency positions continued to emphasize the need for expansion of the State Project and for future additional supplies. Although the agency had begun to make its concerns about the increasing price of SWP water more visible, its leaders continued to insist that additional water was needed in the county. "We have to declare this water surplus to Kern County," KCWA director Fred Starrh said of the unwanted Wheeler Ridge–Maricopa and Berrenda Mesa entitlement water, "even though we don't have a surplus in the county."[74] It was not the water itself that was the problem, water industry leaders declared, but its price.

Toward that end, several Kern water districts began to pursue the possibility of obtaining unutilized federal Central Valley Project water, which had a price ten or even twenty times cheaper than the entitlement water in the State Project system. By 1987, the Bureau of Reclamation had tentatively begun to explore offering CVP "surplus" water on a short-term basis at the low CVP rates, since not all the water potentially available in the federal system had been contracted. But if this "excess" water was offered for sale, as the bureau had attempted to do during the dry summers of 1987 and 1988, that much less water would be available to flow through the delta to the bay, thus intensifying already existing concerns about inadequate flows. Environmental groups and congressional critics immediately objected to this bureau policy, and the transactions were temporarily postponed.[75] For the Kern water industry, however, the CVP "excess water" deal highlighted their long-term concern. Their water "crisis," KCWA board members argued, was simply "a cheap water crisis."[76]

By the end of the decade, the Kern County Water Agency had become an agency with an uncertain future, with many of its key issues still unresolved. The market question—the sale of water entitlements—remained a paramount issue, as did the matter of price. The relationship with the City of Bakersfield over taxes and representation was still uneasy, while the interest in an effective conjunctive-use approach still remained tentative. Water quality, over which KCWA maintained some jurisdiction, had grown to be a problem from which agency managers unsuccessfully tried to extricate themselves as public concerns continued to increase. And with the sudden and possibly long-term decline in the county's agricultural industry, the future direction of the agency seemed up for grabs.

Part II

Accountability

Wide public participation in setting water policy has
always been uncommon. By the turn of the century, a
tight-knit community of development interests—the
"water industry"—had set up an institutional framework
that removed subsequent water issues from public view.
During the 1970s, however, this long-established system—
based on alliances between local and sectional actors, their
powerful congressional representatives, and the various
federal agencies—came under challenge, and the policy
process appeared to be opening to new, public constituencies. This challenge began at the national level, where
opponents of the status quo challenged the established
goals and practices of the water community and promoted
alternative legal, legislative, or administrative scenarios. In
consequence of this new politicization of federal water

policy, many of the traditional strategies and objectives of the local water industry, which had depended on claims for large-scale investment by the big federal or state agencies, were no longer viable.

So, accountability, public input, political evaluation, and public exposure came to matter at the national level and, increasingly, at the local level as well. At the national level, the policy vacuum (particularly regarding new water development) that emerged seemed to increase the interest of "outsiders" in water issues. Water analyst Helen Ingram's observation in 1976 that "opportunities for the participation of new publics are greatest when decision-making arrangements are in flux"[1] was to prove even more relevant in the turmoil about water issues of the following decade. But for the agencies themselves (the basic unit of decision making within the water industry), this challenge of accountability did not mean they should transform their own agendas and practices; it meant they should rethink how to approach the public. The public information (or public relations) function of the agencies became a much more prominent focus.

As a result, despite this apparent opening of discourse and participation, water policy decisions have by and large remained narrowly conceived and drawn. Water issues continue to be defined in "technical" terms, that is, as dependent on expertise, with policy matters then to be settled within discrete, "apolitical" agencies (often still responsive to their old constituencies). This argument, that water questions are technical questions and that the agen-

*cies themselves are public servants, not political actors, has
been widely used by water industry leaders struggling to
maintain control over policy formation, though they may
now justify this control with a somewhat different
rhetoric. By appearing to be more visible and open to
public input, the water industry has hoped to deflect the
skepticism of "outsider" constituencies and to appear to
construct a new agenda* without abandoning earlier
objectives and alliances.

*The increasing tension between the agencies' "status
quo plus" position and the continuing pressure for change,
now from both outside and inside the water industry, has
made the question of accountability increasingly prominent. It has revealed through greater exposure of agency
choices and alternatives a now fractious and unsettled
policy and an incoherent and disorganized structure of
decision making and power among the traditional participants in the water community. The water industry, somewhat more visible and much more in flux, finds that it can
no longer—as easily—control the terms of the debate and
keep the public out.*

6

How Decisions Get Made
and Who Gets to Make Them

≋≋≋≋≋≋**M**ost water purveyors are public institutions. Unlike the electric utilities where investor-owned or privately held utilities, regulated by statewide public utility commissions, generate more than three-quarters of the country's electricity, public water agencies deliver water to more than 75 percent of the country's population.[1] Though they are government structures, these agencies are often subject to little direct public review other than through their boards of directors. These boards, in turn, are largely responsive to, and often composed of representatives of, the interest groups that have traditionally dominated water policy at the local, regional, state, and national levels.

There is a wide array of agencies in California: more than nine hundred at the state level and nearly four hundred in the Southern California region, including the Kern and Imperial areas.[2] The six Southern California agencies under review here are representative of the diversity of arrangements for agency governance, though we have found them remarkably similar in their response to challenges of their accountability, openness to input, and patterns of oversight. The six agencies include a regional water district, MWD, which serves a huge area through its twenty-seven retailer and wholesaler client-members; a county water wholesaler (San Diego County Water Authority) with primarily urban clients; a county water agency (Kern County) with predominantly agricultural clients; a county-wide[3] irrigation district (Imperial); a regional water "pass-through" agency covering most of a groundwater basin (Upper San Gabriel Valley); and a municipal water utility drawing on a portion of a groundwater basin (Burbank). These agencies are chartered and governed in various ways. Two were established as special-purpose districts through enabling legislation at the state level; two others originated through votes by the electorate at the county level; another was organized by a vote conducted within the new agency's service area, which corresponded to a portion of the groundwater basin but not to any combination of existing political boundaries; and one was organized as a municipal public service department. All of the agencies have boards of directors, though in one case—the Burbank utility—that board is only advisory. Each is also ultimately responsible to the political entity linked to its original formation: the state legislature, county board of supervisors, or city council. But this relationship is distant: the agencies operate with little or no supervision from those political entities. Despite this lack of direct political accountability, as government agencies with the power to set water rates, to raise and spend public monies, and to influence land use decisions, these water agencies are immensely influential in political matters.

This relatively insulated yet politically sensitive nature of water agency governance has tended to reinforce the water industry's prevailing culture. Over the years, the selection, organization, and activities of the governing boards of the water agencies have contributed to the closed, self-contained nature of decision making and policy formation. Water policymakers have generated their own policy loop, separate from most other structures of governance in the society. Though many water directors are perceived by various people, including some of the directors themselves,[4] as "politicians," they are essentially politicians without a public, decision makers accountable only to each other and their water-industry constituents. How this pattern of government developed, and whether it can continue, has become an important question to the debate over future water policy.

The Boards of Directors

Board members in the six agencies reviewed here, as in most water agencies, are either elected by the voters in their service area or appointed by their city governments—the mayor or city council—or (for the "wholesaler" agencies San Diego and MWD) by the boards of the client agencies. In either case, until recently, serious challenge to the selection of particular board members has been rare or nonexistent. Most board members appear in, or are chosen from, a limited pool of candidates who have already made a place for themselves within the larger water industry. Those few who are new to water issues, moreover, are quickly socialized and often seem eager to be accepted into the "water fraternity" environment that pervades water agency activities. Once in, a director can normally expect a long tenure, significant perquisites, access to power, and little review. The rewards for directors are self-determined.

The Selection Process: Elections

Where directors are elected (KCWA, IID, and the Upper District), these elections have rarely involved open and substantial debate over issues or thorough review of candidates and their positions. In Kern and the Upper District, the retention of incumbents before 1988 was phenomenal (97.5 percent for Kern; 100 percent for the Upper District).[5]

Elections in Imperial have been more contentious (and the circumstances of directors thus more volatile) due to the more openly political character of IID (and thus its board elections) and also to the importance of electric power issues in the outcome of those elections.[6] This has costs and benefits for the directors themselves; unlike most other water agencies where politicians may decide to "retire" by joining local water boards, a candidate for an IID board position may well "see it as a stepping stone to higher elected office," as one board member commented.[7]

The one defeat of an incumbent in Kern is also instructive of the limited electoral recourse available to challengers. In the early 1980s the death of a director left a vacancy on the Kern board. When vacancies occur, Kern directors invariably have appointed a new board member then able to run as an incumbent in the next election.[8] In this instance, the board selected Fred Starrh (an active participant in the County Farm Bureau—and Republican Party politics—from the Shafter area) who was well known to Kern water industry participants.[9] The first time Starrh (now an incumbent) came up for election, he was opposed by Larry Wedel, a farmer from the Wasco area which, like Shafter, was located in the district represented by Starrh. Neither candidate campaigned intensely, there were no debates, disagreements, or accoutrements (advertisements, canvassing, mailers, and so forth) typical of a contested election. Nevertheless, to the surprise of the KCWA board and of Starrh himself, Wedel won the election.[10]

Wedel's brief tenure on the board was not marked by controversy; he usually supported KCWA policies and was easily integrated into the board. He did not complete his term, however, since he died in office a few months before the next election. Rather than keeping the seat open for the upcoming election, the KCWA board once more appointed Starrh, allowing him to run again as an incumbent when Wedel's term came due. Starrh was again opposed by a candidate, James Payne, who did not campaign, did not criticize Starrh's role at the agency, and did not present any overall policy position of his own. Regional issues and continued mistrust of Starrh still had some effect but this time the incumbent won, albeit by just twenty-six votes. Despite his loss and subsequent narrow victory, Starrh, who had the right background and associations, had already become a power within the KCWA board and became KCWA chair just a year after his second campaign. At his third election in 1986, Starrh ran unopposed, his tenure and position at KCWA now secured indefinitely.[11]

Elections in Kern are affected by four crucial factors: the nature of the districts; the timing of the elections; the power of incumbency; and the agency's identification with agribusiness. The KCWA service area was divided into five different districts, each to select a board member every four years. The district boundaries, however, corresponded neither to existing political subdivisions (for example, supervisorial districts) nor to geographic boundaries (city limits, groundwater basins, etc.). The Bakersfield metropolitan area is divided into three different district areas, and there is no single *urban* district as such. The power and involvement of KCWA's client member agencies intensify the public perception that the agency deals exclusively, or at least predominantly, with agricultural issues and that urban representation is insignificant. Finally, the practice of appointing new board members prior to elections, thus giving them the benefits of incumbency, is complemented by the board's practice of selecting these new appointees from those candidates who are "groomed for the job," as one board member put it, because of their ties to the water industry and to the agribusiness interests which dominate local politics.[12]

The system that evolved at about the same period in the San Gabriel Valley paralleled the closed structure of electoral representation in Kern. Of the four Valley-wide water organizations in San Gabriel, two—the San Gabriel Valley Water Association and Watermaster—have had no effective public oversight. The association is not a public body; as the organization of the different water companies and industrial interests with water rights, it functions directly as the water industry lobbying group. Watermaster, created out of the adjudication process, has nine appointed members: six representatives from among the association groups and three "public" members: one from the Four Cities District (San Gabriel Valley Municipal Water District) and two by the Upper District (Upper San Gabriel Valley Municipal Water District). The dominant private (water industry) representation on Watermaster was the primary reason community and environmental groups challenged its attempt to assure greater powers in the San Gabriel Basin cleanup.

The Upper District Board, a presumably more public, elected body, has attracted "politicians," those individuals interested not just in the circumstances of their own agencies but in broader policy issues facing the water industry.[13] Typically, the five Upper District board members each hold additional responsibilities that give them broader areas of concern: two members are appointed to the MWD board; two are appointed to Watermaster; and at least one member represents the Board to the Association of California Water

Agencies (ACWA), a key state water industry lobbying organization. ACWA members, moreover, like MWD representatives, frequently also participate in other state and national lobbying organizations, such as the California Water Resources Association, the California Municipal Utilities Association, and the National Water Resources Association.[14]

Despite the more-obviously political nature of the agency, selection of Upper District board members has been limited by the same factors present in Kern. For one, the five electoral districts, redrawn every ten years (after the census) to maintain equal populations, do not correspond directly to any particular community, political, or even groundwater boundaries. Moreover, unlike KCWA, with its coincidence with county boundaries and ostensible oversight by the board of supervisors, the Upper District boundaries run through a series of bedroom communities in an area (the San Gabriel Valley) with no other common identity. The Upper District is an artifact of water issues, and its "public"—as well as its board—is made up of those already involved with the water industry.

Board members of the Upper District, even more than their equivalents at KCWA, have consistently been appointed to their positions. In the Upper District, incumbents do not need to run for office if they are not opposed in a specific election, and for many years incumbents never seemed to be challenged. Without a challenge, the unopposed incumbent would be reappointed to his or her position by the Los Angeles County Board of Supervisors, not even having to appear on the ballot of the voters whose district the board member represented.

In the first twenty-five years after the district was founded, only one board member ever ran in a contested election (other than the first election, where there were no incumbents).[15] In that one instance, the incumbent, Conrad Reibold, an engineer with Pacific Telephone and a member of the Arcata City Council who was himself appointed to the Upper District board to fill a board vacancy, had an opponent in the first election (1970) after his appointment. "I couldn't tell you much about my opponent," Reibold recalled in a 1986 interview, "since I never debated him, nor even saw him on any occasion. It was somebody who probably just decided to file. There were never any public appearances, nor were we ever questioned. The only 'campaigning' I did was to run a three-by-five-inch ad in the San Gabriel section of the *Los Angeles Times* the Sunday before the election."[16] Reibold won easily, reinforcing the board's perception that incumbency—and lack of debate—were sufficient to be reelected.

The appointment-as-election process is compounded by the role of the board chairman, who has the power to initiate all appointments subject to majority approval of the board. This has centralized power in San Gabriel even more than in Kern or MWD (after 1975) which rotates the position of chair every two or four years.[17] In San Gabriel in 1986, Reibold decided to circumvent the chair's power to appoint by arranging for *his own* replacement. Reibold, who had been one of the two Upper District representatives to Watermaster, had decided, without telling other board members, to retire. As the filing deadline approached, Reibold continued to assure board members he would file, while privately notifying *his* choice for replacement, Robert Nicholson, the general manager of a private water company and also a member of Watermaster, that he did indeed plan to retire. At the last day prior to filing, Reibold and Nicholson sprung their surprise: Reibold never filed but Nicholson did. As expected, nobody else filed, so Nicholson became the ipso facto incumbent, filing unopposed and, therefore, automatically appointed to the board by the County Board of Supervisors.[18]

In 1988, however, this self-perpetuating system of appointments in lieu of elections was finally challenged. That year, two candidates, William Robinson (an air pollution chemist) and Royall Brown each filed against incumbents up for reelection. This extraordinary challenge had come about because of the extensive (though unorganized) concern among valley residents over groundwater contamination, the passivity of the water agencies, and the snail-like pace of Superfund response. Though they lacked any organizational or funding base, the two challengers put forth, through a door-to-door campaign, a position about water quality that addressed voter concerns. Both candidates also raised questions about the accountability of the board and the lack of public input into board decisions, making the *process* of governance as much an issue as the actual policy decisions.[19]

The two challenged board members decided to employ the strategy successfully used in the one previous challenge of an incumbent. Incumbent Howard Hawkins anticipated the endorsement of the local newspaper, the *San Gabriel Valley Tribune*, given his twenty-five-year tenure on the board and prominent position as past chairman of both MWD and ACWA. Hawkins and fellow incumbent John Maulding did receive the newspaper's endorsement but were nonetheless both defeated by nearly three-to-two margins, to their shock and indeed the shock of the entire Southern California water industry. This new electoral reality was further dramatized two years later, when two more incumbents, including Robert Nicholson, were defeated.[20] The era of the nonexistent election in the San Gabriel Valley had come to an end.

The Selection Process: Appointments

The dramatic results in San Gabriel suggested that under pressure the system of selecting members of water agency boards, at least where elections were required, could not foreclose challenge to the industry—even at the relatively insulated local level—once decision-making arrangements and policy agendas were called into question. That same pattern—traditional insularity and unexpected challenge—also appeared in the strategy of member selection by appointment favored by the two large urban wholesalers, MWD and the San Diego County Water Authority.

As water wholesalers or "pass-through" agencies, MWD and CWA had been further removed from any direct accountability or oversight. Their clients are not individual customers but member agencies, municipalities as well as smaller water districts in turn made up of municipalities or other retailers. According to the charters of both MWD and San Diego, the water districts and the municipal member agencies each appoint representatives. Typically, cities have selected individuals who have themselves been agency water managers or have had some other direct association with the industry. This might include civic leaders, such as real estate developers, bankers, attorneys, or other business figures, or, occasionally, local elected officials (mayors or city council members) both past and present. The same sort of appointments have been characteristic of the water districts, although nearly all make appointments to the larger (MWD or CWA) board from among their own directors. These "wholesaler" boards are thus quite removed from direct public oversight, though it is here that major regional policy choices are made.

Often, these representatives seem to have been appointed in perpetuity. Although most representatives are appointed to four-year terms, most leave their boards only by choice or circumstance, not by the intervention of the appointive body. Through the 1970s, many directors with long board tenures continued as representatives until their deaths, and the average age of the MWD and CWA board members was quite high. As late as 1981, the average age of MWD directors, for example, was sixty-seven; six years later the average had decreased, but only to sixty-one.[21] "There was a time around 1975," one long-time MWD board member recalled, "when we seemed to be going to one funeral after another in just a short period of time."[22]

The length of tenure on the boards (averaging 11.5 years at MWD in 1981, still more than 10 years in 1987)[23] often reinforced the lack of feedback and integration between the board representatives' actions and the specific positions or goals of the appointive municipality or water district. Board representatives operated as if they had carte blanche on most broad policy issues, with the primary exception of rate setting. Most city councils or mayors did not require any direct reports from their representatives, and some of the most powerful directors, such as Joseph Jensen and Fred Heilbron during the 1950s and 1960s, and Earle Blais, Howard Hawkins, Harry Griffen, and Hans Doe during the 1970s, were effectively free from any ongoing reports to or oversight from their agencies. Moreover, board representatives maintained an *exclusive* relationship with the larger agency; all policy communication flowed through them. This lack of direct communication ultimately forced MWD management to establish their own channels through formal monthly meetings with member agency managers, to better acquaint the client agency staff about matters of operational concern.[24]

These problems of communication and absence of oversight were intensified by the centralization of power within the structures of governance of the boards themselves. For nearly twenty-five years, at the formative stage of both agencies, MWD and CWA decisions and policies were tightly controlled by their long-standing chairmen, Joseph Jensen and Fred Heilbron. In each case, these powerful chairmen had been appointed by the largest member agencies, the cities of Los Angeles and San Diego. However, both operated independently of their appointing agencies, at times urging policies of agency growth and expansion potentially antithetical to the direct self-interest (at least in financial terms) of their own agencies. Most importantly, both men's power was personal, not just due to the relative standing of their appointive agency but also due to their conceptions of the larger agency's mission and objectives.

After Jensen and Heilbron finally died in the early 1970s, the leading board members of MWD and CWA, all loyal to their chairmen until their deaths, decided to reform the system *within* the agencies. Both agencies set time limits on the position of board chairman and sought to establish a somewhat broader leadership structure by enhancing the role of the other officers and committee chairs. These changes, however, did not translate into time limits for board appointments or other structural constraints on the relationship between the appointed board member and the appointing agency. Most importantly, the actual selection of the new board chair remained in the hands of a small Special Nominating Committee whose members had been appointed by the previous board chair. These nominating committees reviewed potential candidates behind closed doors without public scrutiny or input, then nominated a single candidate for chair, a candidate who would be approved unanimously and without debate by the full board. In that context, when E. L. Balmer was selected as chairman in 1986, his predecessor, E. Thornton Ibbetson, sent a telegram congratulating Balmer on his victory even though the vote of the full board had not yet taken place.[25] In MWD's most recent selection, the pro forma nature of the board vote was underlined when an official MWD press release was issued announcing the new chair, Lois Krieger, after the Special Nominating Committee announced its decision but *prior* to the full board's vote.[26]

During the 1970s, officials from the cities of San Diego and Los Angeles began to be concerned about these closed relationships and power blocs at the big water agencies. Despite the power of their appointees, Jensen and Heilbron, the two city-member agencies had felt increasingly under-represented in terms of policy and clout of individual board members. The issues of cost allocations and revenue generation were particularly important, since both MWD and CWA relied for most of their history on revenues from property taxes—paid primarily by the developed cities—as fixed income sources to help finance agency expansion. At the same time, as growth shifted to other areas, the voting power of the two largest client members declined, challenged especially by the high-growth member agencies in the MWD and CWA service areas. Moreover, the system of governance by centralized, behind-the-scenes decision making that had evolved out of the practices of Jensen and Heilbron exacerbated those disparities between costs and benefits and between investment and subsequent power. Power was, in practice, still controlled by a handful of directors, not based on the actual voting power (by assessed valuation) of particular member agencies. The use of "weighted" votes (votes calculated on the basis of property-tax payments, as the agency's charters laid out) was never frequent; in the CWA, in fact, this only occurred when it was necessary to achieve a quorum, on matters of no disagreement among board members.[27]

During the 1970s, under pressure from the local city water utilities, the autonomy of Los Angeles and San Diego representatives began to be reduced. For the first time both city utilities established regular meetings between board representatives and utility staff.[28] Moreover, the mayors of both cities, who were responsible for the city's appointments to these boards, changed the cast of participants by appointing their political supporters and financial contributors, not just water industry participants. In a precedent-breaking move, these mayors also selected a few women and minorities, the first such appointments to their previously all white, male boards.[29] By the 1980s, both San Diego and Los Angeles had an entirely new set of directors, several drawn from outside traditional water industry ranks, though some key appointments (particularly from San Diego) were still of individuals from leading law firms or businesses engaged in the political life of the region.

The new San Diego and Los Angeles appointments, however, did not immediately translate into changing policies or restructured mechanisms of governance. In a system of extended tenure, new appointees, particularly those without direct water industry ties, were often kept outside the centers of board power. Moreover, many new appointees expressed little interest in learning the details and intricacies of water policy, a situation compounded by the specialized and often-incomprehensible "language" of water issues. Board involvement was simply another perk, a political payoff for past and anticipated future support for those appointed. Most new board members accepted the terms of discourse and went along with the dominant arrangements, in policy or board relations. The most active new board members were absorbed into the board elites, who continued to maintain a high level of control over the internal structures of board governance.

This kind of socialization was also effective in integrating potential critics into the dominant board approach. In San Diego, for example, the City of San Diego's maverick then-mayor, Roger Hedgecock, chose to appoint

Philip Pryde, considered a leading community environmentalist. Pryde, a former flood control supervisor and county planning commissioner, had been especially active in fights to save riparian habitat. Despite Hedgecock's desire to "make a statement," he still needed to obtain formal backing from city council members; to do so, he needed to gain support from other key officials, particularly Water Authority powerhouse Michael Madigan, who had influence with several council members. A meeting was arranged between the mayor's top aide, Madigan, and Pryde. Madigan bluntly told Pryde that to obtain his backing the environmental advocate would have to be the type of director who would not "make waves," especially on the Pamo Dam issue where opposition among environmentalists was strong. Pryde assured Madigan that, in regard to Pamo, he would be a team player and that generally his style would not be "confrontational." On that basis, Madigan agreed to support him, the council votes were lined up, and the new director took his place and quickly came to embrace the general thrust of CWA policies.[30]

In distinction to San Diego and Los Angeles, a more direct challenge to the system of MWD governance emerged during the late 1970s and 1980s from some of the smaller and more developed municipalities. These cities were experiencing a range of new concerns about water quality and regional patterns of development. These particular member agencies—including Beverly Hills (during the late 1970s), Santa Monica, Pasadena, and Burbank within the MWD system—for the first time appointed as representatives "outsiders" who were prepared to critique existing policies and decision-making processes. Though these directors were heavily outnumbered by others who affirmed, or at least accepted, existing arrangements, they challenged what they considered the closed nature of the system. The issue of accountability became especially prominent, both in terms of board procedures and in reference to the role of the member agencies. Several of these directors, including Tim Brick from Pasadena and Michael Nolan from Burbank, though differing among themselves on particular substantive issues, nevertheless shared a common perspective about public input and agency accountability.[31] In turn, these directors made extensive efforts to report back about activities and to engage their councils and mayors in the ongoing debates about water policy. "What links us most directly," Brick said of himself and Nolan, his Burbank counterpart, "is our appreciation of politics, in the best sense of the word; that is, representation and engagement; elevating issues through debate."[32]

With the interjection of these new appointments, the board setting was finally being "opened up," such that both policies and procedures were coming under review. In a way similar to the unexpected defeats of incumbent water directors in those agencies with elected boards, these "outsider" appointments indicated a claim for debate and change on the related questions of governance and accountability.

The Culture of Governance

Although some change has begun, debate and "outsider" input at the agencies under review has not been pronounced. Water agency governance is still dominated by insiders who see themselves as functioning within a closely defined water industry. Other board members must either await their entry into the informal centers of power or remain essentially excluded, particularly most new board members who come to accept their peripheral status. Debate is still discouraged by board members ill-at-ease with conflict and sharp interchange. These tendencies are reinforced by the mechanisms of socialization and the system of benefits and advantages associated with board membership and water industry participation. Joining a large and powerful board of directors—such as MWD, the San Diego CWA, or the Kern County Water Agency—is attractive in its own right; the additional perquisites associated with the position make membership all that much more appealing.

These benefits take several forms. Most directors receive some form of financial compensation, varying from agency to agency. This might include payment for expenses, per-meeting fees, or an overall annual fee. More importantly, a wide range of expenses are assumed by the agency, including attendance and participation in the wide variety of periodic water industry meetings, conferences, workshops, and tours. In a large agency such as MWD and CWA, such meetings might occur frequently, as often as once or twice a month. These meetings and events are often held at resort hotels, with schedules arranged to allow substantial recreation time.[33] Some agencies have absorbed spousal expenses as well, although these and similar procedures such as reimbursement for first-class air travel came to be challenged and ultimately eliminated with the modest increase in public scrutiny of agency procedures. At MWD, where the annual budget for director fees and expenses has averaged more than $1 million for most of the 1980s, several unsuccessful attempts were made to reinstate both first-class air travel and spousal reimbursement for all directors, after these were eliminated in the late 1970s following a county grand jury inquiry. Those reimbursements remain in place for top management and board officers.[34]

The continual round of meetings and gatherings has been complemented by other, related accoutrements of power and prestige. MWD directors, for example, are encouraged to invite prominent local citizens in their communities to participate in carefully arranged tours of water facilities that are also appealing for the free food, lodgings, and scenic vistas available in such settings. Directors in nearly all the agencies are asked to be part of specially arranged fact-gathering sessions or exchanges with top public officials on particular proposed projects or matters of policy and legislation. Water agency directors are also frequent speakers at civic and business organizations, who rely on "one of their own" to elaborate on the more technical issues of water policy.[35]

The culture of governance is also marked by the informal, clublike atmosphere both at board meetings and at the formal and informal exchanges between water industry participants. "Water people talk to themselves" is a frequent refrain among both participants and critics of the water industry. Banter and pleasantries mark the tone of meetings, particularly when "outsiders" are less visible or involved, such as at lobbying organization functions.

This level of informality and pleasantry has been especially pronounced among some of the larger agencies. For most of MWD's history until the mid-1980s board meetings followed a set routine. The first half of the meeting would be devoted to a pledge of allegiance, a prayer led by an MWD staff member who invoked God on behalf of water industry objectives, tenure presentations (for five-year intervals—that is, for five-year service, ten-year service, twenty-year service, etc.), swearing-in ceremonies for new members, introduction of special guests in the audience (spouses, member agency staff, etc.), and finally special awards or ceremonies. At that point, as much as thirty to forty-five minutes later, the meeting would finally attend to board business. The "substantive" part of the meeting would consist mostly of general monthly reports from staff (complete with slides and charts about sales, income, etc.), and occasional commentary from the board chair or general manager. Actual discussion or debate among board members about any particular item was limited and often nonexistent. MWD meetings almost always lasted from 10:30 A.M. to noon, when board members would retire to a special board lunch room. At nearly all the meetings of the different water agencies under review (with the recent exception of IID during its debates over the SWAP), the only audience attending the water board meetings have been member agency staff and other interested water industry observers, for example, an attorney interested in a particular agenda item.[36]

The absence of discussion and debate at the larger agencies has often been justified by the size of the board and its reliance on the committee structure, where more extended discussion is considered appropriate.[37] Though discussions within committees are often more detailed than at board meetings, most such discussions evolve around staff presentations. Often, debate will occur on procedural matters, such as the timing of a decision. Decisions to revise items involve the most powerful directors, such as the board and committee chairs, and include management input and consent. Critics of the MWD committee structure complain that the press and public, while occasionally attending full board meetings, almost never attend committee meetings.[38]

Even when lively debate takes place, as in occasional discussions at meetings of the Kern County Water Agency, these interchanges are between staff of the member agencies and the elected board members but not between board members themselves. Most of these disputes, moreover, occur outside the public meetings, as did the disagreements that emerged during the mid- and late-1980s over various water transfer proposals. In fact, a two-year sample of KCWA board votes between January 7, 1986, and November 24, 1987, indicates only *one* split vote by the board members.[39] Again, the exception has been the sharper and more contentious debates—and more frequent split votes—at the IID board meetings over the SWAP issue, due to the prominence and visibility this issue developed during the five-year negotiation period.[40]

At the urban agencies, more extensive debate is most likely to involve contrary points of view *within the established confines of water industry objectives*. Distributional conflicts are most notable in this category. Questions such as apportioning costs between fixed and variable sources of income, operational conflicts between regional water agencies and smaller units, and siting and financing distribution systems can create protracted conflicts that are frequently resolved through trade-offs. While open debates at board meetings over such issues can occur, the issues are far more likely to be raised (and resolved) earlier in the decision-making process through informal negotiation outside public arenas.[41]

The limited nature of debate has transformed the formal mechanisms of agency governance, such as board meetings, into social events. The social character of the board meeting itself, for example, has been institutionalized through informal, after-meeting lunches (at MWD, the Upper San Gabriel District in conjunction with Watermaster, sometimes Kern), and dinners (San Diego) that become the highlight of the day's activity.[42] The advanced age of directors, plus the fact that many tend to be retired from their work, added an element of leisurely pace and set patterns for such meetings. In that context, water agency gatherings, as one MWD director put it, "used to be fun."[43]

Less so today. With the increase in debate and in "outsider" participation at the board level, and with increasing public scrutiny from critics, legislators, and the press, the culture of agency governance has also begun to change. Meetings are longer and include more debate, at each of the agencies. In the process directors have also become more visible figures, subject to challenge for the first time. In San Diego, for example, the idea of a public takeover by CWA of the San Diego Gas and Electric utility created a degree of public scrutiny of Water Authority directors and their actions unprecedented for the large agency. "Some of the directors felt uncomfortable with this new situation," reflected CWA general manager Lester Snow. "Most others realized that the more relaxed atmosphere of earlier days when public review was almost non-existent might no longer be the case."[44]

This acknowledgement of a transition is still tempered by the degree to which the organizational culture and the system of perquisites and rewards

has remained intact. "Trying to say no is still difficult," commented Burbank's Nolan, whose sharp and insistent style has particularly rankled some
of the older directors at MWD. "You'll hear a nervous cough by one, perhaps
a smirk or laughter by another. The body language of those uncomfortable
with criticism is striking."[45] The technical complexity of the issues presents
another obstacle; criticism is often dismissed as unfounded or inappropriate
because it is not *expert enough*. Directors, especially those with only a limited background regarding water issues, hesitate to criticize for fear of being
ridiculed for their lack of knowledge, a problem even more telling for members of the general public—who are often criticized or intimidated for their
lack of technical knowledge or background.[46]

The importance of technical knowledge and the apparently diminished
role of allocation and distributional issues have also reduced the role and
power of the governing bodies. A major debate within the water industry
has emerged, not so much in terms of governance and accountability but
over the role of management and its focus of activity. With the demise of the
era of the forceful (often autocratic) chairman, and the relative erosion of
the closed system of governance, power over agency policy has shifted to the
staff. Once seen as technicians following their marching orders, water managers have begun to take—or at least share—center stage.

The Managerial Evolution

For most of this century, water systems management has
been the province of engineers. With the widespread introduction of chlorination and filtration in most metropolitan water systems by World War I
(and the expanding interest in irrigation in California and the West), water
issues came to be defined as supply issues. These were perceived as political
in nature *but as requiring technical capabilities for effective implementation*.
The governing bodies of the local agencies, along with politicians and ad-
ministrators at the federal level, formed the coalitions which passed legislation authorizing the major water supply systems that were then built. But
the engineers were the ones who built and operated such systems, both at
the local-agency level and within the large federal bureaucracies such as the
Bureau of Reclamation and the Army Corps of Engineers.

As a consequence, most chief executives or general managers of both
large and small agencies were classified as *chief engineers*. In the larger agencies such as Kern, MWD, Imperial, and San Diego, the primary task of management was to oversee the construction and ultimate operation of the major
imported water systems serving Southern California, the Colorado River
Aqueduct, and the State Water Project. The leadership of the groundwater
agencies, though somewhat differently structured, still required significant

input from engineers, whether as consultants (as with the Upper San Gabriel District), or in a staff capacity (as with the City of Burbank's utility).[47]

This engineering function had significant effects on policy. Where to site an aqueduct and its various facilities, for example, had major distributional impacts and often provoked the most difficult and contentious debates among member agencies. How to allocate costs, though at times disguised as a technical question, also became a point of dispute. Yet the engineer-managers often deferred to the lawyers or the powerful, politically oriented board members on matters of overall policy, such as MWD's Laguna Declaration, San Diego's relationship to MWD, the IID decision to negotiate a SWAP, or Kern's delay in pursuing the Peripheral Canal in the late 1960s and early 1970s.[48]

That reliance on the separation of political decision making and engineering skill, embodied in the division between the governing board and an operations-oriented management, began to make less sense by the early 1970s when traditional water development goals were successfully challenged. At the federal level, a National Water Commission was established that brought together sociologists and political scientists, economists and geographers, as well as civil engineers, to review the state of national water policy. Their recommendations, such as establishing markets, restructuring pricing policies, more planning, and increased efficiency, all required a different kind of "expertise" of the "chief engineers" at the agency level.[49] And although the recommendations of the National Water Commission were never incorporated by water agencies, they signaled some of the new agenda that would be considered in the next decade, when the demise of the big water project could no longer be ignored.

Each Southern California agency experienced that transition on some level, through some major political event such as the Peripheral Canal referendum; through unanticipated administrative problems such as the withdrawal of San Diego's Pamo project; or through legal constraints such as the conservation-related lawsuits brought against the Imperial Irrigation District. Even the smaller agencies, like Burbank or other cities in the MWD system, came to be swept up in the debates over the Peripheral Canal. Furthermore, by the mid- and late-1980s, concern also had shifted from supply issues to the difficult and intractable questions of water quality, an area most water managers and board members knew little about.[50]

In encountering such transitions at the most immediate, operational level (for example, how to meet—and continue to encourage—anticipated growth, or how to stay within maximum contaminant levels for various organics), water agency managers found themselves forced to respond more directly than their board counterparts. On the one hand, the political and lobbying activities of the water leaders continued to revolve around the recreation of old political alliances and the reestablishment of traditional agendas.

On the other hand, water agency managers were being obliged to consider different programs if they still wanted to accomplish long-standing objectives. Some managers, as a result, began to clash with their boards, as did MWD's John Lauten during the mid-1970s. Other managers, like Kern County's Stuart Pyle, proceeded cautiously when introducing new approaches such as groundwater storage and conjunctive use. Most importantly, however, managers became increasingly preoccupied with *nonengineering* functions, and those who felt uncomfortable in such areas, such as Lauten's replacement at MWD (E. L. Griffith), were never able to adjust to the altered responsibilities and direction of the role of chief engineer–general manager.[51]

By the mid- and late-1980s, it had become a truism to suggest that the era of the engineer-manager was coming to an end. What had replaced it, however, was still open to interpretation. "Chief engineer" or "engineer-manager" began to disappear from the job title of top agency management positions. Some boards began to select nonengineers, such as lawyers, to these top positions. Even the engineer-managers, recognizing the changing dimensions of policy, began to familiarize themselves with the new issues or to delegate additional authority to staff familiar with such issues.[52]

The general manager's role came to be defined in a variety of new ways. For some, political lobbying and negotiating skills were now required to accommodate to an era where reallocations, market transfers, legislative intervention, and the breakdown of the traditional consensus on water development now prevailed. Others saw the increasing visibility of water agencies (and a potentially more adversarial press) as requiring a manager skilled in public relations. Water lawyers argued that the manager needed to confront the legal and institutional questions that were coming to the fore. Financial advisers and staff insisted that their area had become more significant, and they pointed to the growing role of the commercial and financial caucuses in water lobbying organizations.[53]

These interpretations also reflected conflicting assumptions about management roles and the possible alternate directions they offered for the agencies. The most pronounced debate of this kind occurred during the selection of the general manager of the San Diego County Water Authority. When CWA's long-time general manager, Linden Burzell, decided to retire in 1984, there were two leading candidates to replace him: John Hennigar, the general manager of the Valley Water District (a CWA member agency), and Larry Michaels, an engineer supervising CWA's quest to build the controversial Pamo Dam storage facility. Hennigar, a prominent member of the rising new leadership group of CWA board members, which included board officers Michael Madigan and Francesca Krauel, did not have an engineering background. He argued, on his behalf, that public relations and politics had become dominant, while engineering and operational responsibilities could be left to the staff. Michaels, on the other hand, found that his engineering background helped him with those directors who preferred an engineer for the position but did not hurt him with other directors who feared the growing power of the new leadership group and were concerned that the politically oriented Hennigar would consolidate their power further. After heated debate Michaels was unexpectedly selected by a narrow margin in closed, executive session (by a nineteen-to-sixteen vote according to one participant).[54]

During his short stint as general manager, Michaels argued that both political and engineering and technical duties remained essential to the position, especially given the CWA's small staff (80 compared to MWD's 1675). Michaels insisted that all water decisions had a technical component, standing on its head the old argument that technical water decisions are also political. But the new leadership group countered that politics had become too important to the position, and that the chief engineer's responsibilities should be split off from the general manager's role and relegated to the second tier.[55]

This time, the new leadership group convinced a majority of the board that Michaels—and his approach—had to go. Once again, however, they were unable to elevate their candidate, Hennigar, to the position. Instead, the board selected Lester Snow, who also had a technical background from his training at the University of Arizona, though his responsibilities in Tucson had been heavily oriented towards political and community issues. Like Michaels, Snow saw his position as expanding both the focus of the general manager's role and the scope of County Water Authority activity. Unlike Michaels, Snow also emphasized efficiency measures, conjunctive use programs, and conservation and reclamation activities, and was particularly focused on issues of public scrutiny of agency performance.[56] The transition from Burzell to Michaels to Snow testifies to the growing role of politics in shaping agendas.

In the agricultural agencies, the general manager and staff have continued to defer to the more politically oriented and engaged board and member agency participants. Stuart Pyle, the long-term general manager of the Kern County Water Agency, whose tenure lasted from 1973 to 1990, conceived of his role as reflecting the interests and objectives of his board of directors, and, beyond that, of the interest groups in the region that dominate the area-wide water industry. During the mid-1970s Pyle got caught, at times, between contending member agencies and board members on a variety of allocation issues. As a result, according to several KCWA directors, he began to take a less affirmative role, despite initial forays into such developing areas as groundwater storage. "It takes time to float alternatives," Pyle said of his board.[57]

Pyle's counterpart at the Imperial Irrigation District, Charles Shreves, a former regional supervisor with the Army Corps of Engineers, immediately found himself forced to confront the politically explosive and unresolved issue of the water SWAP with MWD and the series of lawsuits that had boxed the large agricultural agency into a corner. Like other agricultural agency directors, the IID Board wanted to control the conditions and terms of any future negotiations. At the same time, however, the politically oriented board members also found appealing the vision of IID's new role as market brokers being offered by certain outside consultants. The technically oriented Shreves, as a result, was bypassed by his board through their various arrangements with those consultants. Thus, ironically, the board, operating in the context of a highly charged and politicized situation, decided nevertheless to reduce the political functions of the general manager.[58]

The dramatic changes experienced by the groundwater agencies also did not fully translate into a new role for agency management. The discovery of contaminated wells in the San Fernando Basin only exacerbated a management crisis for the Burbank utility, which went through five general managers in fifteen years.[59] Without either direct technical background or a forceful political approach to the issue of water quality and the question of "polluter" responsibility, the Burbank management deferred to other agencies. At the same time, its interim decisions, such as closing wells and increasing its reliance on imported MWD water, failed to address the long-term consequences of the pollution. Moreover, utility managers and staff were offered little direction on these issues from their governing bodies, whether the city council or the even more passive advisory board.[60]

The San Gabriel situation was also fraught with technical and institutional complexities and passive water agencies. The first general manager of the Upper San Gabriel Valley Municipal Water District, Carl Fossette, established a management style particularly effective in handling adjudication negotiations between potential adversaries. Fossette, with his adept, low-key, conciliatory style and long experience within the water industry, managed to oversee several different adjudications and then ultimately to assume management responsibilities for all the different agencies involved. At one point Fossette had a management position with five different bodies: the Upper District, the Main San Gabriel Watermaster, the San Gabriel Water Association, the Central Basin District, and the West Basin District. This extraordinary arrangement, with its elaborate potential for various conflicts of interest, was accepted by the different interest groups involved on the grounds that Fossette, as attorney Ralph Helm pointed out, "would somehow always find that middle ground."[61]

Fossette's replacement, his assistant Jane Bray, had no engineering experience and little background in water issues when Fossette hired her from the Chamber of Commerce in the late 1960s. Bray, unlike others in the world of San Gabriel water politics, was most adept at public relations and outreach. Bray also quickly demonstrated an ability to learn and talk the language of water that was eventually considered sufficient to enable her to assume Fossette's roles at all three of the San Gabriel groups. In her position, Bray relied on others, such as the Upper District's consulting engineer, Tom Stetson, to formulate the details of policies. Bray, however, was also interested in using her public relations skills to help recast her managerial functions. This possibility was enormously strengthened when Bray succeeded in obtaining for the Upper District the EPA Community Relations/ Outreach position regarding the San Gabriel Superfund site, allowing her to wear yet another management hat.[62]

Bray eventually decided to leave the Upper District (as well as her related positions at Watermaster and the Water Association) to consult for others. Her replacement, Robert Berlien, formerly general manager of the city of Alhambra's water agency, returned to a more traditional definition of the agency manager. Like other managers among the forty-six different purveyors in San Gabriel, Berlien, however, found himself required to redefine his and his agency's approach when it came to the issues of contamination, cleanup, and prevention. Superfund came as a rude shock to these managers, Berlien included, who had never before needed to confront the kinds of regulations, costs, community concerns, and larger social and economic ramifications involved with the deterioration of the basin's water quality.[63] Superfund created the necessity but not the means for agency manager redefinition.

The water quality issue was a primary but not exclusive reason for the breadth and urgency of such redefinition. Those pressures were particularly felt at MWD, the largest and most comprehensive of the agencies, whose scope of activity brought it to the fore in each area of change and innovation, including water quality, reallocations, and pricing and conjunctive use. The importance of politics had long been recognized within the MWD system, and all general managers, even in the days when the position was more exclusively oriented towards construction and operations, assumed some political functions. During the 1970s, however, the political upheavals throughout the water industry were reflected at MWD, where both the board and management tended to be divided about policy directions. Even when a strong, single-issue chairman, Earle Blais, came to the fore during the Peripheral Canal fight, his presence in that issue only disguised the fact that both the board and management had not yet made a clear transition in defining their respective roles in policy.[64]

The selection of Carl Boronkay as MWD general manager in 1983 appeared in some ways a crucial turning point both for governance and management issues and for the direction of the agency. Boronkay, MWD's general counsel at the time of his appointment, sought to strengthen the role and position of agency manager in both its political and technical dimensions. He did this partly by bringing in new staff to develop various "alternative supply strategies," such as the IID SWAP, the Arvin-Edison arrangement, and a wide range of surface and groundwater storage programs.[65] Boronkay also expanded his management group by upgrading the Water Quality and Planning divisions and elevating the role of chief economist.

At the same time, Boronkay became a forceful champion of management control over policy formation, with the board assuming final review and approval. But with the increasing complexity of issues, especially those— such as water quality or transfers—that were new to many in the water industry, the traditional relationship between the board and management was being essentially reversed. A form of "incremental decision making," as one board member put it, increasingly characterized the process, with board members finding themselves reviewing decisions *already made in some other context*. As a consequence, board input became far more specialized and fragmented than ever before.[66]

This management approach was complemented by Boronkay's emphasis, supported by key board members, of the *corporate* nature of the position. Although board members and management of most water agencies had long assumed their participation in a water *industry* that included both private interests and public agencies, that concept of industry was more parochial than broad. While water development had long been considered essential to major interest groups in urban and agricultural areas, water policy was more narrowly defined as the infrastructure activity that made such growth and development possible. The breakdown of a community-wide consensus on development, however, forced water agency managers to seek new ties and to strengthen relations with other elites in the community and, by doing so, to place water policy issues high on the agenda of these elite groups.

At MWD, Boronkay quickly sought to develop those kinds of relationships, joining a variety of organizations, such as the Central City Association for downtown Los Angeles businessmen, the Los Angeles Business Council, and the Hazardous Waste Project of the California Council for Economic and Environmental Balance, which was dominated by the big oil and chemical companies.[67] At the same time, Boronkay sought to raise his salary and those of his top assistants to a scale more commensurate with the status of a *chief executive officer* of a major resource-based organization. These salary raises, which became an ongoing point of contention with several board members critical of this corporate-style approach, were the most visible expression of a management philosophy that assumed not only greater authority for management but also an approach to policy and governance that increased rather than reduced the distance between others in the community and the agency.[68]

Water agencies had indeed begun a transition, but in directions that still remained largely unresolved. New challenges at the board level and changing definitions of management had created a partial "new look" at the agency and recognition that some traditional approaches were no longer applicable. But the issue of public input and accountability remained as crucial as ever, as the evolving structures of governance and management did little to provide an opening for public engagement. Change was in the air, but resistance to change and new and continuing obstacles to public input made the challenge of accountability as compelling as ever.

7

Debating the Language of Policy

The power of the water industry is related to the industry's ability to control the conceptual language within which policy questions are posed. This language of public benefit was protected for years by positive public perception of water agencies and their activities, framed in part by press coverage and "civic" support networks responsive to the industry. Water agencies and their leaders were touted as men of vision and action, laying the groundwork for urban growth and agricultural expansion. Urban growth and agricultural expansion, in turn, were presented as essential to the future prosperity of the region or the state. The grand era of the dam and pipeline builder, which peaked between the 1930s and the early 1960s, placed the water agency at the center of the policy process, guiding public works projects, land use decisions, and the allocation of public resources. Water development was big business for the public sector and those private interests most directly affected by such decisions.

Though agency boards—and, recently but increasingly, agency management—make agency policy, they do not always do so in circumstances of their own choosing. When the agencies themselves are not a focus of controversy, their boards and management may pursue their agendas unimpeded. When the agencies, the vast resources they control, and the potential social impact of their decisions attract public attention, as they have in the past decade, several critical groups of outsiders become important participants in the debate over agency accountability. These actors raise two questions: *Who is the agency to be held accountable to?* and *What is the agency held accountable for?* Of the various groups now engaged in water agency policies, one—the businessmen and land developers who are most often appointed or elected to agency boards—function in effect as industry insiders, not outsiders. This chapter addresses three other groups that are outsiders in one or another sense: the complex of industry consultants, the press, and the community groups that have now challenged the industry's traditional agenda. The first group—industry consultants—are "inside" outsiders, closely integrated with the agencies through both contracting relationships and the complex of water industry institutions and generally sharing the conception of agency goals that is common among management and board members. The other two—the press and the community groups—are "outside" outsiders, and their role has been to challenge the circumstances of agency decisions, and now, increasingly, to challenge the language and conceptions within which these decisions are made and justified.

Advice and Consent:
Water Industry Experts and Consultants

In the area of water policy, the expert, whether engineer, lawyer, or financial adviser, has always played a central role. While some of those functions were met by experts employed within the agencies themselves, over the years a substantial amount of "expert" work has been contracted out to private, non-agency individual consultants or firms. These consultants, who often have previous public agency or government experience, occupy a prominent role within the industry, attending its functions, serving in an official or semi-official capacity in its organizations (such as the National Water Resources Association), and developing a familiar and easy working relationship with the individual managers and board leaders of the agencies themselves. Ultimately, the consultant has become as central to the formation of policy at the regional, state, and national level as any single public official.

Water industry consultants are a specialized and tightly coherent community of powerful "experts" who move in and out of the agencies, who are active in agency associations, who represent the agencies as lobbyists or counsel it as attorneys, financial experts, or technical experts (engineers). The services they provide tie agencies together behind the scenes of everyday policy and management choices, supporting a confluence of interests against what may often, in fact, be a structural conflict of interest among the various agencies. Their "expertise" provides authority to support policy choices (or allows them to substitute for staff and boards in making these choices). The consensus among this community—a consensus which results in part from the imperatives of their own structural position as outside consultants—establishes as industry standards a series of decisions that have substantial political content but which are not open to public view. Though the work of particular consultants may be of high quality by the standards of their particular professions, the overall result of this dependence on outside consultants is an impediment to real innovation, unless it provides a market for particular new technologies (physical or intellectual) in which the consultants themselves have found a stake.

The reasons for this conservatism are complex. First, consultants are normally hired to address particular problems or tasks already identified by management or agency boards: the definition of the problem is set for them by the agency that is their contract employer. Second, consultants offer technical support, whether their technique be legal, economic, or engineering, based on the standards and practices of particular professions; and those standards and practices change very slowly unless there is some substantial pressure for their reexamination.[1] Third, the economics of consulting (since consulting firms, though not chosen on the basis of least-cost bids, are subject to some competition about the price of their services) encourage firms to standardize the solutions they offer various clients as much as possible; their own costs are reduced if their technical staff can use existing work and prior knowledge to address the current problem adequately, rather than spending time to find a perhaps-more-effective but unique solution.[2] Finally, selection of particular consultants for particular contracts depends on management assessment of their competence and effectiveness, an assessment based on a complex of social and business relationships and encounters built up over years and often reinforced by the movement of individuals between agency staffs and agency consultants. In this situation, iconoclasts are unlikely to find a place.

Industry consultants fall generally into three professional categories: lawyers, financial experts, and engineering firms. Lawyers most often take a political role, in lobbying government agencies and in negotiating disputes among various agencies over water rights. They also may represent agencies in the regulatory process where questions of adequate compliance are raised. Financial experts are most often engaged when capital projects need to be funded (and bonds sold), since day-to-day strategies of agency financial management—rate setting, taxation levels and so on—are usually worked out by agency management and boards. Engineering firms have been the most important group of consultants to the agencies, in designing the physical infrastructure (dam and aqueduct construction) and, more recently, in evaluating the technical alternatives that agencies might consider in addressing new questions of water quality or conjunctive use. Engineering firms also provide a number of services that arise out of new management concerns, including environmental impact analyses and other specialized management support (cost estimates, etc.).

The use of expert consultants provides a series of benefits for the agencies that hire them. They need not maintain staffs of experts across all the technical areas which they may need to address; though this would of course be impossible for the smaller agencies, it would be difficult even for the giants, like MWD.[3] Through the use of consultant firms that also serve other agencies, they can open a window into the decisions these other firms may be making; where there are common interests (as in lobbying lawmakers or regulatory agencies) agencies will often join forces with a common consultant. Finally, where apparently technical information is a focus of dispute (as in estimating the costs of complying with water-quality regulations, or the potential for conservation in lieu of additional imported supply) consultants, as outside experts, offer a position of technical knowledge that seems at arm's length from the more openly political choices of agency boards and which therefore appears disinterested.

At the national level, the political role of consultants has been especially important. Phil Swing, first a congressman and water industry leader from the Imperial Valley and later a consultant—the "special water counsel"—for the City of San Diego, provided an early model for this role. In the 1930s, legislative and administrative actions affecting Southern California water agencies were strongly influenced by another prominent consultant-lobbyist Northcutt "Mike" Ely. An attorney, Ely was a negotiator for the City of Los Angeles on Colorado River matters. From his office in Washington, D.C., Ely played a pivotal role in nearly all of the major national water debates that affected Southern California. He obtained the Imperial Valley's exemption from the 160-acre limitation of the 1902 federal reclamation law; he helped to defeat—or at least, to postpone for long periods—legislation deemed hostile to California, such as the Central Arizona Project (CAP) or the Colorado River Storage Basin Project; and he represented, at different times, all the major California users of Colorado River water, especially Imperial.[4]

By the mid 1960s, Ely had become a truly powerful and forceful figure within the water industry, though he never held a staff position with any agency during his years as "consultant." Water industry lobbyist Robert Will recalled that the key compromise between California and Arizona—a compromise that finally allowed passage of the Central Arizona Project legislation—only occurred after great efforts were made to exclude Ely.[5] The other participants considered this essential, since the powerful lobbyist-consultant had become so strongly associated with the Southern California position, which opposed the Central Arizona Project, that they feared he would somehow upset the negotiating process. The eclipse of this colorful and forceful figure occurred at about the time that the overall fortunes of the water industry began to ebb on Capitol Hill.

Despite their diminished role in national policy, consultants and other experts have continued to be influential at the agency level, not only by providing critical information and analysis on particular issues but also by providing a broader and longer-term perspective on agency goals. While some political and technical consultants are hired to justify decisions already made by agency management, others—particularly those with a long and close relationship with particular smaller agencies—effectively control development of broader policy initiatives. The engineering and legal consultants for the Upper San Gabriel District, for example, have played a central role from the very outset of the agency, helping determine the two adjudications, the decision to annex to MWD, and the agency's various approaches to the problem of water quality. Consulting engineer Tom Stetson, on retainer to the Upper District since its founding in 1963, has taken the lead in forming and implementing both general policy and the agency's specific response to a number of issues. Stetson and consulting attorney Ralph Helm (and later with his replacement Arthur Kidman) function as *de facto* management for Upper San Gabriel, just as they do for the other major San Gabriel agencies: Watermaster and the Water Association.[6]

While the relationship between Upper San Gabriel and its consultants is unusual in degree, elsewhere consultants also play dominating roles in particular situations. San Diego attorney Paul Engstrand, a well-known water attorney, has had a contractual relationship with the San Diego County Water Authority for more than fifteen years as CWA general counsel.[7] At the same time, he and his firm have served as consultants and "experts" in a range of water matters for other water industry clients. This representation of various agencies has led to some changes in position for Engstrand: as the lead attorney representing IID before the State Water Resources Control Board regarding IID wasteful water practices in the early 1980s, he argued strongly that IID was not wasting water and that any conservation–water trade agreement between IID and MWD was not feasible. But later, when SWAP negotiations commenced, the San Diego CWA (and its counsel, Paul Engstrand) became strong advocates of such an arrangement.[8]

In the Imperial and MWD SWAP negotiations, three sets of consultants were enlisted, each playing a substantial, though differing, role during the five years prior to final agreement in 1989. The Ralph M. Parsons Company, a Fortune 500 engineering, construction, and resource-development firm based in Southern California, was chosen after a search that considered some of the largest construction and consulting firms in the country. Once selected, Parsons became involved at several levels at once, from the relatively technical work of writing the environmental impact report to the political and policy choices involved in designing negotiating tactics and strategies. Parsons's critics, including local residents who feared a multinational company might overwhelm the local district and take over the crucial decision on negotiation and agreement, successfully focused on the potential conflict of interest embedded in the contract signed between the district and Parsons as a way of forcing the big contractor out.[9]

Though Parsons's role in the SWAP was short-lived, individual consultant Tom Havens, who had first introduced the Parsons executives to IID board members,[10] remained involved at the periphery of the SWAP for most of the five years of negotiations. In contrast to the huge and diversified Parsons company, Havens, who worked alone and who had little technical or engineering experience in water matters, attempted to inject himself in the situation in the hope that his force of personality and strong advocacy of "markets" would be sufficiently compelling.[11] While several IID board members were willing to contract with the affable and energetic Havens, he was forcefully opposed by IID general manager Shreves and dismissed by MWD management who saw him as an unwanted intruder.[12] As a consequence, Havens was ultimately displaced by IID's third and most successful consultant, Robert Edmonston of Bookman-Edmonston, one of the premier Southern California consulting firms. In IID's selection of Edmonston (and MWD's eventual selection of its negotiator, one-time consultant and MWD assistant general manager Myron Holburt), the SWAP negotiations were turned over to the engineer-technicians, who worked out the final agreement.

Consultants have also been hired as an extension of management on particular issues. MWD, for one, has often turned to consulting firms to work out the details of a policy already established in outline form, such as the decisions about new water quality treatment technologies. Both MWD and San Diego have hired former management and staff members as consultants to lay out policies and positions that those individuals had already worked on in their previous staff capacity (and the reverse).[13] Water agencies seem particularly inclined to work with the best-known consulting firms, several of whom hire individuals who had either held management or board positions at those same agencies.

Where consultants themselves approach agencies to offer unsolicited information on potential innovations, it is usually those in which they have some stake. An interesting case in point involved a controversial MWD decision in 1988 regarding a proposed nuclear-powered desalinization plant. As early as the 1960s, MWD officials had expressed interest in constructing a nuclear power plant along the Southern California coast, possibly in the Bolsa Chica area in Orange County where MWD had secured a large parcel of land.[14] By the late 1970s and early 1980s, however, the idea had faded, given the increasing political and financial costs associated with nuclear power. MWD board member A. B. "Doc" Smedley, though, continued to be a strong proponent of the idea, and worked closely with those companies still eager to locate new markets for a declining domestic industry. That opportunity arose when a San Diego-based firm, G. A. Technologies, enlisted Smedley's support and convinced the MWD management team under Carl Boronkay to explore a new graphite-core technology system as a way to revive the nuclear-powered desalinization idea. Once the proposal became public, elected officials throughout the region, especially the city of Los Angeles, expressed outrage that such a plant, to be located along the populous coast, might actually be considered. One Los Angeles Council member, Ruth Galanter, calling the proposal "a bad April-Fool's joke," introduced a resolution banning such a facility within the Los Angeles city limits.[15] But despite the political uproar and even though the initial cost estimates ($600 to $900 an acre-foot) were far higher than other alternatives, the MWD board still voted to fund an initial $300,000 feasibility study, undertaken by none other than G. A. Technologies.[16] MWD management, moreover, instructed their lobbyist in Washington to champion this new nuclear technology, and by extension the nuclear power industry.[17]

These arrangements with consultants raise problems of both accountability and potential conflict of interest. Consultants make decisions among alternatives based on their own practices, which include judgments about acceptable thresholds of risk, about appropriate time frames for which to construct benefit-cost analyses, and about how to estimate unpriced (but real social) costs such as environmental damage and the distributional effects of social disparities. They also suggest choices among technological alternatives with which they may not have equal familiarity. These are policy decisions, in which experts have no special expertise.[18] When they are left to consultants, the social choices they reflect disappear into the consultant-management dialogue, a process with little public accountability.

At times, particularly given the increasing move toward negotiations between agencies over transfers, there is a potential conflict of interest in consulting for several agencies at once. In the San Gabriel situation, consulting engineers and attorneys have functioned in a quasi-staff position for different agencies with conceivably different interests at stake. For example, the Upper District, whose role depends on contracting for additional imported water from MWD, might choose to encourage increasing reliance on such supply while advocating a more conservative stance in terms of groundwater use in the basin. This position could be in conflict with a potential Watermaster policy, given that Watermaster is dominated by purveyors who might favor less conservative use of the less expensive groundwater. Yet the general manager of the Upper District, and its two primary consultants-quastaff, serve in the same capacity for Watermaster.[19]

Consultants thus represent a kind of common meeting ground between public and private components of the water industry, establishing, in effect, a *confluence of interest* with respect to water industry values, procedures, goals, and development and operational strategies. Several top management figures at the large agencies have at one time or another served as consultants, while others, who retire from agency activity, enter the consulting business in some capacity. This second layer of activity, parallel but separate from decisions at the agency level, serves as a less accountable, more invisible part of the water industry. It is where the world of technical expertise not only prevails but reenters the decision-making framework in a period when politics has become more significant. While the water agency has been obliged to begin to appear to alter its ways, the interlinked community of consultants and experts serves as a reminder that the industry as a whole still functions as a world apart, with common and often-unexamined assumptions about the imperatives of water policy and with its own language of power.

"Public Information" and the Press

This special language serves as a barrier to effective and continuing press coverage of agency choices and practices. The public information officers of the agencies present agency decisions in a language of technical inevitability, using technical information as a justification rather than educating the press (or the public) about the basic scientific and economic questions implicated in agency decisions. The water quality issue presents a prime example of this—agency positions dismissing water contamination as a significant and pressing problem are justified by reference to only one side of what is an active and contentious scientific and technical debate. But this one-sided explanation has been increasingly challenged, by the press and by public interest, community and environmental groups. The water industry's ability to control the language and definition of water issues first began to erode during the 1970s, and this erosion accelerated during the 1980s. While distributional issues, that is, contending regional disputes over allocations, had often been the source of conflict during the heyday of water development, the problems the industry now encountered were of a different nature, involving direct challenges to the whole rationale of agency decision making. Changing press coverage and policy debate reflected those differences to some degree, forcing the water agencies to an uneasy reevaluation of their policies and programs. Sharp and often unresolved debate has emerged over new issues such as water quality, water transfers, and the need for new supplies to support further growth.

Until recent years, press coverage of water agency activity was routinely related to rate-setting matters, dry-year concerns, or promotion of particular agency programs, such as ground-breaking on new facilities. More extensive coverage was reserved for those issues with direct political overtones, such as the 1960 bonding election for the State Water Project or distributional conflicts such as the fight over the San Bernardino annexation to MWD. Similarly, the public information, or public relations, activities of the agencies were limited to the routine of press releases and promotional events, while the more significant political maneuvering took place outside the public spotlight. At an agency like MWD, with its extensive political impact and behind-the-scenes lobbying, the public information officer was charged as much with keeping the agency *out of the news* as in it. During the 1970s, this function was ably performed at MWD by Alan Williams, a former political reporter with the *Los Angeles Examiner.*[20] As a low profile, and publicly aloof, agency, MWD didn't worry about "image" issues; if anything, during the Jensen era the district fostered the notion that it was a power unto itself when it came to water matters.[21] The "image" issue, however, became a factor when the agency itself became a public issue. This emerged for MWD—and other agencies such as San Diego CWA—during the Peripheral Canal campaign. Both MWD and San Diego had directly intervened during the election through an aggressive public relations effort, complete with a major multimedia campaign aimed at convincing Southern Californians of their serious vulnerability if they were not able to obtain additional imported water. And although substantial local majorities, particularly in San Diego, supported the canal, there were other indications, including surveys of public attitudes toward the agencies, that skepticism towards agency programs and activities had become more pronounced.

By the mid-1980s, several agencies had responded by attempting to "professionalize" their image-related activities. At MWD, the Boronkay management sought to institutionalize a "government relations" program, aimed at improving MWD's standing with elected officials.[22] At the same time, a new public information director, Tom Spencer, was hired from Getty Oil. Spencer prided himself on his "professional" and image-oriented approach to the public information post.[23]

Other agencies also became concerned about image problems, particularly when issues became politically volatile. During the zone-of-benefit-tax controversy in Kern, the agency, led by one of its directors skilled in those issues, hired a public relations firm oriented toward "public involvement"–image issues.[24] By holding public hearings, group workshops, and involvement sessions, "all that touchie-feelie type nonsense," as one agency director complained,[25] the firm, James Ragan and Associates, helped KCWA defuse the issue of accountability.

These approaches, moreover, were most directly oriented toward reestablishing the once favorable treatment by the press of water agency issues, a treatment which had lately taken a more unpredictable turn. With growing public information programs aimed at mobilizing the public about the agencies' agenda for further expansion through warnings of future scarcity, the agencies drew press attention to themselves, and this attention, once stimulated, supported new press investigations of the structures of power and benefit behind agency policies. At papers like the *Imperial Valley Press*, the *Bakersfield Californian*, and the *San Diego Union*, reporters, several of them new to the water beat, both increased and shifted the focus of their papers' coverage of the agencies. At the *Imperial Valley Press*, for example, water coverage of the IID had been limited and sporadic, due in part to a turnover in reporters assigned to the "agriculture" beat, which included water issues, and an unwillingness by long-time reporters to take on such a difficult and unrewarding task.[26] Thus, the beat was often assumed by young reporters, some fresh out of journalism school, who would rely heavily on the district's public relations staff as they tried to absorb the intricacies of water politics in the valley.

When the SWAP negotiations began, two young reporters, Jim Cole and subsequently Willy Morris, were assigned the task of reporting the complex negotiations. Unlike others before them, Morris, especially, decided to plunge into the issue, working long hours, developing a spectrum of sources and breaking a number of stories directly or tangentially related to the SWAP that other papers, including the *Los Angeles Times*, failed to cover. Morris's strong coverage helped bring the issue to public attention and provided one of the rare instances where water coverage was detailed, ongoing, and informative to both water insiders and outsiders alike.

While the circumstances of the SWAP made Morris's coverage possible, the sense of crisis and turmoil in San Diego water issues in the wake of the Peripheral Canal defeat also opened up the possibility for unusual and substantial coverage in the conservative, establishment-oriented *San Diego Union*. This opening was also influenced by the development of a San Diego edition of the *Los Angeles Times*, which promised to compete with local coverage, particularly on such complex issues as water. As a consequence, the *San Diego Union* in 1983 established a full-fledged water beat, assigning to it a new reporter, Cheryl Clark, recently hired from the *Sacramento Bee*.[27] Clark's timing was propitious, as a series of events (including Galloway, the IID SWAP, a short-lived but crucial strain in relations between CWA and MWD management, and the development of opposition in the community on growth issues), provided a diverse and rich source of stories.

Like Morris, Clark also began to attend agency meetings, both for CWA and MWD, and was able to combine background and feature stories with ongoing coverage and occasional breaking news.[28] She earned the wrath of some of those she interviewed, including MWD's Boronkay, by featuring their remarks in stories even when they were direct and blunt, remarks they assumed would not be seen in print. Boronkay, in fact, actually attempted to intervene with Clark's editor over one striking comment he made about the

Galloway proposal.[29] While the *Union* editors backed their reporter in this and other instances, the water story began to decline in significance in their eyes, once it shifted from a sexier supply-scarcity question to the kind of background story about institutional power and the details of policy about which they assumed their readers had less interest.[30]

Growing reader interest in water-quality issues, however, generated a different level of press coverage. The discovery of widespread contamination of wells in the Los Angeles and Long Beach areas during the 1980s stimulated the interest of an editorial writer at the Long Beach *Independent Press-Telegram*, Larry Lynch, who began to explore the complex maze of water agencies and their approach to this issue. In 1987 Lynch began a series of editorials linking the question of lack of input and accountability to the relatively passive approach of the agencies to the issue. Lynch argued for greater public attention and involvement, even keying some editorials to the little-known, uncontested elections for agency directors.[31] Though the *Press-Telegram*'s appeals on the issue did not lead to any upsets of incumbents, as in the San Gabriel Valley, there were, for the first time, serious election challenges and concern among agency directors. Despite this extraordinary coverage, however, the *Press-Telegram*'s analysis and advocacy came to an end when Lynch was transferred to the paper's Sacramento bureau.

Definition of the story and persistent editorial interest were also essential to the coverage provided by the *Los Angeles Times*. By dint of its extensive circulation and political clout, the *Times* came closest to being a region-wide newspaper, though in fact it focused more on national and international events. Until the 1970s, water coverage in the *Times* included boosterism (on infrastructure-related growth and development issues such as freeways and water projects) as well as the limited, routine agency-generated stories of the kind favored during the Alan Williams era at MWD. By the 1970s, however, the *Times* faced strong criticism for its inadequate local coverage and, as a consequence, established a "City-County Bureau" headed by veteran political reporter Bill Boyarsky.[32]

The Boyarsky group decided that expanded water coverage would be part of its task of uncovering some of the lesser-known yet crucial institutions of power in the region. For a short period during the 1980s, water issues (in general and the MWD in particular) became an informal beat at the *Times*, though no single reporter provided ongoing coverage. Finally, Boyarsky, interested in California history and sensing that water could provide a colorful backdrop to larger regional issues, began to do occasional stories himself. His coverage, however, was sporadic, partly as a result of lack of demand from editors at the paper and partly due to Boyarsky's own judgment that the new, Boronkay-led MWD management team now provided a more open and less paranoid relationship with the press. As an institutional story, water was a "serious" story that needed coverage but that never sustained reader (or editor) interest.[33]

By the late 1980s, water coverage in Southern California had changed, but only in an uneven and episodic way. Coverage in papers like the *Los Angeles Times* and *San Diego Union* at first increased in frequency and critical content, but then declined. Reporters felt constrained by the closed nature of the water industry and some had moved on to other beats (or papers), feeling they had encountered a hiatus of support from their editors. Other papers and other reporters, such as those at the *Los Angeles Herald-Examiner* and *Pasadena Star-News* subsequently came to the fore.[34]

Yet the press still remained a peripheral party in water issues, increasing the visibility of water-policy questions and thus generating greater public awareness, but not, ultimately, by much.

Critics and the Community

With the water agencies on the defensive and water policy in transition, the question of community support and coalition-building became prominent. The public information function of the agencies shifted from a low-key, behind-the-scenes approach, designed to keep the agencies out of the news, to a higher-profile attempt to reconstruct a positive image for the agencies. For the first time, agency managers were selected almost as much for their political and public relations capabilities as for their technical knowledge.

At the same time, water agencies actively sought to re-create the political coalitions which had supported their earlier legislative success. These new industry coalitions, however, had to contend not only with a general reduction in public support but with the beginning of opposition both to specific projects and to the overall agenda of the water industry. Water politics, once simply an extension of the public consensus on growth and on the need for infrastructure to support such growth, now became divided contentiously over both issues and values. As a result, water agencies were now both visible and challenged.

The limited increase in awareness of water agencies paralleled the emergence of a new set of observers—and critics—of the water industry. Though water issues had long stimulated involvement of the industry's own constituencies and occasional broader public concern about distributional issues, monitoring of water agency activities was limited at best. Some "good government" groups, such as the League of Women Voters, had sought to keep abreast of water issues, but their involvement tended to focus on broad institutional or statewide matters, such as the development of the State Water Project.[35]

During the 1970s, the emergence of a more expansive environmental movement increased the scrutiny of water issues, primarily in response to proposed large water projects and water-quality legislation. The staff-based environmental organizations, headquartered in Washington or San Francisco, challenged some of the key legislative and administrative initiatives of the water industry effectively, helping contribute to the water agenda stalemate. These national environmental groups, such as the Environmental Defense Fund, the Natural Resources Defense Council, the Sierra Club, and the Environmental Policy Institute, were sufficiently effective that water industry organizations grudgingly began to accept them as "legitimate," if adversarial, parties to the tradeoffs necessary to accomplish long-standing industry objectives. The prominence of the larger environmental groups did not, however, necessarily translate into effective review and input locally within Southern California and *at the agency level*, in part because of the location of their offices and staffs outside the Southern California region.

Some Southern California water-industry proponents sought to use this outside location to deflect their environmental opponents by characterizing their concerns in regional or distributional terms, that is, as an expression of "Northern California" concerns about "in stream" protection for the natural environment.[36] At the same time, they presented themselves—given the supply-side alliance between industry groups throughout the state—as free of such regional biases and commitments and as interested only in the common public good. The most effective "outsider" claims on agency accountability occurred where local environmental and community groups, or local offices of regional or national organizations, found a constituency within Southern California and addressed agency policy choices specifically as well as in general terms.

Where such efforts took place, as in Citizens for a Better Environment's (CBE) involvement in the San Gabriel Superfund process, they often were not sustained over time. During the early 1980s, CBE had become increasingly interested in groundwater contamination issues throughout the country.[37] The group, headquartered in Chicago but maintaining a number of regional offices including one in San Francisco, decided to open a branch in Los Angeles. It immediately plunged into a complex of related activities, addressing the question of leaking underground storage tanks and of the new San Gabriel Superfund site, the first such site to deal with groundwater contamination.

In San Gabriel, CBE immediately made its presence felt. Staff member Greg Karras, recently arrived from San Francisco to set up the Los Angeles office, began attending (uninvited) key committee meetings that were part of the Superfund process. "The water people on the committee immediately got uptight and even discussed whether to close the meetings so I couldn't attend," Karras recalled, but they ultimately decided that to do so would violate the state's Brown Act governing such meetings.[38]

As CBE increased its involvement, it forced both the water agencies and EPA to consider the question of public input and possible scrutiny, effective in this as it had been on the underground tanks issue that it had helped publicize.[39] But CBE, a staff-run organization dependent on canvassing to raise funds, suddenly pulled out of San Gabriel and Los Angeles just as it began to have an impact. Concerned about the limited funds available from canvassing an area less familiar with environmental organizations (though facing some of the most severe environmental problems, from air quality, to landfill problems, to the extraordinary groundwater situation), CBE decided to refocus its activities in San Francisco, with its potentially lucrative market for canvassing and abundance of related organizations.[40] In San Gabriel, meanwhile, community input remained unorganized and sporadic, though at times explosive.[41]

In some important cases the impact of an environmental organization on a particular agency resulted less from organizational priorities or commitments than from the efforts of individuals who developed passionate concerns and willingness to tackle organizations previously resistant to public input. In San Diego, one such individual—Sierra Club member Emily Durbin—had a substantial impact. Durbin, who moved to San Diego in 1975, had little previous interest in either water or environmental issues.[42] She joined the Sierra Club because of her interest in hiking and began to focus on new development plans in the backpack areas of the northern and eastern ends of the county. In 1982, she also began to hear of plans to build the Pamo Dam in the undeveloped Pauma Valley. Moved by the beauty of the area and convinced the valley "did not deserve to be under water," Durbin decided that this would be her issue.

As a consequence, Durbin, who got herself appointed to head the local Sierra Club's then mostly moribund Water Resources Committee, began attending CWA meetings, learning the technical details of Pamo and of overall CWA and water-industry activity, and expressing her concerns. "I remember being absolutely terrified the first time I went to a CWA meeting," Durbin recalled. "It felt like an older men's club, given their age and gender. And when I asked to address the board, it came as a shock. 'Who the hell is Emily Durbin?' I heard one board member whisper."

"Up to then," Durbin commented, "when someone wanted to address the board, they'd send a note to the committee chair, and, with his consent, they'd then address the committee. But here I was asking to address the full board, telling them that I could put my pants on one leg at a time just as they did. They didn't appreciate that. Then I read a prepared statement about Pamo suggesting they consider alternatives as part of their review. There wasn't much response to that either. It was a sobering experience."

It was not long before Durbin became CWA's most thorough and tenacious critic, her position strengthened by the expanded coverage then appearing in the *San Diego Union*. Though most CWA board members vigorously opposed Durbin and considered her a "troublemaker" (and she became a particular *bête noire* of then-general manager Larry Michaels),[43] her arguments on Pamo eventually became integrated into the review process by EPA and other agencies. EPA's intervention ultimately killed the project, an extraordinary personal triumph for Durbin. But the intensity of that particular issue was never translated into a more powerful organizational response to SDCWA on the part of the Sierra Club. Durbin's passion for saving a valley, with all its attendant personal costs in time and emotional energy, did not establish a more permanent mechanism for accountability, despite its consequence in helping steer the San Diego agency toward some new directions.[44]

The problem of intimidation and resistance to change experienced at first by Emily Durbin in San Diego was magnified at the even more distant and austere Metropolitan Water District. Those who wished to monitor MWD faced a herculean task in contending with a huge fifty-one-member board with no effective oversight at the city or county level, and a format for conducting business that provided little space for public input, let alone impact. When consumer advocate Ellen Stern Harris was appointed to the MWD board from Beverly Hills, she decided to establish a support and advisory committee of utility activists and environmentalists in the Los Angeles area.[45] Most of those who participated, including a Westside housewife named Dorothy Green and a Pasadena activist named Tim Brick, had little knowledge about or experience with the MWD. Though at first frustrated by the difficulty of challenging any MWD policy, several of the participants, especially Green and Brick, became the core of the organization in Southern California opposing the Peripheral Canal. Their success in mobilizing opinion on the issue and in focusing attention on MWD itself, however, did not translate into an effective post-election organization. Harris had since departed from MWD, and while Brick himself was appointed to the MWD board (joining a handful of other "outsiders" in that position), Green and many of the others in the original group began to drift away from their monitoring function.

"I frankly became discouraged," Green recalled. "Here was this very powerful government agency, almost secretive and monolithic in the way they operated. There they were, with no checks and balances, without any real ability for us to develop effective public input. I also wondered whether we could even sustain the effort to monitor them, given the difficulty of translating their complex and inaccessible language and policy decisions in ways accessible to people. Even with our success with the canal issue, it had become an apparently insurmountable barrier."[46]

Dorothy Green's experience illustrates the dilemma faced by community groups contending with agency positions on technical issues divorced from their political and social setting. While such groups are capable of this challenge and succeed in elevating certain otherwise overlooked issues in the process, they find it difficult for such groups to sustain that input and translate it into a process of continuous review, given their limited resources. Still, though limited, such community challenges represent the most direct form of outsider participation in agency activity.

The question of public input and accountability, while growing in importance, remains unanswered by changes in agency activity and behavior. The impact of increasing monitoring by the press, public officials, and members of the community has been felt on particular issues and has helped translate to the local level an awareness that the old agendas have indeed been called into question. But while the method of governance and management has been subject to review, extensive change is still to be seen. The struggle over the language of "technical" information remains crucial, particularly in relation to the matter of access and accountability.

Can water issues be made comprehensible to the public, and, as a consequence, bring about innovation and change? Dorothy Green's dilemma suggests one answer. After drifting away from her monitoring role with MWD, Green still maintained an interest in water and environmental issues, becoming chair of the local Los Angeles League of Conservation Voters. In that capacity, she helped initiate a new organization called Heal the Bay, set up to deal with ocean contamination. The group had formed, in part, out of the efforts of a Culver City public school teacher, Howard Bennett, who had himself also persisted in monitoring agencies dealing with complicated—and inaccessible—sewage treatment and storm drain issues.

Bennett had become concerned that the city of Los Angeles would be granted yet another waiver on sewage treatment requirements for its Hyperion plant, which discharged into Santa Monica Bay. By 1985, when the waiver hearings were scheduled, the ocean near Hyperion had become a brew of DDT, volatile organics, high counts of coliform bacteria, and other contaminants, making it hazardous for fish and swimmers alike. Bennett, with support from Green and others, mobilized an enormous outpouring of support and enthusiasm. "The beach and the ocean are something special to people, the environmental degradation very real in terms of their lives," Green commented about the rapid growth and influence of Heal the Bay.[47] Heal the Bay became a *local* environmental success story, not only marshalling thousands of people, but eventually helping transform policy, presenting perhaps the broadest set of conservation-oriented growth-management policies ever suggested in Los Angeles. Included was a major new water conservation plan, dramatic in its scope (compared to earlier efforts) and also essential if the capacity problems at the treatment plant were to be eased and thus the level of ocean contamination reduced. Green herself was appointed to the City of Los Angeles' five-member Board of Water and Power Commission overseeing the city's Department of Water and Power, while another Heal-the-Bay activist, Felicia Marcus, was appointed to the city's Public Works Board.

To support the pressing need for water conservation Heal the Bay made the connection between growth and water backward from the other end of the pipeline, showing that limitless water-use not only destroyed the areas from which water was taken, it also damaged the areas where this water (now carrying industrial and human wastes) was later discharged. For Dorothy Green, the issue—and the means—had come full circle. For the water agencies themselves, however, the role of these "outsiders" and thus the question of public input remained problematic.

Part III

Innovation: A Problem of Management, Not Technology

In the last decade, water agencies have been forced to reconsider their traditional strategies and agendas in response to public discovery of complex new problems and of the inadequacy of old solutions. The rise of public criticism of the old agenda of tax-subsidized, large-scale, new water development broke the consensus the agencies had established with federal agencies and congressional supporters, making new water development more difficult. At the same time, the discovery of widespread water contamination, largely by industrial chemicals, challenged the agencies to respond to public concern about the health issues of water quality.

These new problems have challenged the agencies in many ways, bringing to light the inflexibility of their traditional strategies of agenda setting and management.

147

They have also forced a reconsideration of the solution water agencies had found to potential conflicts of interest among them—to avoid the question of how to allocate water among their own users and among the various agencies, under conditions of potential future scarcity, by making sure that such scarcity would never occur through committing public investment to more and more water development. Finally, they have forced agencies to look at alternative strategies of demand management, though progress in this area has been limited.

These are managerial, not technological, innovations. Even in the area of water quality, where agency choices among alternative technologies appear to be based on the technologies available, the selections agencies have made have been determined more by their traditional agenda (to meet the needs of their growth constituency) than by an emphasis on constructive, proactive planning for public health.

To achieve these objectives, the issues of water quality, reallocation of water among agencies, and more efficient management have become paramount. The agencies today face two different (but related) water-quality questions: the problem of disinfection by-products, which appears as a result of disinfection of water with relatively high concentrations of dissolved organic substances; and the problem of groundwater contamination, which has overwhelmed groundwater agencies who have found themselves without the resources (financial or managerial) to take an active, effective role. The agencies have also begun to address the question of water transfers—negotiations among agencies (particularly, between the urban and the agricultural agencies) to reallocate water initially committed to agriculture where it is not now needed (at the current price). Finally, agencies have been challenged to manage the water to which they have entitlement more efficiently, by attempting to integrate surface and groundwater management and by encouraging local agencies to use both groundwater resources and pricing strategies to diminish the summer peak demand they place on imported water supplies, thereby reducing the maximum capacity otherwise required of the importing systems.

As these areas of innovation have come to the fore, they have accelerated the pressure for a transition in agency governance. But the key to change remains effective public redefinition of the agencies' mission, which has continued to be dominated by the policies of growth and expansion.

8

Water Quality: New Issues, Old Priorities

Until recently water agencies found little about water quality truly troublesome, except under unusual conditions of biological or industrial contamination. Once chlorination was discovered to be effective in controlling pathogenic bacteria in drinking water at low cost, only extreme industrial contamination or high levels of dissolved salts (hard water) seemed to present water-quality problems. Agencies avoided industrial contaminants where they could by collecting their water upstream of manufacturing centers and could often blend hard water to dilute its concentration of salts.

Now, for most water agencies (in Southern California as throughout the country), water quality has become an urgent problem. *New scientific evidence suggests that the technological revolution in manufacturing and agriculture has led to widespread (not just local) contamination of water supplies and that many new substances once thought innocuous may be hazardous to human health even at low doses. Even established water-treatment technologies (such as chlorination) are now known to be potentially hazardous.* Increased public concern (and dissatisfaction with agencies' responses) has led to expanded monitoring and review, rapidly evolving legislation and regulations, and new costs of treatment, all of which have contributed to the issue's changing status within the agencies. To date, agency response has been reactive—driven by federal and state regulation and primarily concerned with minimizing agency costs for treatment of contaminated water.

But as these issues develop they are likely to force the agencies to confront deeper questions of their priorities and goals, and to take up the question of responsibility for, and prevention of, further water contamination.

The changing definition of what is safe drinking water has been reflected in two parallel events: the discovery that water agency disinfection practices themselves may create a contamination problem; and the finding that, even where disinfection by-products are not a significant problem, both urban and rural water agencies need to address extensive chemical contamination of their water sources. Water agencies have responded first by denying that there is a water-quality problem, despite their increasing loss of public legitimacy as a consequence of this strategy. Water-quality issues bring to light the institutional inertia of traditional political and engineering solutions, which structure and constrain the agencies' willingness to fully consider innovative but unfamiliar alternatives. Agencies' choices about how to address water-quality issues are still strongly influenced by established patterns of accommodation to the claims of their traditional constituencies: developers, large farmers, and major manufacturing industries. Public concern about water quality, however, will not allow these agencies to avoid the realignment that current water questions require. How well these agencies will adapt may ultimately depend on how seriously they can bring themselves to take the new questions of water quality.

What Is Safe Drinking Water?

For much of this century, water quality took a back seat for Southern California agency managers absorbed by their perceived primary mission of growth and expansion. Chlorination and filtration, in controlling bacterial contaminants, appeared to have eliminated any significant public health problems associated with water quality. Agencies prided themselves that the high-quality water they provided had become a model to emulate around the world.

This sense of accomplishment resulted, in part, from the distinction the agencies accepted, after the introduction of chlorine disinfection, between "safe drinking water" and the actual quality of water in rivers and streams. Water-agency managers, with public health officials and legislators, separated treatment and health standards (such as *Escheria coli*[1] levels) for drinking water from any intervention regarding waste discharges into surface water or groundwater. This distinction depended on the conviction that disinfection treatment had essentially eliminated concerns over water contamination, whatever the level of discharge. Thus it seemed unnecessary to regulate municipal (or industrial) discharges and reasonable to allow rivers, lakes, and bays to be used as sewers to disperse municipal and industrial wastes. Officials argued that if the water was safe when put to human use, it did not matter how pristine the rivers were.[2]

Through the 1960s and early 1970s, agencies in Southern California continued to believe that the water they delivered was of high quality. To be sure, there were still a few water-quality problems, especially the alkalinity and total dissolved solids (TDS)[3] of the Colorado River supply and the issue of taste and odor.[4] The high concentration of salts in Colorado River water stimulated utilities with their own wells to use their local water as much as possible. Some MWD member agencies looked to completion of the State Water Project for its "softer" and thus higher quality water from the north.[5] But for domestic users these were aesthetic issues; like the agencies, the public believed that it was getting safe drinking water.

Thus, water-quality issues did not compete for the attention and resources that agency directors and management continued to focus on supply and system expansion. The annual reports of the various Southern California agencies made small mention of water quality from year to year, in contrast to their lengthy coverage of expansion plans. The groundwater agencies were especially unconcerned about water quality, convinced that their well water was of far higher quality than the supplemental imported water MWD provided from the Colorado River.

Even when concerns about chemical contamination arose at the national level during the early 1970s, these seemed distant to the Southern California agencies. Local water managers perceived these problems as restricted to the industrialized corridors of the East and Midwest. Chemical contamination was thought to be a *surface water* issue, and the four major surface water sources for Southern California—the Colorado, the Sacramento River, the Owens Valley–Mono Lake system of Los Angeles, and the Kern River—all brought water from mountainous areas distant from the industrial discharges then associated with these problems.

As a consequence, the Southern California agencies were observers when eastern and midwestern water agencies lobbied to limit legislation to regulate industrial contaminants. The water industry elsewhere made a battleground of passage of the Safe Drinking Water Act in 1974 and of subsequent rule making by EPA; eastern and midwestern agencies (through national water-industry associations such as the Coalition for Safe Drinking Water) fought to limit both the contamination standards to be established and the regulations governing treatment.[6] Though the Southern California agencies, as members of these associations, supported these efforts, they did so passively, directing their primary political energies to lobbying for construction of the Peripheral Canal.[7]

By late 1979, however, two events, one month apart, signaled that water quality would be of regional as well as national interest. In November of 1979 EPA, pursuant to the Safe Drinking Water Act, finally published the first of two maximum contaminant level standards (MCLs) to deal with the wide variety of organic chemicals present in water supplies. This first MCL set a limit of one hundred parts per billion for trihalomethanes (THMs)—then recently discovered to be a by-product of chlorination. The standard itself was less stringent than water agencies had feared, due primarily to water industry lobbying. But MWD found that it might have difficulty meeting the standard, nonetheless. Then, in December, Aerojet-General announced discovery of TCE contamination at a well site in the San Gabriel Valley. This announcement led both the public and the agencies to realize that groundwater contamination in several areas throughout Southern California might indeed be quite serious, and that industrial contamination of water sources was not restricted to surface water. In fact, it appeared that where groundwater had been contaminated, the contaminants were often present in higher concentrations than in surface water. This raised the specter of additional water-quality standards and of potential limitations on the use of the well water that made up a substantial share of the water resources of the region.

These two events—establishment of a THM standard and recognition of the potential extent of groundwater contamination—had direct consequences for Southern California agencies. It was now not enough that drinking water be disinfected and palatable; it had to be free of chemical contamination. At the least, new (and possibly expensive) treatment would be required to meet these standards. These new scientific discoveries changed the definition of safe drinking water in a way that took water agencies by surprise and threatened to undermine their established funding and policy priorities.

The Disinfection By-product Debate

When research detailing the hazards of trace amounts of industrial chemical contamination of water supplies first emerged during the early 1970s,[8] much of the water industry expressed skepticism about its methods and conclusions.[9] This skepticism increased when parallel research began to focus on a whole separate class of contaminants resulting directly from chlorination. The interaction of chlorine with natural and manmade organic material present in the water supply produced, according to these studies, by-products that were potentially carcinogenic. This water-quality problem was a result of the unexpected chemical combination of the organic contaminants present in certain water sources with the disinfection substance, chlorine gas. Moreover, the class of by-products that was formed in this unintended synthesis—THMs—included chloroform, a known carcinogen.[10]

Given nearly universal chlorination of municipal water, THMs were to prove far more common than some of the industrial trace organics (such as trichloroethylene (TCE), a widely used solvent) then also being discovered to be widespread contaminants in municipal water supplies. But the likelihood of a THM standard, let alone one governing all disinfection by-products, seemed at first improbable to the water agencies, which thought that the fact that every utility—and by extension all local governments—would face substantial costs made stringent regulation unlikely.[11] This argument about costs was effective in EPA's decision, when publishing the first MCL for THMs, to weigh these anticipated costs against public health and to set the initial standard at one hundred parts per billion (ppb).[12] If EPA had used the more conservative basis of setting a standard at the concentration where this toxic chemical was estimated to increase the probability of cancer by one case per million people exposed (otherwise the normal threshold of regulation for carcinogens), THM levels might have been set at 2.5 ppb or even lower.[13] Thus, the November 1979 announcement of a standard based on this relaxed threshold was welcomed by most utilities, which had THM levels ranging anywhere from 10 to 75 ppb of more.[14] These levels were especially elevated in Southern California, however, including in the water provided by MWD and several of its member agencies.

By 1980, MWD chemists began to discover that system-wide MWD THM levels, monitored quarterly, were approaching 100 ppb and during some periods actually exceeded the standard.[15] Moreover (depending on where the chlorine was introduced and the subsequent distance to the water's destination), the treated water delivered to certain member agencies, including Santa Monica and Orange County, exceeded the 100 ppb standard. THM levels were particularly elevated for those member agencies that relied, primarily or exclusively, on State Project water. This water, which flowed from the Sacramento River through the Sacramento–San Joaquin Delta before it was withdrawn for delivery to Central and Southern California, picked up greater amounts of organic matter, or "precursors" (both natural and manmade), that combined with chlorine during disinfection to produce these high concentrations of THMs.[16]

Suddenly, MWD had to confront its THM problem, since the MCL was to take legal effect in November 1981. In response, the agency began its first substantive review of techniques to reduce THMs below 100 ppb: it hired consultants and new staff who generated reports, and in the end MWD decided to select the estimated-least-cost alternative among the various treatments reviewed. This least-cost alternative involved substituting for chlorine a new disinfectant complex, chloramines, made by combining chlorine and ammonia. Chloramines combined with the organic precursors less reactively than did pure chlorine and thus produced lower THM concentrations when Delta water was treated.

Chloramine treatment appeared in MWD estimates to be the least-cost alternative to existing practices of chlorine disinfection in part because it was so much *like* chlorination, in both direct engineering and system management. Like chlorination, chloramine treatment is a *disinfection* strategy based on adding something to water in the system, not on taking contaminants out. Chloramine treatment is done by injecting the disinfectant into water in pipelines at sufficiently high concentrations to kill bacteria within the water in the time before the water is used, just as is chlorination. If MWD selected chloramines, the basic system engineering could stay the same; only the disinfectant substance would be changed. Furthermore, the substitution of chloramines for chlorination implied no rethinking of the origins of this new water-quality problem. MWD could continue to use one disinfection process for all the treated water it delivered, regardless of its source.[17] In choosing a water treatment technique that merely substituted one chemical disinfectant for another, operating engineers would not need to consider the source of the water (or the particular contaminants it might carry) before disinfection, as well as the nature of the disinfectant itself. Disinfection, with chlorine or chloramines, is a prophylactic strategy; when water is tested, it is to ensure that disinfection is adequate, not to discover whether actual bacterial contamination of a particular supply makes it necessary nor what by-products might result.

In selecting this particular alternative technique MWD management justified their choice primarily on the estimated initial cost of implementing a new disinfection process. According to their analysis, the most feasible alternative to chloramines—granular activated carbon filtration (GAC)—was too expensive. While a shift to chloramines as the disinfectant seemed likely to reduce THM levels below the first federal standard of 100 ppb, chloramines did have potential disadvantages, including possible taste and odor problems and, most significantly, still unknown health effects. MWD staff alerted board members and management that their use in the MWD system would leave unresolved certain risks and uncertainties.[18] Initial staff estimates suggested that the cost differences between the two technologies might be as much as several hundred million dollars, with the substitution of chloramine for chlorine disinfection considered the "low cost alternative," according to the general manager.[19]

GAC technology would reduce the synthesis of THMs in MWD deliveries by a completely different mechanism, since this technology depends on taking contaminants out of water, not on putting particular disinfectants in. Granular activated carbon filtration is based on a principle familiar to anyone who had a fish tank as a child. Water is passed through a filter filled with small particles of activated charcoal; the contaminants (organic contaminants and some mineral salts) adsorb to (are electrochemically attracted and attached to) the surfaces of the charcoal, and the water which flows from the filter thus has substantially lower contaminant levels. GAC systems require prior physical filtration to remove particles and suspended sediments (the glass-wool chamber in the aquarium filter) and do not in themselves control bacterial growth.[20] But water passed through GAC filtration has much lower concentrations of organic contaminants, and thus it can be subsequently disinfected without the formation of significant concentrations of THMs.

GAC thus has substantial general purification benefits in addition to its effectiveness in reducing the concentrations of THMs in delivered water but these were not considered in MWD's decision. MWD's primary concern with GAC was its high capital and energy costs. Even though GAC was known to be more effective than chloramines in reducing THM concentrations, since it acted by removing the organic precursors of THMs—GAC might reduce THM concentrations by 90 percent or more, while chloramines would reduce THMs, at best, to about half the existing levels—MWD chose to meet then-current standards at the lowest possible cost and with the most limited engineering change, not to seek the more expensive though most thorough or extensive reduction of organic contaminants (and by extension the broadest public health benefits).

While the shift to chloramines as the disinfectant was able to reduce THM levels below the first federal standard of 100 ppb, when it was implemented in 1984 MWD immediately encountered two unanticipated problems: chloramines were not safe for patients on dialysis machines and for fish-tank owners. Chloramine treatment was stopped for nearly a year, while MWD staff sought ways to control those effects, and then reintroduced.[21] At this point the district believed that it had finally resolved the THM problem, nearly four years after the EPA deadline.

Though this commitment to a new treatment technology might have significant long-term implications, much of the THM discussion occurred without public input. At one critical juncture, an environmental representative of the Los Angeles district attorney's office along with the chair of the Health and Environment Committee of the American Pediatrics Association argued at an MWD Committee meeting that the health effects of chloramines were still under review and that GAC filtration was a more proven and effective, albeit more costly, alternative.[22] But the MWD board and management dismissed these arguments and proceeded as planned, believing that if chloramines were adequate to meet existing federal standards the issue of disinfection by-products could be put aside.[23]

It wasn't long, however, until the issue reappeared, threatening to unravel MWD's least-cost response. While MWD treatment systems were being modified to substitute chloramines for chlorine disinfection, Congress was deliberating amendments to the Safe Drinking Water Act. Though these amendments did not address disinfection by-products as explicitly as other organic contaminants (such as TCE), the clear intent of Congress (and EPA's interpretation of the amendments) left little doubt that the 100 ppb standard would be subject to review, and that Congress also wanted GAC to be considered as a benchmark technology for the treatment of water contaminated with all synthetic organic chemicals.[24] Furthermore, new research pointed to a range of other disinfection by-products, including certain chlorinated acids, which EPA was also to review for possible health effects and which might also face restrictive standards. Some of these by-products, EPA staff members noted, could well have greater health impacts than did THMs.[25]

Before these revised EPA THM standards were released, MWD staff began to propose an ambitious research program to analyze new alternative water-quality treatment methods. The staff warned the MWD board members that these treatment technologies might be required if EPA, as anticipated, established more stringent standards for THMs and other possibly carcinogenic by-products of disinfection. Less than two years after chloramines had been introduced, MWD management was now estimating that another reworking of the system would be required, this time costing at least hundreds of millions of dollars.[26]

Most of MWD's directors and management were unfamiliar with the terms and concepts now necessary to consider water-quality issues. They knew that disinfection techniques had to be changed: they had, after all, hired experts—both new staff members and consultants—to deal with a problem that would soon have legal force. But the huge costs involved—the research effort alone (both by EPA and water-utility groups) was to cost several million dollars—seemed an unnecessary diversion from the agency's real matter at hand, providing water for continued regional growth.[27]

With a significant share of its budget at stake, MWD, which had taken a back seat in the earlier standard-setting, now decided to intervene forcefully in the hope of forestalling even-more-stringent regulations. While amendments to the Safe Drinking Water Act were being debated in Congress, the Southern California agencies, particularly MWD and LADWP, with support from the city of San Diego and the San Diego County Water Authority, initiated an intensive lobbying campaign. This Southern California water industry coalition, no longer passive about water-quality regulation, instead became the harshest critic of the proposed amendments. "The Southern California agencies came in here like gangbusters," recalled Jerry Dotson, an aide to Los Angeles Congressman Henry Waxman and the top staff member to the House Subcommittee on Health and the Environment, which was reviewing the legislation. "They pulled out all the stops, arguing as if this legislation might well bring about a terminal crisis for the agencies. They complained that they would be forced to move to far more expensive treatment if forced to meet new standards that would be totally unjustifiable. But that's what the public was insisting they wanted [more restrictive standards] and that's why Congress was responding."[28]

Water-industry lobbying in Washington was duplicated by efforts to block parallel legislation at the state level.[29] Here again MWD and LADWP took the lead, arguing in Sacramento that more restrictive standards would force agencies to shift to GAC and that this would "bankrupt the treasury".[30] Though the Southern California agencies were initially successful in Sacramento, they were increasingly isolated in the congressional debate. The Safe Drinking Water Act amendments passed both houses of Congress by overwhelming majorities, without one member of the Southern California delegation supporting MWD and its allies. Shortly thereafter, EPA formally launched its review of disinfection by-products, privately telling the utilities to expect a new standard anywhere from five or ten to fifty parts per billion.[31]

With the Safe Drinking Water Act Amendments in place, MWD knew it could not meet any more-stringent standard without again changing its treatment method, reducing the concentrations of organic THM precursors in its State Water Project supplies and/or restructuring its methods of disinfection. The district found itself forced to respond to a regulation it had tried to forestall. In response, MWD launched a second major new study of treatment alternatives. This study had two goals: to see whether GAC could be shown to be infeasible, and to examine an entirely new technology called peroxone, an ozone-based system that used hydrogen peroxide to treat organic precursors followed by some disinfectant, probably chloramines.[32] Though peroxone treatment would be costly—new MWD estimates ranged from $200 to $300 million, depending on whether chloramines were used as the disinfectant—it was also presented as far less costly than GAC, now estimated to cost at least $1.5 billion for systemwide application.[33] Like chlorination and chloramine disinfection treatment, peroxone depended on putting something into water, not taking something out: hydrogen peroxide reacts with certain organic contaminants chemically, causing them to be less reactive with subsequent disinfectants, but it does not remove contaminants from water.

The central issue for MWD was still the specific cost of meeting the new THM standards, not a more general goal of reducing overall water contamination; this criterion led both management and the board to support the new peroxone technology. But the peroxone system, unlike GAC, had never been applied to drinking water treatment at a commercial scale. Though MWD staff made plans to test the system at the bench and pilot scales, what full-scale operational issues might emerge remained unknown.

As the study continued, it brought to light a series of disturbing new questions about peroxone, which were treated as peripheral to MWD's discussions about how to proceed.[34] There were indications that peroxone treatment had potential unknown health effects that might be even more significant than the engineers' uncertainties about the costs of full-scale operation. MWD researchers (staff and consultants) discovered that ozonation generated its own class of by-products, a complex of aldehydes including formaldehyde. "It's almost as if we were back in 1974 when they first discovered

THMS," one MWD staff member noted, "and the consequences of that discovery had to be sorted out."[35] As information about aldehyde by-products became available, EPA decided to study the public-health impacts of these, particularly formaldehyde, although it estimated that such information might not be available until well after utilities had made choices among treatment technologies.[36]

MWD management remained wary of the health impacts issue, dismissing its significance but concerned that any negative information might undercut what appeared to be a promising new technology. But the concern over health effects of peroxone from ozonation by-products was compounded by the continuing health-related uncertainties about chloramines. When MWD management first proposed chloramine treatment in the early 1980s, it had been aware that EPA health studies of chloramines were still incomplete.[37] In pursuing the peroxone research, MWD became further committed to chloramines as a residual disinfectant, since neither peroxone nor ozone removed enough reactive organic precursors to reduce THM levels to the new standard if free chlorine were again used as the system disinfectant. Thus chloramine disinfection continued to be essential to the strategy MWD was pursuing.[38]

As EPA worked out new standards (due to be released in 1991 or 1992)[39] and research on the health effects of both peroxone and disinfection by-products continued, MWD moved toward full-scale use of peroxone without public debate (or even thorough discussion by the MWD board). In its public relations campaign in support of the new technology, MWD did not choose to inform the public about the complexities and uncertainties of the by-products issue. Emphasizing peroxone's lower cost and assumed ability to meet anticipated federal THM standards, the district also justified its rejection of GAC as motivated by its environmental concerns regarding disposal of the spent carbon,[40] an issue that it had not seriously investigated in the multi-million-dollar research review of GAC and peroxone.

This posture of environmental concern also appeared in a study (sponsored by MWD, the San Diego CWA, the Los Angeles DWP, and three urban Northern California agencies) of the accumulation of organic precursors in the water that flowed through the Sacramento–San Joaquin Delta.[41] If concentrations of these precursors could be reduced, the study suggested, THM levels could also be reduced significantly, perhaps by 30 to 50 percent. And the study recommended that the best way to bring about this reduction was to construct a bypass facility to take Sacramento River water around the delta: that is, to build a Peripheral Canal.[42]

By 1990, MWD's search for the least-cost alternative had itself become costly but had yielded no clear solution. MWD management justified its preference for peroxone on its estimate of immediate costs and on its conviction that it should plan only to comply with existing federal standards for disinfection by-products, not to address water-quality issues more deeply. In disregarding broader health effects issues, MWD continues to risk future costs and new more-stringent regulations that would require yet another search for the new least-cost alternative. The study of organic precursors, which might have suggested the value of other treatments, strategies that emphasized reducing ongoing contamination of water or removing contaminants before blending and treatment, seems instead to have been politically motivated and supply-oriented.[43] It did not stimulate a more integrated plan of response to disinfection by-products and other water contaminants. The even more difficult issue of whether or how to reduce reliance on chlorination seems even more removed from the process of policy review. Instead, MWD's approach to innovation is still framed by its response to regulation— and resistance to change.

MWD's pattern of response to water-quality issues to date is best characterized as a kind of "disjointed incrementalism."[44] Taken by surprise by the challenge to address significant water-quality problems, MWD's management responded in ways conditioned by the institutional inertia of earlier solutions: it sought to use its political power, built and consolidated in the years of successful claims on federal and state governments for new water supplies, to contain the "damages" of these new health questions; it selected those new technologies that most closely resembled conventional disinfection strategies, in engineering and system management terms; and it subordinated its responsibility to consider innovative strategies for reducing disinfection by-products to its continuing effort to bring about construction of a delta bypass facility.

In addressing the problem of disinfection by-products in this way, MWD has overlooked an opportunity to exercise its regional leadership in the necessary public discussion of a larger set of questions, questions related to the very structure of water-quality treatment and intervention. Disinfection, which seemed for years to allow agencies to focus on the amount rather than the quality of the water they collected, is now an inadequate response to broader water-quality problems and different kinds of contamination. This broader issue is likely to become more difficult, more complex, and more costly in the future, as the general problem of chemical contamination of water is better understood.

"Blame it on the Gas Chromatograph"

While MWD grappled with disinfection by-products, other Southern California agencies found other contamination problems more compelling.[45] In fact, many of these agencies, including the Upper San Gabriel Valley District and the City of Burbank, increased their use of MWD water when their own wells were found to be contaminated with other regulated chemicals. This groundwater contamination was often due to loss or disposal of industrial solvents or other petrochemical products. The problem resembled that of disinfection by-products in that both issues appeared with new scientific knowledge of the potential hazards posed by chlorinated organic compounds and both involved still largely unexplored public-health questions. Yet these parallel problems were often presented as a point of contrast between the effects of contaminant regulation on MWD and on the smaller agencies, especially by those agencies whose wells had been shut down and whose local supplies were jeopardized. These agencies contrasted TCE standards, for example, with the THM standards that had been set at a less rigorous health-effects level. The different agencies began to play "who's got the bigger risk," and to argue in public statements that those risks for which they themselves were responsible were, relatively, insignificant.[46]

This intra-agency rivalry over risk reflected the confusion within the urban Southern California water industry that followed the emergence of the question of chemical contamination during the early 1980s. Just a decade earlier, chemical contamination of surface and especially of groundwater supplies had seemed only rarely important. The extent and severity of the problem were not well known, since agencies then monitored water contamination less frequently, had less sophisticated instrumentation, and looked for fewer potential contaminants.[47] Extensive nitrate contamination of groundwater in the San Gabriel Valley, for example, had been recognized as early as the 1960s, when this contamination was first found in samples of well water from the northern and eastern margins of the valley. But key San Gabriel water leaders dismissed the relationship between nitrate concentrations and chemical-fertilizer use and minimized the health effects associated with nitrate contamination of drinking water.[48] The San Gabriel agencies then made no significant effort to analyze any prospective water-quality issues, other than the nitrate problem, or to incorporate such water-quality considerations as part of their overall responsibility.[49] In minimizing the problem of nitrate contamination, they anticipated the response most agencies would later make to other problems of chemical contamination.

In December 1979, however, when Aerojet-General announced its discovery of polluted wells, several new factors had intensified both public and agency response to the question of water contamination. On the one hand, public concern over hazardous waste sites and toxic chemicals had grown rapidly, in the wake of Love Canal and other similar discoveries of serious industrial contamination of residential neighborhoods. Though the enactment of Superfund[50] was still a year away, the links between chemical discharge and soil and groundwater contamination had been firmly established. Public pressure on the regulators and Congress had begun to mount. The names of chemical contaminants, such as the solvents trichloroethylene (TCE) and perchloroethylene (PCE), were finding their way into the public vocabulary, and this growing public concern would soon transform the way both monitoring and standard setting took place.

On the other hand, while most agencies were ill prepared to review and analyze chemical contamination of their own water in December 1979, the technology to monitor and analyze chemical constituents of water had significantly improved as new instruments with greater detection capabilities, such as the gas chromatograph, were developed. These were not yet widely used by smaller agencies but they were available in the large private testing laboratories; in the major regulatory agencies, such as the California Department of Health Services; and in laboratories of the largest water agencies such as MWD. While the machines themselves could not determine whether what was there was hazardous, or identify particular substances without specific analysis for the presence of each individually, they could be used to find very low concentrations of specific contaminants. These machines could detect traces of many chlorinated organics in parts per billion, as compared to the parts per million or even parts per thousand capabilities of earlier less-sophisticated monitoring instruments. The explosive revelation that groundwater contamination was widespread in Southern California was supported when these new instruments found contaminants where none had previously been detected. At the same time federal and state agencies began to mandate testing for a rapidly growing number of chemicals of concern. A groundwater-quality crisis was in the making.

Emergence of this sudden and unexpected issue sent water agencies searching for ways to minimize the problem's importance. "Blame it on the gas chromatograph" became a common refrain at agency meetings and water industry discussions. Even in 1989, Myron Holburt (MWD's assistant general manager for planning and resources) told a UCLA graduate seminar that "if it had not been for the organic chemists who had come up with these [more sophisticated] instruments, there would not have been the problems we have today."[51] For agency managers and board members, the low levels of contamination now detectable and the still-incomplete scientific investigation of the potential health effects of this contamination seemed insufficient to support the standards being set by federal and state regulatory agencies. Other agencies were setting these standards, but local water agencies were required to commit the resources necessary to comply.

Agency boards and management often had difficulty with the regulatory concept of a health effects *threshold*.[52] The health effects of bacterial contamination are immediate, acute, and often widespread; small samples of bacteria grow satisfyingly large colonies rapidly in water-quality laboratories, and besides, everyone learns in school that germs cause disease. In contrast, the health effects of chemical contamination, where health risks are stated as probability estimates based on mathematical projections of chronic long-term exposure and on more complex epidemiological or experimental connections between contamination and disease, seemed to water-industry officials to be scientifically inadequate to justify the level of response agencies were now to be required to make. If the trace levels detected were equivalent to "a drop of vermouth in a sea of gin," as one MWD official asserted at a board meeting,[53] *and if health risks at these concentrations might be insignificant* and could therefore be denied, then the new measuring instruments, which had made it possible to identify contamination at such low concentrations, could be said to be a part of the problem (for the water agencies at least) and perhaps its cause.

This position was bolstered by public, political, and scientific debate over the importance of chemical hazards. There were three components to this debate: public perception that prior and continuing industrial contamination put people's health at risk; the political posture of the Reagan administration, whose industry-supported agenda of "regulatory reform" to roll back the health and safety and environmental legislation enacted under earlier administrations was justified by the assertion that this regulation was scientifically unsupported and constrained economic growth; and the scientific debate about how to deal with the extent, source, and policy implications of scientific uncertainty in assessing health risks.[54]

Water-industry officials who sought to minimize the health risks of chemical contaminants turned particularly to the arguments of one faction in this scientific debate. The most vocal proponent of this position—that the hazards of industrial chemicals were not adequately proven[55] and that they were possibly insignificant in comparison with other "voluntary" risks—was Bruce Ames, chair of the Department of Biochemistry at the University of California at Berkeley. Ames and his colleagues made use of the comparative-risk argument in the suggestion that synthetic carcinogens may be insignificant, based on their research on carcinogens in certain foods such as spinach and peanut butter.[56] The water agencies immediately embraced Ames's argument as substantiating their belief that the magnitude of the problem did not justify the estimated costs of their mandated response. MWD published 250,000 copies of a commentary (and editorial) written by Ames, which dismissed the seriousness of groundwater contamination.[57] Ames was often invited to lecture before water-industry audiences and his specific comparisons, such as the suggestion that peanut butter posed a greater public danger than did TCE, were widely used in agency statements, which failed to mention that this controversy was unresolved within the scientific community.[58]

MWD's position on this issue—that it was more a matter of external regulation and public hysteria than a serious new question which should stimulate water agencies to rethink their priorities—made it more difficult for the smaller, subordinated agencies to respond effectively or directly to the water-quality problems they suddenly faced. Though MWD was formally responsible only for the quality of the imported water it delivered, the district had so clearly taken the lead in setting Southern California water policy that its resistance to serious consideration of this question left its member agencies without encouragement or technical and political support.[59] MWD's antagonism to GAC filtration of its own, imported Sacramento Delta water discouraged local agencies from considering this technique, and its assertion that all treatment practices under consideration should be universal (rather than specific to the particular contamination of the source) set a model that made it less likely that local agencies would choose flexible, situation-specific treatment strategies responsive to their own complex and particular problems of contamination. While both Upper San Gabriel and Burbank grappled with groundwater contamination sufficient to have led their local sources to be designated as Superfund sites, MWD remained disengaged from these difficult local problems, using the increasing discovery of widespread groundwater contamination only as a further justification for increased dependence on imported water.

Local water-agency resistance to stringent standards for chemical contaminants in drinking water has been based on several factors: board and staff discomfort with the complexity of the scientific and technical information that supports such regulation; the counter-claims of industries concerned about more stringent regulation of their own activities; and the fact that these agencies have been challenged to respond to this new agenda without a climate of technical and financial support to help them address this new burden. Federal and state regulation of toxic chemicals and of chemical contaminants of water is poorly integrated; and the local agencies face demands, in these new regulations, that they take on a responsibility that they are neither financially nor technically prepared to address. But these smaller agencies are also unaccustomed to public controversy; faced with challenges to their own expertise and their set agendas, they tend to be captured by the most organized constituency, which is often their industrial customers. The irrigation agencies addressed in this study provide an illustration of this point.

Agriculture: Natural
and Unnatural Contamination

As water-quality issues began to force their way into the agendas of the water agencies, much of the attention of policymakers and the press focused on the problems of urban contamination. A less well-known yet equally pressing set of problems, however, was emerging in rural areas, where agriculture-dominated agencies also confronted new and disturbing issues. During the 1980s, as the monitoring and reporting of contamination increased, widespread problems began to be identified in agricultural areas such as Fresno and Kern counties. In the Fresno area alone during the late 1980s, thirty-three wells were closed because of excessive levels of DBCP, a potent pesticide whose use had been outlawed more than ten years earlier. DBCP contamination was also found in the Chino Basin in Southern California.[60]

As for the urban agencies, water-quality issues have been an intrusive and potentially disruptive issue for agencies like Kern and IID. Water quality in these agricultural areas had historically been defined as a *drainage* issue, since both areas had potentially serious problems of disposal of return flows. In Imperial, discharge and drainage problems were intricately bound up with the fate of the Salton Sea. The drainage issue in Kern was potentially also serious and complex, since the area was part of the Upper San Joaquin Valley basin, a closed basin (and former marshland) with no effective natural drainage. In both cases, low natural rainfall on the desert or semi-desert soils had left relatively high concentrations of soluble salts in the soil column. Though local growers applied large volumes of water to their land to flush out these soluble salts, in the absence of effective drainage this flushing was not effective and irrigation could cause extensive salt accumulation in the root zone, reducing the productivity of the soil and the profitability of local agriculture.

Flushing new soil to bring it under profitable cultivation required large amounts of water, as much as five to six acre-feet per acre for the first several years of cultivation. Even irrigation intended only to support crop growth required more water here than in most California growing areas. So agricultural activity and expansion depended on a continuing (and, in Kern's case, potentially expanding) source of imported water, and quality and supply issues were linked from the beginning.

In Kern, resolving the drainage problem meant finding some way to take the waste water off the land, by constructing a master drain for the San Joaquin Valley or by selling the water for some other use. The San Joaquin Master Drain proposal, part of the original design for the State Water Project, ran aground with the crisis at Kesterson Wildlife Refuge. The discovery of widespread selenium poisoning of birds at Kesterson, which had been used as a temporary storage area for return flows from the Westlands Water District, not only forced suspension of delivery of irrigation return waters into Kesterson but ultimately ended any consideration of the Sacramento–San Joaquin Delta and San Francisco Bay as the final destination for valley drainage waters.

While addressing its problem of surface drainage, KCWA simultaneously began to collect information on regional groundwater flows and potential sources of groundwater contamination. From this, the agency's staff developed a series of maps detailing their Groundwater Flow Model that could also potentially provide a model for water-quality data in the county.[61] As the data base expanded, it became clear that groundwater in Kern was subject to a range of problems, including elevated concentrations of nitrates, arsenic, fluoride, and other contaminants in excess of drinking water standards. In December 1978 the area's Regional Water Quality Control Board, the lead agency responsible for review of water-quality problems in the region under the Clean Water Act, mandated a study of groundwater contamination under the aegis of the Kern County Health Department. The regional board had first approached KCWA to undertake the study, but it had declined, "anticipating the possibility of controversy," according to one agency staff member.[62] KCWA, nevertheless, provided staff and logistical support for the study, and the first draft of the results was completed in early 1980.

In March 1980 the draft Groundwater Quality Report was released for public comment. This document provided the most extensive analysis of county water-quality issues to that time and included an extensive data base tracing the location, direction of flow, and nature of groundwater contamination. The report also made a series of recommendations, of which the most controversial were pumping guidelines and restrictions and the establishment of an Agricultural Chemical Use Council to initiate guidelines for pesticides and related agricultural chemicals.[63]

The draft report caused strong reaction, particularly among KCWA member agencies and their agricultural landowner-clients.[64] The County Board of Supervisors and the County Health Department were surprised and ultimately intimidated by the intensity of the attack from landowners and the water industry.[65] On the request of these opponents, the supervisors first pulled the report from circulation and then established a new Groundwater Quality Committee to be charged with rewriting the report. This Groundwater Quality Committee, in turn, was given heavy agricultural representation, which quickly dominated its discussions and decisions. The committee placed KCWA itself in charge of the review process.

The KCWA rewrite became, as one of its critics described it, a "function of advocates rather than experts."[66] Information was modified or eliminated altogether, and the recommendations as a whole bore little resemblance to the original draft report. New recommendations included a proposal to make the existing Groundwater Quality Committee permanent, with further studies and a modified well ordinance to be developed by KCWA management, which doubled as the Groundwater Quality Committee's staff. The second draft, released in 1982, was immediately accepted by the supervisors as the final report, fulfilling the requirements of the Clean Water Act.[67]

During the mid- and late-1980s, the water-quality issue in Kern continued to trouble the agency. The discovery of contaminated wells in and around Bakersfield exacerbated the tension between agricultural interests fearful of restrictions on pumping or pesticide use, and urban (or urbanizing) areas discovering contamination problems. New community-based organizations, such as the Kern Valley Action Network, raised potential conflicts of interest in an agency monitoring an issue while it served clients partially or fully responsible for that problem.[68] By 1989, this tension led the agency to complain that it remained hampered in carrying out the agricultural well-monitoring ordinance and that ultimately it would like to reduce its exposure on an issue it had never wanted to confront.[69]

Formed to support the growth of a particular industry (agriculture), irrigation agencies find it impossible to escape their clients' claims that they minimize or deny any public hazards that result from industry activity. Even when the contaminants are naturally occurring, as with selenium, arsenic, and other mineral toxins in Kern, this antagonism appears. They may be natural substances, but they become health problems as a result of inappropriate use or inadequate management. And the public, in Kern and elsewhere, has become increasingly impatient with the inability of water agencies to find solutions to the problems of water contamination.

The Issue of Source Reduction

The water industry's rejection of the need for water-quality monitoring and of the health importance of chemical risks has failed to convince a public increasingly concerned and restive about water contamination and exposure to potentially toxic chemicals. In 1986, environmentalists, labor, and community groups concerned with chemical hazards qualified an initiative, Proposition 65 (The California Safe Drinking Water initiative), for the statewide ballot. This initiative sought to prohibit discharge of known carcinogens, mutagens, and teratogens[70] into drinking water, to require firms to disclose publicly any release of such chemicals into the ambient environment, and to subject public officials who did not disclose known chemical hazards to criminal sanctions.

The water agencies, including agricultural agencies such as Kern, opposed Proposition 65. Though some agencies (including MWD) eventually retreated to a neutral public stance, most water agencies, including the five others considered here, maintained their opposition to this proposition. Their arguments in opposition broadly paralleled those of the main industrial opponents of the initiative, the petrochemical industries and the agricultural users of chemical pesticides.[71] Opponents of the proposition argued that it was unnecessary, unwieldy, costly, would stop economic growth within the state, and had too many exemptions (based on the exemption of government actions from its reporting requirements).

Proposition 65 was endorsed by voters throughout the state by the largest margins ever given an initiative proposition. The Proposition 65 vote was one of several indicators that the water agencies needed to revise their position if public confidence in the water agencies was not to erode even further. Many water customers had switched to bottled or filtered drinking water—more than 48 percent of all households in Southern California, according to one *Los Angeles Times* poll.[72] Though this shift (in drinking water only) was insignificant in terms of overall water use in Southern California, it represented a major embarrassment to the agencies' assumed mission of serving safe drinking water.[73]

Agency managers are still treating the water-quality issue as a *public relations* issue, requiring a better effort at "risk communication"—that is, convincing the public that the agency position is scientifically justified. As public support for Proposition 65 demonstrates, this effort had become crucial if the agencies were to reverse the growing public presumption that they had become part of the problem—not of the solution—without taking public concerns seriously and opening their existing agendas to full public debate over the priority to be given to safe drinking water, the costs and benefits of the various alternatives, and how these costs should be met.

Shortly after the Proposition 65 election, MWD was offered a significant public relations opportunity by one of the architects of the initiative, the Environmental Defense Fund (EDF), which had become interested in estimating the economic value of groundwater lost to contamination. EDF thought this might support a new approach where public agencies could offset industry resistance to regulation by offering economic incentives to encourage firms to reduce their toxic discharges.[74] EDF also wanted to identify industrial processes or products that could be replaced by less hazardous alternatives. EDF had not had a lot of success raising money for its study, but recognized that its long-time nemesis on delta issues, the MWD, might be interested in the proposal, given its substantive (and image-related) water-quality problems.

For MWD, the proposal came at the right time and under the right circumstances. EDF wanted to hire Katy Wolfe, a chemist and Rand Corporation analyst who specialized in water quality. Wolfe had known MWD chief economist Tim Quinn when Quinn had been at Rand, and it was with Quinn that EDF initially explored the arrangement.[75] Quinn was part of a group of young staff members at MWD, including the director of planning, Wiley Horne, who were eager to promote incentive and market-related programs as part of the kind of new thinking they felt they represented within the water industry.[76] For MWD top management, however, an EDF alliance on this issue represented not so much an innovative breakthrough as a public-relations coup.[77]

EDF and MWD management eventually worked out a partnership arrangement they called the Source Reduction Research Partnership, with 50 percent of the expenses to be assumed by MWD. Wolfe, the project director, would be located at MWD headquarters in downtown Los Angeles. The study, as Wolfe framed it and MWD approved it, would entail a generic review of industry practices rather than exploring the specific sources of contamination in a particular groundwater basin. A study of this kind, Wolfe argued, would obtain industry support, since it would offer (in effect, *gratis*) information about alternatives for industry through research funded by public monies.[78] The alternate research strategy—focusing on specific practices leading to specific problems—while potentially offering invaluable information about particular Southern California Basin areas, was also seen as less universally applicable and as more controversial since it inevitably touched on the issues of responsibility and liability. To secure industry support, *a condition mandated by the* MWD *board*,[79] a project advisory committee would be formed with strong industry representation. This source reduction approach, according to both sets of partners, could only succeed as a cooperative—not an adversarial—relationship with industry, with incentives rather than regulations its likely outcome.

For MWD management, while these arrangements, in the abstract, were acceptably framed, they mattered most for the concrete (and crucial) public relations benefits they contained. On several occasions, MWD Manager Carl Boronkay emphasized this aspect, even telling recalcitrant and powerful board member Charles Barker (also a former Chevron executive) that "MWD had already gotten its return in publicity" on the basis of press reporting of the initial project announcement. For the urban water agencies, water quality still remained a question of controlling perception, not of controlling contamination.[80]

The water agencies have not yet come to terms with the eventual implications of a source-reduction approach to water quality. In the end, source reduction is likely to mean intervention to protect water quality at two points: in removing existing contaminants from water and in preventing further contamination. Both will require that the agencies and the public directly address the question of who should pay the costs of such intervention. The question of constituency and perspective ultimately remains crucial in sorting out the role of water agencies with regard to water-quality matters. In the interim, water agencies have allowed themselves to be placed in the uncomfortable position of being themselves held responsible for response to problems of industrial contamination, whatever the source and by whatever means. As a result, they have been forced to shoulder the expenses of monitoring and treatment, while contending with the questions of source, risk, and priorities.

Nearly all agencies, urban and agricultural, wholesale or retail, have so far opted to the side of the polluters rather than the polluted, minimizing rather than concentrating on issues of public health. Water agencies not only see themselves as part of an *industry* but as sharing the values—and the objectives—of other industries. These alliances are the result of the close historical relationship between the agencies and the development and industrial communities whose interests they have served in the past. These are essentially growth and expansion but not water-quality agendas, since the extensive contamination—and the costs associated with such contamination—potentially threaten water quality. These perspectives, and the underlying choice of constituencies they imply, place agencies in a continuing course of confrontation with the public. This confrontation is by no means inherent in the situation or the actual role of the agencies but only in the decisions the agencies themselves are making.

9

Groping Toward Reallocation

The various systems of allocation that govern the supply and transfer of water from one location to another, in California and the West, are based on complex and varying institutional arrangements. No single legal or institutional mechanism prevails, whether at the federal, state, or local agency level. Though allocation of each major source of water, such as the Colorado River, has been guided by a complex of agreements, legal rulings, and institutional arrangements, these allocations themselves have been fluid and somewhat uncertain. Whether the Colorado's "Law of the River" or the State Water Project's contracts, these compacts have always been subject to new economic and political inputs, to renegotiation.

At the same time, the highly complex and technical nature of the language of such allocations, with the detailed distributional arrangements they often entail, surrounds these agreements with an aura of *immutability*. This is based in part on the carefully constructed historical compromises that have characterized each particular arrangement. Resistance to any potential reduction in allocations is often strong, and opponents argue that by tampering with one part of an allocation agreement one could potentially undermine it in its entirety. And yet such change occurs. The Law of the River, for example, appears as an integrated structure, but in fact it is an edifice constructed out of more than sixty years of different building blocks, each resting on its predecessors.

These apparently contradictory aspects of water allocation institutions do have a common point of reference: water is viewed as an economic good, a necessary factor of production that must be put to private use in order to be socially useful. Allocation agreements are essentially agreements about what are taken as *ownership rights*, established divisions of a common resource between water agencies (and thus among their clients) or among private individuals with historical rights to water. The actual water user—the agricultural landowner, urban resident, industrial firm, mining operation, or real estate subdivider—is granted rights to water on a basis implicitly (and at times explicitly) justified by the water's economic or commodity value. But this value is attributed, not directly measured, through exchange: there are no real markets for water.

Water Markets

If water is an economic good, should it be bought and sold? Economics, it is often said, is the science of the management of scarce resources. Economists generally advocate markets as the social institutions that best allocate these scarce resources among competing needs; the greatest aggregate wealth is produced when a commodity is put to its "highest and best use," and this "highest and best use" will support, and thus is discovered by, a higher bid for that commodity. Like other commodities, the worth of water put to a particular use (what economists would call the "factor productivity" of water for a particular user—the dollars earned per dollar's worth of water used) varies among different uses and changes over time as broad patterns of regional economic activity change and develop. Advocates of water markets argue that this change in the value of water is best accommodated by allocating water through a market.

As a general case, markets for natural resources—resources which are captured, not produced, by human activity—differ from markets for produced goods and services in that an increase in demand is not necessarily met by an increase in supply such that price reaches a new equilibrium.[1] At present, water allocation agreements and their associated claims appear both fluid and immutable because the current economic value of water is relative, not absolute. This value varies in two ways: with regard to the use to which the water will be put, and with regard to the amount of water otherwise available. It is in this context that the current controversies over potential water market and transfer proposals should be viewed. There is currently no general market for water. Land appears as a commodity; it can be alienated—bought and sold—and in this market transaction land acquires a price.[2] But though land is privately held and most resources (mineral rights, forests) sold *with* the land can then be separated and sold *from* it, private water rights are (normally, and in California) not separable from land title: water rights are tied to landownership, and water must be used on the land to which it is tied.[3] Where landowners have established particular rights, either directly by virtue of landownership or indirectly by rights through a particular water agency, these reflect land use at the time the rights were established.

There is now no private market for water separate from the market for land. Only government agencies can acquire water rights without tying them to particular landholdings, through appropriation of water to which no other claim has been established. In fact, one historical purpose of these agencies has been to acquire rights to this water, to assure that water scarcity within their service areas would not eventually limit urban or agricultural growth, and to capture water for developed areas from less developed regions before these areas might find local uses for this resource.[4]

Justification of this taking of water from one area to meet the potential water needs of another has been based on two peculiarities of water as an economic resource: the amount of water available fluctuates unpredictably (in environments where rain- and snowfall vary wildly from year to year) and substantial investment and time are needed to build facilities for its long-distance transfer. Water agencies have thus acted to increase supply, by importing water, in order to avoid controversial future decisions, should water become scarce as a result of either natural fluctuation or growth in demand. They have not considered internal markets as a strategy to allocate the water they control among competing uses in their own service areas. Agencies have chosen, also, to price their water to their own customers at the average, rather than the marginal, cost of its provision, thereby protecting new users from paying the actual cost of the expansion in supply which their demands have made necessary.

Water is generally useful, of course, and so available water in California and the West has always been "booked" (claimed)[5] and quite frequently "overbooked," as with Colorado River allocations. Markets are supposed to accommodate this by shifting water among alternative uses: but water markets are necessarily highly imperfect, because of complex patterns of rights, the high capital costs of transportation (and the use of taxes to repay these capital costs), the role of government agencies as intermediaries (whose policies reflect the desires of their particular constituencies, rather than general public debate which includes all those they serve), and because of unpredictable variations in supply. We have seen that users are not willing to pay the marginal cost of new water supply—*ad valorem* taxes are justified by the argument that any regional development has a positive effect (through its multipliers) on the entire regional economy, so that the cost of new water development should be paid from the entire regional tax base, not just by those who get immediate economic benefits from this new, additional water supply.[6]

Much of the discussion of water markets has evolved out of the debates over the current state of water development, including political and economic constraints on future construction of water projects and the difficulty of otherwise "finding" additional water to meet new claims. But it should be noted that the markets under discussion are negotiated exchanges among agencies, not competitive bids among all users; they are external, not internal, markets.

The discussion of water markets reflects a shift in economic power throughout California and the West, away from agriculture and other rural economic activities and towards a greater urban role. This shift has had relatively slight effects on actual water use, in part because manufacturing's need for water is less, in part because of institutional inertia, and in part because of the absence of a mechanism to shift rights to the water itself. But the changing structure of economic power, coupled with the current restructuring of some parts of California agriculture, have led to a growing interest in *reallocation* of water already developed. As a consequence the water industry, though long suspicious of the objectives of the advocates of water markets, now finds itself seriously considering a major new institutional strategy. The discussion of water markets has drawn to the surface both the institutional resistance and the new opportunities markets or reallocations may offer for achieving certain agency goals. As this focus on reallocations by way of water markets and water transfers gains credibility, it could well become the new forum for distributional politics in the 1990s and beyond.

Laying the Groundwork

If water flows uphill toward money (even without a market), as one is reminded in examining the history of California and other western water allocation systems, then these allocation systems have always been economic constructs in some sense. Most have involved some form of government intervention, whether in project construction, in management of the allocation (in part or whole), or through taxing powers or other subsidies to underwrite such systems. While such government activities have been essential to the development of western water facilities, they have always been framed on behalf of those local interests that have most directly benefited. Local water agencies have been intermediaries between these local constituencies and higher levels of government. As these systems have become more complex and elaborate, the agencies have become even more influential.

This agency-led system functioned effectively during much of the first half century of western water development, in concert with the rise of major agencies at federal and state levels, such as the federal Bureau of Reclamation, which built dams throughout the West, and California's Department of Water Resources, which helped underwrite and manage the State Water Project. A different allocation system was worked out for each water source, with relative allocations based on the particular political and economic power of the interested parties at that point in time; there was no consistent formal logic that structured allocation among or within states or even regions. During the heyday of the large surface water projects, these massive public undertakings, only made possible through legislative action and broad tax financing, minimized the burden on local interests while expanding their benefits.[7]

In this setting, the notion of an open or "free" market to allocate water found little support within the water industry, though certain local markets were gradually appearing in California and other areas of the West. In Southern California, formal and informal markets appeared in several of the adjudicated basin areas in Los Angeles County, including the Central, West, and Main San Gabriel basins. After adjudication of the Central and West basins during the 1940s and 1950s, an "exchange pool" system was organized among basin groundwater users.[8] The adjudication agreement had established specific allotments to various users based on historical use. In the West Basin, transfers were allowed between different users at a price that reflected the costs of MWD imported water, pumping costs, and other assessments and fees. In the Central Basin a free floating price for the purchase, sale, or lease of groundwater rights also evolved; historically, these prices tended to lie below MWD rates, though they increased steadily during the 1960s and 1970s. Prices for water in these markets rose considerably during the 1980s, following the defeat of the Peripheral Canal. This early water market concentrated ownership rights, reducing the number of rights holders from 508 in 1966 to 194 in 1985.[9]

A more limited and informal market or transfer system developed in the San Gabriel Valley after its 1973 adjudication.[10] Since quantitative determination of water rights here also had been based in part on past production, certain rights holders, particularly farm and dairy owners who had once been a significant presence in the valley, found they had an additional source of income or value attached to their properties. Though the valley became largely urban by the time of the adjudication or soon after, urban users, such as the City of Covina, had to deal with other rights holders to expand their water use. For Covina, the city's expansion depended on obtaining rights and securing shares within the Covina Irrigating Company, the second largest holder of groundwater rights in the San Gabriel Valley.[11]

These market systems, however, were contained within the adjudicated areas themselves and did not involve private bidding, a net reduction of water withdrawals, or a transfer of water outside the basin boundaries. These rights transfers tended to intensify existing uses of water and paralleled the growing reliance on imported water as a *peaking source* to supplement the consolidated system of groundwater use that had evolved. Thus these limited markets were not seen as challenging the larger system of allocations and new water development that agencies in Southern California and throughout the West had come to depend on.

As these larger-scale allocation systems matured through the 1950s and 1960s, agency activities continued to focus on the construction of distribution facilities. By the 1960s, growing criticism of the economic efficiency of new development projects, and of their impacts on the environment at the point of origin of this "new water," had emerged. These arguments were put forth primarily by traditional conservationist groups, such as the Wilderness Society and the Sierra Club, but were also supported by "good government" organizations (the League of Women Voters) and by various academic analysts and research think tanks (such as Resources for the Future).[12] These groups criticized existing allocation systems as inefficient precisely because of the government role in arranging and underwriting such systems. If local interests were not required to assume the full costs of a water project, the critics argued, water development would necessarily be skewed, in the projects selected and the uses to which water was put, particularly heavily subsidized agricultural use. Large water projects, costly and environmentally destructive, perpetuated cropping patterns and irrigated development in areas that could never support such activity without subsidies (and resulting economic inefficiencies). Economic inefficiency, a focus of the National Water Commission, became the byword for one strategy of criticism of the overall system of allocations.

Through the 1960s and into the early 1970s, the inefficiency argument was increasingly linked to the related concept of water markets. Critics argued that by removing government subsidies from water development, one could eliminate systematic inefficiencies responsible both for poorly conceived projects and poorly designed uses.[13] Markets, critics asserted, would create greater efficiencies by eliminating marginal projects and marginal uses. Those most in need of additional water, primarily urban users, would find it far more expensive to build new facilities than to purchase water through an open market. Moreover, certain agricultural users would find it to their advantage to sell their existing rights to the water rather than continue to obtain it from increasingly expensive water projects. For the water industry, arguments for markets were an attempt to undermine existing allocation structures and especially to oppose any plans for expansion. Moreover, the water agencies saw the position of the conservationist and environmental groups in distributional terms and defined their efforts to protect the areas from which sources of new water might be drawn as a kind of interest group–geographic focus. Even market advocates such as the Rand Corporation were viewed with suspicion, though they couched their arguments in entirely economic terms. Resistance to the idea of markets within the water industry was so strong that the Rand analysts, dependent on funding support from interested parties, became convinced by the early 1980s that the issue, while still an important long-term objective, did not have enough current standing to support their activities full-time.[14]

In the 1982 Peripheral Canal campaign, water market advocacy became linked explicitly to criticism of the water industry and its perspective on water development. The idea of the Imperial–MWD Water SWAP, first broached by the Elmore brothers as litigants in the State Water Resources Control Board Hearings, was seized upon by water industry critics as a canal alternative.[15] As a consequence, the idea was immediately dismissed not only by the primary parties within the potential SWAP, but also by other water industry groups such as the Farm Bureau.[16] Other efficiency-oriented ideas proposed in this period, such as the merging of the California State Water project with the federal Central Valley Project (CVP), were also seen by the water industry as back-door attempts to reduce the amount of water that might flow through the delta into Central and Southern California.[17]

At the moment of strongest resistance to markets and other "efficiency" concepts, however, the water industry found itself subject to events beyond its control. These represented a watershed in terms of supply issues. While the defeat of the Peripheral Canal became the political symbol of this transitional point, the rapid retrenchment of large, newly irrigated agricultural businesses in 1983 and 1984 became its economic symbol. During this same period, the economics of new water development itself also began to change with rising costs and rising prices. All these changes most directly affected those marginal users who had been effectively shielded by the complex of arrangements at both the federal and state levels. Suddenly, the most vocal opponents of water markets found themselves thrust into unanticipated situations, as either prospective buyers or sellers. Water markets had become a new and unknown possibility in a period of diminishing new supplies and water development paralysis.

Family Squabbles

These issues were most pronounced in the agricultural areas, particularly in Kern County where the water industry became divided over how to approach the subject. Though the Imperial-MWD SWAP was the first to generate widespread attention, a far more striking and dramatic dispute was taking shape between the board of directors of the Kern County Water Agency and certain of its member agencies. At stake were both key economic issues for the agricultural water industry and the whole question of agency role and priorities.

The idea of establishing specific water markets in the Kern area had been raised through much of the 1970s and early 1980s, as both water use and irrigated acreage increased dramatically throughout the KCWA service area. Two Rand economists, Tim Quinn (later hired by MWD) and Nancy Moore, had sought to interest Kern landowners and water-agency managers in the concept of water rights as a saleable commodity, to no avail. Armed with charts, tables, and figures demonstrating the economic advantages for certain landowners, the Rand economists thought they might find an interested audience, given the Kern landowners' conservative biases and stated preference for private sector choices over governmental intervention, at least in the matter of groundwater management. "We thought the whole idea of markets would be naturally appealing," Moore recalled, "but we never overcame the suspicion that we were really critics or that such arrangements were actually advantageous." [18]

A different and more novel approach to markets was proposed at about the same time by Henry Vaux, a professor in the Department of Soil and Engineering Sciences at the University of California at Riverside, and, subsequently, director of the UC Water Resources Research Center. [19] Vaux argued that the Kern agencies might be interested in the idea of a water market as prospective *buyers* rather than sellers of water. Vaux's idea, elaborated in a 1985 Assembly Office of Research proposal, specifically proposed a water transfer between Stanislaus County as the seller and KCWA as the buyer. [20] At the same moment as these proposals were made public, two of KCWA's most powerful member agencies, Wheeler Ridge–Maricopa and Berrenda Mesa, had begun their own exploration of ways to market their water allotments as *sellers*, not as buyers. The two big member agencies, the largest in the KCWA system, had similar concerns. Both were located in areas with poor or nonexistent groundwater resources. Investment in irrigation development in these two areas during the 1970s and early 1980s thus depended on State Project water. Growers within the territories of both agencies, moreover, had planted a lot of cotton, one of the crops most directly impacted by the recession, and there had been a number of bankruptcies by 1985–86. Both agencies, each dominated by a handful of landowners, had been among the most aggressive supporters of the Peripheral Canal, arguing that expansion of the State Project was essential for future agricultural prospects. [21]

Both agencies had first discussed the question of markets or transfers as a *cost reduction* measure. The price of State Project entitlement water had increased significantly during the early 1980s, partly as a function of increased energy costs both within the state system and for the distributional systems established for each member agency. Increasing bankruptcies among the smaller landowners meant that the per unit cost for all landowners would increase as well, since the fixed costs of the water systems had still to be paid. As a result, both agencies sought ways to deal with unpaid bills and with those landowners wishing to opt out of the system.[22]

While the two agencies shared a set of common dilemmas, their approach to the issue of markets was significantly different. At the Wheeler Ridge–Maricopa agency, attempts were made to identify which landowners wanted to abandon their entitlements to State Project water and which landowners might be willing to buy such entitlements.[23] These entitlements had been established through contracts between landowners and member agencies, with the landowners held liable in case of any default. Wheeler Ridge then contracted with KCWA for a portion of KCWA's overall State Project entitlements. Once the Tejon Ranch and Tenneco, the two biggest landowners within the agency, indicated that they would be sellers rather than buyers, Wheeler Ridge knew it had to seek buyers beyond its own landowner-clients, either within Kern or outside the county.

Tenneco and Tejon had different strategic interests. Tenneco had decided to get out of the farming business altogether and began to seek various ways to increase the value of its properties in a period of declining land prices. The Tejon Ranch, on the other hand, had decided to explore changing the use of its land. Tejon, controlled by the parent company of the *Los Angeles Times*, was particularly sensitive to negative forms of publicity and wanted a "minimum of political fallout," as the company president put it.[24] The company wanted to set up an arrangement that would quickly and quietly recoup its investments, including the cost of distribution facilities built to serve its speculative irrigation ventures.

At Berrenda Mesa, the early discussions of cost reduction quickly turned into a search for profit. Led by Ron Khachagian, an executive with the Blackwell Land Company, vice chairman of the Berrenda Mesa board, and a major political figure in the county, this KCWA member sought a price for the sale of its entitlement water in excess of the costs of the water and investment in facilities. Khachagian differentiated his agency's approach with that advocated by the Tejon Ranch on behalf of Wheeler Ridge–Maricopa. "The Tejon Ranch is afraid of making an extra buck on this because they fear the *Los Angeles Times* will get bad publicity," Khachagian asserted in 1986. "They are ultra, ultra conscious of bad publicity. They want to assign no value to the water other than the assumption of all their encumbrances. We, on the other hand, are in this to realize a return on our investment, to get paid for the value that has built up on our land."[25] The price Berrenda Mesa was suggesting, ranging from $800 to $1000 per acre-foot, was immediately perceived as antagonistic to the interests of KCWA, whose staff and board members had focused on how to keep all the agency's entitlement water within the county.[26]

In 1985, when Wheeler Ridge–Maricopa announced its "middle course" price of $175 an acre-foot and Berrenda Mesa indicated its intention to seek a significant profit from its new rights to State Project water, the KCWA board was thrust into the middle of the debate. The agency discovered that even on the terms suggested by Wheeler Ridge, there were no likely buyers among its other member agencies. Despite this, board members still argued that all entitlement water had to be kept within the county, insisting that the decline in agriculture was transitional and that increases in irrigated production would resume once economic conditions for agriculture improved.[27]

In April 1986, the agency board released a position paper on the entitlements issue that focused these arguments on the overall question of markets in the Kern area.[28] According to the document, any reallocations or restructuring of entitlements had to take into account two factors: that the "County remains short of water," and that "present financial problems will probably not go on for a long period of time." As a consequence, it was stipulated that the "agency's first priority," once entitlements were offered for sale, would be "to assure that the State Project allocation to Kern County remains available to Kern County users."

This position immediately placed the agency in conflict not only with Berrenda Mesa, now perceived as a kind of Peck's Bad Boy by the agency staff and board, but also with the publicity-shy Wheeler Ridge–Maricopa agency. Part of the conflict was based on differing perspectives over the state of Kern agriculture and the future prospects for both irrigation and water use in the county. Some KCWA directors argued that cost factors could change again and that Wheeler Ridge and Berrenda Mesa might in the future reverse themselves and even request additional water as they had in the past. But Tejon President Jack Hunt argued that "the restructuring of the United States farm economy will get a lot worse before it gets any better."[29] As a consequence, more marginal forms of irrigation, Hunt asserted, would become increasingly "unviable" and the economics of farming itself in Kern County, and, by extension of irrigated water use, "had to be reevaluated."

These differences in perspective were compounded by differences in approach. By 1986, Wheeler Ridge had identified three potential buyers, all located outside the Kern service area. These included the Castaic Lake Water Agency, situated between Tejon's properties and the MWD service area, the Coachella Valley Water District, and the Desert Water Agency, the latter two located in the Palm Springs area near neighboring Imperial Irrigation District. For more than a year the prospective buyers and sellers, along with KCWA, MWD, and the state's Department of Water Resources, negotiated whether or how to structure such an arrangement.[30] The two large state contractors, KCWA and MWD (with DWR), opposed any outright sale but considered various "buy back" plans whereby the entitlements would revert back to the state that would then be able to offer the additional entitlements, either on a temporary or permanent basis.

For KCWA, the key issue remained keeping entitlements available to Kern, particularly during dry-year periods when the State Project could not provide enough water for everyone and agriculture was obliged to take the first reductions. This concern became particularly compelling during 1987 and 1988, when a drought raised the possibility of immediate cutbacks. The focus on the buy-back plan shifted back to Kern as the agency made renewed efforts to find buyers for the Wheeler Ridge water. At one point, KCWA board members even explored increasing the zone-of-benefit tax on the grounds that keeping the water in the county benefited all, groundwater and surface-water users alike.[31] This idea, however, also was problematic, given recent battles over the tax and continuing urban and oil company concerns over their share of payments. Finally, the agency succeeded in at least partially resolving its dilemma when it maneuvered the sale of about one-third of the entitlements at a reduced price to the urban-based Improvement District (ID No. 4), whose board overlapped with that of KCWA. This arrangement, justified by reference to future urban growth, failed fully to satisfy either Wheeler Ridge landowners or the urban water officials, but it got KCWA off the hook temporarily and kept the entitlements in the county.[32]

The problems with Berrenda Mesa, on the other hand, seemed insurmountable. By 1987, the Kern member agency had turned to the Environmental Defense Fund, a major water-market advocate, to help in its quest to sell the water. Although the memorandum of understanding signed between the environmental group and the agricultural agency made no mention of price or profit, the intention of the agreement was clear: to further the deal.[33]

It was less the relationship with environmentalists than the impact of the drought, however, that helped position Berrenda Mesa in its quest to become the first significant seller—and profit taker—in what it considered inevitable: the establishment of a market for water in California. By 1988, at the height of the drought, Berrenda Mesa had located its own prospective buyers: three Orange County agencies.[34] Announcement of this immediately escalated the war of words between Berrenda Mesa and KCWA and also brought MWD into the picture. KCWA board members vowed to block any such arrangement in the courts if and when Berrenda Mesa sought to pursue its agreement. MWD supported KCWA's claim that State Project entitlements could not be traded and that the contracts for water between the state and various contractors such as MWD and KCWA were inviolate. Furthermore, MWD remained adamantly opposed, as it had with Galloway, to an attempt by any individual agency in its service area to secure water that it felt rightfully belonged to MWD or other recognized contractors.[35]

Berrenda Mesa, meanwhile, sought to buttress its own position. It actively lobbied for new, market-related legislation introduced by Southern

California Assemblyman, and sometime MWD critic, Richard Katz. It also hired an attorney to explore legal avenues for a deal including bringing suit against KCWA and other state contractors to insure that a sale could take place. And it prepared an initial study and proposed negative declaration to facilitate any future transfer of its entitlements.[36]

During 1988 and 1989, as the drought preoccupied water agencies throughout the state, both Berrenda Mesa and KCWA played a waiting game, marshalling their resources and presuming that the showdown over markets would once and for all resolve the question of who controlled the water and how it could be sold. Waiting in the wings were other prospective sellers, including other KCWA member agencies as well as other landowners in Kern and the Central Valley. Now attention turned to the potential buyers, whose actions would determine whether this new interest in reallocations would become significant to water supply discussions in California.

Hedging Their Bets

A market could only be sustained in California if it became buyer-driven. When the first indications of interest in selling water rights (as entitlements or the land itself) appeared in 1985 and 1986, many sellers turned their sights south, particularly to the Metropolitan Water District. The San Diego County Water Authority was also approached, particularly after the Galloway proposal was made public; but the cautious approach of CWA, which had decided to refer all prospective deals first to MWD, appeared to leave potential sellers with only one major game in town.[37]

The response from MWD was ambiguous at best. During 1985 and 1986, more than half a dozen prospective sellers, including George Nickel and Tenneco (inheritors of the Miller and Lux fortunes), trooped down to Sunset and Beaudry in downtown Los Angeles, headquarters of the big urban district, to explore a possible sale, lease, or other transfer mechanism allowing water to flow south.[38] MWD management dampened enthusiasm about an immediate deal in most instances, particularly regarding those proposals involving outright purchase of land or of the water rights attached to the land.[39] MWD management was sensitive to the charge that the big urban wholesaler might recapitulate the Owens Valley "land grab" of the Los Angeles Aqueduct seventy-five years earlier.[40] Still, MWD management wanted to keep the district's options open and so were unwilling entirely to foreclose any option, including land purchases.[41]

As water markets began to preoccupy water industry discussions in California, MWD, the central actor in most proposals, attempted to maintain its position of studied ambivalence. On the one hand, the district continued to oppose and criticize any attempts to pose markets as an alternative to its long-standing objective to expand the State Water Project supply. The district also maintained a public posture of opposition to entitlement transfers in the State Project system or purchases of land in the Central Valley, though it advocated such transfers in the Colorado River system.[42] But district management also encouraged its new chief economist, Tim Quinn, recently hired from Rand, to explore arrangements other than an outright sale of land or water rights. One of Quinn's first activities was to help organize and secure MWD participation in a heavily attended water markets conference arranged by the UCLA Extension Program.[43] At MWD, water markets were becoming an acceptable agenda item, though the terms of discussion still had to be defined.

MWD's interest in markets was also tempered by the realization that its long-anticipated water-supply shortfall—tied to failure to expand the State Water Project—had still not occurred. During the Peripheral Canal campaign, water industry leaders had warned that completion of Phase One of the Central Arizona Project in 1985 would create a dramatic shortage of water for Southern California. By 1990, however, more than four years after the CAP had come on line and even after an unprecedented four consecutive dry years, MWD still found itself with a sufficient supply of water. This available supply was reflected in part by the continuing high storage levels—upwards of 90 percent during the summer months—in MWD's own reservoirs.[44] This continuing indication of a sufficient supply, available well into the 1990s, gave MWD far more flexibility in its supply options than its public posture seemed to suggest.

It was also clear that any future shortfall would occur during dry or drought-year conditions, not during a normal year. The State Project system had been built to accommodate the peaking needs of the contractors, with much of the planning and construction designed around those peak-load requirements. This overcapacity-based system was still capable, even in its "semi-built" status (that is, without a better mechanism to channel water through or around the delta), of delivering sufficient imported water supplies during normal-year cycles. The problem, for both MWD and the other contractors, was how to handle those less frequent dry-year occurrences.

With such needs in mind, Tim Quinn, MWD's front-line "markets" negotiator, began to approach agencies about potential transfer arrangements focused on this long-term "dry yield" factor.[45] These arrangements contrasted with the MWD-IID SWAP, which benefited MWD more, in the increase in baseline Colorado River entitlements the urban district obtained in exchange for funds for conservation facilities. The SWAP offered MWD a more *secure* supply, since it would have contractual rights to an additional 100,000 acre-feet of water. But that water represented only a "paper" benefit (for at least the near and medium term) since that 100,000 acre-feet was already, in terms of available Colorado River supply, above MWD's own paper entitlements.

MWD had been drawn into the negotiations on the Imperial SWAP partly as a result of the strong public support of the arrangement, after the State Water Resources Control Board Hearings had forced IID to seek negotiations.[46] The lengthy maneuvering between the two sides in part reflected concern about whether to consummate an agreement, with much of the debate centered on the final price to be set. Both sides, however, also knew that failure to complete a deal also might leave them with substantial political and regulatory problems.[47]

MWD's Quinn quietly began to arrange other transfer deals to meet MWD's future requirements for additional water during dry years. Quinn explored both possible State Project and Colorado River opportunities and was soon successful in convincing several agencies that meeting MWD's needs would bring substantial benefits to their own areas. In the Kern area, Quinn approached the Arvin-Edison Water District, a member agency of the Kern County Water Agency as well as a Central Valley Project contractor. Arvin-Edison, situated on the west side of the KCWA service area, also relied on an extensive groundwater basin which was still being overdrawn, despite additional CVP water (which had also allowed new irrigated development). Aware of this dilemma, Quinn proposed to Arvin-Edison managers that MWD store its unused State Project entitlements in the Arvin-Edison groundwater basin.[48] This would aid the agricultural agency's attempts to reduce the overdraft and would lower pumping costs since the groundwater tables would be higher. Then, if and when MWD experienced a shortfall in State Project water during a dry year, MWD would simply take Arvin-Edison's CVP water, while the agricultural agency instead pumped the MWD water that had been stored in the ground. Furthermore, MWD would pay for the additional facilities needed both to store the water and to connect CVP water to the State Project system. MWD management estimated that the full cost of the project would amount to about $128 per acre-foot, with as much as 100,000 acre-feet of water potentially available during that future dry year.[49]

In 1986, a Memorandum of Understanding was signed and ratified by the two agencies. Obstacles still remained, however, in the form of objections from both the Kern County Water Agency and other Central Valley Project contractors. KCWA had long relied on the availability of MWD's unused State Project entitlements as cheap "surplus water," and although the changing circumstances in both Kern and the State Project suggested that such "surplus" supplies might be less available to KCWA's customers in future years, the Kern water leaders wanted some leverage over the arrangement. KCWA board members were also concerned that this dry-year agreement might also, indirectly, affect State Project supplies, since the CVP water also flowed through the delta and the amount of water made available through one system could conceivably affect the other.[50]

This trade in CVP water also stimulated objections from the CVP contractors.[51] Above and beyond their concerns over a transfer of CVP water, these parties were also wary that this supply, now reserved to agriculture, would ultimately be captured for an urban user. This action, CVP agricultural contractors feared, would set a precedent, raising the whole question of agricultural water use in a period when both the price of agricultural water and the environmental consequences of such use were being challenged. These concerns impeded completion of the deal, though MWD modified the arrangement to meet certain of the objections.[52] By 1989, Arvin-Edison, anxious to secure the benefits of additional water stored in its basin, worked out an arrangement whereby MWD would begin to make its unused State Project entitlements immediately available, even prior to a successful resolution of the obstacles that had emerged. Despite some unhappiness among MWD directors, this proposal, with strong backing from MWD management, was accepted.[53]

While the Arvin-Edison deal was being pursued, Tim Quinn also ventured to the Palo Verde Valley in the desert areas north and east of Imperial. This agricultural district, like Imperial, held a higher priority for its share of Colorado River water than did MWD. Quinn discovered that several landowners in the area, including the San Diego Gas and Electric company, which owned a 6,000-acre ranch that had been tied into its plans for the defunct Sundesert nuclear power plant, might be interested in a possible dry-year–related agreement. MWD proposed that it would pay landowners in the area a set fee—$200 per acre—to sign up to be part of the proposed dry-year exchange.[54] If and when a dry year occurred, MWD would then pay these landowners—at an additional $400 an acre—not to use their water and instead to make it available to MWD. MWD would provide six months notice of when it intended to use such water. And then, once the dry-year conditions had subsided, the water would revert back to landowner use.

Quinn told the landowners that such an arrangement, like the Arvin-Edison situation, offered strong benefits for both parties.[55] The landowners could continue farming (or, as in San Diego Gas & Electric's case, maintain title to the land and water rights for any future power plant) with the exception of that dry year when the water would be transferred. At the same time, they would obtain a fee for their participation in the program and a fee at the time the water was transferred. MWD, on the other hand, would obtain a dry-year yield of approximately 100,000 acre-feet based on the 22,000 acres of land held by those interested in signing up. Since each acre in Palo Verde used about 4.6 acre-feet of water per acre, this arrangement for MWD was quite inexpensive: a start-up cost of about $130 an acre-foot, and less than $90 an acre-foot as implemented.[56]

In March 1987 the Palo Verde arrangement was brought to the MWD board's attention. The agreement, MWD management told directors, was close at hand. As with Arvin-Edison, however, obstacles quickly undermined the potential agreement. Some Palo Verde landowners began to have second thoughts about the low fees set for the arrangement and were particularly wary of criticism within the Palo Verde Valley that an Owens Valley situation was in the making. One local Palo Verde newspaper headlined its story of these criticisms, "MWD: Drop Dead," suggesting that MWD would have to offer a considerably higher price in order to consummate the deal.[57]

Price—and timing—it appeared were as much a factor in concluding these arrangements as the kinds of institutional constraints and agency opposition experienced in the Arvin-Edison and Berrenda Mesa–Wheeler Ridge and Maricopa situations. The Palo Verde arrangement also interested a number of Imperial landowners who had eagerly awaited the more favorable political climate resulting from completion of the SWAP to pursue a possible deal. MWD also proposed a variation of this dry-year arrangement to Indian tribes who had been engaged in a long legal battle with MWD over rights to Colorado River water. But MWD remained reluctant to secure these arrangements without a favorable price for itself as the buyer, given its flexibility on future supply needs.[58] Moreover, MWD was most interested in its dry-year options, which ultimately framed its approach to any discussions over markets. Defining its position on markets as "(tailored) to the many different situations that will be considered and taking cognizance of the present long-developed water scene,"[59] MWD management sought a position not as an advocate and champion of markets, but as still a buyer when the circumstances were right.

Win-Win, or Lose-Lose

By the late 1980s, water markets, for the water industry, had become an acceptable, albeit unresolved, part of the discourse on water issues. Even organizations such as the Association of California Water Agencies, long a bastion of anti-market sentiment, would in 1989 co-host, with a leading academic advocate, a water markets conference.[60] All were coming to agree that "water now devoted to agricultural use (84 percent of the developed water in California) will be a major source for meeting future urban needs," as MWD general manager Carl Boronkay put it.[61]

This recognition of an eventual, inevitable shift toward reallocations was also being defined—both by advocates of "markets" and by potential transfer participants—as a "win-win" situation. The scenarios suggested that while agricultural water use would probably decline (either through changing cropping patterns or withdrawal of land from production), urban use would escalate with anticipated growth in such urban regions as Southern California's South Coast Basin. This new variant on the Laguna Declaration—water will be made available, whatever the source—became a standard point of departure for potential buyer or seller, environmental advocate, or water industry skeptic. Both parties in such transactions would thus be winners. Agricultural landowners would benefit because they would have found a mechanism to "bail out" (the Wheeler Ridge case), to respond to external constraints (IID), or to make some profit (as advocated by Berrenda Mesa). Urban buyers, meanwhile, would be able to increase their overall supplies and could avoid the difficult and potentially contentious matter of demand management. Reallocation became another way to continue the growth agendas of the urban areas.

These scenarios were contingent on making explicit the underlying presumption of water rights: their value as a commodity. At the same time, water agencies were finally beginning to reconcile themselves to the diminished role of the federal (and, possibly, the state) government in securing additional allocations. As part of this change, agencies and landowners now sought a new role from federal agencies such as the Bureau of Reclamation; where earlier they had argued that their interest in water from federal or state projects was not modifiable, they now sought the transfer of these rights from higher agencies directly to local agencies and landowners as a first step toward establishing a market.[62] State control of the water systems was presented as appropriate at that point where costs were met by taxes and thus users were subsidized. But when water rights became a commodity (and water markets became a bid-price system), water agencies and their clients argued that water should be a commodity owned by the entitled users, not the taxpayers who had paid for its development. After sharp and divisive debates over market issues during much of the eight years of the Reagan administration, the announcement by the Bureau of Reclamation in late 1988 that this market approach would become policy was almost anticlimactic.[63] The resistance of the water industry to the general notion of markets had eroded by the end of the decade. Translating general acceptance into specific deals, however, still remained difficult. While the position of the water industry on water markets had evolved, divisions among environmentalists and other water industry critics over the "win-win" perspective toward markets had also surfaced. A number of groups began to raise the question of "public welfare values" or "third party impacts," especially to the environment.[64] While markets might reduce pressure for construction of new facilities, they did not necessarily result in reduced water use, an issue of particular note in the Bay-Delta situation. By transferring water to an expanding urban user from a marginal agricultural user (who might otherwise have reduced or eliminated water use as a result of price increases or other economic factors), inter-agency markets perpetuated existing water-supply export patterns. Some environmental groups, such as the Natural Resources Defense Council, also argued that markets helped perpetuate inequities in the federal water reclamation systems, where agricultural users had long benefited from a variety of subsidies. By transferring the heavily subsidized water rights to local agencies and landowners who in turn were then able to sell and profit from such rights, the cycle of subsidies would then be extended.

Some of the most extensive criticisms of "third party" impacts, however, involved questions of relative regional development emerging out of the experiences in Arizona and other parts of the Southwest, where cities such as Phoenix and Tucson (as well as real estate and commercial development interests) had aggressively attempted to secure water rights by purchasing land from farmers in depressed rural counties.[65] Similar efforts were pursued with various southwestern Indian tribes who claimed significant rights to both the Colorado River and other water sources.[66] These activities had significant negative economic impacts in the rural areas through reduced tax rolls, employment opportunities, and available income. Furthermore, by reducing water to a commodity, markets or transfers created significant negative *cultural* impacts, particularly among Indian tribes where water and its uses were associated with crucial noneconomic values central to community life.[67] In a major survey of rural southwestern communities, one University of Arizona institute discovered that these "third party impacts" were widely associated with urban efforts to establish markets.[68]

The possibility of negative impacts associated with transfers, a "lose-lose" scenario rather than a "win-win" perspective, is perhaps most apparent in one of the less visible but more instructive deals proposed between a water agency located in Kern and Kings counties and a Southern California urban water user. The Kern-Kings agency, the Devil's Den Water District, was formed by the Producers' Cotton Oil Company, a farming and cotton-ginning operation whose lands constituted 90 percent of the Devil's Den service area. The agency had secured State Project water (independently of KCWA) to irrigate the company's 15,000 acres of cotton first planted in the late 1960s.[69] In line with the decline and restructuring of the cotton industry in the 1980s, Producers' Cotton Oil went through a series of corporate owners, to be taken over finally by a Tennessee-based cotton broker, Dunavant Enterprises. Dunavant decided to get Producers' Cotton Oil out of the farming end of its cotton business and as a consequence offered its land in the Devil's Den District up for sale. In the interim, the company leased its land to a local grower who continued to plant, employing forty workers full- or part-time.[70]

Within a short period Producers' Cotton Oil/Dunavant found a buyer, the Castaic Lake Water Agency, which had been one of the parties interested in purchasing State Water Project entitlements from the Wheeler Ridge–Maricopa agency. Castaic Lake Water Agency had only limited State Project water available to serve one of the fastest-growing areas in Southern California, the newly developing lands north of the Los Angeles city limits, just south of the Tehachapis. Castaic Lake was seeking not just a dry-year supply but an overall increase in a secure future supply, anticipating increased growth.[71]

Once the Devil's Den lands became available, Castaic Lake Water Agency was a willing buyer, hoping to thus secure Devil's Den's State Project contract entitlement.[72] Though the deal was opposed by KCWA and concerns were raised by other contractors, as well as the state's Department of Water Resources,[73] on the face it appeared to meet "win-win" criteria—an agricultural entity bailing out, while a high-growth urban area obtains its additional water.

But the Devil's Den–Castaic Lake Water Agency deal also had all the attributes, once third-party impacts are accounted for, of a "lose-lose" arrangement. If the land and the water rights were sold, the local area would experience the same impacts as had rural Arizona: declining employment, income, and economic benefits associated with farming. Moreover, the grower leasing the land from Producers' Cotton Oil had wanted to explore another possible alternative to outright sale of the land, including more efficient water use and crop rotation, as well as a possible dry-year transfer arrangement where the lands could remain fallow while the water rights were made available to an urban user.[74] Such an alternative would not only reduce third-party impacts, at least, but could also lead to a net reduction of water use.

In the urban area, meanwhile, the whole question of growth in the Castaic Lake area was a controversial and unresolved policy matter.[75] By focusing on a transfer arrangement instead of confronting demand-side issues of price and possible growth-management strategies, the Castaic Lake Water Agency opted for the growth scenario that had long dominated Southern California. In this way, the Castaic–Devil's Den deal did, in fact, replicate the Owens Valley experience at the turn of the century, where Los Angeles' own unresolved growth debate was settled in part by the activities of a nascent water industry. At the same time, the acquisition of land and transfer of water rights from the Owens Valley precluded other forms of rural development and transformed the area into a water colony of the metropolis, a political act that still haunts both regions.

This question of third-party impacts raises larger issues about long-term water industry objectives. The water markets that agencies are seeking to develop are not real markets; at best, they are market transactions between agencies, not private individuals. Therefore, the interests of individuals are only well represented if individuals are adequately represented in the agencies themselves. Markets, once resisted by the industry, are gradually evolving into a supply-side solution to the decline of additional imported water allocations in both agricultural and urban growth areas. At the same time, irrigated California agriculture, an economic enterprise dominated by corporate farms and increasingly dependent on large imported water—supply systems, has needed to restructure itself to contend not only with changes in the sphere of agricultural production but with the changing nature of water policy as well. Though still constrained by resistance at the institutional level, and by concerns among agencies about their share, water markets have emerged as one solution that might allow long-standing water industry objectives to remain intact. Instead of transforming water systems, as its advocates had long hoped, the water market has been taken up by the industry as one way to restructure such systems to better save them. Whether this represents a "win-win" or a "lose-lose" scenario depends on the perspective and the interests involved.

10

The Role of Efficiency

![D]uring the 1970s—facing rapidly increasing oil prices, fear of shortages, difficulties in siting and constructing new power plants, and public anger over higher rates—the electrical utility industry discovered "efficiency." This took the form of better management practices in the generating and distribution of energy, more energy-efficient building standards and product designs, and a revised pricing system. At the same time, long-standing assumptions about consumer habits and the link between economic growth and energy use were questioned at last. The electric utility industry, though it had long been wedded to construction of huge central-station power plants, now found itself required to pursue efficiency-related programs and to turn away from these costly and wasteful habits.[1]

Just a few years earlier, these utilities had insisted that any such changes would have disastrous consequences. Utility managers argued that the overall economic well-being of society was dependent on high-energy use. Rate structures were designed to encourage greater energy use. Inefficient, *expansive* use was considered a mark of distinction, a sign of prosperity for consumer and utility alike. These arguments, however, quickly dissipated in a transitional era, when both public input and the shifting economics of the industry forced a reevaluation of utility management practices.

Similarly, the water industry in the 1980s, confronting new dynamics in both the water-supply and water-quality arenas, also had begun to discover "efficiency." Water agencies had long regarded efficiency programs as secondary, inconsequential efforts—designed as much for public consumption as for substantive planning. Water conservation was seen as *voluntary* activity, as a measure of good citizenship to be pursued by an individual urban resident, industrial plant or farmer, not on an institutional or structural basis. Water rate structures, like electricity prices, were based on the principle that the greater the use, the cheaper the price; such rates discouraged conservation and rewarded overuse and inefficiency. These problems were magnified in agricultural rates, where subsidized prices and the availability of imported water allowed inefficient cropping patterns and irrigation practices to flourish. Water systems were designed for overcapacity to meet future anticipated peaks, like the central-station power plant. The substantial costs of such plants were justified on the basis of "economies of scale." By the 1980s, however, the large water development project had reached the same impasse as had the big power plants, a casualty of escalating costs, environmental impacts, and new public agendas.

These trends were particularly pronounced in California, where debates that emerged during the Peripheral Canal campaign reflected differing conceptions of efficiency and development.[2] Water-industry critics, elaborating on arguments that had been effectively presented by the National Water Commission, criticized California water systems as grossly inefficient and wasteful. At the same time, they promoted efficiency programs, such as the conjunctive use of ground and surface waters, and pricing initiatives, such as seasonal rates, as alternatives to the cycle of expansion symbolized by the Peripheral Canal.

During the debates, leading Canal advocates, including MWD, the San Diego CWA, and the Kern County Water Agency, adamantly insisted that their systems had achieved more-than-adequate levels of efficiency.[3] They dismissed arguments about conjunctive use or pricing reform as politically motivated and suggested that "conservation" efforts had reached their full potential.

Prior to the 1980s, water-supply planning, in fact, had disregarded conservation or efficiency-related programs in projecting future demands and supply needs. Urban and agricultural agencies based planning estimates directly on estimated population growth and expansion of irrigated production. New development projects were defined as necessary to sustaining future prosperity. In the aftermath of the defeat of the Peripheral Canal and of the growing recognition that future water development had become increasingly problematic, water agencies quietly and cautiously began to review the management of their systems. The agricultural agencies discovered that certain previously taboo strategies, such as groundwater management and storage, offered alternatives less expensive than continuing expansion of facilities. The urban agencies also found that conservation and efficiency programs could involve a lot more than had their previous "educational" efforts aimed at a passive public. Though most urban agencies presented only limited, and often *pro-forma*, analysis of conservation possibilities in the state-mandated reports they prepared during the early- and mid-1980s,[4] by the end of the decade they came to recognize that efficiency measures also represented *additional yield*. To the surprise of critics, agencies such as MWD began to explore such programs. Efficiency was finally becoming a management and planning tool, though still designed more to maintain system goals than to change them.

Upgrading Conjunctive Use

In February 1986, MWD management released a letter to its board of directors outlining various strategies to secure additional water supplies on both short and long-term bases.[5] What distinguished this document, and subsequent annual updates, from previous descriptions of prospective supply-side efforts was the preponderance of what MWD managers characterized as "alternative supply projects." These alternatives included the IID SWAP; acknowledgement that the expected completion of Phase One of the Central Arizona Project would nevertheless leave significant surpluses in the Colorado River system for the foreseeable future; and a range of proposals for increased surface and groundwater storage (and possible conjunctive use programs) within the MWD system.

Groundwater management and conjunctive use had long been attractive "efficiency" concepts, often raised in contrast to traditional water industry reliance on new water development to meet future demands. Such concepts suggested that the use of a particular resource (whether groundwater or surface water, local or imported supplies) could be *controlled* for some larger public benefit. Using imported water and groundwater conjunctively (that is, designing the system to draw from different sources at different periods), required both a planning mechanism and an instrument for enforcement, whether through pricing incentives or taxes or some other method of control. Moreover, groundwater management was a catch-all phrase, ranging from extensive controls over pumping and pricing to the more limited goal of increasing storage capacity. In the absence of conjunctive-use programs, groundwater management remained "incremental": groundwater provided an additional, but discrete, source of local water supplies.

"Conjunctive use" is a term used to refer to a whole dimension of alternate strategies of integrated management of surface and groundwater supplies.[6] When fully in place this integrated management can resolve many of the problems water agencies otherwise encounter: variations in local demand (especially seasonal variation—the "summer peak" problem); variation in available supply due to changing rainfall from year to year; the costs of constructing surface storage facilities in areas of rapidly rising land prices; the engineering problems of surface storage in an area with significant hazard of earthquakes; and substantial evaporation losses from surface storage in semi-arid climates. Conjunctive use encounters two problems: it requires coordinated management of water resources which may currently be controlled by various distinct agencies, each with its own institutional agenda; and, where aquifers are contaminated with agricultural or industrial chemicals, new water introduced into the aquifer may pick up these contaminants.

For MWD, the strong emphasis on new groundwater storage—the most limited and easily implementable of the groundwater management-efficiency possibilities—was particularly compelling. For nearly fifty years the MWD system had been designed with an emphasis on shifting local agencies away from local groundwater sources toward imported water supplies. During the 1940s and 1950s, that approach had been constrained by limited member-agency interest in the more expensive and lower-quality Colorado River water. By 1949 (during the entire first eight years of the aqueduct's operation) only a total of 146,000 acre-feet of Colorado River water had been delivered in Southern California, less than four percent of the system's capacity. Even by 1961, after San Diego, Orange County, and major Los Angeles County agencies had annexed to the MWD system, little more than 5.5 million acre-feet of Colorado River water had been delivered to local Southern California agencies, still less than half of the system's capacity.[7] Local agencies continued to rely on their groundwater, even those agencies that had annexed to MWD in anticipation of future shortfalls from future growth.

During the 1960s and 1970s, the Southern California water system tilted toward greater imported water use and a considerably more limited reliance on groundwater. On the one hand, several of the groundwater basins had been or were in the process of adjudication. These adjudication arrangements, in turn, were worked out in part on the assumption that parties could purchase imported water to meet needs above and beyond the safe yield of the groundwater basins. Thus, growth in areas that had previously relied on groundwater was now keyed to the availability of imported water, particularly after State Project water became available to Southern California in 1972.

At the same time, however, local agencies made little effort to expand their storage capacity or to use the imported water other than directly, as an additional supply. As a consequence, imported water eventually evolved into a *peaking source* for a number of local agencies, which relied on groundwater production up to the amount allowed under the adjudication and then "peaked off" the imported water to handle any increased demands (particularly during high-use periods such as the summer months). This tendency, which became especially prevalent with the arrival of State Project water, further reinforced the pressures on the imported water system where competing demands (including environmental claims for *reducing* exports out of the delta during the high-use periods) created the political dynamics that culminated in the Peripheral Canal legislation and referendum.

Thus, tension developed between the local agencies, which had come to accept imported water as a peaking source but still resisted any coordinated program, and the regional agencies such as MWD, which wanted access to groundwater basins to store the imported water. MWD had long maintained that local agencies needed to provide their own storage, including groundwater storage. That policy, however, was essentially disregarded as agencies relied on MWD to meet their peak needs from its main distribution lines. As long as there was plenty of capacity left in the lines, the notion of local storage and coordination remained elusive. But the rapid growth of the 1960s and the expectation that the boom would continue through the next several decades made the question of additional storage more pressing.

The key concern for MWD involved the difficult and potentially expensive problem of securing new storage capacity to accommodate the addition of State Project water into the system. Some of the fiercest inter-agency battles in Southern California during the 1960s and 1970s occurred over the siting of new surface storage facilities[8]; these debates were related to where and when the most rapid growth in the basin was anticipated or would be stimulated. At the same time, MWD continued to encourage local storage as a way of increasing the system's capacity to handle the anticipated rapid growth, but often to no avail. Studies during the 1960s and 1970s pointed to a phenomenal volume of unused groundwater storage capacity in the region, four and a half million acre-feet or more.[9] But the groundwater agencies had little interest in assuming the expense of expanding storage capacity, let alone providing MWD (or the State Department of Water Resources) with storage rights.

The divisions that emerged between the regional need for storage and local resistance to such plans were more than simply a conflict over regional planning versus local autonomy. Both positions, in fact, represented self-interest in light of an expanding system, strategies to deal with growth in the manner least costly to the particular agency. And MWD, which might have benefited most from local storage since it would avoid the capital costs of constructing systems that could meet peak summer demand, remained focused primarily on expanding its own infrastructure; its proposals to induce additional local storage were of lower priority than efforts to expand the State Water Project.

By the late 1970s, attempts to expand local groundwater storage and to coordinate groundwater and imported water use seemed at an impasse. Though Southern California groundwater basins were no longer being overpumped to the extent still occurring throughout the Central Valley, they remained essentially a separate system providing incremental rather than conjunctive benefits. With MWD still emphasizing expansion of the State Project, there was a vacuum around any regional efforts toward conjunctive management of local and imported water supplies for Southern California.

Into this vacuum tentatively stepped the new Brown administration in Sacramento, which seemed particularly amenable to the "efficiency" arguments of environmentalists, academics, and other critics of the water industry. Brown's Department of Water Resources, for example, launched a number of studies to explore the feasibility of expanding groundwater management programs by using existing storage sites or by expanding or creating new ones.[10] A governor's commission also released a report discussing the framework for groundwater management in both urban and agricultural areas.[11]

The emphasis on groundwater management in the Brown administration helped revitalize efforts to expand groundwater storage in Southern California. The DWR studies included preliminary investigations of the Chino, San Gabriel, and San Fernando basins (among other areas) as potential sites for storing imported State Project water. The most attractive appeared to be the large underused Chino Basin which, stretching 220 square miles east from Los Angeles, was part of the Upper Santa Ana River Watershed and ultimately drained into the Santa Ana River. The basin traversed a wide stretch of undeveloped, agricultural, and urban-industrial lands (where there had been rapid population growth during the 1970s and 1980s), encompassing one part of the high-growth Inland Empire at the eastern edge of urban Southern California. The area's population was projected to increase even more dramatically into the twenty-first century with the expansion of Ontario airport and with new subdivisions in the Chino Hills, Ontario, Rancho Cucamonga, Fontana, and elsewhere.

During the late 1970s, the Chino Basin underwent an extensive and complex adjudication that established three classes or "pools" of water users: agricultural, nonagricultural (industrial users), and appropriative (municipal users). Each of these pools was allowed to pump up to a specified amount, and the sum of these shares collectively constituted the basin's safe yield—set at 140,000 acre-feet a year.[12] As in other adjudications in the region, any excess pumping would require users to pay funds to the Chino Basin Watermaster, which would then replace such "overproduction" with supplemental, imported water, to be purchased from MWD. After the adjudication, the Chino Watermaster (designated as the Chino Basin Municipal Water District, also a member agency of MWD) steadily increased its amount of imported water from 14,244 acre-feet in the year prior to the adjudication to 36,025 acre-feet ten years later.[13] Those figures were expected to continue to grow significantly over the next couple of decades.

The DWR preliminary study, completed about the time that adjudication was coming to a close, strongly urged a new storage program that would be more directly tied into conjunctive-use objectives, including relieving peak period pressures on the state system. Though MWD staff were also interested in peak-reduction measures, the strongest concerns expressed, particularly among MWD board members at the time, were related to the intervention of the state agency within the Southern California area. Moreover, complex and delicate negotiations were still taking place between the Brown administration and State Water Project contractors over the Peripheral Canal and related facilities. The administration wanted to link the canal water development package to more innovative, environmental, and efficiency-oriented efforts, particularly groundwater management and conjunctive-use programs.[14] These efforts were strongly resisted by the agricultural agencies, which received tacit support from MWD.[15] As a result, the groundwater management proposals were separated from the canal package.

While these statewide issues were being debated, MWD, trying to separate advocates of conjunctive use from opposition to the Peripheral Canal, agreed to undertake (with DWR) a joint feasibility study on a Chino Basin Groundwater Storage Program. Four years later in March 1983, less than a year after the Peripheral Canal package was defeated, the report was finally released.[16] The joint DWR-MWD study was optimistic about prospects for storage and conjunctive use in the Chino Basin. Identifying three possible project sites, the study estimated that a large-scale groundwater storage program, based on storing an annual average of 81,000 acre-feet when excess State Project water was available (with nearly 1.7 million acre-feet of water to be ultimately stored) could increase the firm yield of the State Water Project by as much as 184,000 acre-feet per year.

The joint DWR-MWD report, however, was never implemented. Direct DWR participation was soon terminated and the plans put forth in the joint report were quickly scaled down.[17] Though the Chino Basin Municipal Water District (the Basin Watermaster and an MWD member agency) remained favorably inclined toward a storage project, the numerous municipalities and industrial and agricultural interests in the area had not yet given their full attention and support to such a program.[18] Some program, however, still seemed attractive to MWD both in terms of cost and in the amount of storage capacity available.

The Boronkay management team launched another review on the Chino Basin, this time by MWD alone (in consultation with the local agencies). After several more years of review and negotiation, including exploring new issues of groundwater contamination, a Draft Environmental Impact Report for a smaller but still substantial program was released in 1988.[19] The scale of the project was reduced to 700,000 acre-feet of SWP water, to be stored in the Basin to meet emergency and critical dry-year needs. Though the report described "an increment of flexibility toward optimizing use of Metropolitan's water delivery facilities,"[20] the conjunctive-use aspect of the project (in particular those provisions aimed at reducing peak demand on, and establishing additional firm yield in, the State Project) were not spelled out.

Most significantly, the revised MWD program was obliged to deal with the new question of water quality. The 1983 joint report had noted several water-quality concerns: whether it was appropriate to introduce State Project water (with high THM precursors) into a water basin where such precursors were minimal; the existing high nitrate levels in the basin; and the level of total dissolved solids in basin groundwater, which had precluded storage of the even-more saline Colorado River water.[21] By the late 1980s, however, these issues were overshadowed by the discovery of other widespread groundwater contamination throughout the basin. The first indications of such contamination appeared in State Department of Health Services tests in the early 1980s in response to new legislation mandating monitoring.[22] In its own review MWD also did extensive monitoring and testing. These tests indicated that basin contaminants not only included high pesticide levels (especially the now-banned pesticide DBCP), stemming from the area's agricultural activities, but also a wide range of synthetic and volatile organics (from industrial discharges and landfill sites, among other sources). All these tests suggested that the contamination might be spreading and that the sources of contamination had not been eliminated. When monitoring results were made public, the issues of water quality and storage were joined. At MWD, a few directors expressed concern that such contamination might ultimately affect a potential MWD supply source, though staff argued that any contaminated wells in the basin would not be included in MWD's storage program.[23] At the same time, local agencies and municipalities began to be concerned that higher water levels from any storage program would exacerbate their own contamination problems. (As often with contaminated groundwater sites, the higher the water table, the greater the contamination.)[24] MWD agreed that concentrations of organics could well increase as a result of the program but suggested that such increases could not be directly quantified.[25] And although MWD also agreed that such impacts could not be eliminated, the agency argued that some could be mitigated through the overall project design.

With new discoveries of well contamination during 1988 and 1989, the intersection of storage and quality problems became even more compelling. Some municipalities, such as the city of Chino and the city of Norco, worried that water quality problems were not being sufficiently addressed. These two cities, with another local water district, went to court in early 1989 to try to compel the Chino Basin Watermaster to give far greater consideration to water quality even at the risk of completion of the storage program.[26] MWD was drawn into this conflict, hoping that the long effort to expand storage in the Chino Basin might yet be resolved favorably.

The experience with the Chino Basin was the first substantial effort by the Boronkay MWD management team to elevate storage and conjunctive use to a central role in the emerging MWD "alternative supply" regional strategy. Within four years, MWD staff identified more than twelve additional potential storage sites and programs and set up studies with member agencies as diverse as the Upper San Gabriel Valley MWD and the San Diego County Water Authority to identify future potential storage capacity.[27] While many local agencies remained wary of what one agency manager called "intrusion into our own affairs,"[28] MWD did interest several agencies in potential storage programs that would benefit the local agency as well as the district. Unlike earlier periods when local agencies assumed they could simply continue to peak off the MWD system, local agency managers were now concerned about both potential supply shortages and water-quality problems that might reduce their own operating flexibility.[29] A number of agencies, such as Burbank, had been forced to turn substantially or exclusively to MWD in the wake of discovery of severe contamination of their own sources. The shift towards MWD as a primary, not just a supplemental, supplier had become even more pronounced.

Despite these new challenges, conjunctive use was not a widely held objective in Southern California. Rather than using local sources as peaking supplies to reduce reliance on MWD water during the high use summer months, local agencies (including the groundwater agencies) continued to increase their demands for more imported water.[30] By 1985, a peaking crisis had erupted within the MWD system as several of the MWD distribution lines came close to capacity during an exceptionally hot July.[31] Though some limited engineering changes alleviated the peaking problem through the next several summers, this again brought up the question of the peak and overall distribution capacity. Expanding storage capacity, the heart of the alternative supply strategies, could eventually help alleviate the issue of the peak, but only through related changes in the way water was being utilized at the agency level. The more traditional approach to peaking, expanding both the distribution system and its capacity, still remained the focus for most agencies, and this was reflected in MWD's plans for a $3 billion expansion of its distribution system.[32] The costs of this, however, would be far higher than a peaking program, which could address the demand-side of the water management equation. For MWD and several of the local agencies, expanded storage was a goal, but it was a hollow objective without further incentive to change agency demand-side habits. By the late 1980s, all these issues had come to the fore, placing in relief questions of expansion and equity as well as the effort to construct a more efficient system.

While the urban agencies began to implement their well-publicized search for alternative strategies for storage, the agricultural agencies were tentatively exploring possible new uses of the groundwater basins within their own territories. Through the 1970s, the primary focus for Kern, as with other Central Valley agricultural agencies, was to expand their use of imported water as a way to deal with overdraft.[33] Despite the increase in State Project water, groundwater overdraft continued through the 1970s. The notion that imported water would reduce the overdraft—essential to the political rationale for the State Project—had been obviated by the expansion of irrigated acreage. This failure was compounded by the growing pressure (ranging from the Governor's Commission to environmental groups and other opponents of State Project expansion) for an overall groundwater management program in the San Joaquin Valley. These were complemented by specific suggestions from Governor Jerry Brown and his staff, calling for basin storage and conjunctive-use programs throughout the state (including in Kern County).[34]

The response of the Kern landowners and the water agencies was immediately hostile. Much of the opposition was exacerbated by the "strong negative reaction" (as Stuart Pyle characterized it) toward Brown and Ronald Robie (Brown's head of the State Department of Water Resources). The landowners feared that any management program would ultimately raise the issue of "property rights," either through adjudication or through other restrictions on pumping (to prevent further overdraft). Opposition to "groundwater controls" had become a fundamental tenet for the Kern landowners and other water industry interests.[35]

While the Brown administration did not succeed in its modest plans to develop storage sites in the Kern area, water officials with the City of Bakersfield quietly began to develop their own management program that would eventually influence the agency's activities. The city's interest stemmed from its long conflict with the Kern County Land Company (subsequently Tenneco), which had rights to the Kern River in areas that had become increasingly urbanized. After a series of court actions and failed negotiations, the City and Tenneco finally agreed to a purchase price for sale of those properties by the land company to Bakersfield. Included in the acquisition was approximately 2,800 acres, located in and along the Kern River channel, which could be used as a groundwater recharge site.[36]

After the 1976–77 drought, the city decided to explore storing water at the site and began developing this program the next year. The surrounding agricultural districts and a number of other KCWA member agencies were wary of the city's banking program, since it had the potential of making the underground water supply "accountable." "The [agricultural] districts did not want to see a formalized accounting of groundwater," Bakersfield Water Manager Gene Bogard recalled. "They saw that as the first step toward adjudication."[37]

Despite these concerns, the KCWA staff, led by General Manager Pyle, saw some distinct advantages to the agency if it were able to participate in the banking program. Groundwater extractions had increased during the drought, increasing fears that the groundwater supply could at some later time become unusable. "Before the drought," Stuart Pyle recalled, "there had been a feeling that the groundwater basin could continue to decline forever and that maybe at some point it could eventually run out of water. The drought brought that eventuality home."[38]

When the county experienced heavy rains during 1978 and 1979, Pyle cautiously began to maneuver on the recharge program. In 1981, after concluding an agreement with Bakersfield, the agency began its own banking program, based on the concept of "positive balance," that is, that the "water extracted cannot exceed the water put in," as Pyle put it.[39] This cautious approach, limiting the amount of water that could be used conjunctively at any given time, largely allayed the fears of some but not all of the member agencies and board members who had thought this might approximate the much-feared groundwater-management–groundwater-controls strategy. To begin with, the amounts of water banked by the agency were relatively small, far less than the storage undertaken by the city.[40] Agency managers were also quite tentative concerning the conditions governing withdrawal, an approach that became even more striking several years later, when the agency debated how (and even if) the stored water should be withdrawn during the third and fourth drought years in 1989 and 1990.[41] Despite the caution of the KCWA staff, the storage plan continued to generate strong opposition within Kern, particularly from the Rosedale–Rio Bravo water district, a KCWA member agency drawing water from nearby wells.[42]

The Foibles of Pricing

If there has been another issue within the water industry as sensitive as water rights and local control over the terms of water availability and use, it is the matter of price. For agricultural users, the price of water is a central factor in production decisions. Resistance to price changes has been particularly pronounced among users of federal water, though it has also become significant among contractors within the State Project system. The water crisis for California agriculture (as Kern County Water Agency directors argue) has essentially been a *cheap* water crisis, as the costs for delivering imported water have risen at the same time as subsidies structured into the system became less available.

While price has always been a central concern for the agricultural agencies, it is an equally compelling, though less visible factor, among urban water agencies. In the imported water system, wholesalers, such as MWD, the San Diego County Water Authority, and the Upper San Gabriel Valley Municipal Water District, either structured their systems to maintain a low and attractive price per acre-foot, particularly to new customers, or functioned simply as "pass-through" agencies, adding a small surcharge to cover costs.

At the local utility level, the price of water was also kept low, particularly for larger users favored by the flat or declining-block rates most prevalent throughout Southern California. Neither wholesalers nor local utilities structured rates around *time of use*, on a seasonal or daily basis. Water rates not only encouraged use, including peak demands, they favored the newest and largest users, which often controlled the terms of debate on price.

These pricing arrangements functioned without challenge through design and construction of the region's elaborate water systems, but they encouraged increasing use of imported water. Within MWD, annexation rates were heavily subsidized, most operational and capital costs were paid through tax assessments rather than user charges, and overall user charges were set on the basis of a "postage stamp" rate, that is, through averaging all costs, including the incremental marginal costs of additional construction. At the local utility level, most rates were designed on the assumption of "economies of scale" which presumed that increased use ultimately saved money. To encourage this, utilities set up a "declining block" pricing structure—the larger the increment used, the lower the cost per unit. There was no recognition that water was a limited resource, which should be allocated in a way that put it to the most desirable uses: following the Laguna Doctrine, the agencies assumed that imported water would be available to meet any increase (present or future) in water requirements. Some utilities even assumed that the cost of imported water might match (or even be lower than) the cost to store and pump water locally. In the mid-1970s, when stresses on the State Project system were already visible, the city of Beverly Hills abandoned its local water supply and capped its wells, deciding that the costs of upgrading its own system were too high and anticipating that MWD imported water would be *permanently* available at lower cost.[43]

For the power utilities, the energy crisis had led to pressure to change their management strategy. The declining block pricing structure, favored by both electric and water utilities, came under sharp attack from consumer groups outraged by escalating electric bills and energy industry critics who focused on issues of conservation and efficiency. As a result, electric utilities set aside declining-block pricing and explored a range of new rate structures designed to lower per capita use and address questions of equity. This directly affected those utilities, such as the Los Angeles Department of Water and Power (DWP) and the Burbank Public Service Department, which delivered both electricity and water. These agencies were the first to revise their water-pricing policies. Burbank established an "inclining-block" approach based on a scale that inclined *upwards* the larger the meter size. It also instituted a demand charge based on the highest monthly use during the peak use summer-month periods of July through October, with new rates reestablished annually beginning with the July usage. The demand charge was explicitly designed to link peak reduction with an overall reduction in per capita use.[44]

In the 1980s, these innovative rate structures were more the exception than the rule among Southern California water agencies. Most agencies still maintained either a declining block or flat rate and seasonal charges were almost nonexistent. Even the Los Angeles DWP, which in 1986 instituted a seasonal pricing program based on higher summer charges, structured the program with a relatively small price differential, estimating only a modest reduction in use as a result.

The strongest incentive to change local rates during the early 1980s was related to the changing *wholesale* price of water. During this period, rates for imported water delivered to local agencies escalated dramatically (at one point doubling in less than three years) in contrast with the minimal price increases that had occurred during much of MWD's earlier history.[45] These sudden increases in price were related to a number of factors, including the decision to reduce the role of taxes in meeting capital and operating costs, increases in state charges that were related to increased energy costs in the State system, and a significant drop in water sales in one especially wet year, which left the wholesale agencies with operating deficits. These increases created a new perception among local utilities, making the price of water a new factor in planning. As a result, several agencies did begin to modify their rates, including phasing out declining blocks.[46]

This shift primarily reflected the change of perception about future prices. Through the 1970s, imported water, though still more expensive than the costs of pumping local water, was perceived as a stable and relatively inexpensive source of supply. This was due in part to the significant contribution of real-property taxes to meeting MWD's operational and capital costs. In the first forty years of such taxes within the MWD service area, more than $1.13 billion in tax receipts had been collected, of which the city of Los Angeles alone had contributed nearly $350 million, or more than 30 percent of the total.[47] Though the actual tax rates had steadily declined (from a 1946 peak of 50 cents per $100 assessed valuation), the total tax receipts available to the district were considerable and continued to climb, reaching $93 million (based on 9.5 cents per $100 assessed valuation) in fiscal year 1983–84 when several financial issues came to a head.[48]

This issue of tax subsidies had long been a sensitive matter between different member agencies within MWD. The high tax rates of the 1930s through the late 1940s, made necessary by low sales, had been justified as a long-term investment in a system that every one, including Los Angeles, would require to support future growth. Though the tax rate did begin to decline during the 1950s (in part as a result of new annexations that increased both the tax base and overall water sales), objections to the *equity* of this system had become even more pronounced. The City of Los Angeles, which paid the giant's share of taxes but took a dwindling share of water purchases, felt particularly aggrieved, but its directors were not fully able to restructure the system.[49] They did win certain compromises, particularly Resolution 5821, passed in September 1960, which stipulated that water purchasers (rate payers) would absorb operation and maintenance costs and at least half of all remaining capital charges after annexation fees.[50]

During the 1960s and 1970s the tax-rate issue had continued to fester within MWD, pitting the City of Los Angeles against the San Diego County Water Authority, the largest user of water in the MWD system. Los Angeles initiated a lawsuit over the issue in 1975, resulting in another out-of-court compromise resolution, this time establishing a complex "proportionate-use formula" to allocate costs between taxes and rates.[51] This compromise was quickly subject to criticism, which became more intense during the political maneuvering about the Peripheral Canal. Canal critics pointed out Los Angeles's vulnerability on the issue, which would be exacerbated with the additional costs resulting from the canal package of facilities. Dissatisfaction with this compromise was not limited to canal critics; Los Angeles's continuing substantial tax burden had long been a focus for complaint of both the City Administrative Office (CAO) and certain council members. The CAO prepared several reports exploring whether the City of Los Angeles should actually withdraw from the MWD system.[52] By 1983–1984, legislative maneuvers had once again forced the issue to a head. This time, it was agreed that tax payments to MWD would be significantly reduced by 1990. This latest compromise strongly suggested that the MWD's long reliance on taxes was finally drawing to a close.

If taxes were reduced, then rates would invariably go up. By how much, however, depended on a range of other circumstances, such as volume of sales and other available sources of income. The recognition that a new pattern of increased rates had set in was dramatically experienced during the same 1983–84 water year when the taxes issue became so visible. During the summer and fall of 1983, MWD for the first time in its history experienced the first stage of a fiscal crisis. Reserve funds had been rapidly depleted in the face of an unexpected, extraordinary drop in water sales during a particularly wet year, combined with additional costs associated with the State Water Project. Water industry critics dubbed the issue the "pray for drought" water crisis, since the problems were related to a *decline* in sales caused in part by greater-than-anticipated rainfall. MWD management, which had long sought to increase rates, used the opportunity to initiate an unprecedented $53 an acre-foot (more than 25 percent) mid-year rate increase, the first out-of-cycle rate increase in MWD history.[53] In the next few years other new fiscal policies were also established, including bigger fund reserves, a "rate stabilization" plan that eliminated significant rate decreases even when end-of-year balances were positive, and a more conservative method of calculating projected sales and revenues.[54] What failed to emerge was any significant rate restructuring, either by establishing new, fixed sources of income or by dealing with the equity issues associated with the existing "postage stamp" rate. Though MWD managers raised the possibility of such discussion of new rates or charges (to be adopted before the 1990 changes on taxes),[55] the board failed to take up this possibility through a systematic public airing of the issues. Instead, in the next several years, in the midst of a new dry-year cycle, the focus shifted to the question of peak demand and to the pricing issues associated with it.

As early as 1969, in anticipation of the arrival of State Project water and continuing high growth rates, MWD managers had raised the idea of a pricing policy designed to reduce peak demand within the MWD system.[56] Such a policy might address several related problems: the possibility that demand might outstrip capacity prior to construction of new distribution facilities, the need for incentives to encourage greater local storage, and the search for another source of revenue without instituting a large, overall rate increase. The idea of a peak or seasonal rate was raised again in 1974 and 1977.[57] But initiation of any such program was effectively blocked by agencies with large agricultural clients and those with limited storage facilities (San Diego and several of the Inland Empire agencies).[58] Without a strong bloc of supporters for seasonal rates, the idea was each time withdrawn in favor of pricing policies that focused on dry-year or emergency storage needs.[59]

As peaking problems came to preoccupy MWD during the mid 1980s, several district staff, including its new chief economist Tim Quinn and Director of Planning Wiley Horne, began to explore the possibility of a seasonal rate once again. Horne and Quinn felt such a program could delay the need for new distribution facilities, which would cost the district billions of dollars. "The figures look good," Quinn would comment to other MWD staff and directors in explaining how the system would pay off for both MWD and member agencies. Such a program, Quinn argued, would postpone the anticipated system expansion expenses and, at the same time, would provide local agencies with an additional incentive to expand storage capacity, to take advantage of the seasonal price differential. Quinn and Horne, however, were reluctant to present seasonal pricing as a conservation effort, since stimulating effective conservation (reduction in summer use) would require local agencies also to take up seasonal rates, and might thus seem to violate local agency prerogatives in setting their own rates.[60]

After more than a year of research and lobbying, MWD staff—at a "System Overview" workshop—presented the conceptual outlines of their seasonal pricing program, though without any specific figures or recommendations.[61] It was identified primarily as part of the effort to deal with the system's need for expansion. Nevertheless, the plan was immediately subject to strong criticism, led by San Diego directors who continued to fear that such a pricing program would disadvantage their agency. Once again, seasonal pricing (the "S" word, as Quinn ironically dubbed it)[62] had to be shelved, only to be brought back in 1989 in the form of a seasonal "storage" program.[63] Instead of constructing a price differential on higher summer month rates, this plan offered price *reductions* for the winter months. MWD staff argued that this program merely extended previous efforts to use price as an incentive to increase water availability during critically dry periods.[64]

Seasonal pricing, with its explicit conjunctive use and conservation-related goals, had given way to a storage incentive program with price reduction incentives to increase storage capacity. Where seasonal pricing would also have encouraged MWD clients to reserve their own local supply, particularly groundwater, for peak demands and to back off on the claims they made for increased capacity for imported summer water, the storage incentive program sought to set up more insurance against severe drought by expanding storage capacity, not to contain increasing demand. Tentative exploration of a demand-side strategy had been reduced to another supply-oriented mechanism for meeting the dominant system objective: expansion for a growth-driven future.

The Cycle of Expansion

By the late 1980s, as water agencies sought to adjust to an era of alternative supply strategies, the long-standing mission of the Southern California urban water industry (embodied in the Laguna Declaration) remained expansion of the system to meet any possible growth. Growth and expansion, water agency managers liked to say, were as inevitable as birth itself, and it would not only be wrong but foolish to try to tamper with it. Those innovative supply strategies the agencies adopted—such as water marketing, other reallocations of costs, or incentives for increased storage—did not contradict the mission of expansion but strengthened the resolve to sustain it, in response to what were seen as setbacks to future water development. Even the peaking efforts, such as the seasonal storage pricing initiative, were a cost-savings device to extend the time before new infrastructure and new supplies became necessary.

The commitment to expansion was most clearly articulated in the continuing agency focus on new facilities within the region. These facilities further strengthened the emphasis on imported water as the "final solution" for a permanent cycle of expansion. All the high growth areas in Southern California (the eastern and northern ends of San Diego county, the south coast areas of Orange County, the Inland Empire areas of Riverside, San Bernardino, and Orange counties, and the border area between Los Angeles and Ventura counties) were in need of new or expanded imported water facilities to sustain continuing high growth rates. The discussions of the mid- and late-1980s about system expansion, culminating in MWD's $3 billion facilities plan, paralleled earlier discussions about the need for facilities to sustain widening growth. The physical location and timing of development of new water infrastructure in Southern California still paralleled the lines of growth and development through the region. Water availability and growth were still interchangeable concepts.

By the late 1980s, alternative supply strategies had become essential to this relationship. Innovative programs were directly related to the need to secure additional supplies. Even conservation programs, long a stepchild of agency policy, received additional support during the late 1980s precisely as a form of securing additional supplies. The Conservation Credits Program (a new and innovative program established during the late 1980s) elaborated this theme.[65] The program was modeled after the "Local Projects Program" which had been initiated during the Peripheral Canal period, then dropped, and finally revived in a modified form in the late 1980s. The revised Local Projects programs, most of which were essentially local agency reclamation efforts such as desalinization or waste water reuse, were financially supported by MWD, which subsidized them with credits set at no less than the avoided energy cost of pumping State Project water into Southern California.[66] This notion of "replacement value" associated with the effort did not imply cutting back imported water supplies; it meant additional support in securing necessary supplies. Similarly, the Conservation Credits program, first employed to help subsidize a Santa Monica program to convert the city to the use of low flush toilets, was justified as a form of additional support for supplies, albeit by reducing demand.[67] The notion of conservation as a supply source, which came into prominence with electrical utilities during the 1970s, was now at last seen favorably by the water agencies more than a decade later.[68]

This recognition of demand reduction as a supply source, however, was not extended into the area of pricing. For one, water planners in much of Southern California were skeptical of any relationship between price and demand. The concept of price elasticity for example—an inverse relationship between price and demand based on demand being sensitive to price—had long been rejected at MWD on the basis that water was too essential for its use to be influenced by price. At the local agency level, the average residential unit price of water had remained low enough over the years that local rate structures, including declining blocks, which disadvantaged smaller users, escaped public attention. The rise in the cost of wholesale water, however, elevated the issue of price at the agency level and highlighted the growth and equity issues associated with long-standing pricing policies. These issues would once more come into play with the construction of additional—and expensive—facilities to meet the new growth scenarios in the region.

How to allocate costs in the regional system was not a new issue. The construction of the State Water Project had led several more-developed agencies to question the method of average cost pricing—sharing costs on an equal basis, no matter what the benefits. Both Los Angeles and Santa Monica initiated proposals during the 1960s to differentiate water rates according to sources of supply, which would have set up the basis for marginal pricing where new users would pay the costs of new and more expensive water.[69] Several more-developed agencies, most located in Los Angeles County, also objected to the significant subsidies associated with annexation rates.

Annexation rates during the 1940s and 1950s had been heavily subsidized on the justification that the district desperately needed to increase its level of sales of Colorado River water and could only do so by expanding the MWD service area. During the 1960s and 1970s, annexation fees were modified, partly as a reflection of changing assumptions about water availability.[70] Still, annexation charges were significantly underpriced relative to any criterion which measured the expense to the district of supplying additional water to new areas. When the issue flared during the Peripheral Canal campaign, General Manager E. L. Griffith justified the policy by suggesting that by restructuring the annexation fees, MWD would ultimately influence and redirect growth patterns—a taboo subject—since there were still undeveloped lands within the existing and already annexed service areas of the high growth agencies.[71]

By the late 1980s, yet another annexation study had been initiated, presenting a series of alternative pricing proposals which highlighted both the significant price breaks and the range of pricing alternatives. The largest price increase was associated with an approach that identified the *marginal* costs (to the district and other existing member agencies) directly related to the costs of an additional increment of supply. The marginal rate—an astounding $4,000 to $40,000 per acre-foot for the cost of developing new water supplies—was quickly dismissed as essentially eliminating any potential for annexation.[72]

The notion of "marginal pricing," which contrasted directly with averaging costs to all agencies (the basis of the postage-stamp rate), began to gain currency during the late 1980s among a handful of agencies (particularly Pasadena and Burbank), which were concerned about the inequities of spreading the $3 billion costs of the new system expansion program. Though a distinct minority, these agencies and their representatives began to raise issues that cut to the heart of the water industry mission. They argued that the rationale behind system expansion (based on the fact that MWD, as its Planning Director put it, was "becoming the primary supplier to growth areas"[73]), significantly disadvantaged the developed areas, where increases in water use were minimal or associated with the loss of local water supplies due to contaminated wells.[74] A pricing system where costs would be directly allied to benefits would not only be more equitable, but would more directly identify the costs of system expansion. In this way, the costs of expansion could be defined as marginal costs, since additional facilities were based on obtaining that additional—and more costly—unit of water.[75]

Opposition to marginal pricing—and justification of existing water industry arrangements—was linked to the conception of the distribution of benefits of growth and expansion. During the debates over MWD tax policy, San Diego argued that the benefits of a subsidized rate structure were growth benefits[76]: the entire Southern California region, including its developed areas, gained in this way from the cycle of expansion that brought with it greater population growth, industrial activity, jobs, and other forms of economic activity. Growth, they argued, was a regional and not a local benefit and the presumed mission of water agency activity—meeting the growth, whatever the circumstance—remained as compelling as ever.

To carry out that mission, efficiency as a supply strategy had become a new and crucial component of water industry activity. The form of that activity, whether increased storage, expanded conservation, or reduction of interim capacity problems coexisted with the traditional agenda—new distribution facilities, increased long-term capacity,[77] and ultimately (if the political will could be reestablished) new water development in Northern California. The water industry was indeed changing, only the better to carry out its mission and extend its role as integral to the patterns of regional growth.

11

Toward a New Mission

In Southern California water development has been integral to the growth agenda. Water agencies, led by vigorous entrepreneurs who sought aggressively to capture and secure distant sources of supply so that their service areas could flourish and expand, became central to the political and institutional setting that promoted and sustained the urban, industrial, and agricultural expansion of the region. Water agencies were closely tied into the growth coalitions: their leadership was drawn from the business and political elites who shaped the growth agendas; and they helped frame the conceptual basis of the legislation, planning, investments, administrative actions, and cultural perceptions that moved this region toward extraordinary economic expansion.

Today water leaders say that water development has not caused growth. It has, however, both created growth's essential preconditions—through unlimited water availability, pricing subsidies, and the commitment of capital to a huge public works infrastructure—and allowed each cycle of expansion to continue unchecked by physical or environmental limits. Now that explicit growth agendas have become less popular, the water agencies have become more defensive in justifying their activities. "People will still have babies," water leaders assert, suggesting that the source of growth is human nature, and that growth is thus inevitable. The agencies predict greater population growth, greater economic activity, and more urban expansion, and then assert that they must secure the new supplies necessary to meet those needs. According to this scenario, the people of Southern California demand such water because they know they will need it. The agencies' concern is not whether but how to secure such supplies, particularly given increasing constraints on new water development. Innovative supply strategies have thus become part of the quest to meet the inevitable requirements of growth.

There are signs, however, that these growth agendas have reached an impasse, or at least have run up against compelling limits. We see an exhaustion of environmental resources—contaminated water, polluted air basins, sewage capacity problems, intractable hazardous waste sites, solid waste disposal crises—as a result of such growth. Transportation grid lock, a crisis of affordable housing, and abandonment of public education are other signs; so too, the deepening of the "widening divide" between rich and poor, through the creation of a two-tier economic system. "Boom" and "growth" in this context are really misnomers that disguise issues of equity and of the quality of daily life. At the same time, the political structures and institutions designed to deal with such problems appear inaccessible and often paralyzed. In each area of policy, traditional agendas are at stake, and the reevaluation of long-standing activities and objectives has become of great importance.

For the water agencies, this process of review and evaluation has been uncertain and has not been pursued with enthusiasm. Agency boards and management see accountability more as a matter of improving public relations or obtaining political clout than of opening up the policy process to new input. Where outsiders have been able to influence policy, it has almost always been through adversarial relationships and through outside pressure such as legal action or political initiatives. The water agencies still remain locked into the narrowly drawn culture of the water industry, despite new public challenges, increased awareness, and resistance on such key matters as water quality, environmental impacts, and the allocation of the costs of new development.

In the area of water quality, agency actions have been regulation-driven (reactive, not proactive) and focused primarily on minimizing agency costs of treatment. At the same time, water agencies have been leaders in opposition to new regulations and in seeking to encourage public skepticism about the significance of chemical contamination. In this they have not only sided with the polluters (and joined their coalitions) but, as with the Safe Drinking Water Act Amendments, have taken the lead in challenging key provisions of legislation and implementation. Where agencies have explored more innovative solutions, such as MWD's Source Reduction Study or the San Gabriel agencies' search for mechanisms to reduce contamination, they have been motivated by concern over potential losses—of supply, due to regulation of water quality, and of public credibility.

The intense public interest in water-quality matters has not led agencies to reevaluate their policies; rather, agency responses reflect a desire to improve their public image through more effective public relations, the better to dismiss those public concerns. Though water agencies were at the forefront of public health when bacterial contamination was the hazard in question, now these agencies treat water-quality issues as externally imposed regulations that threaten their use of groundwater or of groundwater basins for storage, not as a public health problem in which they might take a constructive and leading role.

Similarly, agencies' new interest in water markets and transfer arrangements, though innovative by contrast to their earlier exclusive focus on new source development, reflects the problematic state of water policy. When new construction to establish new allocations has been blocked (perhaps permanently) both by rising political opposition and by the real marginal costs of this new development, then reallocating existing supplies becomes the obvious next step. The variety of market and transfer proposals reflects the benefits of this strategy, both from the point of view of the sellers, since the restructuring of certain agricultural sectors makes these water transfers more profitable than continued cultivation, and of the buyers, since urban water agencies, in a growing urban economy, are fast becoming the major "water seekers." Transfers between agencies serving different regions, however, raise major equity and "value" issues from the perspective of both buyer and seller communities. Most water transfers are intended to extend growth through providing more cheap water, not to reallocate water to its best use. Though some transfers have been tied to conservation and conjunctive-use concepts rather than to outright sale of land or water rights, they fail to address the more encompassing issues of cultural, social, and economic impacts of such transfers on the affected communities. By avoiding this, agencies still remain aloof from those larger matters of regional policy that their actions influence but which they themselves fail to address.

More importantly, as a result the water agencies continue to refuse to enter the debates on growth and quality of daily life, choosing instead to maintain their special relationship to the growth constituencies and growth policies they have so long supported. The apparent transition in water development has included expanded interest in a variety of innovative "efficiency" strategies, including storage, pricing, and expanded efforts at conservation, but these have been structured as supply-side measures designed to stretch existing supplies to allow continued unlimited growth, rather than demand-side strategies designed to reduce the overall demand for water. Such demand-side approaches, including marginal pricing, annexation policies, and user fees would shift agency focus toward a balanced consideration of allocation within, not just between, agency service areas and would thus directly address the question of how to manage urban growth and the related questions of equity, economic imbalance, and the quality of daily life.

By entering the arena of growth management of this kind, water agencies would more directly link questions of accountability and innovation. Water agency leaders have argued that they are ill-equipped to deal with growth-management issues such as land use and that these are more appropriately addressed by other agencies. But water agencies, as former MWD board member Ellen Stern Harris has stated, have long been land-use planners de facto; to continue to deny this makes effective and democratic debate over land-use policy impossible. Water agencies, of course, cannot make growth management decisions in isolation, but if the role of water agency decisions in this issue is better recognized by the agencies and the public at large, this recognition highlights the social, not just the technical, nature of water-policy choices. This would encourage access and participation by a public increasingly concerned about such matters.

How can such a shift in emphasis and activity be accomplished? Although the agencies remain relatively insular, the expanded debate on issues of growth, environmental degradation, and quality of daily life has brought more attention to and interest in water agencies and their activities. What has been lacking is a systemic critique of the agency itself and its link to the related matters of democratic scrutiny and restructuring of local government. This study is intended to begin that critique and to explore the basis for new forms of agency planning, governance, and public policy.

These new forms would directly touch the matters that this study explores: the nature and process of agency decision making and how such pivotal issues as water quality, reallocations, and management perspectives are being addressed. What follows are proposals that suggest directions for these changes, flowing directly from our analysis here.

Change the Mission
of the Water Agencies

Water agencies have seen their mission as one of continuous expansion: to paraphrase the Laguna Declaration, agencies have chosen to provide water to whoever claims it, no matter the circumstances or the direct or indirect costs. Factors of cost, social consequence, and environmental impact have been ignored or poorly addressed. *A new mission would see water decisions as contributing to the quality of daily life in fact and not just rhetorically, by linking water subsidies to questions of equity and of socially acceptable and desirable land-use patterns, and by elevating water quality to a central concern.*

That could be accomplished by launching an extensive, public debate and discussion, aimed at evaluating and structuring a new, inclusive, mission statement. This discussion and debate should include both wholesale and retail, and urban and agricultural agencies and all of those they serve.

Make Water Quality a Priority

Since chlorination and physical treatment were introduced more than eighty years ago, water agencies have distinguished what goes into the water from whether the water is safe to drink. But water contamination results from historical and contemporary patterns of industrial, agricultural, and urban activity. In addressing the new problems of contamination only, or primarily, in terms of treatment costs (and through attempts to limit the stringency of standards), the agencies have avoided confronting the sources of pollution. Instead, they have focused on their own potential internal costs and on whether they will be "let off the hook" by some political agreement that these hazards are an inevitable "public risk," just another unfortunate but necessary side effect of the benefits of modern life. Water agencies have not taken the lead in raising the importance of a conservative and effective focus on protecting public health. Water agencies should lead the efforts to reduce contamination, while selecting clean-up and treatment-alternative decisions on the basis of their responsibility to public health; alternative technologies, both engineering and management, must be compared on the basis of their long-term effectiveness, not just the lowest short-term cost. *It is not reasonable for agencies to plan for supply needs for the following fifty years but then to choose among water-quality policies based only on short-term cost. It is not reasonable because it is not balanced, but also, because supply and water-quality questions are so inextricably entangled that it is impossible to separate the two issues in planning for the future of the region.*

Water agencies need to establish policies, join coalitions, and use their lobbying powers to promote effective source-reduction programs, both within their own service areas and on a larger regional, state, and national scale. Water agencies should also seek to address the principle of "the polluter must pay," while promoting the most comprehensive, long-range clean-up strategies.

Renegotiate the Relationships Among Agencies

In the past, wholesaler agencies like the Metropolitan Water District have made decisions that have substantial effects internal to the territories of their client-member agencies. They have used the tax base of already urbanized areas (based primarily on residential land use) to support the construction of delivery systems that make possible urban expansion outside these settled areas. They have used their political power to establish a standard agenda for the whole Southern California region, an agenda that has not been sensitive to the particular interests of local communities. It is time to turn this around. *Where there is a compelling common interest in water problems in Southern California today, it is in the area of water quality.* MWD *should set aside its growth agenda and take the lead in addressing the water quality problem, and in offering technical and financial support to its member agencies where those problems are most severe.* Groundwater contamination, both existing and continuing, is likely to have a greater effect on successful management of the Southern California water supply in the foreseeable future than any shortfall in imported water. MWD has argued that its mission is to import water, not to manage it—but it has acted to construct a regional water economy that has used imported water as a drug to allow denial of accumulating local problems. Only MWD is in the institutional and financial position to support the agency initiatives that will be required to address this issue successfully, and to manage the negotiations and adjustments between Southern California agencies this problem will require. In developing a new common mission statement, with all its policy implications, the Southern California agencies, as part of their public outreach and program of accountability, need explicitly to elevate water quality to the top of their agendas.

Ground Reallocation Decisions in Social As Well As Economic Criteria

Interest in transfers between agencies has stemmed largely from the shifting economic and political constraints on new water development. As such, new arrangements have a largely (and limited) economic rationale; are the costs favorable for the buyer and the selling price advantageous to the seller? There are related questions of jurisdiction and control, but even these institutional impediments are often addressed in economic terms. *Transfers, however, have immediate and indirect regional, social consequences that must be addressed as part of evaluating any such arrangement. The rising economic power of urban Southern California does not justify closing off development alternatives for agricultural communities, though the corporate owners of this agricultural land might choose such local closure if it offers greater benefits to their enterprises.* Effective evaluation of these consequences might include, as in the case of the IID-MWD SWAP, a community impact analysis (and result, perhaps, in compensation through a community impact fund) or, as in the Devil's Den–Lake Castaic deal, an evaluation of economic development alternatives as part of the community review process. Reallocation decisions also need to be evaluated in the buyer communities, as part of the overall "mission" restructuring process.

Establish a Demand-Side Planning Focus

The new interest in efficiency and alternative supply-side management strategies has not led to development of a demand-side focus, which would more directly address questions of growth and its social, economic, and environmental consequences. *A demand-side approach would explore—through pricing and other social policies—questions of equity (not only who should pay, but how much they should pay), how growth might or might not be directed, and other community goals.*

Create New, Democratic Structures

This most crucial change in agency activity is central to the establishment of new policies. *Public input and accountability must become central to the procedures and purposes of agencies* that *have long functioned as quasi-private institutions.* This process of democratization must address selection of the governing bodies as well as redefinition of the organizational culture. Elections should be made viable, particularly for municipalities. For regional wholesalers, those appointed to boards must also be held more accountable—and their activities made more visible—to both elected officials and the public. Member agencies of wholesaler organizations, like MWD, San Diego CWA, and KCWA, should be provided the legal option of electing rather than appointing their delegates to the wholesaler agency boards. Time limits on appointments should be explored. More organized public interest should also be encouraged, perhaps through a utility dues check-off system, as has been established in several states for electrical utilities. Ultimately, the water industry, including the water agencies, has to be opened up to greater scrutiny and new forms of participation if any change in agenda is to occur.

If we link accountability and innovation, we can begin to change the discourse about water in Southern California and other areas of the country. The commodity value of water (to the industry's particular constituency), which has for so long shaped the discourse and set the policy framework, is essentially what is at question in this debate. In its place can emerge a conception of the *community* value of water, and with it, a new public agency, central to community life and to fulfilling the community's objectives.

Part IV

Reference Material

Notes

Research for *Thirst for Growth* relied almost entirely on primary source material, including agency publications, letters, memoranda, interviews, personal observations, government reports, and a wide variety of financial and technical documents. In its attention to the activities and agendas of local agencies, this study covers new ground.

Few scholars have previously studied the development of water policy at the local level. Most published work on water issues addresses federal and state agencies and their impact on water resources decisions, implying that the initiative in such decisions appears above the local level. To evaluate the importance of local initiatives, we thoroughly reviewed a huge body of local documentary and participant sources. We contrast our findings with the existing literature on state and federal initiatives, referred to where appropriate in notes to the text.

The notes to the text identify the specific documents and sources from which our analysis is developed. Where the notes refer to documents or internal memoranda, researchers are most likely to locate them through the libraries or archives of the agencies concerned. The nature of this research, like that of much historical research which returns to primary sources, rests on the depth and complexity of the primary evidence and makes the footnotes the best basis for bibliographic inquiry.

Introduction

Note: Through 1990, MWD's Southern California reservoirs averaged 90 percent of capacity, and although storage levels were down considerably in Northern California reservoirs, MWD planners envisaged a series of alternative scenarios to allow the district to secure sufficient additional supplies. MWD's limited mandatory rationing plan adopted in December 1990, reduced deliveries to most urban users (noninterruptible water contracts) by 5 percent and to agricultural and other users covered by interruptible water contracts by 20 percent. These imposed restrictions were far less stringent than any of the other mandatory plans adopted elsewhere in the state. See "Incremental Interruption and Conservation Plan—Selection of Appropriate Conservation Level," letter of general manager to the MWD Board, December 10, 1990. See also General Manager's reports for the months of June, July, and August 1990, Metropolitan Water District of Southern California; interviews with Carl Boronkay, Richard Balcerzak, Duane Georgeson, and Wiley Horne (all 1990).

Chapter 1 *"The Mighty MET": A Center of Power*

1. The Metropolitan Water District of Southern California (MWD), *Annual Report* for the Fiscal Year July 1, 1987, to June 30, 1988, Los Angeles, 1988 (hereafter cited as MWD *Annual Report*).

2. See Memorandum from Bob Gomperz, Metropolitan Water District Public Information Department, to Robert Gottlieb, July 27, 1987; see also 1989–1990 MWD *Annual Report* (1990).

3. MWD 1987–88 *Annual Report* (1988); San Diego County Water Authority *41st Annual Report* (1987); *LA 2000: A City for the Future* (Final Report of the Los Angeles 2000 Committee, Los Angeles, November 15, 1988); Edward W. Soja, Rebecca Morales, and Goetz Wolf, 1983, "Urban Restructuring: An analysis of social and spatial change in Los Angeles," *Economic Geography* 59:195–230; Edward W. Soja, Allan D. Heskin, and Marco Cenzatti, 1985, "Los Angeles: Through the Kaleidoscope of Urban Restructuring," UCLA Graduate School of Architecture and Urban Planning.

4. The legislation was approved by the governor on May 10, 1927, and went into effect July 29, 1927. Metropolitan Water District Act, State of California, Chapter 429, Statutes 1927, p. 694.

5. See *The Metropolitan Water District of Southern California: History and First Annual Report*, for the period ending June 30, 1938, (compiled and edited by Charles A. Bissell), Los Angeles, 1939.

6. See Vincent Ostrom, 1953, *Water and Politics: A Study of Water Policies and Administration in the Development of Los Angeles*, Los Angeles: Haynes Foundation; Robert Gottlieb, 1988, *A Life of Its Own: The Politics and Power of Water*, San Diego: Harcourt Brace Jovanovich.

7. See MWD, *History and First Annual Report*, pp. 333–353; "1976 Analysis of Annexation Policy of the Metropolitan Water District of Southern California," prepared by the offices of the general manager and general counsel, February 1976.

8. Joseph Jensen, 1970, "Developing California's Natural Resources," UCLA Oral History Program (hereafter Joseph Jensen oral history); "Joseph Jensen," Biog-

raphy, Metropolitan Water District, February 1, 1973.

9. Whitsett, who had been called "the founder of Van Nuys," was an active real estate developer and banker and had been part of the land syndicate (organized by *Los Angeles Times* owner Harry Chandler and other local leaders) that subdivided large areas of the San Fernando Valley. Whitsett, who remained chairman of the MWD Board for nearly eighteen years, set the model of an aggressive, expansion-oriented leader as the district chair. William P. Whitsett, 1938, [untitled biographical statement], MWD; "William P. Whitsett, Van Nuys Founder, Philanthropist Dies," *The Valley News*, April 9, 1965.

10. MWD, *History and First Annual Report*, 1939; Joseph Jensen oral history; Jerome W. Millman, 1957, "Economic Problems of the Metropolitan Water District of Southern California," *Proceedings of the 32nd Annual Conference of the Western Economic Association.*

11. See Metropolitan Water District of Southern California, "Reply to Memorandum of Roy L. Donley, Councilman, Fifth District," " 'Does the Colorado River Aqueduct Mean Economic Suicide for the City of Los Angeles?' " Los Angeles, April 3, 1933.

12. Cited in 1976 Analysis of Annexation Policy of the Metropolitan Water District of Southern California, February 1976.

13. See Metropolitan Water District of Southern California, *Report on Forecast of Growth of Metropolitan Area and Permissible Rates for Colorado River Water,* May 21, 1931, Los Angeles.

14. 1976 Analysis of Annexation policy, MWD, February 1976.

15. See 1950 *Census of Population*, volume 1, Number of Inhabitants, United States Department of Commerce, pp. 5–10.

16. Joseph Jensen oral history. For the first fifteen years of operation, deliveries of Colorado River water amounted to only 12.14 percent of the aqueduct's capacity (*Eighteenth Annual Report* [1955–56]), MWD of Southern California, 1956, pp. 42–43).

17. 1976 Analysis of Annexation Policy, MWD, February 1976, p. 4.

18. The actual amount derived from tax collections, however, continued to increase even as the rates later went down, reflecting both the increased value of regional land and the expanding district service area. For a composite portrait of the district's first thirty-five years of tax collections, see MWD 1972 *Annual Report*, Tables 36 and 37.

19. Joseph Jensen oral history; 1976 Analysis of Annexation Policy.

20. 1976 Analysis of Annexation Policy, MWD.

21. MWD *Annual Reports* 1943, 1947; San Diego County Water Authority *First Annual Report* (1944–46).

22. Joseph Jensen oral history.

23. Joseph Jensen oral history: *William H. Jennings: Water Lawyer*, UCLA Oral History, 1967.

24. Calculated from MWD *Annual Report*, 1987–88.

25. MWD *Annual Report*, FY 1954–55, 1955.

26. See "Statement of Conditions Governing Annexation to the Metropolitan Water District of Southern California," Special Water Problems Committee, Board of Directors, Metropolitan Water District of Southern California, October 26, 1938.

27. "Laguna Declaration Statement of Policy," Metropolitan Water District of Southern California, approved by the Board of Directors of the Metropolitan Water District of Southern California, December 16, 1952.

28. Joseph Jensen oral history; see also "Ramifications; engineering, legal and financial if the City withdraws from the Metropolitan Water District of Southern California," Report from the City Administrative Officer to the Water and Power Committee, Los Angeles City Council, May 12, 1970.

29. See "Gigantic Water Battle of 20 Years Ago Recalled," Harvey Feit, *San Bernardino Sun*, December 23, 1985; also, Interviews with Howard Hawkins (1987); Ralph Helm (1986); MWD *26th Annual Report* (1964), p. 143.

30. See James H. Krieger and Harvey O. Banks, 1962, "Ground Water Basin Management," *California Law Review* 50:56–77; Albert J. Lipson, 1978, *Efficient Water Use in California: The Evolution of Groundwater Management in Southern California*. Rand Corporation, Santa Monica R-2387/2-CSA/RP (November 1978).

31. Interview with E. Thornton Ibbetson (1987); for a background to the development of the Central Basin and West Basin areas and the formation of their local water industries, see Elina Ostrom, *Public Entrepreneurship: A Case Study of Groundwater Basin Management*, unpublished dissertation (Political Science), UCLA, 1965.

32. Interviews with Howard Hawkins (1986); Earle Blais (1987); Robert Gough (1986); Donald Brooks (1987); E. L. Griffith (1983).

33. During the late 1940s and early 1950s, the district had even entertained constructing *its own* Northern California supply system, undertaking engineering studies of the Eel River in Northern California as one possible source. Moreover, its initial acceptance and participation in the California Water Project were fraught with tension, since MWD leaders insisted on both firm contracts and massive projections of growth in the region and of water entitlements required to meet those future needs. Wary of signing on with the system without such firm contracts, Jensen even insisted that MWD withhold support for the state project during the bonding election to fund the system, until the MWD board overruled him and came out in support less than a week before the election. (See Minutes, Meetings of the Board of Directors, MWD of Southern California, August 9, September 13, 20, 23, 25, October 4, 11, 18, 25, November 1, 1960; see also *Contract Between the Metropolitan Water District of Southern California and the State of California Department of Water Resource, for a water supply,* November 4, 1960). Contracts were finally signed and MWD entitlements set at the figure of 1.5 million acre-feet of water (later increased to 2.1 maf, with 4.23 maf to be provided in the system as a whole). These figures were based on projections of population growth to 23 million in Southern California and 42 million in the state by the year 2000. (See *Management of the California State Water Project*, Bulletin 132 series, 1963–66; also Bulletin 78, Department of Water Resources, State of California, December 1959.)

34. See Table B-5B, "Annual Water Quantities Delivered to Each Contractor," *Management of the California State Water Project*, Bulletin 132-83, November 1983.

35. Interviews with John Lauten (1987); Donald Brooks (1987); see Memorandum from Assistant Engineer J. A. Rinn to Principal Engineer R. W. Thompson, MWD, February 21, 1975; Memorandum no. 55, "Kern County Water Agency surplus water

requests," from Senior Engineer Glen W. Smith to Assistant General Manager, MWD, December 18, 1969.

36. One MWD document called these plans "a second stage of the State Water Project that would utilize surplus water from the Eel River and other rivers in the north coastal area of California. . . . Construction plans of the State and the District are designed so as to be able to take delivery [of this water]." *Official Statement,* Metropolitan Water District of Southern California, May 14, 1968, p. 32.

37. Interviews with William Gianelli (1987); John Lauten (1986); William R. Gianelli, "The California State Department of Water Resources 1967–1973" (interview conducted by Malca Chall, 1985, Government History Documentation Project oral history), University of California, Berkeley, 1986.

38. Stephanie Pincetl, 1985, "The Environmental Policies and Politics of the Brown Administration," unpublished doctoral dissertation (Urban Planning), UCLA.

39. Interviews with John Lauten (1986), Howard Hawkins (1986), Robert Gough (1986)

40. Interview with E. Thornton Ibbetson (1986).

41. Interviews with Howard Hawkins, Earle Blais, Robert Gough, Robert Will (all 1986). While the jockeying within management was taking place, the board leadership, in 1975, decided to establish a two-term limit for the position of board chairman. Hawkins, the first chair to whom this restriction applied, thus stepped down at the end of 1978, to be replaced by Earle Blais.

42. The phrase "completing the State Water Project" was often used by MWD staff and board members in the late 1970s and early 1980s to indicate that the intent of the original plan for the State Water Project had included a Delta transfer facility. However, partly in response to opposition in Northern California and partly due to problems of limited funding (made available through the initial $1.75 billion state bond authorization), a Delta facility only began to be considered seriously *after* construction of the State Project was completed in 1972.

43. Interviews with Robert Gough (1986), E. L. Griffith (1986), Earle Blais (1987); Howard Hawkins (1986); untitled press release, (E. L. Griffith's background), MWD, August 19, 1977; untitled press release, (Earle Blais's background), MWD, December 12, 1978.

44. Blais used the term "final solution" (without irony) on a number of occasions at MWD board and committee meetings and other public occasions. "Final solution" was another way of stating that the canal represented the necessary, additional infrastructure for transporting water from the Sacramento River to Central and Southern California. Author's notes, Executive Committee meeting, MWD, March 9, 1982; also Comments at Executive Committee, December 7, 1982.

45. "Groundwater Management," letter from Earle Blais to Robert E. McCarthy, president, Board of Directors, Kern County Water Agency, January 30, 1981; letter from Rex Pursell to Earle Blais, July 7, 1981; letter from Earle Blais to Rex Pursell, president, Friant Water Users' Association, September 2, 1981.

46. These priorities could be seen in such forms as a beefed-up public relations program and enlarged speaker's bureau, discussions at board meetings, or allocation of time spent by the leadership, especially Blais and Kennedy. Blais, in particular, constantly exhorted his fellow directors to take up the cause, suggesting that they each ask themselves, "Have I really done today what I should be doing on this project

[the Peripheral Canal]?" (Author's notes, comment by Earle Blais, executive committee meeting of the board of directors, April 13, 1982). See also the Budget vs. Cost Report (1981−1982 fiscal year, period ending Sunday, February 28, 1982) showing the "overbudget" expanded activities of the Public Information Program; also MWD Press Release "Water Agency Chief Announces Public Information Program," January 12, 1982, where Blais described MWD's "responsibility to inform people about issues affecting their water supply," and MWD (via Vice Chairman Carl Fossette) argued that once "the people are aware of the facts, we have no doubt they will support a plan [the Peripheral Canal] which will get much-needed water here."

47. Most of these comments were made outside the board's meeting rooms, given Blais's dominant role in this period. (Author's notes, comments by Harry Griffen [MWD director from San Diego County Water Authority], April 13, 1982; author's notes, conversations with Robert Gough, Gerald Lonergan, Jay Malinowski [April and May 1982].)

48. Author's notes, debate before the staffs of Senator Alan Sieroty, Assemblymen Howard Berman and Mel Levine, comments by MWD Director Sam Rue, July 6, 1981.

49. See "Responses to Analyst's Questions and Comments Prepared by the Staff of the Metropolitan Water District of Southern California," 1981, Municipal Buyers Conference, San Diego, California, January 27, 1981.

50. *Los Angeles Times*, June 10, 1982.

51. *A Survey of Public Opinion Toward Water Issues and Major Water Agencies*, Novick-Rappaport Associates, report prepared for the Metropolitan Water District of Southern California, August 30, 1983.

52. Minutes, Meeting of the State Water Project Planning Subcommittee, March 23, 1983.

53. See "Completion of the State Water Project," a position of the State Water Contractors, draft, February 22, 1983; "California's Water Future: Policy and Plumbing Go Hand in Hand," A Call to Action by Governor George Deukmejian, April 5, 1984.

54. "Political Clout," letter from Ray Corley, Jr., legislative representative to MWD directors and member agency managers, September 26, 1984.

55. Author's notes, conversations with MWD directors Lester Carlson, Katherine Dunlap, Edward Kussman, Sam Rue, Ken Witt (all January through March 1984).

56. Key Boronkay appointments included Wiley Horne, director of planning; Greg Leddy, director of finances; Rich Atwater, director of resources; and Tim Quinn, chief economist.

57. Author's notes, conversation with Wiley Horne (1986).

58. See "A Case for the Peripheral Canal," Earle C. Blais, *Los Angeles Times*, October 11, 1981; "Colorado River Article," letter from Evan L. Griffith, MWD general manager, to Thomas J. Graff, regional counsel, Environmental Defense Fund, October 9, 1981; letter from Thomas J. Graff to Evan Griffith, October 21, 1981; "Report on Imperial Irrigation District," letter from David Kennedy to Jack J. Coe, chief, Southern District, Department of Water Resources, August 26, 1981.

59. Interview with Carl Boronkay (1987); author's notes, conversations with Myron Holburt (1985), Wiley Horne (1984), Howard Hawkins (1984).

60. See chapter 8; for the MCL standard, see Federal Register, 44, no. 231, 68624–68707, November 29, 1979.

61. The interest in utilizing groundwater basins for storage, and, at the same time, increasing sales of imported water, dated back to the 1940s and 1950s when the Colorado River Aqueduct was substantially underutilized. See chapter 10.

62. See "A case for the Peripheral Canal," Earle Blais, *Los Angeles Times*, October 11, 1981.

63. "Seasonal pricing" refers to a price structure that includes an additional assessment for water used during high demand periods; this attempt to reduce peak demand can also be institutionalized through ascending scale charges. "Marginal pricing" refers to the concept of charging new users the marginal, not the average, cost of the water they require; this marginal cost reflects the higher capital costs of facilities built with present dollars and to capture water from less-accessible sources (see chapter 10).

64. "Status of Current Activities to Increase Metropolitan's Water Supplies," letter from the general manager to the board of directors, Metropolitan Water District, February 3, 1986; "An Update on Increasing Metropolitan's Water Supplies," letter from the general manager to the board of directors, Metropolitan Water District, January 27, 1987.

65. Author's notes, comments by MWD Director Tim Brick (1987).

66. See "Board Briefing Summary on System Overview Study," Metropolitan Water District, February 1987; author's notes, System Overview Study Workshop, February 18, 1987.

67. Interview with Carl Boronkay (1987); presentation by Myron Holburt, UCLA Urban Planning Program, April 18, 1989; also "Water Supply—Is there a Regional Population Ceiling?" Donald C. Brooks, director of planning, MWD, presented to SCAG Development Guide Advisory Committee, January 21, 1981; see also "Can There Be Gain With No Pain," Ed Ely, *Focus*, Metropolitan Water District, 1989.

68. Author's notes, discussion with Tim Brick (1988).

69. See "Position on Proposed Delta Legislation," letter from general manager to board of directors, MWD, February 24, 1987; also "Who is Winning," letter from Ray Corley, legislative representative, to MWD member board and agency managers, July 9, 1987.

70. Minutes, Adjourned Regular Meeting of the Board of Directors, The Metropolitan Water District of Southern California, September 22, 1987; author's notes, comments by Tom Spencer, public information director, meeting of the MWD executive committee, September 22, 1987.

71. *United States v. State Water Resources Control Board* (1986) 182 Cal. App. 3d 82 [also known as the Racanelli decision].

72. Water Quality Control Plan for Salinity (Draft) and Pollutant Policy Document (Draft), San Francisco Bay/Sacramento–San Joaquin Delta Estuary, State Water Resources Control Board, October 1988.

73. See "Drought Proposal Could Harm Homes, Business," MWD Press Release November 2, 1988; "San Francisco Bay–Delta Draft Plan Deviations from the Racanelli Opinion," letter from general counsel to MWD board of directors, Decem-

ber 20, 1988; letter from general manager to MWD board of directors, November 21, 1988.

74. Author's notes, conversation with MWD directors Tim Brick, Chris Reed; notes, board meeting, December 13, 1988; "Status of Bay-Delta Hearing," letter from general manager to MWD board of directors, January 31, 1989; "A Water-Grab Plan That Would Make Shortages a Way of California Life," Carl Boronkay, *Los Angeles Herald-Examiner*, January 26, 1989. In late 1989, MWD management formally initiated discussions with the Dolphin Group, a Republican-oriented political consulting firm, to launch a coordinated lobbying and influence-brokering campaign on the need for Northern California water. "Metropolitan Water District Public Action Program Plan and Budget, February 1, 1990–January 30, 1991," presented by the Dolphin Group, Inc., December 5, 1989.

75. At a meeting with former MWD directors on May 2, 1989, Boronkay stated that MWD use of "politics" for pressuring the governor to intervene with the state board was responsible for withdrawal of the Draft Report. (Author's notes, comments by Carl Boronkay.)

76. *Delta Drinking Water Quality Study*, Brown and Caldwell, report prepared for nine agencies, May 1989 (see chapter 8).

Chapter 2 Growth and Identity

1. The area served by CWA members has averaged a population growth rate of about 4 percent throughout the more than forty years since CWA was formed; see San Diego County Water Authority, *42nd Annual Report*, 1988.

2. San Diego County Water Authority, *41st Annual Report*, 1987.

3. San Diego County Water Authority, *42nd Annual Report*, (1988); *Water in the San Diego Region, 1985* (Published by the San Diego Association of Governments [SANDAG], 1985); MWD *Annual Report*, 1987, p. 42.

4. *Water in the San Diego Region, 1985*. SANDAG.

5. William H. Jennings, oral history, UCLA, 1967.

6. See San Diego County Water Authority, *1st Annual Report*, 1946, p. 27; William Kahrl, 1982, *Water and Power* (Berkeley: University of California); Richard F. Pourade, 1967, *The History of San Diego: The Rising Tide* (San Diego: Union-Tribune Publishing Co.), pp. 54–56.

7. "Requesting the Division of Water Resources of the State of California to Apportion California's Share of the Waters of the Colorado River Among the Various Applicants and Water Users Therefrom in the State, Consenting to Such Apportionments, and Requesting Similar Apportionments by the Secretary of the Interior of the United States," Seven Party Water Agreement, August 18, 1931.

8. The figures assigned to the various signatories to the Seven Party Agreement were based on two sets of claims—a larger set of figures (totalling 5.362 million acre-feet) assuming California would continue to obtain its full claim to Colorado River water, and a lower set (totalling 4.4 million acre-feet) based on Arizona's interpretation of the division of water between it and California. It was this latter interpretation, upheld by the U.S. Supreme Court in 1963 in *Arizona v. California* (373 U.S. 546 (1963)), that ushered in the contemporary search for an additional source of

imported water to "make up" the loss of Colorado River water for the combined fourth and fifth priorities of MWD and the San Diego CWA.

9. San Diego County Water Authority, *1st Annual Report*, 1946, p.28.

10. William H. Jennings oral history.

11. Shelly J. Higgins (as told to Richard Mansfield), 1956, *San Diego: This Fantastic City* (official history of city and county policy), City of San Diego.

12. Figures on the navy presence in San Diego County Water Authority, *1st Annual Report* (1946); see also Richard F. Pourade, 1977, *The History of San Diego: City of the Dream* (San Diego: Copley Books).

13. San Diego County Water Authority, *1st Annual Report*, 1946; William H. Jennings oral history; Shelly J. Higgins (as told to Richard Mansfield), *San Diego: This Fantastic City*.

14. County Water Authority Act (Cal. Stats. 1943, c 545, p 2090 sec. 1.); also, Shelly J. Higgins, *San Diego: The Fantastic City*, p. 212; Richard F. Pourade, *The History of San Diego: City of the Dream*.

15. San Diego County Water Authority, *1st* and *2nd Annual Reports* (1946, 1947); William H. Jennings oral history.

16. The navy's presence, even after the war, was still overwhelming. As late as 1947 the navy, while occupying 10 percent of the San Diego area, still used more than 40 percent of the region's water. (Statement by Rear Admiral John J. Manning, chief of the navy's Bureau of Yards and Docks, cited in Richard F. Pourade, *The History of San Diego: City of the Dream*, p. 73; see also William H. Jennings oral history.)

17. See San Diego County Water Authority, *1st Annual Report* (1946); *2nd Annual Report* (1948); San Diego County Water Authority, *Administrative Code*, Article 2, Sec. 2.9.

18. San Diego County Water Authority, *2nd Annual Report*, 1948; MWD *Annual Report* (1947).

19. See San Diego County Water Authority, *2nd Annual Report*, 1948.

20. William H. Jennings oral history; interview with George Yackey (former general manager of Fallbrook Public Utility District), 1989.

21. William H. Jennings oral history; Joseph Jensen oral history.

22. William H. Jennings oral history. The City of San Diego, by the late 1940s, had developed a number of reservoir sites to make use of its own local sources. For example, during 1946–47 (prior to deliveries of imported water), the City of San Diego obtained 56,000 acre-feet from local sources. Three years later, with the first barrel of the aqueduct complete, total deliveries for the city had actually *declined* to 49,000 acre-feet, and 20,000 acre-feet of that was Colorado River water. The next year, city deliveries increased slightly, to 51,000 acre-feet, though Colorado River use jumped to 35,000 acre-feet (68 percent of total deliveries). As the city expanded, it let its own storage system function as a supplement to imported water, which became the city's margin of growth. (See San Diego County Water Authority, *3rd Annual Report* [1949], Table 7, p. 21, and San Diego County Water Authority, *4th Annual Report* [1950], Table 7, p. 26, and Table 9, p. 29).

23. Robert S. Melbourne, 1986, "San Diego County's Water Crusader: Fred A. Heilbron," *Journal of San Diego History* vol. 22, no. 4, Fall 1986; William H. Jennings oral history.

24. See chapter 1. Joseph Jensen, William H. Jennings oral histories; see also interview with George Yackey (1989). Yackey's brother, Harold, was head of the neighboring Vista Irrigation District at the time. See comments by Harry Griffen on San Diego's role with respect to Laguna Declaration, minutes of the Subcommittee on Finance and Policy, board of directors, MWD, May 9, 1988.

25. The first year CWA acquired MWD water, it purchased 41,000 acre-feet, more than one-third of all Colorado River sales to MWD member agencies and about three times the amount purchased by the two other largest users, the cities of Pasadena and Los Angeles. (See Table 15—Water Sales by Metropolitan Water District to Member Agencies, in San Diego County Water Authority, *3rd Annual Report*, 1949, p. 47; see also MWD, *26th Annual Report*, 1964, Table 14, p. 48.)

26. "Fred A. Heilbron," untitled biography, Metropolitan Water District, n.d.; Robert Melbourne, "San Diego County's Water Crusader: Fred A. Heilbron."

27. Interview with Linden Burzell (1986).

28. Interview with Linden Burzell (1986); the two previous general managers, J. L. Burkholder and Richard S. Holmgren, had also been MWD directors during their tenure as general managers.

29. Quoted in Robert E. Melbourne, 1986, "San Diego County's Water Crusader: Fred A. Heilbron," San Diego County Water Authority.

30. See MWD, *37th Annual Report* (1975), Table 12; also *23rd Annual Report* (1961). Per capita water use figures are in San Diego County Water Authority, *Water Distribution Study*, November 1987, p. 12.

31. See MWD, *27th Annual Report* (1965), Tables 1 (p. xxxiv) and 14 (p. 48).

32. Joseph Jensen oral history.

33. During the 1976−77 and 1987−89 "droughts" or critically dry years, MWD never implemented its preferential rights system, since it was able to meet its clients' needs from its Colorado River supply without even claiming the State Project water to which it was entitled under the state's own "preferential rights" system. (See Management of the California State Water Project Bulletin 132−87, September 1987, and Bulletin 132−79, November 1979; also MWD *Annual Report*, 1988.)

34. William H. Jennings oral history; interview with Linden Burzell (1985); see also "Reappraisal of Impact on San Diego County Water Authority of MWD's Section 135 (Preferential Rights)," general counsel, San Diego County Water Authority (revised), March 12, 1987; "A Generalized Discussion of Cost Allocation Policies by MWD," presented by Paul Engstrand on Behalf of the San Diego County Water Authority, to MWD, December 6, 1983.

35. Interview with Linden Burzell (1985); "Hans H. Doe," untitled biography, Metropolitan Water District, n.d.; "Harry Griffen," untitled biography, San Diego County Water Authority, March 1985; author's notes, conversations with Harry Griffen (1980, 1982, 1983); see also "Study of Alternative Methods of Meeting Forecasted Water Demands of San Diego County Water Authority," MWD Report no. 929, September 1978.

36. Interviews with Al Ziegaus (1986), Pete Rios (1986); see also "Imported Water: Our Way of Life," transcript of advertisements prepared by Phillips-Ramsey Co. (SDCWA's advertising firm), Work Order No. SWA-82-20-701, March 9, 1982.

37. *Los Angeles Times*, June 10, 1982; *San Diego Union*, June 14, 1982.

38. Interview with Larry Michaels (1986); interview with Paul Engstrand (1986).

39. Interviews with Larry Michaels (1986), Mike Madigan (1986), Paul Engstrand (1986); see also *Economic Value of Reliable Water Supplies*, State Water Contractors' Exhibit No. 51, Bay-Delta Hearings, State Water Resources Control Board, Sacramento, 1987; *Economic Value of Reliable Water Supplies for Industrial Users*, by Thomas C. Thomas and Richard C. Carlson, prepared for the Metropolitan Water District, June 9, 1987; State Water Contractors' Exhibit No. 57, Bay-Delta Hearings.

40. See County of San Diego, *Water Supply Outlook for San Diego County, 1980–2000*, 1982; *Final Report—Water Independence Project*, Technical Advisory Committee to the County of San Diego, County of San Diego Office of Special Projects, 1983; see also CWA's own analysis: "A study of potential water supply for San Diego County," San Diego County Water Authority, July 1983; and minutes of the meetings of the board of directors, San Diego County Water Authority, July 14, 1983.

41. Interviews with Will Sniffen (1986), Rod Donnelly (1986), Larry Michaels (1986). See also "Agreement with San Diego County Water Authority for Construction of Pamo Dam and Reservoir," memorandum from John Lockwood, Assistant City Manager to Public Services and Safety Committee, San Diego City Council, November 19, 1982; "Draft Environmental Impact Report–Environmental Assessment for the Pamo Reservoir," prepared for San Diego County Water Authority, Mooney-Littieri and Associates, November 18, 1983.

42. The San Diego County Water Authority and the Metropolitan Water District of Southern California, Feasibility Study Report on Pamo Dam and Reservoir, July 1983, James M. Montgomery, Consulting Engineers.

43. Letter from L. R. Burzell, general manager and chief engineer, San Diego County Water Authority, to Evan L. Griffith, general manager, MWD, January 26, 1982; "Pamo Reservoir Feasibility Study," letter from general manager to the board of directors, MWD, June 17, 1982; minutes of the Water Policy Committee, San Diego County Water Authority, May 10, 1984; "Metropolitan Water District Participation in the Pamo Project," letter from Lawrence Michaels, general manager and chief engineer, to board of directors, San Diego County Water Authority, July 5, 1984; letter from Edward J. Thornhill, MWD, to Linden R. Burzell, January 20, 1984.

44. Interviews with Richard Lumsdahl (1986), John Musick (1986), Larry Michaels (1986), Paul Engstrand (1986), Linden Burzell (1985); *Meeker Herald* (Colorado), August 30, 1984.

45. Interviews with Larry Michaels (1986); author's notes, conversation with Ray Corley (MWD lobbyist), 1984. Assembly majority leader Mike Roos, representing a district in the City of Los Angeles, precipitated some of these activities by successfully attaching a provision to legislation enacted in September 1983 (AB322), providing that MWD not be able to impose a property tax rate exceeding that set for FY 1982–83, unless at least 80 percent of MWD's board of directors found that a fiscal emergency existed, requiring and approving a property tax increase. See Report to the California Legislature in Response to AB322, MWD, March 1984; also, minutes of the meetings of the board of directors, San Diego County Water Authority, February 9, 1984, and August 8, 1984.

46. Interview with Larry Michaels (1986); San Diego County Water Authority, *Annual Report* (1985), p. 40; see also *Urban Water Management Plan*, San Diego County Water Authority, 1986.

47. See "Analysis of Option Agreement between the Galloway Group, Ltd., and San Diego County Water Authority," letter from general manager and general counsel to the board of directors, Metropolitan Water District, September 11, 1984.

48. Interviews with Michael Madigan (1986), John Hennigar (1986), Dale Mason (1986), Larry Michaels (1986).

49. With General Manager Michaels and the CWA's General Counsel Paul Engstrand, the new leadership had been flown by private jet to the Yampa site for the Galloway project, and then entertained and lobbied by the project backers. Interviews with John Musick (1986), Paul Engstrand (1986), Larry Michaels (1986), Michael Madigan (1986); see also "San Diego makes a water deal," Cheryl Clark, *San Diego Union*, August 30, 1984.

50. "Analysis of Option Agreement between the Galloway Group, Ltd., and San Diego County Water Authority," September 11, 1984.

51. "Analysis of Option Agreement"; "Analysis of Legal Opinions re: Proposed Water Service Agreement between the Galloway Group, Ltd., and San Diego County Water Authority," letter from general counsel to board of directors, MWD, November 9, 1984; interview with Carl Boronkay (1987).

52. "Colorado River Scheme May Set Off a New Outbreak of Western Water Wars," David Smollar, *Los Angeles Times*, September 9, 1984; *Denver Post*, September 2; 1984, August 31, 1984; *Rocky Mountain News*, August 31, 1984.

53. Interviews with George Nickel (1986), Bill Balch (1986), Ron Lampson (1986), Larry Michaels (1986).

54. Owned by the Copley family who are important in San Diego politics.

55. Press release, Assemblyman Larry Stirling, September 15, 1984.

56. Interview with Mike Madigan (1986); see also minutes of the meeting of the board of directors, San Diego County Water Authority, January 8, 1987; also, author's notes, discussion, board of directors meeting, San Diego County Water Authority, January 8, 1987.

57. See minutes of the meeting of the board of directors, San Diego County Water Authority, September 19, 1984; Ballot Argument for Proposition B: Pamo Reservoir Bonds; press release, Metropolitan Water District, statement by E. Thornton Ibbetson, chairman of the board, MWD, October 10, 1984; minutes of the board of directors, San Diego County Water Authority, October 9, 1984; "MWD Denies Pamo Dam Aid Promise," Cheryl Clark, *San Diego Union*, October 11, 1984.

58. *San Diego Union*, November 6, 1984; interviews with Emily Durbin (1984), Larry Michaels (1986), Mike Madigan (1986).

59. See San Diego County Water Authority, Transcript of Proceedings, Public Hearing, Pamo Reservoir, San Diego, November 19, 1986; "A Great World City," *San Diego Union*, January 1, 1986; interview with Paul Peterson (1986); comments on "water policy" by Paul Peterson, CWA Director to Public Facilities and Recreation Committee, San Diego City Council, May 7, 1985; interview with Don Wood (Citizens Coordinate for Century 3), 1986; see also "Transcript of Proceedings, Public Hearing: Pamo Reservoir," San Diego, Army Corps of Engineers, November 19, 1986.

60. "Pamo Dam Gets EPA Rejection Slip," Janny Scott, *Los Angeles Times*, March 14, 1987; *San Diego Union*, March 14, 1987.

61. Interviews with Larry Michaels (1986); Art Bullock (former assistant general manager, San Diego County Water Authority, 1987), Mike Madigan (1986), Janet Erickson (1986).

62. Interview with Larry Michaels (1986), Mike Madigan (1986); see comments by Mike Madigan, minutes, meeting of the board of directors, MWD, August 19, 1986, p. 9.

63. IID, in fact, continually sought to pursue a separate relationship with San Diego, but to no avail (see chapter 5). See, for example, letter from Tony Gallegos to board of directors, San Diego County Water Authority, September 20, 1988.

64. Interviews with Charles Cooper, Janet Erickson, Phil Pryde, Mike Madigan, Larry Michaels (all 1986); minutes of the meeting of the board of directors, San Diego County Water Authority, February 9, 1984; February 23, 1984.

65. Interviews with Larry Michaels, Mike Madigan, Charles Cooper; *San Diego Union*, March 13, 1987.

66. Interview with Lester Snow (1989); "Emergency water storage: Pamo Reservoir" *San Diego Union*, October 6, 1988; letter from Lester Snow to the board of directors, San Diego County Water Authority, July 8, 1988.

67. Interviews with Lester Snow (1989), Wiley Horne (1988); "San Diego County Optional Storage Study," letter from general manager to the board of directors, MWD, February 27, 1989.

68. According to CWA's own estimates, these new efforts were capable of developing 75,000 acre-feet of additional water from existing sites, and 150,000 acre-feet from new storage. (Interview with Lester Snow, 1989.)

69. Part of the resistance to increased storage capacity was related to the City of San Diego's long-standing policy limiting storage in its reservoirs to 60 percent of capacity. This policy, first initiated in the 1950s, emerged directly out of "end-of-the-pipeline" fears. By 1989, Snow was estimating that CWA could still use about 25,000 acre-feet from a seasonal storage program, but as new capital improvement projects came into service, CWA could expand *its* participation. "Seasonal Storage Water Service," letter from Lester Snow to the board of directors, CWA, June 2, 1989.

70. See "Proposition C—Regional Planning and Growth Control Measure," letter from Lester Snow, general manager to San Diego County Water Authority board of directors, October 7, 1988; *Los Angeles Times*, October 16, 1988.

71. San Diego County Water Authority, 1987 Distribution Study; "Authorization for South Riverside–San Diego County Area Study," letter from director of planning to assistant general managers Richard W. Balcerzak and Myron B. Holburt, MWD, October 30, 1987.

72. They also often saw themselves excluded from the highly valued and inexpensive arrangements shared by other California utilities (such as Edison), including the much-coveted hydroelectric power from Hoover Dam.

73. *San Diego Union*, November 16, 18, 19, 1988; January 24, 1989.

74. SDG&E maintained via MWD an allocation of Colorado River water for a potential future energy plant, while the CWA was obliged to pay for SDG&E electricity at rates the water authority leaders considered excessive. See "San Diego Gas & Electric Acquisition Study," letter from Lester Snow to board of directors, San Diego

County Water Authority, January 6, 1989; "SDG&E Study: Public Ownership Alternatives," prepared for the San Diego County Water Authority, R. W. Beck and Associates, October 1989.

75. See, for example, "SDG&E Reportedly Plots to Destroy Water Agency," Michael Richmond, *San Diego Tribune*, November 22, 1986.

76. Presentation by Lester Snow, UCLA Urban Planning Program, June 6, 1989.

Chapter 3   The Politics of Groundwater

1. It should be noted that, like most discoveries of water contamination, this did not occur spontaneously. The problem of nitrate contamination of agricultural groundwater was identified as a result of the rise (elsewhere) in incidences of disease that were eventually traced to this cause. Once the possibility of nitrate contamination was known, agencies began to test for this contaminant, and widespread contamination was found as a result of this testing.

2. Concentrated nitrates in drinking water cause methemoglobinemia, an anemia of young mammals (including children). Nitrates may be implicated in the synthesis of nitrosamines, which may be carcinogens. But neither of these potential health effects has been taken as a serious, common problem. "Nitrates get little attention as pollutant," Lee Garber, *San Gabriel Valley Tribune*, July 3, 1989.

3. D. Anderson, 1977, *Riparian Water Rights in California.* Staff Paper #4. Governor's Commission to Review California Water Rights Law.

4. The law of riparian rights grows out of this exclusion of nonriparian owners because they have no access to the water through title to land adjoining the watercourse. (D. Anderson, 1977, *Riparian Water Rights in California.* Staff Paper #4. Governor's Commission to Review California Water Rights Law, p. 101.)

5. (*Katz v. Walkinshaw*) "Where the total water supply including surface water and groundwater is limited, the court decided that it is necessary to have a doctrine which protects existing investment and provides certainty for future capital expenditure." (A. Schneider, 1977, *Groundwater Rights in California.* Staff paper #2, Governor's Commission to Review California Water Rights Law, p. 4.)

6. A. Schneider, 1977, *Groundwater Rights in California.* Staff paper #2, Governor's Commission to Review California Water Rights Law, p. 1.

7. Merrill R. Goodall, John D. Sullivan, and Timothy de Young, 1978, *California Water: A New Political Economy.* Montclair, N.J.: Universe Books.

8. See Patricia Ballard, 1980, "And Conflict Shall Prevail: Reclamation Law, Water Districts, and Politics in the Kings River Service Area..." Unpublished master's thesis, Graduate School of Architecture and Urban Planning, UCLA.

9. Table 32, "Area and Population of Member Agencies," MWD *Annual Report* (1988), p. 104. Burbank's 1980 population, according to the U.S. Census, was 84,625; the 93,800 figure is estimated population as of January 1, 1989. See "Population Estimated of California Cities and Counties: January 1, 1988, to January 1, 1989," Department of Finance, Demographic Research Unit, May 1, 1989, Report 89E-1.

10. *City of Los Angeles v. City of San Fernando*, Superior Court, Los Angeles County, Case No. 650079, 1968.

11. MWD, *30th Annual Report*, 1968, Table 14, p. 38.

12. See testimony by Fred Lantz, Water System Manager, Public Service Department, City of Burbank at San Fernando Superfund Site Burbank Well Field Community Meeting, Burbank, November 9, 1988.

13. Jackson Mayer, 1974, *Burbank History.* Burbank: Soldado Publishing Co.

14. Interview with Goodwin Glance (1985); see City of Burbank, "Annual Budget," FY 1986–87, (1987), pp. 155–175.

15. For example, during FY 1974–75, Burbank's total water production was 23,394 acre-feet of which 13,502 acre-feet (58 percent) was well water and 9,892 acre-feet (42 percent) was MWD water. (MWD, *37th Annual Report,* 1975, p. 30.)

16. See "Burbank: An Abbreviated History" in City of Burbank *Annual Budget,* FY 1986–87, p. A-2; also Jackson Mayer, 1974, *Burbank History.*

17. Jackson Mayer, 1974, *Burbank History,* pp. 55–60.

18. Jackson Mayer, 1974, *Burbank History,* p. 79.

19. Cited in Jackson Mayer, 1974, *Burbank History,* p. 80.

20. Vincent Ostrom, 1953, *Water and Politics.*

21. "Description of Electric System," City of Burbank, Public Service Department, April 1983.

22. *Of Men and Stars: a History of Lockheed Aircraft Corporation,* March 1957, Lockheed, Burbank.

23. Jackson Mayer, 1974, *Burbank History.*

24. City of Burbank, Water and Electric Fund, report on examination of financial statements for the years ended June 30, 1985, and 1984, Coopers and Lybrand, pp. 9–11.

25. See "Water Rate Analysis and Financial Study," prepared by City of Burbank Public Service Department, March 1983.

26. Los Angeles, in fact, had filed a suit during the 1930s against Burbank and Glendale to secure its San Fernando Basin rights. Though it obtained a judgment in its favor in this case, it was never able to enjoin the defendants since a substantial water surplus existed at that time. Letter from Alan E. Capon to April Smith, August 23, 1989.

27. *City of Los Angeles v. City of San Fernando,* Case No. 650079, 1968; see also Albert J. Lipson, 1978, *Efficient Water Use in California: The Evolution of Groundwater Management in Southern California,* Rand Corporation, Santa Monica, CA R-2387/2-CSA/RF.

28. See Bulletin 186, "A Ground Water Storage Program for the State Water Project: San Fernando Basin Theoretical Model," May 1979; "Preliminary Evaluation of State Water Project Ground Water Storage Program: San Fernando Basin," Larry L. Peterson, State of California Department of Water Resources, Southern District, February 1979.

29. From 1975, the year Los Angeles's suit was upheld, to 1980, Burbank's purchases of MWD water increased from 42 percent to 92 percent of its total distribution. MWD *Annual Reports,* 1975, 1980.

30. This MWD program, the interruptible pricing program, was first proposed in 1979, in part to ward off efforts to establish a time-of-use, seasonal pricing program (see chapter 10). Burbank began to receive interruptible water during the early 1980s, attracted by its favorable price. But the discovery of well contamination created problems with continuing the program, since those agencies participating in

the program were obliged to "interrupt" their purchases of MWD's imported water (and rely on their own supplies) during critically dry years, when the interruptible provisions were to be implemented. Since Burbank's wells could no longer be used because of contamination, it was technically in violation of the program's requirements. However, MWD never needed to enforce the program, even during the "drought period" of 1987 and 1988. The Burbank utility managers, meanwhile, only suspended their purchases after their new MWD director, Mike Nolan, became aware of the problem and brought it to the utility's attention. Interview with Mike Nolan (1987); testimony of Fred Lantz, San Fernando Superfund site community meeting, November 9, 1988.

31. See "Planned Utilization of Ground Water Basins, San Gabriel Valley, Appendix A: Geohydrology." Bulletin No. 104–2, Department of Water Resources, State of California, 1966.

32. Figures derived from *Annual Report* of the Main San Gabriel Watermaster, FY 1986–1987, November 1, 1987.

33. "Upper San Gabriel Valley Municipal Water District. What it is, what it covers, what it does." USGVMWD, n.d.

34. *Upper San Gabriel Valley Municipal Water District v. City of Alhambra et al.*, Case No. 924128, judgment signed and filed: December 29, 1972; and entered: January 4, 1973, Book 6741, p. 197.

35. Final Community Relations Plan, Environmental Protection Agency, Region 9, San Francisco, 1984.

36. See *Annual Report of the Board of Water Commissioners*, Los Angeles, 1901–1902; Robert Gottlieb and Irene Wolt, 1977, *Thinking Big: The Story of the Los Angeles Times, Its Publishers, and Their Influence on Southern California.* New York: Putnam.

37. "West Covina, California: Differentiation of a Suburb from Central Cities with Emphasis on Land Use," Bill Hideaki Takizawa, unpublished master's thesis, (Geography), UCLA, October 1961.

38. Carl and Ruth Fossette, 1986, *The Story of Water Development in Los Angeles County.* Downey: Central Basin Municipal Water District.

39. See "The Need for Supplemental Water: A Report for the Upper San Gabriel Valley Municipal Water District," Koebig & Koebig, Inc., September 14, 1961, p. 40; see also "Population estimates of California Cities and Counties, January 1, 1988 to January 1, 1989," Report 89 E-1; Department of Finance, Demographic Research Unit, Sacramento, May 1, 1989.

40. Agriculture may use large volumes of water, but much of this filters back through the soil into the groundwater pool. Domestic and industrial water, once used, ordinarily enters the sewer for disposal, though it can, with appropriate treatment, be reclaimed for further use. Agriculture thus may require more water but, in a given region, it currently uses it less consumptively.

41. "The Alternatives and Recommendations in the Stetson Report on a Supplemental Water Supply for Upper San Gabriel Valley Municipal Water District," to the Upper San Gabriel Valley Water Association, May 9, 1962, Carl Fossette, field secretary; Elina Ostrom, 1965, *Public Entrepreneurship: A Case Study in Ground Water Public Management*, unpublished dissertation (political science), UCLA, 1965.

42. *Long Beach et al. v. San Gabriel Valley Water Co. et al.*, Los Angeles Superior Court, Case No. 722647, September 12, 1965.

43. Joseph Jensen oral history; MWD, 1976, "Analysis of Annexation Policy."

44. Hotchkiss would later become an MWD director representing the small, wealthy enclave of San Marino.

45. See Carl and Ruth Fossette, 1986, *The Story of Water Development in Los Angeles County.*

46. Elina Ostrom, 1965, *Public Entrepreneurship: A Case Study in Groundwater Public Management*; Albert J. Lipson, 1978, *Efficient Water Use in California.*

47. Interview with Ralph Helm (1986).

48. *A Supplemental Water Supply for Upper San Gabriel Valley Municipal Water District*, final report, Stetson, Strauss, and Dresselhaus, Inc., prepared for the Upper San Gabriel Valley Municipal Water District, October 16, 1962.

49. See "Voters OK Water District Formation," *Alhambra Post-Advocate*, July 22, 1959; *Feasibility of Serving the San Gabriel Valley Municipal Water District from the State Water Project*, Bulletin No. 119–6, Department of Water Resources, State of California, May 1964.

50. In fact, the Upper San Gabriel Valley uses very little MWD water in comparison to that from local sources. In 1987–88, the USGVMWD took only 13,000 acre-feet of water from MWD for its direct use (only 6.94 percent of the water distributed by its member agencies). It took another 37,000 acre-feet as replenishment deliveries, to meet the adjudication levels. Source: MWD *Annual Report*, 1988.

51. Interview with Howard Hawkins (1986); see also the alternatives and recommendations in Thomas Stetson, "Report on a Supplemental Water Supply for the Upper San Gabriel Valley Municipal Water District," Report to the Upper San Gabriel Valley Water Association, May 9, 1962.

52. Interviews with Ralph Helm (1986) and Howard Hawkins (1986).

53. Interview with Howard Hawkins (1986).

54. Interview with Ralph Helm (1986).

55. "Annexation of Sierra Madre to Upper San Gabriel Valley Municipal Water District and Metropolitan," memorandum from the general counsel to the chairman of the board, MWD, August 14, 1968; "Detachment of the City of Sierra Madre from the San Gabriel Valley Municipal Water District," memorandum from P. A. Towner to W. R. Gianelli, Department of Water Resources, June 9, 1967; letter from W. R. Gianelli to Ernest Lee, manager, San Gabriel Valley Municipal Water District, March 8, 1967.

56. Interview with Howard Hawkins (1986); "Proposal by the San Gabriel Valley Municipal Water District for Joint Use of Facilities," letters from General Manager Frank Clinton to the board of directors, MWD, March 9, 1972, and April 5, 1972; minutes of the meeting of the board of directors, MWD, April 11, 1972, Item 29166.

57. *Long Beach et al. v. San Gabriel Valley Water Co. et al.*, Case No. 722647, September 12, 1965.

58. See Albert J. Lipson, 1978, *Efficient Water Use in California.*

59. Interviews with Ralph Helm (1986), Tom Stetson (1986), Don Howard (1986).

60. Interviews with Tom Stetson (1986), Jane Bray (1986), Don Howard (1986); also Albert J. Lipson, 1978, *Efficient Water Use in California.*

61. Interviews with Robert Munro, manager of Special Services, Blue Diamond Materials (1986), Jane Bray (1985), Tom Stetson (1985), Ralph Helm (1986).

62. *Upper San Gabriel Valley Municipal Water District v. City of Alhambra et al.*, Superior Court, Los Angeles County, Case No. 924128, January 4, 1973.

63. *Upper San Gabriel Valley Municipal Water District v. City of Alhambra et al.*, Superior Court, Los Angeles County, Case No. 924128, January 4, 1973.

64. Bray had replaced Carl Fossette, her mentor and a pivotal figure in the Valley. Fossette had been appointed the Upper District's first general manager at the same time that he was general manager for the Upper District's downstream rivals, the Central and West basin districts. This extraordinary overlap of functions was testimony in part to Fossette's low-key, behind-the-scenes influence in all three groundwater areas. Fossette would eventually retire from his management duties to become the Central Basin District's representative to the MWD board of directors where he served for more than thirteen years until his death in 1986. (Interviews with Jane Bray [1986], Ralph Helm [1986], Howard Hawkins [1986]; see also Fossette's autobiography, *The Story of Water Development in Los Angeles*, written with his wife Ruth Fossette and published privately in Los Angeles in 1986, shortly after his death.)

65. Interview with Wiley Horne (1986). This can be seen in terms of MWD purchases during the summer months by such groundwater agencies as Central Basin, West Basin, the Municipal Water District of Orange County, and the Upper District, which *increase* substantially. See "Monthly Water Use by Member Agencies for FY 1984–85 through FY 1987–88," Office of the General Manager, MWD, prepared by Operations Planning.

66. "Main San Gabriel Basin Groundwater Management," Thomas Stetson, prepared for the 82nd annual meeting of the Cordilleran Section of the Geological Society of America, California State University, Los Angeles, March 25–28, 1986.

67. *Los Angeles Times*, January 17, 1980; January 18, 1980; interviews with Robert Berlien (1989), Jane Bray (1986), Howard Hawkins (1986), Burt Jones (1986).

68. San Fernando Superfund Site, "Agencies Announce Completion of North Hollywood Groundwater Treatment Facility," U.S. EPA, May 1989.

69. See "Organic Chemical Contamination of Large Public Water Systems in California," Department of Health Services, State of California, April 1986, C18–C20.

70. California state action levels, set by DOHS at levels designed to protect public health, were nonetheless advisory, not enforceable, water quality standards. Legislation introduced through the mid- and late-1980s unsuccessfully sought to change the status of action levels to enforceable standards. This legislation was strongly opposed by water agencies. See "Sacramento Report," letter from Ray Corley to MWD board and member agency managers, July 1, 1985. Compromise legislation agreed to by the water agencies and key state legislators was finally arranged in the late 1980s. This agreement separated those "maximum contaminant levels" which were to have the force of law from "health-based recommendations" that were still only advisory, and also established public notification requirements.

71. Presentation by Neil Ziemba, UCLA Urban Planning Program, May 2, 1989.

72. See "Organic Chemical Contamination of Large Public Water Systems in California," Department of Health Services, State of California, April 1986, C18–C20.

73. Interviews with Neil Ziemba (1989), Cass Luke (field representative for Assemblywoman Sally Tanner) (1985).

74. Interviews with Paula Bisson, EPA Region IX (1986), Jane Bray (1986); Final Community Relations Plan, EPA, May 1984.

75. Presentation by Neil Ziemba, UCLA, May 2, 1989.

76. Record of decision for Suburban Water Systems, Bartolo Well Field Operable Unit, September 1988, EPA Region 9, San Francisco.

77. Testimony by Robert Ghirelli, Regional Water Quality Control Board, presented to State Water Resources Control Board hearing on San Gabriel Valley ground water problem, June 28, 1988.

78. "EPA to Propose Basinwide Technical Plan," Fact Sheet 7, San Gabriel Valley Superfund Sites, EPA Region IX, August 1989.

79. Interview with Neil Ziemba (1989).

80. "Summary of Estimated Costs and Schedules for Different Remedial Action Approaches," EPA, exhibit presented at State Water Resources Control Board Hearing, El Monte, June 28–29, 1988.

81. Interview with Neil Ziemba (1989); see "San Gabriel Superfund Sites 1–4, draft overall enforcement strategy to be developed jointly by EPA Region 9 and the California Department of Health Services," Regional Water Quality Control Board, April 1988.

82. Interview with Robert Berlien (1989).

83. At a meeting designed to explore the ability of local water districts to take on a greater share of the cleanup-enforcement workload associated with leaking underground tanks, local water agency representatives (including Jane Bray from the Upper District) complained that, "as utilities, water purveyors are not 'regulators' and don't feel comfortable taking on enforcement responsibilities," and that "water purveyors prefer continuing to work with the regulatory agencies to ensure actions are taken to protect groundwater quality, rather than becoming responsible for initiating these actions." Memorandum, "Groundwater Clean Up by Local Water Districts," from Robert Ghirelli, Regional Water Quality Control Board, to Darlene Ruiz, member, State Water Resources Control Board, June 14, 1983.

84. Interview with Robert Ghirelli (1988); see Toxic Substances Control Division, Department of Health Services, State of California, written testimony before the Environment and Labor Subcommittee of the Committee on Small Business, Baldwin Park, California, June 5, 1989.

85. San Gabriel Superfund Site Areas 1–4, draft, *Overall Enforcement Strategy*, April 1988, p.3.

86. Interview with Tom Stetson (1986); see also *Fifteenth Annual Report* of the Main San Gabriel Watermaster for 1986–1987, November 1, 1987, p. 5.

87. Interview with Robert Berlien (1989).

88. See written testimony before State Water Resources Control Board Hearing concerning the San Gabriel groundwater problem, prepared by Arthur G. Kidman,

McCormick & Kidman, lawyers, on behalf of the Basin Water Quality Management Committee of the Main San Gabriel Basin Watermaster, El Monte, June 28, 1988.

89. Interviews with Neil Ziemba (1989), Robert Berlien (1989); see also Robert Berlien, written testimony before the Environment and Labor Subcommittee of the House Committee on Small Business, representing the Upper San Gabriel Municipal Water District, Main San Gabriel Basin Watermaster, and San Gabriel Valley Water Association, Baldwin Park, June 5, 1989.

90. See testimony by League of Women Voters, Southern California Regional Task Force and the East Valley Organization, before the Environment and Labor Subcommittee of the House Committee on Small Business, Baldwin Park, June 5, 1989. In 1990, MWD also entered the fray, suggesting a conjunctive use program to manage the groundwater's supply while MWD resources were also employed to help deal with the contamination.

91. See "Organic Chemical Contamination of Large Public Water Systems in California," Department of Health Services, State of California, April 1986.

92. Underground Storage Tank Investigation, Regional Water Quality Control Board, Los Angeles, 1983.

93. See "Summary of Chemical Analyses for TCE and PCE in Soil at CALAC's Burbank Facilities during 1984–85," Underground Storage Tank Investigation, Regional Water Quality Control Board, Los Angeles, Table 1; also, Lockheed Groundwater Monitoring Program—Testing Well Data, Gregg & Associates, April 30, 1987.

94. Transcript of testimony by Fred Lantz, San Fernando Superfund Site, Burbank Well Field, community meeting before the U.S. EPA, Burbank, November 9, 1988.

95. "Lockheed must clean up ground water at Burbank plant," Karen West, Los Angeles Daily News, August 8, 1987.

96. See "Poisoned Wells," Los Angeles Daily News, August 26, 1987; also Los Angeles Daily News, September 19, 1987.

97. See "L.A. Steps up Groundwater Cleanup Effort," Karen West, Los Angeles Daily News, August 24, 1987; see also letter from Mayor Tom Bradley and City Councilman Marvin Braude to R. R. Heppe, President, Lockheed Corporation, August 7, 1987.

98. A review of the minutes of the Burbank Public Service Advisory Board, January 1, 1984, through November 19, 1987, finds only a few sessions devoted primarily to water, with those mostly dealing with rate matters. Beginning in June 1987, focus on the water quality issue increased, especially at the meetings of June 1, 1987, July 13, 1987, and September 14, 1987.

99. Transcript, meeting of the Burbank City Council, October 20, 1987; see also "Groundwater Contamination," City Council presentation, City of Burbank Public Services Department, October 20, 1987.

100. See record of decision for the Burbank Well Field Operable Unit, San Fernando Valley Area 1, Superfund Site, U.S. EPA Region 9, San Francisco, May 1989, pp. 11–12. The speed of response seems most directly related to the question of liability rather than the extent of the contamination. For example, United Technologies Co., located in the City of Industry in the San Gabriel Basin area, moved quickly to clean up a massive TCE spill after realizing that if it waited until after heavy rains occurred, its liability for clean-up costs would greatly increase as surface trans-

port spread the contamination. Though it had conducted only basic soil and ground-water tests, the company began to implement a full remedial clean-up plan eighteen months after the conditions was identified, a response that sharply contrasted with Lockheed's activity. Meeting of the Los Angeles Water Quality Control Board, November 10, 1987.

101. Air stripping consists of spraying water into the fan-driven air rising through a specially constructed tower. Water bearing organic contaminants, which evaporate more easily than the water itself, enters the moving air, and the concentration of contaminants in the water that falls to the floor of the tower is thus reduced. After public concern about the value of stripping these contaminants from the water by pumping them into the air became intense, EPA and DWP agreed to treat the air passing through the falling water with granular activated carbon filters before releasing it into the ambient environment (see chapter 8).

102. San Fernando Superfund Site Area 1, Fact Sheet #2, Burbank, October 1988, EPA Region 9, San Francisco; see also "San Fernando Superfund Site Burbank Wellfield Operable Unit, Special Notice Letter," May 2, 1989.

103. Presentation by Ed Fader, UCLA, December 6, 1989. Fader also noted that "aerospace companies manufacture chemicals and they never really thought about that [environmental consequences]," a situation applicable to other Superfund parties in the San Fernando Basin, such as Rockwell.

104. A number of the parties held to be responsible by EPA complained that the new relationship with Lockheed might ultimately force the smaller companies to pick up the remaining—and substantial—costs, once Lockheed's liability had been capped (at $52 million over a six-year period, per one Lockheed proposal). *Los Angeles Daily News*, August 26, 1989; August 12, 1989; August 8, 1989.

105. Continuing tests through 1989 indicated that the groundwater contamination even included areas once thought to be free from pollution, thereby upsetting the timetable and cost estimates arrived at as part of the negotiations with Lockheed. "Burbank Water Problems Grow," Jaxon Van Derbeken, *Los Angeles Daily News*, August 23, 1989.

Chapter 4   A Desert Conundrum

1. IID, "Profile of the Imperial Irrigation District," n.d.

2. See "Imperial Valley, Annual Weather Summary: Monthly High, Low, and Mean Temperatures, 1914–1985," Imperial Irrigation District, 1985.

3. Imperial County Agricultural Commissioner, 1989, *Annual Crop Report, 1988*.

4. California, Employment Development Department, 1988. *Annual Planning Information, Imperial County.*

5. Numbers are adjusted to exclude noncounty residents (California, Employment Development Department, 1988, *Planning Information, Imperial County*).

6. See U.S. Bureau of the Census, 1980 Census, Population, General Social and Economic Characteristics of California, Part 1; also *California County Rankings*, 1988, Center for Continuing Study of the California Economy, Palo Alto.

7. See *Water Conservation Plan*, Imperial Irrigation District, 1985.

8. Though in only three years during that period (1973–75) did the water dis-

trict order more than its allotted share of 2.6 million acre-feet as stipulated in the 1931 Seven Party Agreement (later modified by the *Arizona v. California* court ruling in 1963).

9. "Proposal for Funding Water Conservation Programs," Donald A. Twogood, Proceedings of the Specialty Conference Sponsored by the Irrigation and Drainage Division of the American Society of Civil Engineers and the San Antonio Branch and Texas Section of the American Society of Agricultural Engineers, July 1985.

10. Interview with Kristine Fontaine (1988); see "Facing the Future . . . Proud of our Past," 75th Anniversary brochure, Imperial Irrigation District, 1988.

11. "Proposal for Funding Water Conservation Programs," Donald A. Twogood, July 1985.

12. See *Imperial Irrigation District, California*, Charles P. Burgess, prepared for Blythe and Co., and Kaiser and Co., May 21, 1943.

13. See F. C. Farr, 1918, *History of Imperial Valley*, Berkeley: Elms and Franks.

14. The Reclamation Service during this period was making a comprehensive survey of areas where it might intervene to provide federally reclaimed water to farmers with 160 acres or less, under the terms of the 1902 Reclamation Act. Robert L. Sperry, 1975, "When the Imperial Valley Fought for its Life," *Journal of San Diego History* 21(1); also Paul G. Barnett, 1978, "Imperial Valley: the Land of Sun and Subsidies," report prepared for California Rural Legal Assistance, September 1978, Davis, California.

15. See H. T. Cory, 1915, *Imperial Valley and the Salton Sink*, San Francisco: Dodd Mead.

16. Paul G. Barnett, 1978, "Imperial Valley: The Land of Sun and Subsidies"; see also Otis Tout, 1932, "The First Thirty Years 1901−1931: History of Imperial Valley, Southern California, USA," San Diego.

17. Steere, Collis H., 1952, *Imperial and Coachella Valleys*, Stanford University Press; "Southern Pacific Imperial Valley Claim," hearings on House Joint Resolution 48 authorizing and directing the Interstate Commerce Commission to ascertain the loss to the Southern Pacific Co. in closing and controlling the break in the Colorado, U.S. Congress, House Committee on Claims, January 23, 1917.

18. H. T. Cory, 1915, *Imperial Valley and the Salton Sink*; see also Remi Nadeau, 1974, *The Water Seekers*, Santa Barbara: Peregrine Smith.

19. Beverly Bowen Moeller, 1971, *Phil Swing and Boulder Dam*, Berkeley: University of California Press; J. K. Hartshorne, "Water to Make the Desert Bloom: A Brief History," in *Welcome to the Imperial Irrigation District*, IID, June 1982; Norris Hundley, 1973, "The Politics of Reclamation: California, the Federal Government and the Origins of the Boulder Canyon Act—a Second Look," *California Historical Society Quarterly* 52 (4); also Remi Nadeau, 1974, *The Water Seekers*.

20. Norris Hundley, 1973, "The Politics of Reclamation"; Paul G. Barnett, 1978, "Imperial Valley: The Land of Sun and Subsidies."

21. Carey McWilliams, 1943, *Ill Fares the Land*, New York: Barnes and Noble.

22. See Eugene Chamberlain, 1951, "Mexican Colonization Versus American Interests in Lower California," *Pacific Historical Review*, February 1951.

23. Interview with G. K. Roussel (IID, head of land sales) (1987). By 1987, there were still 104,180 acres owned by IID below the Salton Sea, "Report No. 93,

Gross Acreage of Imperial Irrigation District within the A.A.C. Service Area Boundaries," Imperial Irrigation District, March 3, 1987.

24. Paul G. Barnett, 1978, "Imperial Valley: The Land of Sun and Subsidy"; also "The Contribution of the All-American Canal System, Boulder Canyon Project, to the Economic Development of the Imperial and Coachella Valleys of California and to the Nation," Bureau of Reclamation, U.S. Department of Interior Report, Interior and Insular Affairs Committee, House of Representatives, U.S. Congress, May 1956.

25. Table 1, "Distribution of Land Ownerships in the Imperial Irrigation District," in "Economic Impact of the 160 Acre Limitation on Imperial County," Council of California Growers, 1977, San Mateo, California; Paul Barnett, 1978, "Imperial Valley: Land of Sun and Subsidies"; also, Imperial Valley Press, May 17, 1987.

26. Interview with Lester Bornt (1986).

27. See Historic Salton Sea, Munson J. Dowd, Imperial Irrigation District, 1965; "Salton Sea: Nature's Accident in the Desert," Aqueduct, no. 4, 1986.

28. Interview with Lester Bornt (1987).

29. See Salton Sea Mitigation Plan: Phase 1, A proposal to mitigate the adverse effects of salinity on water quality, fisheries, wildlife, and recreation at the Salton Sea, submitted by Imperial Irrigation District and the County of Imperial, May 1988; Salt Balance—Imperial Valley, Soil Conservation Service and Imperial Irrigation District, 1983; "Activists fight for Sea with tainted fish and too much salt," Ken Wells, Wall Street Journal, June 17, 1986.

30. Cited in "The Salty Salton Sea," by M. J. Dowd, Executive Officer, Imperial Irrigation District, in District News, Imperial Irrigation District, vol. 18, no. 5, October 1952; see also "Many District Facilities used for Recreation in Imperial County," District News, Imperial Irrigation District, July 1960; also District News, January 1955, March 1955, October 1958; see Land Sales Contract Between County of Imperial, County Board of Supervisors, and Imperial Irrigation District, executed February 7, 1944.

31. Interview with John Benson (1987). From 1982 to 1984 alone, IID was obliged to pay $1,689,819 in legal fees primarily for litigation related to Salton Sea flooding. Imperial Valley Press, January 9, 1985.

32. "Salton Sea: Danger Ahead," Indio Daily News, December 19, 1985; see also Imperial Valley Press, October 31, 1985.

33. See Salton Bay Marina v. Imperial Irrigation District, Superior Court, Imperial County, 1982; also "Water Surface Elevation—Salton Sea, 1904–1986," Imperial Irrigation District Map, 1987.

34. Interviews with John Elmore (1985), Stephen Elmore (1985), David Osias (1986).

35. See Investigation under California Water Code, Section 275, Of Use of Water by Imperial Irrigation District, District Report, Department of Water Resources, Southern District, December 1981.

36. See Environmental Defense Fund, 1983, Trading Conservation Investments for Water, Robert Stavins (principal author), March 1983; see also an interview with John Elmore (1985). Even as late as the 1983 hearings before the State Water Resources Control Board, only EDF's Tom Graff testified in support of the concept of an MWD-IID arrangement.

37. In a letter attacking the concept of the SWAP, MWD Assistant General Manager David Kennedy wrote to the Southern District Chief of the Department of Water Resources, "We see no practical way in which Metropolitan can acquire any permanent rights to water salvaged within IID, and it would be misleading for the Department to put out a report which raises this possibility as though it had real credibility." Letter from David N. Kennedy to Jack J. Coe, August 26, 1981.

38. See testimony by Imperial County Supervisors Louis Legaspi and Jim Bucher, *Hearing on Alleged Waste and Unreasonable Use of Water by the Imperial Irrigation District*, State Water Resources Control Board, El Centro, September 19, 1983; see also an interview with John Benson (1986).

39. Interview with David Osias (1986).

40. Interview with Paul Engstrand (1987).

41. See Investigation under California Water Code, Section 275, "Of Use of Water by Imperial Irrigation District," District Report, Department of Water Resources, Southern District, December 1981.

42. Testimony by Wiley Horne, State Water Resources Control Board hearings, September 19, 1983.

43. Interview with John Benson (1986); author's notes, conversation with Myron Holburt (1985). Holburt, shortly after the state board hearings came to an end, met with IID officials and strongly urged them to enter negotiations with MWD, in light of their growing political vulnerability.

44. A phrase used by IID board member John Benson. Interview with John Benson (1986).

45. Interviews with Tom Havens, Robert Davidson (vice president, Ralph M. Parsons Company) (1986), Kline Borney (1986), Dennis Parker (1986), Melvyn Brown (1986).

46. Interviews with Tom Havens (1985), Richard Lundahl (1986); in February 1984, shortly before interjecting himself into the IID situation, Havens approached one of the authors (Robert Gottlieb), then still an MWD director, inquiring about ways to relate concepts of privatization, the rhetoric of various initiatives by the Reagan administration, to the Southern California water scene. Havens, like his Galloway counterparts, had focused on the region in the wake of the Peripheral Canal defeat and widely disseminated tales of a potential "shortage."

47. Interview with Robert Davidson (1987). Parsons's acquisition of Engineering Science, a small but active consulting firm in the environmental services area, led to this creation of a new subsidiary, Parsons Municipal Services, which launched its privatization activities. See also "Parsons Tells IID of Program," Terry J. Tripp, *Imperial Valley Press*, December 19, 1984.

48. Interviews with Bill Condit (1987), Leroy Edwards (1986), and Tom Havens (1987).

49. "Imperial-Parson Water Conservation Planning and Development Agreement," letter from Robert W. Schempp, senior engineer, MWD, to Myron B. Holburt, Dec. 16, 1985.

50. See Draft Environmental Impact Report, Proposed Water Conservation Program and Initial Water Transfer, IID, California State Clearinghouse No. 86012903, April 1986; and Final Environmental Impact Report, October 1986.

51. Interview with Robert Davidson (1987); "Water Sale Bypassing MWD Said Feasible," Cheryl Clark, *San Diego Union*, August 9, 1985.

52. Interview with Larry Michaels (1985).

53. Interviews with Charles Shreves (1987), Donald Twogood (1986), Robert Davidson (1987); "Water Swap May Mean Boost to Valley's Economy," Jim Cole, *Imperial Valley Press*, July 29, 1985.

54. The language of the memorandum of understanding (see note 56) reflected the "agree to disagree" concept.

55. Interviews with Bill Condit (1987), Leroy Edwards (1986), and John Benson (1987).

56. See "Memorandum of Understanding—Imperial Irrigation District," letter from the general manager to the board of directors, MWD, July 5, 1986.

57. Minutes of meeting of the board of directors, MWD, July 9, 1985; the IID board, in response to public outcry, deferred their vote on the MOU several times and scheduled a public hearing on the matter before finally voting against it on October 15, 1985.

58. See transcript of public hearing regarding draft memorandum of understanding between the IID and MWD, El Centro, September 30, 1985.

59. *Imperial Valley Press*, September 30, 1985; February 5, 12, 1986.

60. Minutes of the meeting of the board of directors, Imperial Irrigation District, October 15, 1985; also minutes, January 21, 1986; "IID to Review Parsons Deal amid Criticism," Willy Morris, *Imperial Valley Press*, April 22, 1986.

61. Letter from Leroy Edwards, president, board of directors, IID, to board of directors, MWD, August 20, 1986; letter from E. Thornton Ibbetson, chairman, board of directors, MWD, to Leroy Edwards, August 26, 1986. Ibbetson, himself an Imperial Valley landowner, sent his response, essentially handing the issue back to MWD management, without consulting the MWD board itself. This caused some additional controversy, raising the question of Ibbetson's own potential conflict of interest.

62. See the minutes of the meeting of IID board of directors, July 16, 1985 concerning Salton Bay Marina settlement; *Imperial Irrigation District: Alleged Waste and Unreasonable Use of Water*, Water Rights Decision, Decision 1600, State Water Resources Control Board, June 1984; see also Order: 84-12, Affirming Decision 1600 and Denying Petitions for Reconsideration, State Water Resources Control Board, September 1984.

63. Interviews with Willy Morris (1987) and Stephen Elmore (1986).

64. Letter from Gerald L. Moore, president, board of directors, Imperial Irrigation District, to Francesca M. Krauel, chairman, board of directors, San Diego County Water Authority, April 1, 1987; letter from Francesca Krauel to Gerald Moore, April 23, 1987.

65. *Imperial Valley Press*, January 16, 1987; interview with Tom Havens (1987).

66. See the minutes of the board of directors, IID, July 16, 1985.

67. See memorandum, "Increase in Water Rates," from the general manager to the Imperial Irrigation District board of directors, June 20, 1985; minutes, meeting of the board of directors, Imperial Irrigation District, February 17, 1987; *Imperial Valley Press*, September 9, 1987.

68. *Imperial Valley Press*, November 6, 1986; November 7, 1988.

69. Interview with Carl Boronkay (1987).

70. *Imperial Valley Press*, August 13, 1988; *Imperial Valley Press*, June 21, 1988.

71. Interview with John Benson (1987). The "Lord Jim" characterization was widely used by Benson and other IID board members, at a time when Bucher had become the SWAP's—and the district's—leading political opponent.

72. *Imperial Valley Press*, March, 13, 1987 and June 16, 1988.

73. *Imperial Valley Press*, November 23, 1988.

74. Interview with Willy Morris (1987). The group, Salton Sea Coordinating Council, whose statements received considerable attention from both state agencies and the press, more or less disappeared when its key leader and founder, Bill Karr, moved away from Riverside County.

75. Interview with Carl Boronkay (1987).

76. The IID SWAP figured prominently in the public posture adopted by Boronkay and his staff, concerning their new, alternative approaches, particularly in Northern California. Author's notes, conversations with Carl Boronkay, August and September 1987; author's notes, conversations with State Assemblyman Philip Isenberg (1987).

77. Minutes of the board of directors, IID, October 15, 1985.

78. Interviews with John Benson (1987) and Lester Bornt (1987).

79. Quoted in *Imperial Valley Press*, December 18, 1988. See "No Vote," Don Cox, *Imperial Valley Press* , November 20, 1988.

80. "Agreement with Imperial Irrigation District for the Implementation of a Water Conservation Program and Use of Conserved Water," letter from general manager to board of directors, MWD, November 15, 1988.

81. Minutes of the meeting of the board of directors, MWD, December 10, 1988.

82. "Coachella Valley Water District Proposal for Approval of the Imperial Irrigation District—Metropolitan Water Conservation Agreement," letter from the general manager to the MWD board of directors, May 30, 1989; *Imperial Valley Press*, August 20, September 15, and September 19, 1989.

83. *Imperial Valley Press*, November 1, December 13, and January 10, 1989.

Chapter 5   The Search for Cheap Water

1. See Table B–4, "Annual Entitlements to Project Water," and Table B–5B, "Annual Water Quantities Delivered to Each Contractor," Bulletin 132–87, Management of the California State Water Project, Department of Water Resources, State of California, September 1987.

2. See Kern County Water Agency, *Water Supply Report, 1987*, May 1988; also Kern County Agricultural Commissioner, *Annual Crop Report, 1986*.

3. The problem is similar in magnitude to other areas in the San Joaquin Valley. "Conjunctive Use Management Programs in Kern County, California," presented at United Nations Seminar on Conjunctive Use of Surface and Groundwater Resources, New Delhi, India, February 10–13, 1986. Prepared by Stuart Pyle, engineer-manager, Kern County Water Agency.

4. See Table B–4, "Annual Entitlements to Project Water," Bulletin 132–87,

Management of the California State Water Project, Department of Water Resources, State of California, September 1987.

5. "Conjunctive Use Management Programs in Kern County, California," Stuart Pyle, 1986.

6. Margaret Aseman Cooper, 1979, *Land, Water and Settlement in Kern County, California, 1850–1890*, New York: Arno Press.

7. Margaret Aseman Cooper, 1979, *Land, Water and Settlement in Kern County, California, 1850–1890*; also Donald Pisani, 1984, *From the Family Farm to Agribusiness: The Irrigation Crusade in California and the West* (Berkeley: University of California Presss).

8. Donald Pisani, 1984, *From the Family Farm to Agribusiness*; also Donald Worster, 1985, *Rivers of Empire* (New York: Pantheon).

9. *Lux v. Haggin*, California Supreme Court, 1886.

10. Edward Treadwell, 1931, *The Cattle King: A Dramatized Biography*, Fresno, California: Valley Publishers.

11. Donald Pisani, 1984, *From the Family Farm to Agribusiness*; Donald Worster, 1986, *Rivers of Empire*.

12. Interview with George Nickel (1986); *History of Kern County*, W. W. Robinson, Title Insurance, Los Angeles, 1961; H. J. Vaux, Jr., 1985, in *Scarce Water and Institutional Change*, Kenneth D. Frederick (editor), Resources for the Future, Washington, D.C.

13. H. J. Vaux, Jr., 1985, in *Scarce Water and Institutional Change*.

14. Ibid.

15. Kern County Water Agency Act 9098 [Cal. Stats. 1961 ch. 1003 p. 2652, effective July 6, 1961]; see *Kern County Water Agency: First Five Years—1961 to June 30, 1966*, Kern County Water Agency, 1966.

16. Interview with Henry Garnett (1987); see Erwin Cooper, 1968, *Aqueduct Empire*, Glendale: Arthur H. Clark.

17. "Quantitative Economic Study of Representative Kern County Farm Enterprises," Francis A. Moore, Jr. and Park J. Ewart, authorized by the Kern County Water Agency, Bakersfield, 1962; *Fresno Bee*, March 1960; also see letter from Del Ogilvie, engineer-manager, Kern County Water Agency to Francis A. Moore, Jr., April 19, 1962.

18. The issue reappeared in the election fight the following year over the $1.75 billion in construction bonds for the project; see the "Burns-Porter Act: A California High Water Mark," Harvey O. Banks and Jean O. Williams, report prepared for the State Water Contractors, April 1984; also Robert Fellmeth, *The Politics of Land*, New York: Grossman, 1973.

19. Interview with Don Brooks (1987); see *Feather River and Delta Diversion Projects: Investigation of Alternative Aqueduct Systems to Serve Southern California*, Bulletin No. 78, Department of Water Resources, State of California, December 1959, pp. 142–49.

20. See *The Price of Water: Surplus and Subsidy in the California State Water Project*, Michael Storper and Richard Walker, Berkeley: Institute of Government Studies, 1984; see also "Myth vs. Reality: Agricultural Subsidies in the State Water Project," presented by Warren J. Abbott, general counsel, MWD, before the California Senate Agriculture and Water Resources Committee, January 21, 1986, and "Subsi-

dies in the State Water Project: A Reply to the MWD," Michael Storper, UCLA, March 10, 1986; also "Agricultural Subsidies and the State Water Project," letter from the general counsel to MWD board of directors, May 22, 1986.

21. Interviews with John Lauten (1986), E. L. Griffith (1983), and Donald Brooks (1987); see "Overview of the State Water Project: History and Background," Don Brooks, State Water Project Workshop, MWD, January 22, 1986.

22. Author's notes, discussion with David Kennedy (1981); author's notes, presentation by E. L. Griffith, UCLA Urban Planning Program (1983).

23. See Section 14.2 of the Kern County Water Agency Act 9098 (revised, 1985); also "Report to the Board of Directors of Kern County Water Agency on Establishment of Zones of Benefit," Leeds, Hill and Jewett, Inc., consulting engineers, report prepared for the Kern County Water Agency, September 1974.

24. See League of Women Voters, *The Big Water Fight*, 1966. Brattleboro, Vermont: S. Greene Press.

25. *Bakersfield Californian*, November 13, 1963. The vote evolved around approval of the contract between the state and KCWA, which had been formed in 1961, contingent upon voter appropval of the contract. Kern voters, while approving the contract by a small margin (589 votes), voted down a proposal to establish a greater-Bakersfield water district. As a consequence, KCWA subsequently formed Improvement District No. 4 to provide water for Bakersfield and surrounding areas.

26. Tenneco, 1968 *Annual Report*; "Tenneco's Corporate Farming," Ann Crittenden, *New York Times*, April 1, 1981.

27. See Robert Gottlieb and Irene Wolt, 1977, *Thinking Big: The Story of the Los Angeles Times, Its Publishers and Their Influence over Southern California*, New York: Putnam; Form 10K, Tejon Ranch Co., for fiscal year ended December 31, 1985, Securities and Exchange Commission File No. 1−7183.

28. *California Business*, March 1981, p. 28.

29. Don Villarejo, 1981, *New Lands for Agriculture*, Davis, California: Institute for Rural Studies.

30. In 1968, the year the State Project water arrived, there were 719,000 irrigated acres in the county; that figure jumped more than 100,000 acres in less than three years and another 100,000 by 1975. See "The Future of Irrigation in Kern County," Stuart Pyle, engineer-manager, KCWA, presented at American Society of Civil Engineers Water Forum, August 11, 1981.

31. See *Prospectus*, Tejon Agricultural Partners, 1971; "Report on Tejon Ranch Lake Development," 1972, Systems Management, Inc.

32. Don Villarejo, 1981, *New Lands for Agriculture*; for example, one major landowner, J. Norman Dawe, an executive of Getty Oil, was on the board of two different agencies—Cawelo Water District and Lost Hills Water District—while Tejon Ranch representatives were on the boards of three different agencies: Wheeler Ridge–Maricopa, Arvin-Edison, and Tejon-Castaic.

33. The tax shelters were under the provisions of the Federal Tax Code in effect until 1976, which stimulated off-farm investment in particular types of farming (especially perennial crops—orchards, vineyards—and cattle) where initial capital costs were high. (Thomas A. Carlin and W. Fred Woods, 1974, *Tax Loss Farming*, USDA Economic Research Service Report No. 546.)

34. See *The California State Water Project—1978 Activities and Future Man-*

agement Plans, Bulletin No. 132–79, Department of Water Resources, State of California, November 1979.

35. See *The California State Water Project: Current Activities and Future Management Plans*, Bulletin No. 132–80, Department of Water Resources, State of California, October 1980.

36. Interview with Jack Hunt (1986).

37. Interviews with Gene Lundquist, Ron Lampson, Henry Garnett, Stuart Pyle (all 1987).

38. Interviews with William Gianelli (1987) and John Lauten (1986).

39. Interview with Gene Lundquist (1987).

40. "Tables Describing 1977 Water Exchange and Alternatives for a Similar Exchange in 1978 under Various Water Supply and Demand Conditions," from the general manager to the ad hoc committee to study 1978 water exchange program, MWD, December 12, 1977; also "1977 Water Exchanges," from the general manager to board of directors, MWD, December 5, 1977.

41. See "Status Report on 1978 and 1983 Exchange Water Contracts with Kern County Water Agency," from the general manager to the board of directors, MWD, September 20, 1986.

42. Kern County Water Agency, *Annual Report*, 1972 and 1973, p. 29.

43. "Agency Position on Water Supply for Proposed Nuclear Power Generating Plant Near Wasco in Kern County," Kern County Water Agency, June 13, 1974.

44. While opposing the state's efforts, KCWA management was also—without much fanfare—launching its own storage program. (See chapter 10; also chapter 8 for a discussion of Kern water quality issues.)

45. Report to board of directors of Kern County Water Agency on establishment of zones of benefit, September 1974; report to board of directors of Kern County Water Agency on establishment of zones of benefit, July 1981, Leeds, Hill and Jewett, Inc.

46. "'Zone of Benefit' Tax no Longer Defensible, Water Study Reports," Ron Campbell, *Bakersfield Californian*, October 6, 1982.

47. Projections were that it could rise as high as $12 million by 1984 and eventually to $18.8 million. *Bakersfield Californian*, October 6, 1982.

48. "Water tax plan to soak homeowners," Ron Campbell, *Bakersfield Californian*, October 26, 1983. Also *Bakersfield Californian*, October 14, 1982, and October 16, 1982.

49. "Ag water may be heavy tax burden," Gail Schontzler, *Bakersfield Californian*, January 23, 1982.

50. *Bakersfield Californian*, June 5, 1982.

51. See the 1988 report on water conditions, Improvement District No. 4, Kern County Water Agency, February 1, 1989.

52. *Bakersfield Californian*, June 7, 1982, and June 8, 1982.

53. Interview with Gene Lundquist (1987).

54. The firm of James Ragan and Associates characterized itself as a "public involvement" firm, specializing in handling controversial issues. *Riverside Press Enterprise*, August 17, 1987; interview with Gene Lundquist (1987).

55. Interviews with Pauline Larwood, Gene Tackett, Stuart Pyle, John Means, Tom Schroeter (all 1987).

55. Interviews with Pauline Larwood, Gene Tackett, Stuart Pyle, John Means, Tom Schroeter (all 1987).

56. The restructuring, in part, was related to the definition of a groundwater-based agency, which included the Wheeler Ridge–Maricopa Agency though that agency's groundwater resources were generally of poor quality. Interviews with Gene Lundquist (1987), Tom Schroeter (1987), and Gene Bogard (1987).

57. Interviews with Fred Starrh (1987), Philip Kelmar (1987), and Henry Garnett (1987). Kelmar had particularly irked agency officials when he organized efforts to force the agency to use ID No. 4 surplus funds to reduce the City of Bakersfield's zone-of-benefit charges.

58. See *Management of the California State Water Project*, Bulletin 132–85, Department of Water Resources, State of California, September 1985; Kern County Agricultural Commissioner, *Annual Crop Report*, 1983–85.

59. Kern County Agricultural Commissioner, *Annual Crop Report*, 1984.

60. Power costs increased substantially for all state contractors between 1983 and 1985, increasing six-fold for MWD, the largest consumer of power in the State system. See Kern County Water Agency, *Biennial Report* 1984–85; MWD *Annual Reports* for FY 1983–84 and 1984–85.

61. Don Villarejo, 1981, *New Lands for Agriculture*; *Official Statement*, Wheeler Ridge–Maricopa Water Storage District, Kern County California, $7,600,000 1970 Bonds, Series E, October 13, 1971.

62. Kern County Agricultural Commissioner, *Annual Crop Report*, 1981; "Ten Years of Water Management, 1971 through 1980," Wheeler Ridge–Maricopa Water Storage District: Official Statement, $7,600,600 1970 Bonds, Series E, 1971.

63. *Prospectus*, Berrenda Mesa Water District, Kern County, California, $4,150,000 First Issue Series E General Obligation Bonds, Sale Date May 17, 1983.

64. Interview with Jack Hunt (1986); Form 10K Report to the Securities and Exchange Commission, Tejon Ranch Co., for FY ended December 31, 1985.

65. Interview with Ron Lampson, manager, Berrenda-Mesa Water District (1987). By 1986, 18,769 formerly irrigated acres were left fallow (see notices of sale during 1985, pursuant to the provisions of California Water Code sections 36951 and 36952). That same year, Wheeler Ridge–Maricopa reported twelve landowners covering 4,472 acres in delinquency on their accounts. Wheeler Ridge–Maricopa Water Storage District Report of Delinquent Accounts, and Penalties and Interest Accrued, December 8, 1986.

66. Interview with Ron Lampson (1987).

67. See transcript, Kern County Water Agency Hearing, November 13, 1986. See chapter 9 for a full discussion of the Kern transfer issues.

68. Berrenda Mesa's defaults had become so severe that the district itself now held title to substantial land (interview with Ron Lampson, 1987).

69. The Devil's Den Water District, though located in Kern and Kings counties, was not a member agency of the Kern County Water Agency but instead maintained a separate contract for 12,700 acre-feet of water from the State Project (see chapter 9).

70. See Transcript of the adjourned board meeting of the board of directors, Kern County Water Agency, November 13, 1986; Kern County Water Agency, *1986–87 Biennial Report*.

71. "Tejon Ranch wants to ditch water plan," Bob Cox, *Bakersfield Californian*, September 19, 1987.

72. Interviews with Fred Starrh (1987) and Stuart Pyle (1987); see Kern County Water Agency, *1986–87 Biennial Report*.

73. See Resolution 12–88, adopted at the meeting of the KCWA board of directors, May 16, 1988. Also minutes of the meeting of the board of directors of the Kern County Water Agency, April 25, 1988.

74. Interview with Fred Starrh (1987).

75. See Kern County Water Agency memorandum, "Staff Summary and Recommendation for Agency Execution of the Temporary Water Service Contracts with the Bureau and Member Units," from Stuart Pyle and Tom Clark to the State Contract Committee, January 22, 1987; also, *The Water Coalition Newsletter*, July 1987.

76. Interview with Gene Lundquist (1987).

Part II Accountability

1. "The Politics of Information: Constraints on New Sources," Helen Ingram, in *Water Politics and Public Involvement*, John C. Pierce and Harvey P. Doerksen (editors), Ann Arbor, Michican: Ann Arbor Science Publishers, 1976.

Chapter 6 How Decisions Get Made and Who Gets to Make Them

1. Scott A. Fenn, 1983, "The Structure of the Electric Power Industry" in *America's Electric Utilities: Under Seige and in Transition*, Investor Responsibility Research Center, Washington, D.C.; U.S. EPA, Federal Reporting Data System Tape, Fiscal Year 1987.

2. "State-Wide Alpha Listing of Water Service Agencies," Department of Water Resources, State of California, May 1985.

3. Imperial Irrigation District also includes that small portion of Riverside County where the Salton Sea extends.

4. For the use of the term "politician," interviews with Robert Nicholson (1986) and Howard Hawkins (1986). A number of agency officials are either former or current elected officials. Three of the five most recent MWD board chairs were formerly mayors: Howard Hawkins (West Covina), Earle Blais (Burbank), and E. L. Balmer (El Segundo).

5. Calculated from the number of (potential) elections and of defeats of incumbents (one in Kern, none in the Upper District) from the inception of each district to 1988.

6. The most contentious election in recent district history prior to the SWAP period occurred in 1974 when several incumbents were unseated. Those results were largely due to dissatisfaction by power consumers who saw the incumbents favoring the large water users over the individual power customers. Since 1969 nine incumbents have been defeated in IID elections (a retention rate of 64 percent, far lower that the other water districts). (Letter from Patricia B. Warren, assistant director, Public Information, IID, to April Smith, July 19, 1989.)

7. Interview with John Benson (1986).

8. In twenty-five years of elections of Kern directors, not one "open" race (without an incumbent candidate) has occurred.

9. Interview with Fred Starrh (1987).

10. Starrh (who lost by 601 votes—53 percent to 47 percent) attributed his defeat to the "Wasco factor," since Wasco had been the site proposed in the 1970s for a nuclear power plant that had been opposed ("violently opposed" as Starrh put it) by local residents but supported by KCWA. Starrh had strongly backed the plant and believed that the Wasco area residents never forgave him. But there were also significant class and political divisions between the strongly Democratic, lower-income Wasco area and the more Republican and wealthier Shafter community.

11. Letter from Stuart Pyle to April Smith, July 11, 1989; interview with Fred Starrh (1987).

12. Interview with Gene Lundquist (1987). Lundquist, an executive with Cal-Cot, a cotton-related corporation, himself fits this description well. Lundquist was appointed to a board vacancy soon after he completed a political apprenticeship with the California Agricultural Leadership Council. This program, started by the Council of California Growers with grants from the Kellogg and James G. Boswell Foundations, was explicitly designed to create new leadership in the area of politics and public relations among young and upcoming landowners or executives with agricultural businesses.

13. Interviews with Burt Jones (1987), Robert Nicholson (1986), and Howard Hawkins (1987).

14. One identifying mark of water industry membership is participation in the continuing cycle of meetings of the various trade and lobbying associations that tie the industry together.

15. Interview with Robert Berlien (1989).

16. Interview with Conrad Reibold (1986).

17. The Upper District's chair through 1990, E. Burton Jones, was first appointed in 1977.

18. Interviews with Conrad Reibold (1986) and Robert Nicholson (1986).

19. Interview with William Robinson (1989).

20. Final vote tabulations in the 1988 elections gave Brown 58.1 percent to Maulding's 41.9 percent and Robinson 57.4 percent to Hawkins's 42.6 percent (*Los Angeles Times*, November 10, 1988). In the 1990 elections, incumbent Al Wittig came in fourth in a field of five candidates (*Los Angeles Times*, November 8, 1990).

21. The 1987 information was provided by Karen Dorff, MWD; 1981 information can be found in *The Metropolitan Water District: The Institution and Water Supply Planning*, Robert N. Blanche et al., UCLA Graduate School of Architecture and Urban Planning report to the City of Santa Monica.

22. Between 1970 and 1977, there were ten deaths of MWD directors. MWD, *Annual Report* (1977).

23. The 1987 information is provided by Karen Dorff, MWD; 1981 information can be found in *The Metropolitan Water District: The Institution and Water Supply Planning*, Robert N. Blanche et al.

24. Interviews with Linden Burzell (1986) and Duane Georgeson (1985); comments by John Lauten, meeting of former MWD directors, May 2, 1989.

25. Minutes, meeting of the MWD board of directors, October 14, 1986.

26. Interestingly, the press release might have been premature. The Special Nominating Committee had in fact been quite contentiously divided between Krieger, whose symbolic importance as what would be the first female chair was underscored by her supporters, and Burton Jones (of the Upper District), a favorite of several old-guard directors. Rumors were thick the morning of the board vote, that Jones' supporters might nominate their candidate from the floor, breaking with precedent, but this did not occur. The committee's conflict over this nomination, however, was less over differences between Krieger (a long-standing water industry figure who was also chair of ACWA, the industry lobbying organization) and Jones than over personalities and anger stimulated by MWD management's increasingly dominant role. A few months later, the precedent-breaking action was finally achieved when two other names were placed in nomination for vice chairman in opposition to the choice of the Special Nominating Committee, Charles Barker, a former Standard Oil executive who had been a close friend and ally of the late chairman, E. L. Balmer. One of the challengers, Los Angeles Director Marilyn Garcia, was in fact elected, on the third ballot. Santa Monica Director Christine Reed, a Garcia supporter, characterized this battle as between the "old order" and "those directors who do not want to be a rubber stamp for the staff and who do not support policies just because 'it is how we have always done it'. . . . Change comes much more slowly to the MWD than it does to the region. I suppose this thus is true of other indirectly selected agencies where there is a great perceived distance between the agency and the ultimate consumer," Reed concluded. Memo from Christine Reed to the mayor and council members, City of Santa Monica, August 22, 1989; *Pasadena Star-News*, September 20, 1989.

27. The most common occurrence of weighted votes was adjourned sessions related to setting the annual property tax rate, when few directors were present. Analysis of minutes of the San Diego County Water Authority, 1981–1986.

28. Interviews with Willard Sniffen (1986) and Duane Georgeson (1985). Former MWD General Manager John Lauten recalled that when MWD managers first established a monthly meeting with the managers of local member agencies, there was still resistance to the idea by the MWD board. Prior to that time, during the Jensen era, MWD managers were obliged to discuss matters with MWD directors, who had the option of whether to pass on such information to their managers. Comments of John Lauten, meeting of former MWD directors, May 2, 1989.

29. In 1974 Katherine Dunlap, representing the City of Los Angeles, became the first woman even appointed to the MWD Board, forty-six years after the district was founded. In San Diego, Judith McConnell was appointed to the board in 1973, the first woman in the twenty-nine years since the formation of that agency.

30. Interviews with Emily Durbin (1987), Don Wood (1986), Mike Madigan (1986), Phil Pryde (1986), Dave Nielsen (1986), and Roger Hedgecock (1986, 1987).

31. Presentations by Mike Nolan and Tim Brick, UCLA Urban Planning Program, May 31, 1989. When one of the authors (Robert Gottlieb) joined the MWD board in 1980, there was only one other explicit "outsider," Ellen Stern Harris, representing the City of Beverly Hills, who resigned in early 1981. Though several directors from the City of Los Angeles also considered themselves "outsiders" in erms of a variety of issues, the Los Angeles directors never created a unified "bloc" in challenging existing policies and arrangements. By the late 1980s, however, the

role of the "outsiders" had modestly expanded, as reflected in the elections of both Lois Krieger as chair and Marilyn Garcia as vice-chair in 1989.

32. Tim Brick, presentation at UCLA Graduate School of Architecture & Urban Planning, May 31, 1989.

33. Expenses for the MWD board of directors during FY 1988–89, for example, totaled $385,000, much of which included travel and other reimbursements. MWD, *Annual Budget.*

34. See Metropolitan Water District Administrative Code Sections 435.4.5 and 435.6.2; "Amendment to Expense Account Regulations Pertaining to Directors," letter from E. Thornton Ibbetson, chairman of the board, to board of directors, MWD, April 4, 1983; also "Spouse Expense," E. Thornton Ibbetson, statement for discussion at MWD Directors' Workshop, October 5–7, 1987.

35. MWD, for example, has an active speaker's bureau facilitating these speaking engagements for both staff and directors. As an example, there were nineteen different speaking engagements during the month of November 1987, with more than 2,300 people in attendance, at groups such as the Chamber of Commerce, Kiwanis and Rotary clubs, schools, and professional societies. MWD, "Report of the Activities of the Public Information Division," October–November 1987.

36. For board routines, see minutes of the board of directors, MWD, 1980–1984.

37. Letter from E. L. Balmer, chairman, to MWD board of directors, March 18, 1987.

38. Presentation by Mike Nolan, UCLA Urban Planning Program, May 31, 1989. This situation is even more pronounced at special board meetings, such as retreats, where attendance of the press and public is nonexistent. At an October 1987 MWD board retreat, MWD Chairman E. L. Balmer began the meeting by asking, "Is there anybody here from the public? Seeing and hearing none–Thank God!" (Laughter among board members). Author's notes, MWD Board Retreat Meeting, October 6, 1987.

39. Review of the minutes of the meetings of the board of directors of the Kern County Water Agency. The only "split" vote occurred on June 26, 1986, on a four-to-one vote regarding a water marketing bill introduced in the state legislature.

40. Review of the minutes of the board of directors of the IID from 1984 to 1986 revealed thirty-two different split votes during the course of seventy-seven meetings, far more frequent than Kern, but still a small percentage of the total votes.

41. Though this practice continues today, the presence of "outside" directors, who frequently violate the norms of behavior at board meetings, has led to debate that would never have occurred in earlier periods.

42. San Diego's dinners became subject to controversy about possible violations of the Ralph M. Brown Act regarding open public meetings. Water Authority leaders denied that the dinners were policy related or by invitation only, though the dinners were never attended by uninvited citizens. "In a sense, it's a private party," CWA Chair Francesca Krauel said in characterizing the meetings. ("Water Board's Meetings May Violate Brown Act," *Escondido Times-Advocate*, September 7, 1986).

43. Author's notes, comments by Gerald Price, MWD board of directors meeting, August 16, 1986.

44. Interview with Lester Snow (1989).

45. Presentation by Mike Nolan, UCLA Urban Planning Program, May 31, 1989.

46. Interviews with Patty Prickett (Citizens for Safe Drinking Water), Ingrid Markle (League of Women Voters), both 1987. Markle, who represented the League on matters of water quality, attempted to present her views at an MWD Water Problems Committee meeting and felt that she had been subject to harassment both prior to the meeting (through phone calls from MWD staff) and at the meeting. Antagonism focused in part on whether she had sufficient expertise to deal with the matter at hand, legislation which MWD opposed and the league supported.

47. Interviews with Jane Bray (1986) and Tom McCauley (1986). Tom Stetson's role at the Upper District since the district was founded in 1963 has been as quasi-staff, with an ongoing relationship and detailed responsibilities. Burbank, on the other hand, had a regular engineering staff and used consultants only occasionally, though they were crucial to data gathering and strategy planning in the groundwater contamination issues.

48. Kern General Manager Stuart Pyle characterizes the general manager's role as "professional support" of the policies of the institution he represents, a position similar to that taken by Carl Boronkay at MWD. Both general managers, however, have been crucial in the formation of policy (unlike some of their predecessors). Interviews with Stuart Pyle (1987) and Carl Boronkay (1987).

49. See National Water Commission, 1973, "Water Policies for the Future," final report to the president and congress of the United States, Port Washington, New York.

50. Author's notes, comments by Duane Georgeson, assistant general manager, Los Angeles Department of Water and Power, at "Water in the West: Understanding the New Era," A Conference of the Institute for Resource Management, Sundance, Utah, October 19, 1985.

51. Presentation by E. L. Griffith, UCLA Urban Planning Program, 1983; interview with Robert Gough (1986).

52. Interviews with Carl Boronkay (1987), Larry Michaels (1985), and Jane Bray (1986).

53. Interviews with Robert Gough (1986), Jane Bray (1986), Carl Boronkay (1987), and Stuart Pyle (1987).

54. Interviews with Charles Cooper, Janet Erickson, Mike Madigan, Linden Burzell, Phil Pryde (all 1986); the vote at the "open" board meeting, however, was unanimous and without public debate. Minutes of the San Diego County Water Authority board of directors, February 23, 1984.

55. Interviews with Larry Michaels (1986), John Hennigar (1986), and Mike Madigan (1986).

56. Presentation by Lester Snow, UCLA Urban Planning Program, June 6, 1989.

57. Interviews with Stuart Pyle (1987) and Gene Lundquist (1987).

58. Interviews with Charles Shreves (1987), Bill Condit (1987), and John Benson (1986).

59. Interview with Alan Capon (1989).

60. Review of the minutes of the Public Services Advisory Board and Burbank City Council, 1985–1987; interviews with Goodwin Glance (1986) and Dale Kyle (1986).

61. Interviews with Ralph Helm (1986), Jane Bray (1986), Bill Ferry (1986).

62. Interviews with Jane Bray (1986) and Tom Stetson (1985).

63. Interview with Robert Berlien (1989).

64. Author's notes, comments of Robert Gough, November 1982.

65. Interview with Carl Boronkay (1987).

66. Author's notes, discussions with MWD Directors Christine Reed (May 9, 1989) and A. MacNeil Stelle (January 20, 1987). Stelle, a vice chairman of the MWD board, complained that MWD management "think of us [MWD directors] as a bunch of mushrooms. They want to control information and decisions."

67. Letter from general manager, MWD, to the board of directors, MWD, September 19, 1985; letter from Robert Gough, assitant general manager, MWD, to Roger Reidy, *Los Angeles Herald-Examiner*, November 7, 1985.

68. MWD Vice-Chairman (and Upper District representative) Burton Jones defended Boronkay's salary raise, stating that it was justified when "you consider he's the chief executive officer of a corporation as big as [MWD]." Quoted in "MWD panel recommends $17,000 raise for Boronkay," Rick Orlov, *Los Angeles Daily News*, June 13, 1989.

Chapter 7   Debating the Language of Policy

1. For a general review of the role of experts, see Baruch Fischhoff, S. Lichtenstein, P. Slovic, S. L. Derby, and R. Keeney, 1981, *Acceptable Risk*, Cambridge: Cambridge University Press; for a careful review of the conservatism of engineering consulting standards, see E. S. Ferguson, 1987, "Risk and the American Engineering Profession: The ASME Boiler Code and American Industrial Safety Standards" in V. T. Covello and B. B. Johnson (editors), *The Social and Cultural Construction of Risk*, (Dordrecht, Holland: D. Reidel).

2. The standardization of the process of environmental impact analysis provides another example of this dynamic. See "A Disaster in the Environmental Movement," Sally Fairfax, *Science*, February 17, 1978.

3. Certain MWD board members, such as the former chairman of the Finance and Insurance Committee, Carl Kymla, have attempted to expand the role of consultants through monitoring the expansion of staff positions and developing a pro-consulting bias in response to new demands on agency technical staff. Author's notes, discussion with Carl Kymla (1983); see *Quarterly Reports on Consultant Employment*, 1981 and 1982, from the general manager to the Organization and Personnel Committee, MWD board of directors. The issue of hiring additional staff or hiring consultants was also a key area in the debate regarding the district's massive $3 billion expansion plans. See "Engineering: Designs on the Future," *People*, Metropolitan Water District, No. 4, 1989.

4. See John Ross Terrell, 1965, *War for the Colorado River*, 2 volumes, Glendale: Arthur H. Clark.

5. Interview with Robert Will (1986).

6. Interviews with Jane Bray (1985), Thomas Stetson (1985), and Ralph Helm (1986).

7. Interview with Paul Engstrand (1987).

8. *Annual Report* of 1974, San Diego County Water Authority; see State Water

Resources Control Board Hearings, *Alleged Waste and Unreasonable Use of Water by the Imperial Irrigation District*, March 17, 1983, and September 29, 1983. Engstrand also continued to represent IID before the State Water Resources Control Board and on other legal matters at the same time that IID sought out San Diego during the SWAP negotiations. Interview with Paul Engstrand (1987).

9. Interview with Charles Shreves (1987): *Imperial Valley Press*, February 5, 1986; *Brawley News*, April 31, 1986.

10. Interviews with Tom Havens, Robert Davidson, John Benson (all 1987).

11. Interview with Tom Havens (1987).

12. Interview with Carl Boronkay (1987); author's notes, comments by Myron Holburt, October 13, 1987.

13. James Montgomery and Associates, for example, had developed a longstanding relationship with MWD over the disinfection by-products issue, consulting for the agency at different times where the issue was under discussion. Eventually, MWD Water Quality Division hired a former Montgomery staff person to work in this area.

14. MWD, 28th *Annual Report*, 1966, pp. 151–152.

15. Quoted in "Ban Sought on A-Reactors Not Used in Research," *Los Angeles Times*, April 2, 1988.

16. "Appropriation No. 547 for $300,000 to finance Metropolitan's share of a desalination study and authorization to enter into an agreement," letter from the general manager to the board of directors, MWD, January 21, 1988.

17. See "Presentation by Robert P. Will, representative of MWD of Southern California, on FY 1988 Department of Energy Budget Request, High Temperature Gas Cooled Reactor Program" to the Subcommittee on Energy Research and Development, Committee on Science, Space and Technology, U.S. House of Representatives, March 18, 1987; letter from Carl Boronkay, MWD general manager, to Robert A. Roe, chairman, Committee on Science, Space and Technology, February 26, 1987; *Los Angeles Daily News*, February 14, 1989.

18. See Baruch Fischhoff et al., 1981, *Acceptable Risk*.

19. These overlapping roles also reinforce the shift of the locus of policymaking from boards of directors to management and their consultants.

20. Interview with Alan Williams (1975).

21. Jensen fostered that image with his bluster and behind-the-scenes maneuvering. One MWD director recalled an incident when he—by chance—walked into Jensen's office and heard the MWD chairman berating then-Governor Edmund G. (Pat) Brown over a water issue. Interview with Howard Hawkins (1986).

22. MWD *Annual Report*, 1985.

23. Interviews with Tom Spencer (1987) and Carl Boronkay (1987).

24. Interview with Gene Lundquist (1987).

25. Interviews with Henry Garnett (1987) and Fred Starrh (1987).

26. Interviews with Willy Morris (1987) and Jim Cole (1986).

27. Interview with Cheryl Clark (1986).

28. Clark was able to expand the *Union*'s coverage in part because the paper's own interest in and concern about the water issue was increased by San Diego CWA's attempt to mobilize local business and political elites.

29. Boronkay actually told Clark that the decision to pursue Galloway was

"shocking" and he asked whether "members of the Authority actually smoke [controlled substances] before meetings? Do they look woozy in public? Was there any slurring of words?" *San Diego Union*, August 30, 1984. Boronkay, embarrassed by the quote, sent a sharp note to the managing editor of the *Union*, calling the reporter's actions "unethical" and a "breach of trust" because, he asserted, he had made his comments off-the-record; this was denied by the reporter, who had logged the quotes directly on her computer.

30. It was Clark, however, who voluntarily left the water beat to begin covering AIDS and other health issues.

31. "You Can Safeguard Water Supply by Voting," *Long Beach Independent Press-Telegram*, December 13, 1987; "Election Can Affect Drinking Water," *Long Beach Independent Press-Telegram*, July 22, 1988. "Officials who deal with water seemingly are still operating under the belief that the less the public knows the better off everyone is," Lynch wrote in an August 2, 1987, editorial. "If the public is to participate intelligently in the decision-making process that leads to a safe environment . . . ," he countered, "it must have all the information available. Any policy that contravenes that basic point is either paternalistic or just simply dishonest."

32. "The Gray Lady of Spring Street Hits 100," Robert Gottlieb, *Los Angeles*, December 1981.

33. Interview with Bill Boyarsky (1987). Boyarsky, impressed with the new MWD management group, was also a personal friend of a top MWD public information official, Jay Malinowski.

34. See, for example, the series of articles in the *Los Angeles Herald-Examiner*, December 11, 18, 1988 (primarily written by Emilia Askari, recently assigned to the water beat). The series was later reprinted by the paper under the heading "Tapped Out: Our Water—How we get it, use it, abuse it." The demise of the *Herald-Examiner* in late 1989 heightened the crucial regional significance of the *Los Angeles Times*, which was now the only paper with the resources to document the multiple regional roles of the MWD.

35. See League of Women Voters, *The Big Water Fight: Trials and Triumphs in Citizen Action on Problems of Supply, Pollution, Floods and Planning Across the United States*, Brattleboro, Vermont, S. Greene, 1966.

36. Presentation by Tom Clark, Kern County Water Agency assistant general manager, at UCLA urban planning program, April 25, 1989.

37. See Citizens for a Better Environment, *Environmental Review*, Annual Report issue, "1988: The Year in Revue," 1989.

38. Letter from Greg Karras to Tom Bailey, California Department of Health Services, July 26, 1983; interview with Greg Karras and Robert Ghirelli (1986).

39. Comments of Greg Karras on Behalf of Citizens for a Better Environment before the Environmental Protection Agency and the California Department of Health Services, Hazardous Materials Management Section, Regarding the "Field Investigation Team's Draft Report Summarizing Data Gathering Efforts in the San Gabriel Valley Groundwater Basin Superfund Study," Los Angeles, August 28, 1983; "Keeping the Pressure on in Los Angeles," Greg Karras, Citizens for a Better Environment, May-June 1984.

40. Interview with Greg Karras (1986).

41. In one confusing episode, the Department of Health Services advised residents in the unincorporated Hacienda Heights area that their well water had elevated

levels of 1,1-dichloroethylene (DCE) and that bottled water should be used for drinking and cooking. Immediately thereafter, DOHS rescinded the advisory, stating that despite the DCE levels in the water, they did not "pose any imminent public health danger." This turn of events caused a huge uproar in the community. See "To the Customers of the San Gabriel Valley Water Company in Hacienda Heights," letter from Kenneth Kizer, director, State Department of Health Services, October 4, 1985; "Is Hacienda Heights Pollution Problem Being Watered Down?" Betsy Bates, *Los Angeles Herald Examiner*, December 18, 1985. By 1988, the water quality issue finally began to translate into greater community engagement, this time without outside intervention by nationally based environmental groups. New coalitions were formed and certain community organizations, such as the East Valley Organization (EVO) made the water quality–Superfund issue a major organizational priority. See "Testimony of the East Valley Organization before the Environment and Labor Subcommittee of the House Committee on Small Business," Baldwin Park, June 5, 1989.

42. Interview with Emily Durbin (1986).

43. Interviews with Henry Nowicki (1986), Larry Michaels (1986), Emily Durbin (1986). Nowicki, also a Sierra Club member, created an organization called "Dialogue" to stimulate discussions and exchanges between water industry officials and citizen groups. Nowicki, however, felt that the tension between Michaels and Durbin was great enough that he decided not to invite Durbin to the sessions. The organization eventually folded. Nearly two years after her Pamo victory, Emily Durbin, who had been battling cancer for more than ten years, died at the age of fifty-seven.

44. Dialogue, for example, never succeeded in establishing a mechanism for community input to the water agencies, who felt attending the dialogue sessions was not a high priority. Interviews with Art Bullock (former CWA assistant general manager) (1986) and Henry Nowicki (1986).

45. The Harris support group eventually evolved into W.A.T.E.R. (Working Alliance to Equalize Rates), led primarily by Dorothy Green.

46. Presentation by Dorothy Green, UCLA Urban Planning Program, May 11, 1989.

47. Presentation by Dorothy Green, UCLA Urban Planning Program, May 11, 1989.

Chapter 8 *Water Quality: New Issues, Old Priorities*

1. *Escheria coli* is the coliform bacterium that is used as an indicator of the degree of fecal contamination of the water supply and thus, indirectly, of the likelihood of contamination of water with human disease organisms.

2. See "Urban Wastewater Technology: Changing Concepts of Water Quality Control, 1850–1930," Joel A. Tarr, James McCurley, and Terry Yosie in *Pollution and Reform in American Cities*, Martin Melosi (editor), Austin: University of Texas Press, 1980.

3. TDS is a measure of the dissolved mineral salts, or the "hardness" of water.

4. It was taken seriously enough at one time to prod MWD management into exploring alternative treatments, including granular activated carbon (GAC) filtration, which was used by several large eastern municipal agencies to control taste and odor problems. See Appendix, *Annual Report*, MWD, 1977, p.50.

5. When the San Gabriel Municipal Water District was formed, one crucial

argument against annexation to MWD via the Upper San Gabriel Valley Municipal Water District was concern over the TDS levels in Colorado River Water, which could not be as well used for storage, and preference for the State Project water, thus suggesting a separate contract with the state.

6. See "A History of the Attempted Federal Regulation Requiring GAC Adsorption for Water Treatment," James Symons, *Journal of the American Water Works Association*, August 1984.

7. There is, for example, only limited discussion of these issues in MWD *Annual Reports* when these events preoccupied many utilities in the East and Midwest. MWD, in fact, only first established its Water Quality and Research Branch in anticipation of passage of the Safe Drinking Water Act. See 37th *Annual Report* for FY 1974-75, MWD, p. 35; interview with Michael McGuire (1981).

8. See *Safe Drinking Water: Current and Future Problems*, Clifford S. Russell (editor), Washington, D.C.: Resources for the Future, 1978.

9. Interview with Foster Burba, water manager, Louisville utility (1986).

10. See *Trihalomethanes in Drinking Water*, American Waterworks Association, Denver, 1980.

11. Interviews with Foster Burba (1986) and Richard Miller, water manager, Cincinnati utility (1986).

12. Federal Register, 44, No. 231, 68624-68707 (November 29, 1979).

13. A more stringent standard would also have challenged the prevailing reliance on free chlorine as a disinfectant. In a 1988 interview, Peter Rogers of the California Department of Health Services commented, "The current standard for THMs is set at a level which is far higher than the risk levels we use for other contaminants, and the reason it's up there is because if at that time it were lower it might eliminate the use of chlorine as a disinfectant." Transcript, Interview, KABC Channel 7, May 10, 1988. See also "With it, Long-term Cancer Risks," Ron Linden, head of Technical Services Section of the Sacramento Regional Sanitation District, *Sacramento Bee*, March 29, 1987.

14. Interviews with utility water quality managers in Detroit, Chicago, Seattle, Denver, Portland, Madison (1986); see "AWWARF Trihalomethane Study," Michael T. McGuire and Robert G. Meadow, *Journal of the American Water Works Association*, January 1988.

15. During 1979, MWD exceeded the standard both on an annual basis and during two of the four quarters. "Trihalomethane Monitoring Program—Annual Report" from Senior Engineer M. J. McGuire to water quality manager, January 15, 1980. See "Technical Aspects of October 6, 1980, Meeting with MWD Manager on Trihalomethanes," City of Santa Monica inter-departmental memo from E. J. Lash and J. E. Hoagland to C. K. McClain and S. H. Scholl, October 7, 1980. It was estimated at the time that thirty-five utilities in California would not be able to meet EPA's November 29, 1981, deadline for implementation of the THM standards.

16. Though we think of water as pure, water is a solvent; most water sources include low concentrations of many naturally occurring compounds, substances, and organisms. Surface water carries mineral salts and organic acids in solution as well as suspended mineral and organic particles and, sometimes, bacteria and viruses; groundwater often has higher concentrations of salts but is usually free of particles and pathogens due to the filtering effect of flow through the soil column (unless local

contamination occurs). Whether or not these harm human users depends on their concentration and their potential toxicity. Where water passes through (or over) soils with high volumes of organic matter (like the peat soils of the Sacramento–San Joaquin Delta) high concentrations of organic contaminants can be picked up.

17. MWD delivers water to its clients from two primary sources; some clients receive mainly State Water Project water, some Colorado Aqueduct water, some a blend of the two—and adjusts its deliveries constantly on the basis of shifting seasonal and local water demands and variations in supply.

18. "Proposed Study of Alternative Disinfection Methods," letter from the general manager to the board of directors, MWD, April 30, 1981.

19. Capital cost estimates for GAC were estimated at $181 million, with total annual costs of $42 million. "Use of Chloramines as an Alternative Disinfectant for Trihalomethane Control," letter from general manager to the board of directors, MWD, August 2, 1982.

20. In fact, home systems can present a health problem if inadequately maintained, since the filter and the sediments it can accumulate may provide a substrate for bacterial growth if not disinfected or replaced.

21. "Water Purification Method Changed," MWD statement, May 15, 1985.

22. "Use of Chloramines in Metropolitan Water District Supply," letter from Ira Reiner, Los Angeles County district attorney to board of directors, MWD, July 5, 1985. Though Reiner's representative had been engaged in previous meetings and discussion, board members dismissed the letter—and the arguments—as a "stunt."

23. Minutes of the meeting of the Water Problems Committee, MWD, July 8, 1985.

24. See "Regulating Organics: An Interview with Michael Cook, EPA," *Journal of the American Water Works Association*, January 1987.

25. "Potential Health Risks of Drinking Water Disinfection Byproducts," Jennifer Orme and Edward V. Chanian, Office of Drinking Water, United States Environmental Protection Agency, 1988.

26. See letter from general manager to board of directors, MWD, Dec. 22, 1988, Board Item 8–3.

27. At one point in 1987, a director inquired whether the district's financial plan, then being prepared to detail the costs of these future supply expansions, included the potential new water quality–related expenditures under discussion at the meeting. With some embarrassment, the general manager replied that it did not, but that management would include such potential costs in any future draft of the financial plan. This "oversight," as the general manager termed it, was evidence of the agency's initial inability to comprehend the long-term implications of the changing definition of water quality, other than through regulation-driven discussions of least-cost ways to meet external standards. A year later the general manager would complain that the district's major capital programs were now being "driven, in great part, by water quality requirements." See minutes of the Subcommittee on Financial Policy, MWD, March 7, 1988.

28. Interview with Jerry Dotson (1987); "Comments on Proposed Regulations," letter from Carl Boronkay to Joseph A. Cotruvo, Office of Drinking Water, EPA, February 14, 1986; interview with Duane Georgesen (1987).

29. At an October 1987 board of directors retreat, MWD lobbyist Ray Corley

spoke of the alliance of the water agencies with the "ag-chemical" industry in killing water-quality legislation introduced in the previous session of the state legislature, an alliance that had effectively blocked initiatives at the state level. Author's notes, comments by Ray Corley, MWD board retreat, October 6, 1987.

30. Author's notes, comments by Michael McGuire, meeting of the Special Committee on Water Quality, April 19, 1987. McGuire, in earlier testimony before the California legislature, explained that MWD's expenditures in the water-quality area "are important, to try to retain the public's trust in its water supply. We have seen an erosion of this trust over the past few years as a result of widely publicized contaminant problems in the state's groundwaters. Hysterical media coverage, in many cases, has caused the public to lose faith in its drinking water." Presentation to California Senate Committee on Agriculture and Water Resources, March 5, 1985.

31. Safe Drinking Water Act Amendments of 1986, Public Law 99–339; author's notes, comments by Michael McGuire, Special Committee on Water Quality, April 9, 1987.

32. Letter from general manager to board of directors, MWD, Board Item 8–4, Appropriation No. 536, July 22, 1987.

33. Letter from general manager to board of directors, MWD, December 22, 1988. When projecting these costs in terms of average water rates, however, the differential in cost per acre-foot between a construction program with oxidation facilities and a base construction program with GAC facilities was just $33 per acre-foot ($427 for oxidation, based on average sales, versus $460 for GAC). See "Projected Average Water Rates," Table 5, in "Long-Range Finance Plan Update," letter from the general manager to the Finance and Insurance Committee, MWD, November 25, 1987.

34. Author's notes, comments by William Glaze and Michael McGuire, meeting of the Special Committee on Water Quality, January 10, 1989; "Water Quality Division Monthly Activity Report for April 1989," from director of water quality to Assistant General Manager Richard W. Balcerzak, April 19, 1989, p. 4.

35. Author's notes, comments by Dan Ashkenaizer, March 1989.

36. Interview with Jennifer Orme, Office of Drinking Water, U.S. EPA, 1988.

37. Author's notes, comments by Michael McGuire, Water Problems Committee, MWD board of directors, July 8, 1985.

38. Chloramines became the necessary option when it was discovered that chlorine with peroxone would not reduce THM levels substantially enough. Moreover, chloramine health-effects studies were still not completed at the time these decisions were made. (Author's notes, presentations by Michael McGuire and Jennifer Orme [EPA] at the meeting of the Special Committee on Water Quality, MWD board of directors, January 10, 1989. Concern about possible toxicological problems with chloramines was so strong within the water industry that a letter on behalf of the water agencies was sent to EPA Administrator William Reilly. Reilly was asked to "use the influence of your office" to speed up the toxicological review of chloramines. (Letter from Harold E. Snider, president, American Water Works Association, to William K. Reilly, October 19, 1989.) EPA, moreover, was quite aware of agency interest in confirming the safety of what one EPA document called "the most cost-effective means of meeting current and future chlorination by-product standards. . . .

Not being able to use chloramines," the document went on, "would result in many more systems having to use costly precursor removal treatment to meet current or lower standards." "Discussion of Strawman Rule for Disinfectants and Disinfection By-Products," Stephen W. Clark, Office of Drinking Water, WPA, October 11, 1989.

39. By late 1989, EPA had oriented its review process toward the choice between a 25 and a 50 ppb standard for chloramines—that is, the higher range of possible standards—linking the standard-setting analysis with the agencies' concerns about cost and with the question of the ability of utilities to meet the new standards. EPA estimated that only about 40 percent of large water agencies could meet a standard of 25 ppb, while 75 to 85 percent could meet a 50 ppb standard. ("Discussion of Strawman Rule," EPA, October 11, 1989, p. 15.)

40. The carbon collects contaminants and eventually becomes ineffective as a filter. Used carbon can be reactivated by heating at high temperatures, which drives off many of the contaminants as gasses; however, the vapors from this process contain hazardous substances that must be captured and treated or disposed of. If the carbon itself is simply discarded, it may be a hazardous waste. However, there is no new contamination generated by GAC; the technology merely captures the contaminants that are otherwise present, in lower concentrations but at higher volumes, in the water subjected to treatment.

41. *Delta Drinking Water Quality Study*, Brown and Caldwell, consulting engineers, May 1989.

42. It should be noted that this argument was introduced not within the internal review of THM reduction strategies but as part of the agencies' lobbying in regard to the Bay-Delta Hearings, suggesting that its purpose was related more to expanded supply than to reduction of disinfection by-products. When the issue of control of precursors first surfaced during the Peripheral Canal campaign in March 1982 (on release of a DWR study), it did not become a major campaign theme for MWD. The district was concerned about not antagonizing agricultural users, who could interpret such an approach as also leading to possible intervention against agricultural sources such as irrigation runoff, pesticide use, and so forth. Moreover, in 1982, the issue of THMs had received little public attention; MWD was concerned about bringing unwanted attention to the issue by raising it as a campaign issue.

43. This approach was highlighted when new research began to make it clear that ozonation would only be successfully used to reduce THM levels sufficiently if chloride and bromide levels in the Bay Delta waters could also be reduced from present levels. As a result of seawater intrusion, which itself resulted from the increased withdrawal and export of fresh water from the delta, both chloride and bromide levels had increased significantly. To reduce those concentrations, one could either *decrease* exports or construct a bypass facility such as the Peripheral Canal. The canal alternative would avoid having to address either the seawater intrusion concern or the buildup of organic precursors originated in agricultural runoff into the delta. For MWD, there was no real choice between what would have amounted to a pollution-prevention approach (reducing withdrawals and controlling agricultural contamination) and a pollution control (or "avoidance") strategy, since the canal remained the long-term centerpiece of the district's supply-enhancement orientation. "I consider this 'another arrow in my quiver'," commented MWD official Richard

Clemmer of the bromide/seawater/Peripheral Canal connection. (Quoted in *Sacramento Bee*, November 5, 1989. See also letter from Carl Boronkay to Water Pettit, State Water Resources Control Board, October 27, 1989.)

44. This term is normally used in planning to refer to the strategy advocated by Charles Lindblom in his article "The Science of 'Muddling Through'" (*Public Adminstration Review*, 19, 2 [Spring 1959]: 79–99). We use it here in a quite different and critical sense, in reference to a sort of institutional "tunnel vision" by which the institution avoids reconsideration of its established agenda or patterns of response, and therefore escapes innovation.

45. In the San Diego system, which relied primarily on Colorado River water, THM levels ranged around 50 ppb; THM levels for the municipal agencies varied substantially, from 20 to 30 ppb in parts of Los Angeles to 50 ppb or more in Burbank and Santa Monica. Systemwide THM levels in the late 1980s ranged from 60 to 75 ppb. Those few agencies that had difficulty complying with the 100 ppb standard relied on MWD to work out the best means for compliance. See general Manager's report to the MWD board of directors, May 26, 1988, pp. 11–12.

46. Presentation by Larry McReynolds, Los Angeles Department of Water and Power, UCLA Urban Planning Program, November 1987.

47. There are two ways of determining whether water is safe: to administer it to animals and examine them for health effects (bioassays) or to test it for the presence of specific contaminants believed to be hazardous. Bioassays are performed on the effluents of some sewage treatment plants (on an experimental basis), but they are not used to test the potential health effects of delivered water because they would be prohibitively expensive. For example, to discover whether water contaminant levels were sufficient to cause one additional cancer death per million people by biological assay, we would have to administer that water, under circumstances which controlled for other exposures to potential carcinogens, to millions of animals in order to meet statistical standards of reasonable proof.

The alternative way to test water is to examine it for particular substances that are known, or suspected, to be hazardous to health. At the present time, these tests must be made on a contaminant-by-contaminant basis. We do not know whether water is contaminated with a particular substance unless we look for that substance specifically. If we do not look for a particular contaminant, we cannot know whether it is there.

48. Neither did Upper District board member and then MWD Chairman Howard Hawkins, who owned a chemical fertilizer plant. Interview with Howard Hawkins (1986).

49. In the establishment of the Main San Gabriel Watermaster, water quality received only a passing mention, though that mention later provided the basis for Watermaster's increased activity in response to Superfund. (Presentation by Tom Stetson, UCLA Urban Planning Program, November 1985.)

50. CERCLA—the Comprehensive Environmental Response, Compensation and Liability Act of 1980.

51. Presentation by Myron Holburt, UCLA Urban Planning Program, April 18, 1989.

52. Author's notes, comments by Richard Balcerzak, board of directors meeting, MWD, June 12, 1984.

53. See Dorothy Nelkin and Michael S. Brown, 1984, *Workers at Risk* (Chicago: University of Chicago Press); Cambridge Reports, 1978, *Public and Worker Attitudes toward Carcinogens and Cancer Risk* (Cambridge: Cambridge Reports); Lou Harris, 1981, "Substantial Majorities Indicate Support for Clean Air and Clean Water Acts," *The Harris Survey* 47:2–3.

54. See Murray Weidenbaum and Robert Defina, 1978, *The Cost of Federal Regulation of Economic Activity* (Washington, D.C.: American Enterprise Institute); the various chapters by Reagan adminstration officials in V. Kerry Smith (ed.), 1986, *Environmental Policy under Reagan's Executive Order: The Role of Benefit-Cost Analysis* (Chapel Hill: University of North Carolina Press). For a critique of the assumptions used in this approach see R.N.L. Andrews, 1986, "Economics and Environmental Decisions, Past and Present," in Smith, *Environmental Policy under Regan's Executive Order*; R.N.L. Andrews, 1982, "Cost-Benefit Analysis as Regulatory Reform," in D. Swartzmann, R. A. Liroff, and K. G. Croke, *Cost Benefit Analysis and Environmental Regulation: Politics, Ethics and Methods* Washington, D.C.: Conservation Foundation, pp. 107–35; and David Noble and David Dickson, 1981, "By Force of Reason," in T. Ferguson and J. Rogers (eds.), *The Hidden Election* (New York: Pantheon).

55. John C. Bailar, III, Edmund A. C. Crouch, Rashind Shaikh, and Donna Spiegelman, 1988, "One-hit Models of Carcinogenesis: Conservative or Not?" *Risk Analysis* 8 (4): 485–97; Alvan R. Feinstein, 1988, "Scientific Standards in Epidemiologic Studies of the Menace of Daily Life," *Science* 242 (2 December 1988): 1257–63; R. W. Tennant, B. H. Margolin, M. D. Shelby, E. Zeiger, J. K. Haseman, J. Spalding, W. Caspary, M. Resnick, S. Stasiewicz, B. Anderson, and R. Minor, 1987, "Prediction of Chemical Carcinogenicity in Rodents from In Vitro Genetic Toxicity Assays" *Science* 236 (22 May 1987): 933–41; Baruch Fischhoff, S. Lichtenstein, P. Slovic, S. L. Derby, and R. Keeney, 1981, *Acceptable Risk* (Cambridge: Cambridge University Press); and M. Russell and M. Gruber, 1987, "Risk Assessment in Environmental Policy Making," *Science* 236 (17 April 1987): 286–90.

56. A position based on rejection of the whole accepted methodology of testing for carcinogenetic effects, which depended on animal models, high-dosage administration as a substitute for chronic, lower-dose exposures, and statistical tests of experimental results (see The U.S. Agency Staff Group on Carcinogens, 1986, "Chemical Carcinogens: A review of the science and its associated principles," *Environmental Health Perspectives* 67: 201–82). In fact, each of these testing strategies does introduce uncertainty, but the alternatives are not acceptable: If we do not use animal models, do we disregard the possible risks of these substances, or attempt to test them on human subjects instead? If we do not use high-dose exposures as a surrogate for chronic exposure, can we wait seventy years (the standardized human lifetime used in these models) to know whether or not these substances are toxic? Current legislation breaks up responsibility and risk for the assessment of chemical hazards: where suspect chemicals are already in commerce, the burden of regulatory proof is on government; but where new commercial chemicals are proposed, the burden of proof that they are not hazardous is on the firms that seek to introduce them (J. M. Mendeloff, 1988, *The Dilemma of Toxic Substance Regulation*, Cambridge, Massachusetts: MIT Press). In neither case would the responsible party be likely to accept the political costs of recommending human testing or of a seventy-year delay for the results.

57. Bruce Ames, Renae Magaw, and Lois Swirsky Gold, 1987, "Ranking Possible Carcinogenic Hazards," *Science* 236 (17 April 1987): 271–80. Also "New Water Quality Brochures," letter from general manager, MWD to all directors and member public agencies, June 30, 1986. The brochure, "How safe is safe?" was adapted from testimony before the California Senate Committee on Toxics and Public Safety Management and reprinted November 11, 1985, in the *Los Angeles Times*.

58. The area where MWD appeared most willing to offer assistance to local agencies confronting contamination problems was through financial assistance for treatment technology to clean up local wells and thus preserve as a source of supply. In the San Gabriel case, MWD linked its interest in a conjunctive-use program for the Basin with support for constructing treatment facilities.

59. In fact, scientists cannot fully resolve this controversy; science cannot prove relationships, it can only show that alternative explanations are unlikely. But the public, legislators, and the regulatory agencies have decided that, while the controversy about scientific proof of chemical hazards may never be fully resolved, there is sufficient evidence that chemical contamination of water may be hazardous to make it necessary to require water agencies to act in a way that is conservative of public health.

60. Only MWD, with its huge budget, powerful political position, and large technical staff, was really in a position to begin to seek effective solutions to these problems.

61. See "Organic Chemical Contamination of Large Public Water Systems in California," Department of Health Services, State of California, April 1986; "Drought Threatens Lush 'Illusion' of Arid Fresno Area," *Imperial Valley Press*, July 25, 1989.

62. *Kern County Ground Water Model*, Department of Water Resources, San Joaquin District and Kern County Water Agency, District Report, March 1977.

63. Interview with Florn Kore (1987), Mike Rector (1986), and Stuart Pyle (1987).

64. *Groundwater Pollutant Study*, San Joaquin Valley, Kern County California, Kern County Health Department, Leon M. Hebertson, health officer, Vernon S. Reichard, director, Division of Environmental Health, March 1980.

65. "Comments on Groundwater Pollutant Study, Recommended Action Plans," letter from Stuart Pyle, engineer-manager, KCWA, to Daphne Washington, Kern County Health Department, September 22, 1980; memorandum from B. A. Babcock, Bookman-Edmonston Engineering Inc., containing comments on groundwater pollutant study, to Cliff Trotter, Kern County Agricultural Water Well Standards Committee, August 13, 1980.

66. Letter from Vernon S. Reichard, director, Environmental Health Division, to Kern County board of supervisors, October 17, 1980.

67. Interviews with John Means (1986), Florn Kore (1987), Michael Rector (1986), and Stuart Pyle (1986).

68. Groundwater Quality Report, San Joaquin Valley, Kern County, California, approved by the Kern County board of supervisors by Resolution No. 821029, March 1982.

69. Interview with Joyce Johnson (1988).

70. Letter from Richard L. Haberman, Senior Sanitary Engineer, Department of Health Services to Joel Heinrich, director of policy analysis, Kern County Administrative Office, September 19, 1988; letter from Stuart Pyle to chairman, Kern County board of supervisors, September 29, 1988; author's notes, comments by Stuart Pyle, January 1989 meeting of Kern Valley Action Network.

71. Carcinogens are substances that cause cancer. Mutagens are substances that cause mutation of the genetic material of sperm or ova and thus modify the heredity of babies; most mutations are lethal to the embryo but those that are not may be expressed as genetic defects in living infants or in their children. Teratogens are substances that affect the normal development of the embryo; for example, thalidomide was a teratogen that disturbed normal development of the arms of the fetus.

72. There were other connections between the water industry and the petrochemical industry. The chairman of the MWD board at the time of Proposition 65, E. L. Balmer, was a former Chevron executive. The two industries both participated in the Hazardous Waste Management Project of the California Council on Environmental and Economic Balance, an industry-funded lobbying group. The committee, which included both MWD and LADWP as members, had a membership in which oil and chemical companies were heavily represented (letter from general manager to board of directors, MWD, September 19, 1985). And both industries were to discover that their positions on risk and acceptable discharges were decidedly unpopular with the voting public.

73. *Los Angeles Times*, September 20, 1986.

74. A 1989 customer survey for the Los Angeles Department of Water and Power proved even more embarrassing than previous polls. An astounding 64 percent of those surveyed indicated that they used bottled water, water filters, or both. Among DWP's *own employees*, 59 percent used some combination of bottled water or water filters. "64% of DWP's customers steer clear of tap water," Myron Levin, *Los Angeles Times*, September 20, 1989.

75. Interview with Tom Graff (1986).

76. Interview with David Roe (1987).

77. Interviews with Wiley Horne and Tim Quinn (1987); also, presentation by Wiley Horne, UCLA Urban Planning Program, October 1987.

78. Author's notes, comments by Carl Boronkay and Jerald Butchert (manager, Westlands Water District), meeting of the National Water Resources Association, December 3, 1986.

79. In April 1990, three years after the Source Reduction Research Partnership had been formed and a million dollars (almost all of it public funds) spent on the project, MWD fired Wolfe soon after a draft report she had prepared had begun to circulate. Wolfe had clashed with both MWD and EDF participants, both over the substance of her research findings (that source reduction involved difficult choices) and the nature of the personalities involved in the project. The former Rand chemist also claimed that MWD and EDF antagonists had "sent a memo instructing me to alter the results of the study." Ultimately, the report was sent to another consulting firm for rewrite purposes. See letter from Katy Wolfe to Thornton Ibbetson, chairman, Water Problems Committed, MWD, July 17, 1990. Also, draft work plan and initial meeting of the advisory committee, Kathleen Wolfe, project manager, Source Reduc-

tion Research Partnership, April 16, 1987; author's notes, comments by Katy Wolfe, January 1987.

80. Minutes, meeting of the executive committee, MWD board of directors, December 9, 1986.

Chapter 9   Groping Toward Reallocation

1. Donald A. Brobst, 1979, "Fundamental Concepts for the Analysis of Resource Availability." In V. K. Smith, *Scarcity and Growth Reconsidered* (Baltimore: Resources for the Future), 196–236.

2. To the classical economists private property in land arose from the confirmation of private rights to the benefit of particular individuals who thus acquired monopoly over segments of what had been a common inheritance. Confirmation and protection of these rights are part of the role of the state, of the changing structure of government. The historical aspect of this establishment of private rights can be seen in their incompleteness: land (as space and soil) has taken on an almost entirely private form, carrying with it forests and ores; but water, which was not scarce in humid England and the eastern United States, is not everywhere or entirely established as "private" property.

3. D. Anderson, 1977, *Riparian Water Rights in California*, Staff Paper #4, Governor's Commission to Review California Water Rights Law; A. Schneider, 1977, *Groundwater Rights in California*, Staff Paper #2, Governor's Commission to Review California Water Rights Law.

4. It is impossible to know what the development history of the Owens Valley might have been if Los Angeles had not successfully captured rights to Owens Valley water—reducing water scarcity in Los Angeles by imposing it on the valley.

5. This is particularly true where tax subsidies of the capital and operating costs of transport infrastructure mean that the price of water does not fully reflect the cost of providing water.

6. A recent example of this argument appears in a report prepared for the San Diego County Water Authority (and distributed to all MWD directors) by Regional Economic Research (a San Diego consulting firm), entitled "An Analysis of the External Benefits Associated with the Availability and Use of MWD Water Supplies," December 29, 1983.

7. Groundwater activity was more narrowly focused, depending state-by-state on the legal form of ownership rights, but several of the major surface water systems, like the Central Valley Project and State Water Project in California, were designed in part to allow private withdrawals of groundwater to proceed uninterrupted.

8. "Public Entrepreneurship: A Case Study in Ground Water Basin Management," Elina Ostrom, Ph.D. diss., UCLA, 1965; also Albert J. Lipson, 1978, "Efficient Water Use in California."

9. Bonnie Colby Saliba, 1986, "Market Transactions and Pricing of Water Rights in the West," in Steven J. Shupe (ed.), *Water Marketing: Opportunities and Challenges of a New Era*, (Denver).

10. Interviews with Thomas Stetson (1985) and Jane Bray (1985).

11. See *Annual Report, Main San Gabriel Basin Watermaster, 1986–1987*, November 1, 1987; also interview with Howard Hawkins (1986).

12. See, for example, Irving K. Fox and Orris C. Herfindahl, *Attainment of Efficiency in Satisfying Demands for Water Resources*, Washington, D.C.: Resources for the Future, 1964; Maurice Kelso, "The Water is Different Syndrome, or What is Wrong with the Water Industry?" 1967, paper presented to the American Water Resources Association, November 1967.

13. Charles E. Phelps, Nancy Y. Moore, and Morlie H. Graubard, 1978, *Efficient Water Use in California: Water Rights, Water Districts and Water Transfers*, (Rand Corporation Report R–2386–CSA/RF, November 1978).

14. Interview with Nancy Moore (1983).

15. Interview with Tom Graff (1986); see Robert Stavins, *Trading Conservation Investments for Water*, Environmental Defense Fund, Berkeley, California, 1983.

16. See testimony by William Dubois (California Farm Bureau) before the State Water Resource Control Board Hearings on Alleged Waste and Unreasonable Use of Water by the Imperial Irrigation District, September 1983.

17. By the late 1980s, as new water development scenarios became increasingly problematic, various contractors for State Project water became more and more interested in the state takeover of the Central Valley Project as a means to "stretch" existing supplies by consolidating operation of the two systems.

18. Presentation by Nancy Moore, UCLA Urban Planning Program (1983).

19. "Water Scarcity and Gains from Trade in Kern County, California," H. J. Vaux, Jr., 1985, in *Scarce Water and Institutional Change*, Kenneth D. Frederick (editor), Resources for the Future, Washington, D.C.

20. "Water Trading: Free Market Benefits for Exporters and Importers," Patricia Schifferle, project manager, Assembly Office of Research, O58–A (government report), Sacramento, California, February 1985.

21. The Tejon Ranch, for one, had been a substantial financial contributor to the pro-Canal campaign. *Contra Costa Times*, February 25, 1982. See also "Close Up: Khachigian Has Water On His Mind," Margaret Hart, *California Business*, March 1981, p. 28.

22. Interviews with Ron Lampson (1986), Ron Khachigian (1986), and Dennis McCarthy (1986).

23. "Conditions for Transfer or Marketing of Water Entitlement Outside the District," Wheeler Ridge–Maricopa Water Storage District, May 14, 1986; "Conditions for Changes in Surface Water Service Area," Wheeler Ridge–Maricopa Water Storage District, June 17, 1985; interviews with Jack Hunt (1986), Dennis McCarthy (1986), and Stuart Pyle (1987).

24. Interview with Jack Hunt (1986).

25. Interview with Ron Khachagian (1986).

26. Interviews with Ron Lampson (1987) and Stuart Pyle (1987); see Transcript, board of directors meeting, Kern County Water Agency, November 13, 1986.

27. Interviews with Robert McCarthy (1986), Fred Starrh (1987), and Gene Lundquist (1987); see "Transfer of State Project Entitlement Proposals," letter from the general manager to the board of directors, MWD, November 4, 1986.

28. *Kern County Water Agency Plan for Redistribution of State Water Project Contract Entitlement*, Kern County Water Agency, April 1986.

29. Interview with Jack Hunt (1986) and Robert McCarthy (1986).

30. "Position Regarding the Possible Transfer of State Water Project Agricultural

Entitlements," letter from the general manager to the board of directors, MWD, April 34, 1987; also, "An Update on Proposed Transfers of State Project Entitlements," letter from general manager to board of directors, MWD, March 31, 1987; letter from general manager to board of directors, MWD, November 26, 1986.

31. Interviews with Stuart Pyle (1987) and Fred Starrh (1987).

32. Minutes of the board of directors meeting, KCWA, April 28, 1989, and May 26, 1988. The transfer of the nearly 14,000 acre-feet of entitlement water involved one of Tejon Ranch's tax-sheltered partnerships, Pastoria Creek. Though Hunt, president of Tejon, called the arrangement a "half-a-loaf solution," the leading environmental advocate of water markets, Tom Graff (EDF), called it "a victory for the forces of darkness," since Tejon was not able to realize a profit on the sale. "Grower Pays $1.4 Million to Escape Water Contract," Ann Cony, *Sacramento Bee*, May 11, 1988.

33. "Memorandum of Understanding between Berrenda Mesa Water District and the Environmental Defense Fund," July 9, 1987; interview with Tom Graff (1987).

34. *Draft Report: Potential Purchase of Water from Berrenda Mesa Water District*, Kevin Hunt, vice president/general manager, P&D Technologies, report prepared for Moulton-Niguel Water District, March 1988.

35. Presentation by Myron Holburt, UCLA Urban Planning Program, April 18, 1989.

36. Interview with Ron Lampson (1989); "Proposed Transfer of a Portion of the District's State Water Project Entitlement," initial study and proposed negative declaration, Berrenda Mesa Water District, with technical assistance from Jones & Stokes Associates, Inc., July 15, 1988.

37. Interviews with Bill Balch of Tenneco West (1986), Larry Michaels (1986), and George Nickel (1986).

38. In one interesting development that never was consummated, some of the Kern interests explored contracting with the Parsons Company (at that time under attack from Imperial residents for its role in the SWAP) to represent them in negotiating and implementing a transfer to MWD (see letter from George W. Nickel to Myron Holburt, January 3, 1986).

39. MWD management at one time made a distinction between land purchases in different areas (e.g., the Imperial and Central valleys) but the position was not consistently maintained.

40. This criticism had already been leveled by Imperial residents regarding the SWAP negotiations.

41. "MWD Considers Buying Farms," *US Water News*, March 1986.

42. This not only included the IID SWAP, but also involved possible land transactions in the Imperial, Coachella, and Palo Verde valleys. "Purchase of Farms Studies—to Reap the Water," Ronald B. Taylor, *Los Angeles Times*, December 16, 1985; "MWD May Buy Hard-Hit Farms to Obtain Water," Cheryl Clark, *San Diego Union*, December 23, 1985.

43. Ultimately, sixty-one staff or board members of MWD and member agencies attended the conference, called "Buying and Selling Water in California: How Does it Fit into the State's Water Policy Portfolio?" at Santa Monica, February 27-28, 1986.

44. See, for example, "Arizona Project Hits Snag," *Focus* no. 4, 1989, Metropolitan Water District; general manager's report for June 1990, Metropolitan Water District, June 25, 1990.

45. Interview with Tom Quinn (1988).

46. Imperial Irrigation District Alleged Waste and Unreasonable Use of Water, Water Rights Decision 1600, State Water Resources Control Board, June 1984.

47. Interviews with Carl Boronkay (1986, 1987), Charles Shreves (1987), Bill Condit (1987), and Lester Bornt (1987). IID, in particular, was concerned about the State Regional Water Quality Control Board enforcing its ruling, while MWD was concerned about its position with respect to the Bay-Delta Hearings.

48. Interviews with Tim Quinn (1987) and Cliff Trotter (1987).

49. "Arvin-Edison/Metropolitan Water Storage and Exchange Agreement," from the general manager to the board of directors, MWD, April 15, 1986.

50. The KCWA provided the sole vote against the Arvin-Edison plan at a meeting of the State Water Contractors in October 1989, declaring that "it has the right to approve any transfers of state water within its boundaries." "Kern Agency Opposes Water Swap," Christopher Krueger, *Bakersfield Californian*, October 22, 1989. Also, interview with Henry Garnett; author's notes, general manager's report to the board of directors, (Myron Holburt) November 18, 1986; "Revised Principles for the Arvin-Edison/Metropolitan Water Storage and Exchange Program," letter from general manager to board of directors, MWD, August 8, 1988.

51. Interview with Henry Garnett (1987); "Interim Agreement with the Arvin-Edison Water Storage District," January 27, 1989.

52. Interview with Paul Tiegen (1989).

53. Board members were concerned at two levels: that approval of the program would be interpreted as support for the renewal of Arvin-Edison's Central Valley Project contracts with their heavily subsidized rates; and that there was "no absolute guarantee that MWD will get the water in times of drought." Letter from MWD board member Christine E. Reed to city council, City of Santa Monica, November 16, 1989; minutes, meeting of the board of directors, MWD, May 9, 1989; November 14, 1989.

54. Author's notes, comments by Myron Holburt, general manager's report, meeting of MWD board of directors, March 10, 1987.

55. Interview with Tim Quinn (1988).

56. Author's notes, comments by Myron Holburt, general manager's report, meeting of MWD board of directors, March 10, 1987.

57. "Farmers Tell MWD to 'Drop Dead'," Dennis Coffon, *Palo Verde Valley Times*, April 17, 1987. See also *Palo Verde Valley Times*, March 13 and March 19, 1987. A Palo Verde agreement would also raise all the institutional issues regarding Colorado River allocations in California; see "Water Marketing in Southern California," Myron Holburt, Richard W. Atwater, and Timothy H. Quinn, *Journal of the American Water Works Association*, March 1988, pp. 36–45.

58. Boronkay, as early as 1985, complained that San Diego's interest in such arrangements, particularly the IID SWAP, was price-related, declaring, "Why should they get the cheap water?" Author's notes, comments by Carl Boronkay, Water in the West conference, Institute for Resource Management, Sundance, Utah, October 20, 1985.

59. "Water Marketing—Promises and Pitfalls," Carl Boronkay, presented to the Scientific and Technical Information Institute, Ministry of Water Resources and Electric Power, Liukand, Dewa., Beijing, China, September 27, 1988.

60. *ACWA News*, vol. 17, no. 16, August 7, 1989.

61. Carl Boronkay, "Water Marketing—Promises and Pitfalls," 1988; even as early as September 1986, the State Department of Water Resources issued a detailed "Catalog of Water Transfer Proposals," involving thirty-one different proposals.

62. "Voluntary Transfers of Federally Supplied Water: Experiences of the Bureau of Reclamation," Richard W. Wahl in Shupe, *Water Marketing: Opportunities and Challenges of a New Era*, 1986.

63. "Interior Releases Policy on Western Water Marketing," *ACWA News*, January 9, 1989, p. 4.

64. See *Measuring the Community Value of Water*, Helen Ingram et al. The Water and Public Welfare Project, The Udall Center for Studies in Public Policy, University of Arizona and the Natural Resources Center, University of New Mexico School of Law, January 1989.

65. "Urban Use of Arizona's Rural Groundwater," Karl F. Kahlhoff, *Journal of the American Water Works Association*, March 1988.

66. "Leasing Indian Water: Upcoming Choices in the Colorado River Basin," Gary Weatherford, Mary Wallace, and Lee Herald in Shupe, *Water Marketing: Opportunities and Challenges of a New Era*, 1986.

67. See *Water and Poverty in the Southwest*, F. Lee Brown and Helen M. Ingram, Tucson: University of Arizona Press, 1987.

68. See *Measuring the Community Value of Water*, Helen Ingram et al., The Water and Public Welfare Project, The Udall Center for Studies in Public Policy, University of Arizona and the Natural Resources Center, University of New Mexico School of Law, January 1989.

69. Bangor Punta Corporation, Form 10K, submission to the Security and Exchange Commission, 1982.

70. Interview with M. H. Pace (1989).

71. Interview with Robert Sagehorn, general manager, Castaic Water District; "Devil's Den Purchase Was Good Deal For SCV," Robert C. Sagehorn, *Newhall Signal*, December 4, 1988.

72. "Status Report on Possible Transfer of State Water Project Agricultural Entitlements to Castaic Lake Water Agency," letter from general manager to board of directors, MWD, August 8, 1988.

73. Letter from Stuart Pyle to David Kennedy, director, Department of Water Resources, July 29, 1988; also, "Devil's Den Deal was Outside Normal Bounds," Stuart Pyle, *Newhall Signal*, December 4, 1988.

74. Interview with Milt Pace (1989).

75. Even one of Castaic Lake Water Agency's directors opposed the transfer for its potential growth implications (*Santa Clarita Valley Citizen*, October 25, 1988).

Chapter 10   The Role of Efficiency

1. David Roe, 1984, *Dynamos and Virgins* (New York: Random House).

2. See, for example, *Water and Power: The Peripheral Canal and Its Alternatives*,

Harry Dennis (San Francisco: Friends of the Earth, 1981); and "Answers to Arguments against the Peripheral Canal," letter from the general manager to the board of directors, MWD, April 10, 1981.

3. See "The Future of Irrigation In Kern County," Stuart Pyle, engineer-manager, Kern County Water Agency, presented at ASCE Water Forum 1981, San Francisco, August 11, 1981.

4. *Urban Water Management in California: A Report to the Legislature in Response to the Urban Water Management Planning Act of 1983*, Department of Water Resources, State of California, December 1986; *The Regional Urban Water Management Plan for the Metropolitan Water District of Southern California*, July 1985.

5. "Status of Current Activities to Increase Metropolitan's Water Supplies," letter from the general manager to the board of directors, MWD, February 3, 1986.

6. "The Time Has Come to Define the Conjunctive Management of Water Resources," Michael D. Bradley, in *Proceedings of the Symposium on Conjunctive Management of Water Resources*, American Water Resources Association, Arizona Section and the Arizona Hydrological Society, Tucson, Arizona, October 18, 1985.

7. Cited in "Ground Water Basin Management," James H. Krieger and Harvey O. Banks, *California Law Review* 50 (1962): 57.

8. Those fights eventually boiled down to the issue of where to locate the major new distribution lines from the State Water Project. The eventual choice was enlargement of the East Branch of the California Aqueduct, which was designed to increase MWD's capacity to take State Project water. See Environmental Impact Report: Enlargement of the East Branch of the Governor Edmund G. Brown California Aqueduct, Report 956, MWD, October 1985.

9. Report of the Engineering Subcommittee, Karl A. Johnson (chairman), Donald G. Brooks, Mitchell L. Gould, Dennis E. McClain, presented to Duane Georgensen, chairman, Southern California Water Conference, Ad Hoc Committee on Conjunctive Use of Ground Water Basins, June 17, 1974.

10. See *Ground Water Basin Storage Symposium Proceedings*, sponsored by the California Department of Water Resources, Los Angeles, August 8, 1979; *The California State Water Project—1978 Activities and Future Management Plans*, Bulletin 132–79, Department of Water Resources, State of California, November 1979, pp. 35–37.

11. Governor's Commission to Review California Water Rights Law, *Final Report*, December 1978; see especially, A. J. Schneider, "Groundwater Rights in California," staff paper #2, July 1977.

12. *Chino Basin Municipal Water District v. City of Chino et al.*, San Bernardino Superior Court, Case No. 164327, 1978.

13. MWD *Annual Reports*, FY 1977–78, 1978; FY 1987–88, 1988, Table 15, p. 39.

14. See Remarks by Governor Edmund G. Brown, Jr., at the Signing of SB200, July 18, 1980, reprinted in Bulletin 132–80, Department of Water Resources, October 1980, pp. 33–37.

15. Letter from Earle Blais to Rex Pursell, September 2, 1981; for an attack on the Brown proposals, see "State Groundwater Controls Aren't the Solution for Groundwater," in CWRA's *Objectives in 1981*, California Water Resources Association, 1980.

16. *Chino Basin Groundwater Storage Program*, final report, Camp Dresser & McKee, prepared for Department of Water Resources, State of California and MWD of Southern California, March 1983.

17. General manager's report to the board of directors, MWD, September 9, 1983, p. 8. A letter was prepared by MWD linking DWR's removal from the project to the issue of constructing additional State Project facilities.

18. The large number of potential participants was one factor. Groundwater users in the proposed storage program area included 21 municipal water-supply agencies, 11 major industrial users, and about 520 agricultural users. Chino Basin Groundwater Storage Program, Draft Environmental Impact Report, Report No. 975, MWD of Southern California, June 1988.

19. Chino Basin Groundwater Storage Program, Draft Environmental Impact Report, Report No. 975, MWD of Southern California, June 1988.

20. Chino Basin Groundwater Storage Program, Draft Environmental Impact Report, Report No. 975, MWD of Southern California, June 1988, p. I–1.

21. In a May 27, 1982, letter from the general manager to the board of directors on the Chino Basin feasibility study, there is no mention of any potential water quality problem, and the following assertion appears: "There are no major environmental issues that cannot be mitigated except that, in the future, urbanization will limit direct spreading of imported water."

22. *Organic Chemical Contamination of Large Public Water Systems in California*, DOHS, State of California, April 1986. See Appendix B–14 for contamination results in the Chino area.

23. Minutes of the meeting of the board of directors of MWD, October 14, 1986, p. 15.

24. The discovery of contaminated wells during the early and mid-1980s was exacerbated by new studies in 1986 that showed significant contamination at the Kaiser Steel site, a major industrial site in the area. "Pollution May Affect plan to Use Chino Basin for Storage," Gary Polakovic, *San Bernardino Sun*, October 26, 1986.

25. See Response of the MWD of Southern California to motion for review of Watermaster actions and decisions, *Chino Basin Municipal Water District v. City of Chino et al.*, San Bernardino Superior Court, Case No. 164327, February 8, 1989.

26. "Motion Challenges Chino Basin Groundwater Storage," letter from general counsel to board of directors, MWD, November 28, 1988, and "Proceedings Challenging the Chino Basin Watermaster's Groundwater Storage Program," letter from general counsel to board of directors, MWD, December 1988.

27. See "A Progress Report on the Activities to Increase Metropolitan's Dependable Water Supplies," letter from the general manager to the board of directors, MWD, January 31, 1989.

28. Interview with Jane Bray (1986).

29. San Diego, interestingly, discovered that there were also possible contamination threats to potential groundwater storage basins within its territory. See letter from Byron M. Buck, director, Water Resources Planning, to the board of directors, SDCWA, July 6, 1989.

30. See *Monthly Water Use by Member Agency*, FY 1984–85 through FY 1987–88.

31. "Summer Water Shortages," letter from the general manager to the board of directors, MWD, May 16, 1986.

32. The concept of system expansion had preoccupied MWD management through the 1980s. See *The Need for Major Additions to Metropolitan's Distribution System*, Report No. 949, MWD, July 1983; "Treatment Plant Expansion Policy," letter from the general manager to the board of directors, MWD, November 22, 1985.

33. See "Groundwater Overdraft Correction Policy," Resolution No. 27–76, Kern County Water Agency, passed by the board of directors, September 23, 1976.

34. See Bulletin 132–79, Department of Water Resources, State of California, October 1980, pp. 22–24.

35. The 1980 *Groundwater Pollutant Study* released by the Department of Health Services (that had been so strongly criticized by the Kern water industry) also argued in favor of imported water to relieve groundwater problems as its starting point: its proposed restrictions on pumping were not, in fact, related to groundwater management and controls but rather to water-quality controls. Moreover, for the water industry, the term "groundwater controls," used to refer to adjudication and other restrictions on pumping, was contrasted with "groundwater management," which industry figures defined as storage or replenishment programs [interviews with Henry Garnett (1986) and Stuart Pyle (1987)].

36. *City of Bakersfield 2800 Acre Groundwater Recharge Project*, November 1986, City of Bakersfield, pamphlet published by the city.

37. Interview with Gene Bogard (1987).

38. Interview with Stuart Pyle (1987).

39. Ibid.

40. "Recapitulation of Water Spreading by Source, 2800 Acre Recharge Facility," City of Bakersfield, 1986.

41. "1989 Shortages and Local Dry Year Supplies," memorandum from Gary Buchar to Stuart Pyle, George Ribble, Thomas Clark, Kern County Water Agency, March 6, 1989; *Water Age*, Kern County Water Agency, March, April, August 1990.

42. Author's notes, comments by Mary Collup, Rosedale–Rio Bravo Water District, at the meeting of the board of directors, Kern County Water Agency, January 22, 1987; "Water Bank Withdrawal Proposal Brings Lawsuit," Ronald Campbell, *Bakersfield Californian*, March 4, 1987. Despite the opposition, KCWA management continued to see advantages to developing programs around local sources, given the high costs of maintaining (let alone expanding) State Water Project supplies. "Agency planners believe that yield from local sources using when-available, wet-year water and ground water banking will be cheaper than expensive additions to major State Project storage facilities." *Water Age*, January 1990, publication of the Kern County Water Agency. Also, minutes of the Kern County Water Agency, December 28, 1989, p. 8.

43. Interview with Mel Odom, general manager, City of Beverly Hills water utility (1983).

44. Interview with Dale Kyle (1987); *Water Rate Analysis and Financial Study*, City of Burbank Public Service Department, March 1983.

45. "History of Water Rates," Table 38, MWD *Annual Report*, FY 1976–77, 1977, p. 169; MWD *Annual Report*, FY 1983–1984, 1984, p. 107.

46. There was, however, no consistent pattern to the changes, and several utility managers interviewed during the early 1980s failed to associate their revised rate structures to any peak-reduction or conservation goals. Moreover, MWD analysts argued in this period that there was little or no relationship between the price of water and its use. See Carver E. Hildebrand, *The Relationships between Urban Water Demand and the Price of Water*, Metropolitan Water District of Southern California, February 1984; "Southern California's Water Supply: Local Perspectives on Regional Policy," Jeff Archuleta et al., comprehensive project, UCLA Urban Planning Program, June 1983.

47. "Tax Levies and Collections, August 16, 1929, to June 30, 1977," MWD *Annual Report*, FY 1976–77, 1977, Table 36, pp. 166–167.

48. MWD *Annual Report*, FY 1983–84, 1984, Tables 36 and 37, pp. 119–120.

49. This included MWD Chair Jensen whose position on the matter began to change in this period (Joseph Jensen oral history).

50. Resolution 5821, passed by MWD board of directors, September 27, 1960 (MWD *Annual Report*, FY 1960–61, p. 128–129).

51. See MWD *Annual Report*, FY 1976–77, 1977, p. 123; "Informational Material Relating to the Proportionate Use Formula," letter from executive secretary to MWD directors, August 25, 1981.

52. "Ramifications of the City Withdrawing from the Metropolitan Water District," report from the Los Angeles City Administrative Office to the Energy and Natural Resources Committee, Los Angeles City Council, September 9, 1982; "Ramifications: engineering, legal and financial, if the City withdraws from the Metropolitan Water District," report from the City Administrative Officer to the Water and Power Committee, May 12, 1980. In the 1970 report, the CAO complained that "Below-cost water supplies now subsidized by taxpayers will, by the very availability of such supplies, tend to hasten the development and occupation of new areas that are otherwise sub-marginal for urbanizing."

53. MWD *Annual Report*, FY 1983–84, 1984, p. 107.

54. Several of these measures had been long-term objectives of MWD management, which had sought to increase its revenue base in the face of declining tax receipts and increasing costs. Interviews with Robert Gough (1984) and Gerald Lonergan (1984); "Working Capital Reserve Requirements," letter from general manager to board of directors, August 31, 1984; and letter from general manager to Subcommittee on Reserves, September 10, 1984.

55. Author's notes, comments by Gerald Lonergan, 1984; presentation by Greg Leddy and Robert Campbell, UCLA Urban Planning Seminar, 1985.

56. Brown and Caldwell—Robert A. Skinner, Consulting Engineers, *Water Pricing Policy Study*, the Metropolitan Water District of Southern California, June 1969.

57. MWD, 1974, *Water Pricing Study, Volume II: Analysis of the Problem: Policies Affecting Components of Water Rates*, Report No. 912, Los Angeles, November 1974; "Report on Seasonal Water Pricing Proposal," letter from general manager to Subcommittee on Water Pricing Proposals, board of directors, MWD, September 17, 1979.

58. The San Diego CWA was particularly opposed to any seasonal pricing pro-

gram because of its large agricultural constituency and strong advocates such as Hans Doe, one of CWA's MWD directors, who was also an MWD board vice-chair in that period. See "Statements Made at the Water Problems Committee Meeting of MWD Board of Directors by Harry Griffen (San Diego CWA MWD representative) and Anne Thomas, Counsel for Western Municipal Water District of Riverside County," November 9, 1987.

59. In 1979, the seasonal pricing concept, strongly supported by an MWD vice-chairman, Ben Haggott, from the City of Torrance, was tabled at the last minute in favor of an "interruptible" pricing rate that favored both agriculture and those districts purchasing groundwater replenishment water. The issue was further complicated by an intense debate over whether to define "agriculture" for these purposes in terms of one-acre or five-acre lots, given the widespread existence of small avocado groves in residential subdivisions in the Southern California area. Interviews with Robert Gough (1981) and James Krieger (1981).

60. Author's notes, meeting between Tim Quinn, Wiley Horne, Tim Brick, Robert Gottlieb, August 1986.

61. "Workshop on Policy," MWD board of directors, June 30, 1987.

62. Interview with Tim Quinn (1988).

63. "Seasonal Storage Water Service," letter from the general manager to the board of directors, MWD, June 27, 1989.

64. Initial response from MWD member agencies varied. Several agencies, most notably the Orange County Water District, used the establishment of the Seasonal Storage Service program to develop a loan program to help its own member agencies finance the construction of forty to fifty new wells and to rehabilitate existing wells. Other agencies, however, simply saw the program as a price break and downplayed its potential as an incentive for increasing storage capacity or reducing peak purchases. "Status Report on Metropolitan's Activities to Assist Member Agencies in Expanding Groundwater Conjunctive Use in Southern California," letter from the general manager to the MWD board of directors, November 28, 1989; *San Gabriel Valley Tribune*, August 6, 1989; "Water Officials Study New Pricing Plan," Mike Sprague, *Whittier Daily News*, July 28, 1989.

65. "Financial Incentives for Water Conservation," letter from the general manager to the board of directors, MWD, August 8, 1988.

66. The rationale behind this new policy was that each acre-foot developed from a local project under the program avoids the delivery of an equivalent amount of State Project water. "Financial Impact of Local Projects Program on Metropolitan," letter from the general manager to the board of directors, MWD, June 17, 1986.

67. "Proposed Conservation Credits Agreement with the City of Santa Monica," letter from the general manager to the board of directors, MWD, February 23, 1989. The City of Pasadena also sought to develop a similar program; see "Agreement with Planning and Management Consultants, Ltd. to Develop Reliable Estimates of Water Conservation Savings Through Evaluation of Pasadena's Retrofit Program," letter from the general manager to MWD board of directors, October 3, 1989.

68. The concept of conservation both as a supply source and as part of a growth-oriented strategy is also explored in William Martin, Helen Ingram, Nancy Laney, and Adrian Griffin's study, *Saving Water in a Desert City*, (Washington, D.C.: Resources for the Future, 1984).

69. The latter as part of a ballot argument during a 1966 MWD bond election (see *1976 Analysis of Annexation Policy*, MWD, February 1976).

70. See *1976 Analysis of Annexation Policy*, MWD, February 1976.

71. The board, aware of the apparent contradiction between a policy which encouraged annexations and a public posture suggesting anticipated shortages, had a brief moratorium on annexations, until a new report once again justifying that policy was released. See "Review of Metropolitan's Annexation Policy," letter from the general manager to the board of directors, MWD, December 27, 1982; see also "Annexation Policy," letter from S. Dell Scott, MWD director, City of Los Angeles, to board of directors, MWD, February 18, 1983.

72. "Annexation Charge Study and Recommended Change in the Per-Acre Annexation Charge," letter from the general manager to the board of directors, MWD, March 23, 1988.

73. Comments by Wiley Horne, "Workshop on Policy," MWD, June 30, 1987.

74. *Pasadena Star News*, May 9, 1989; May 20, 1989.

75. For a discussion of marginal pricing issues, see "Marginal costs and seasonal pricing of water service," Patrick C. Mann and Donald L. Schlenger, *Journal of the American Water Works* Association 74(1): 6-11, January 1982.

76. "An analysis of the external benefits associated with the availability and use of MWD water supplies," Regional Economic Research, San Diego, report to the San Diego County Water Authority, December 19, 1983.

77. MWD managers, in fact, spoke of *expanding* treatment capacity from 130 percent to as much as 170 percent.

Index

About the Authors

Robert Gottlieb is the coordinator of the environmental analysis and policy area of the UCLA Urban Planning Program. He is the author of six books including *A Life of Its Own: The Politics and Power of Water* and *Empires in the Sun: The Rise of the New American West* (coauthored with Peter Wiley). He was a member of the board of directors of the Metropolitan Water District of Southern California between 1980 and 1987.

Margaret FitzSimmons is an assistant professor of urban planning in the Graduate School of Architecture and Urban Planning at UCLA. She received the Nystrom Award from the Association of American Geographers in 1985 for her dissertation research on agricultural change and environmental consequences and has continued to do research on agriculture, water quality, and toxic substance issues.